Praise for David Foster Wallace's
Consider the Lobster
And Other Essays

"David Foster Wallace's reportorial pieces sparkle with the same sort of odd, telling details and weird little observations that distinguish his liveliest fiction. . . . This collection trains Mr. Wallace's acute eye not inward at the solipsistic terrain of people's minds, but outward at the world — at politicians, at writers, at ordinary and oddball individuals of every emotional stripe. Like his best fiction, it reminds the reader of both his copious literary gifts and his keen sense of the absurdities of contemporary life in America at the cusp of the millennium."   — Michiko Kakutani, *New York Times*

"Wallace is as original and disturbing as a computer worm. . . . *Consider the Lobster* demonstrates a contemporary American master working at the extreme edge of the radar, asking question after question about the mad, mad world in which he finds himself."
                                — Robert McCrum, *Guardian*

"If it weren't for barrier breakers like Wallace, willing to redefine usage in a way that makes other writing seem flat and severely lacking in content, we'd all sound like *Beowulf.* Or worse — cavemen."
                        — Karla Starr, *Willamette Week Online*

"*Consider the Lobster* showcases Wallace's funny, observant side. He attacks subjects as varied as the Vegas porn awards, a Maine lobsterfest, and the humor in Franz Kafka — with a voice that manages to be both Midwestern-front-porch digressive and scientifically rigorous."
                                                — *Details*

"To read Wallace's rendition of these events is to experience the muchness of American life in the way that Tom Wolfe used to deliver it to us. Like the great avatar of new journalism, Wallace is a master of flipping a world inside out through its own lingo, of swallowing it whole and then destroying it from the inside on its own terms."
— John Freeman, *Boston Globe*

"David Foster Wallace is to the footnote what Agassi was to tennis or Jordan was to basketball."
— J Keirn-Swanson, *Cleveland Plain Dealer*

"Good writing graffitis its perceptions over the world, and it's impossible to get through a day without a Wallace line. . . . After reading him, I feel buzzed-up, smarter — I'm better company."
— David Lipsky on National Public Radio's *All Things Considered*

"The big themes — the trivialization of meaning, political corruption, the shift in public interests, the world of pornography — are absorbing and, in Wallace's skilled hands, often make for mesmerizing reading. . . . It's good to read someone who can teach and be irreverent at the same time."
— Carlo Wolff, *Fort Worth Star-Telegram*

"Wallace is the brainiest and most prolific of our young masters."
— Steve Almond, *Los Angeles Times Book Review*

"Can a serious essayist also traffic in style and glitz? David Foster Wallace finds a way. . . . Wallace does not like irony. He does like serious issues, seriously discussed. These appear gradually, however, and reaching them is great fun, as the reader swoops and swirls and doubles back and races down the final reaches of Wallace's prose. It's as if Wallace had been, not a tennis star, but a snowboarder. A snowboarder with a PhD."
— Peter Grier, *Christian Science Monitor*

"Wallace is bracingly insightful. . . . So vast is his intellectual energy and ambition. . . . Few of his young peers have spoken as eloquently and feelingly as he has about the hard tasks of the moral imagination that contemporary American life imposes on them."

— Pankaj Mishra, *New York Times Book Review*

"Entertaining, sharp, and often amusing. . . . Wallace doesn't pretend to have any answers, but at least he knows what the questions are."

— Ashley Gauthier, *Free Lance-Star*

"Wallace's voice is that of a hip polymath's, where slang and obscure jargon intermix and many, many self-conscious digressions take place in voluminous footnotes. . . . The only thing that unites these seemingly disparate essays is Wallace's unique talent for delving past the obvious and reading the profound, all the time remaining both entertaining and erudite."

— Traver Kauffman, *Rocky Mountain News*

"A book you read and read again, and underline, and read to friends, and keep going back to."   — Rich Cohen, Salon.com

"Essays by David Foster Wallace would be recognizable without his name attached. His relentless curiosity, his earnestness, his generous spirit, his often goofy tone, his erudition, and even his use of footnotes in magazines that otherwise eschew footnotes contribute to his recognizability. Wallace's essays, short stories, and novels are so familiar, it seems he has been around forever."

— Steve Weinberg, *Baltimore Sun*

"*Consider the Lobster* is a great collection of Wallace's best nonfiction writing. . . . It's absurd, and inspired, and — like every other Wallace book — it's like nothing else out there."

— Erik Henriksen, *Portland Mercury*

Consider the Lobster

and Other Essays

David Foster Wallace

BACK BAY BOOKS
LITTLE, BROWN AND COMPANY
NEW YORK   BOSTON   LONDON

Back Bay Books / Little, Brown and Company
Hachette Book Group
1290 Avenue of the Americas, New York, NY 10104
littlebrown.com

Originally published in hardcover by Little, Brown and Company, December 2005
First Back Bay paperback edition, July 2007

Back Bay Books is an imprint of Little, Brown and Company. The Back Bay Books name and logo are trademarks of Hachette Book Group, Inc.

The publisher is not responsible for websites (or their content) that are not owned by the publisher.

The following pieces were originally published in edited, heavily edited, or (in at least one instance) bowdlerized form in the following books and periodicals. N.B.: In those cases where the fact that the author was writing for a particular organ is important to the essay itself — i.e., where the commissioning magazine's name keeps popping up in ways that can't now be changed without screwing up the whole piece — the entry is marked with an asterisk. A single case in which the essay was written to be delivered as a speech, plus another one where the original article appeared bipseudonymously and now for odd and hard-to-explain reasons doesn't quite work if the "we" and "your correspondents" thing gets singularized, are further tagged with what I think are called daggers. To wit:

*†"Big Red Son" in *Premiere*.
"Certainly the End of *Something* or Other, One Would Sort of Have to Think" in the *New York Observer* and *The Anchor Essay Annual: The Best of 1998*.
†"Some Remarks on Kafka's Funniness from Which Probably Not Enough Has Been Removed" and *"Authority and American Usage" in *Harper's*.
"The View from Mrs. Thompson's" and *"Up, Simba" in *Rolling Stone*.
"How Tracy Austin Broke My Heart" in the *Philadelphia Enquirer*.
*"Consider the Lobster" in *Gourmet* and *The Best American Essays 2005*.
"Joseph Frank's Dostoevsky" in the *Village Voice Literary Supplement*.
*(at least a tiny bit) "Host" in the *Atlantic Monthly*.

Library of Congress Cataloging-in-Publication Data
Wallace, David Foster.
Consider the lobster and other essays / David Foster Wallace. — 1st ed.
p. cm.
Includes bibliographical references.
HC ISBN 0-316-15611-6 / 978-0-316-15611-0
PB ISBN 0-316-01332-3 / 978-0-316-01332-1
I. Title.
PS3573.A425635C66 2005
814'.54—dc22   2005010886

Printing 28, 2021

LSC-C

Design by Renato Stanisic
"Host" design by Marie Mundaca and Peter Bernard

Printed in the United States of America

Contents

for Bonnie Nadell

Consider
the
Lobster
and Other
Essays

BIG RED SON

THE AMERICAN ACADEMY of Emergency Medicine confirms it: Each year, between one and two dozen adult US males are admitted to ERs after having castrated themselves. With kitchen tools, usually, sometimes wire cutters. In answer to the obvious question, surviving patients most often report that their sexual urges had become a source of intolerable conflict and anxiety. The desire for perfect release and the real-world impossibility of perfect, whenever-you-want-it release had together produced a tension they could no longer stand.

It is to the 30+ testosteronically afflicted males whose cases have been documented in the past two years that your correspondents wish to dedicate this article. And to those tormented souls considering autocastration in 1998, we wish to say: "Stop! Stay your hand! Hold off with those kitchen utensils and/or wire cutters!" Because we believe we may have found an alternative.

Every spring, the Academy of Motion Picture Arts and Sciences presents awards for outstanding achievement in all aspects of mainstream cinema. These are the Academy Awards. Mainstream cinema is a major industry in the United States, and so are the Academy Awards. The AAs' notorious commercialism and hypocrisy disgust many of the millions and millions and millions of viewers who tune in during prime time to watch the presentations. It is not a coincidence that the Oscars ceremony is held during TV's Sweeps Week. We pretty much all tune in, despite the grotesquerie of watching an industry congratulate itself on its pretense that it's still an art form, of hearing people in $5,000 gowns invoke lush clichés of surprise and humility scripted by publicists, etc. — the whole cynical postmodern deal — but we all still seem to watch. To care. Even though the hypocrisy hurts, even though opening grosses and marketing strategies are now bigger news than the movies themselves, even though Cannes and Sundance have become nothing more than enterprise zones. But the truth is that there's no more real joy about it all anymore. Worse, there seems to be this enormous unspoken conspiracy where we all pretend that there's still joy. That we think it's funny when Bob Dole does a Visa ad and Gorbachev shills for Pizza Hut. That the whole mainstream celebrity culture is rushing to cash in and all the while congratulating itself on pretending not to cash in. Underneath it all, though, we know the whole thing sucks.

Your correspondents humbly offer an alternative.

Every January, the least pretentious city in America hosts the Annual AVN Awards. The AVN stands for *Adult Video News*, which is sort of the *Variety* of the US porn industry. This thick, beautifully designed magazine costs $7.95 per issue, is about 80 percent ads, and is clearly targeted at adult-video retailers. Its circulation is appr. 40,000.

Though the sub-line vagaries of entertainment accounting are legendary, it is universally acknowledged that the US adult-film industry, at $3.5–4 billion in annual sales, rentals, cable charges, and video-masturbation-booth revenues, is an even larger and more efficient moneymaking machine than legitimate mainstream American cinema (the latter's annual gross commonly estimated at

$2–2.5 billion). The US adult industry is centered in LA's San Fernando Valley, just over the mountains from Hollywood.[1] Some insiders like to refer to the adult industry as Hollywood's Evil Twin, others as the mainstream's Big Red Son.

It is no accident that *Adult Video News* — a slick, expensive periodical whose articles are really more like infomercials — and its yearly Awards both came into being in 1982. The early '80s, after all, saw the genesis of VCRs and home-video rentals, which have done for the adult industry pretty much what TV did for pro football.

From the 12/11/97 press release issued by *AVN* (visitable also at www.avn.com):

- The nominations for the 15th Annual AVN Awards were announced today.[2] This year's awards show, commemorating AVN's 15th anniversary, celebrates "History". [*sic*]
- Awards will be presented in a record 106 categories over a two night period.
- The adult industry released nearly 8,000 adult releases [*sic*] in 1997, including over 4,000 "new" releases (non-compilation). AVN reviewed every new release in every categroy [*sic*] this past year, logging over 30,000 sex scenes.[3]

---

[1] One porn production company, Caballero Home Video, has its headquarters in a big Van Nuys duplex whose other half is the soundstage for *Beverly Hills 90210*.

[2] The passive mood here's a bit disingenuous — the release itself is announcing them.

[3] At, say, an average of 90 minutes per movie, this means that some person or persons put in 1.4 years of nonstop continuous porn-viewing. Hence your correspondents' alternative for US males so tortured by carnal desire that they are tempted to autoneuter: Volunteer as a judge for the AVN Awards and spend 1.4 years gazing without rest at the latest in adult video. We guarantee that you will never thereafter want to see, hear, engage in, or even think about human sexuality ever again. Trust us on this. All five marginal (and male) print journalists assigned to cover the 1998 AVN Awards concur: Even just watching the dozen or so "big" or "high-profile" adult releases of the past year — *Bad Wives, Zazel, A Week and a Half in the Life of a Prostitute, Miscreants, New Wave Hookers 5, Seduce & Destroy, Buttman in Barcelona, Gluteus to the Maximus* — fried everyone's glandular circuitboard. By the end of the Awards weekend, none of us were even having normal biological first-thing-in-the-morning or jouncy-bus-ride-between-hotels erections; and when approached even innocently by members of the opposite sex, we all now recoiled as from a hot flame (which made our party a kind of strange and challenging breakfast gig, according to our Sunday-AM waitress).

- By comparison, last year there were approximately 375 films eligible for the Academy Awards that these voters [*sic* — meaning different voters from the AVN voters, presumably] were required to see. AVN had to watch more than 10 times the amount of releases in order to develop these nominations [usage and repetition *sic*, though 4,000 divided by 375 is indeed over 10].

From the acceptance speech of Mr. Tom Byron, Saturday, 10 January 1998, Caesars Forum ballroom, Caesars Palace Hotel and Casino complex, Las Vegas NV, upon winning *AVN*'s 1998 Male Performer of the Year Award (and with no little feeling): "I want to thank every beautiful woman I ever put my cock inside." [Laughter, cheers, ovation.]

From the acceptance speech of Ms. Jeanna Fine, ibid., upon winning *AVN*'s 1998 Best Supporting Actress Award for her role in Rob Black's *Miscreants:* "Jesus, which one is this for, *Miscreants?* Jesus, that's another one where I read the script and said 'Oh shit, I am going to go to hell. [Laughter, cheers.] But that's okay, 'cause all my *friends*'ll be there *too!*" [Huge wave of laughter, cheers, applause.]

From the inter-Award banter of Mr. Bobby Slayton, professional comedian and master of ceremonies for the 1997 AVNAs: "I know I'm looking good, though, like younger, 'cause I started using this special Grecian Formula — every time I find a gray hair, I fuck my wife in the ass. [No laughter, scattered groans.] Fuck you. That's a great joke. Fuck you."

Bobby Slayton, a gravelly-voiced Dice Clay knockoff who kept introducing every female performer as "the woman I'm going to cut my dick off for," and who astounded all the marginal print journalists in attendance with both his unfunniness and his resemblance to every apartment-complex coke dealer we'd ever met, is mercifully absent from the 1998 Awards gala. The '98 emcee is one Robert Schimmel, alumnus of *In Living Color* and a Howard Stern regular. Schimmel looks like a depraved, deeply tan Wallace Shawn and is no less coarse than B. Slayton but a lot better. He does a pantomime of someone attempting intercourse with a Love Doll he's been too lazy to blow up all the way. He contrasts the woeful paucity of his own ejaculate with the concussive orgasms of certain well-known male performers,[4] comparing these men's ejaculations to automatic lawn sprinklers and doing an eerie sonic impression of same. All of 1998's marginal print journalists are together at Table 189 at the very back of the ballroom. Most of these reporters are from the sorts of men's magazines that sit shrinkwrapped behind the cash registers of convenience stores, and they are a worldly and jaded crew indeed, but Schimmel gets a couple of them — whose noms de guerre are Harold Hecuba and Dick Filth — laughing so uproariously that people at the Anabolic Video table nearby keep looking over in annoyance. At one point during a routine on premature ejaculation, Dick Filth actually chokes on a California roll.

. . . But all this is Saturday night, the main event. And there are a whole lot of festivities preceding Saturday's climax.

The adult industry is vulgar. Would anyone disagree? One of the AVN Awards' categories is "Best Anal Themed Feature"; another is "Best Overall Marketing Campaign — Company Image." *Irresistible,* a 1983 winner in several categories, has been spelled *Irresistable* in *Adult Video News* for fifteen straight years. The industry's not only vulgar, it's *predictably* vulgar. All the clichés are true. The typical porn producer really is the ugly little man with a bad toupee and a pinkie-ring the size of a Rolaids. The typical porn director really is the guy who uses the word *class* as a noun to mean refinement. The typical porn starlet really is the lady in Lycra eveningwear with tattoos all down her arms who's both smoking and chewing gum while telling journalists how grateful she is to Wadcutter Productions Ltd. for footing her breast-enlargement bill. And meaning it. The

---

[4] (Mr. Peter North, in particular, delivers what seem more like mortar rounds than bio-emissions.)

whole AVN Awards weekend comprises what Mr. Dick Filth calls an Irony-Free Zone.

But of course we should keep in mind that *vulgar* has many dictionary definitions and that only a couple of these have to do w/ lewdness or bad taste. At root, *vulgar* just means popular on a mass scale. It is the semantic opposite of *pretentious* or *snobby*. It is humility with a comb-over. It is Nielsen ratings and Barnum's axiom and the real bottom line. It is big, big business.

Thirty-four-year-old porn actor Cal Jammer killed himself in 1995. Starlets Shauna Grant, Nancy Kelly, Alex Jordan, and Savannah have all killed themselves in the last decade. Savannah and Jordan received AVN's Best New Starlet awards in 1991 and 1992, respectively. Savannah killed herself after getting mildly disfigured in a car accident. Alex Jordan is famous for having addressed her suicide note to her pet bird. Crewman and performer Israel Gonzalez killed himself at a porn company warehouse in 1997.

An LA-based support group called PAW (= Protecting Adult Welfare) runs a 24-hour crisis line for people in the adult industry. A fundraiser for PAW was held at a Mission Hills CA bowling alley last November. It was a nude bowling tournament. Dozens of starlets agreed to take part. Two or three hundred adult-video fans showed up and paid to watch them bowl naked. No production companies or their executives participated or gave money. The fundraiser took in $6,000, which is slightly less than two one-millionths of porn's yearly gross.

As you know if you've seen *Casino, Showgirls, Bugsy,* etc., there are really three Las Vegases. Binion's, where the World Series of Poker is always played, exemplifies the "Old Vegas," centered around Fremont Street. Las Vegas's future is even now under late-stage construction at the very end of the Strip, on the outskirts of town (where US malls always go up); it's to be a bunch of theme-parkish, more "family-oriented" venues of the kind that De Niro describes so plangently at the end of *Casino*.

But Las Vegas as most of us see it, Vegas qua Vegas, comprises the dozen or so hotels that flank the Strip's middle. *Vegas Populi:* the opulent, intricate, garish, ecstatically decadent hotels, cathedra to gambling, partying, and live entertainment of the most microphone-swinging sort. The Sands. The Sahara. The Stardust. MGM Grand, Maxim. All within a small radius. Yearly utility expenditures on neon well into seven figures. Harrah's, Casino Royale (with its big 24-hour Denny's attached), Flamingo Hilton, Imperial Palace. The Mirage, with its huge laddered waterfall always lit up. Circus Circus. Treasure Island, with its intricate facade of decks and rigging and mizzens and vang. The Luxor, shaped like a ziggurat from Babylon of yore. Barbary Coast, whose sign out front says CASH YOUR PAY-CHECK — WIN UP TO $25,000. These hotels are the Vegas we know. The land of Lola and Wayne. Of Siegfried and Roy, Copperfield. Showgirls in towering headdress. Sinatra's sandbox. Most of them built in the '50s and '60s, the era of mob chic and entertainment-*cum*-industry. Half-hour lines for taxis. Smoking not just allowed but encouraged. Toupees and convention nametags and women in furs of all hue. A museum that features the World's Biggest Coke Bottle. The Harley-Davidson Cafe, with its tympanum of huge protruding hawg; Bally's H&C, with its row of phallic pillars all electrified and blinking in grand mal sync. A city that pretends to be nothing but what it is, an enormous machine of exchange — of spectacle for money, of sensation for money, of money for more money, of pleasure for whatever be tomorrow's abstract cost.

Nor let us forget Vegas's synecdoche and beating heart. It's kitty-corner from Bally's: Caesars Palace. The granddaddy. As big as 20 Wal-Marts end to end. Real marble and fake marble, carpeting you can pass out on without contusion, 130,000 square feet of casino alone. Domed ceilings, clerestories, barrel vaults. In Caesars Palace is America conceived as a new kind of Rome: conqueror of its own people. An empire of Self. It's breathtaking. The winter's light rain makes all the neon bleed. The whole thing is almost too pretty to stand. There could be no site but Las Vegas's Caesars for modern porn's Awards show — here, the AAVNAs are one more spectacle. Way more tourists and conventioneers recognize the starlets than you'd expect. Double-takes all over the hotel. Even just standing around or putting coins in a slot machine, the performers become a prime attraction. Las Vegas doesn't miss a trick.

The Annual AVN Awards are always scheduled to coincide with the International Consumer Electronics Show (a.k.a. CES), which this year runs from 8 through 11 January. The CES is a very big deal. It's like a combination convention and talent show for the best and brightest in the world of consumer tech. Steve Forbes is here, and DSS's Thomson. Sun Microsystems is using this year's CES to launch its PersonalJava 1.0. Bill Gates gives a packed-house speech on Saturday morning. Major players from TV, cable, and merchandising host a panel on the short-term viability of HDTV. A forum on the problem of product returns by disgruntled customers seats 1,500 and is SRO. The CES as a whole is bigger than your correspondents' hometowns. It's spread out over four different hotels and has 10,000+ booths with everything from "The First Ever Full Text Message Pager in a Wristwatch" to the world's premier self-heating home satellite dish ("The Snow and Ice Solution!").

But far and away the CES's most popular venue, with total attendance well over 100,000 every year, is what is called the Adult Software[5] exhibition, despite the fact that the CES itself treats the Adult tradeshow kind of like the crazy relative in the family and keeps it way out in what used to be the parking garage of the Sands hotel. This facility, a serious bus ride from all the other CES sites, is

---

[5] Yes: "Software" is a funny misnomer here. It's going to be a constant temptation to keep winking and nudging and saying "no pun intended" or "as it were" after every possible off-color entendre, of which there are so many at the AAVNAs that yr. corresps. have decided to try to leave most of them to the reader's discretion as matters of personal choice and taste.

an enormous windowless all-cement space that during show hours manages to induce both agoraphobia and claustrophobia. A big sign says you have to be 21 to get in. The median age inside is 45, almost all males, nearly everyone wearing some sort of convention-eer's nametag. Every production company in the adult industry, from Anabolic to Zane, has a booth here. The really big companies have booths that are sprawling and multidisplay and more like small strip malls. A lot of porn's top female performers are contract players, exclusive vendors to one particular production company; and one reason why a lot of the starlets seem kind of tired and cranky by Saturday night's Awards gala is that they will have spent much of the previous 72 hours at their companies' CES booths, on their feet all day in vertiginous heels, signing autographs and pos-ing for pictures and pressing all manner of flesh.

The best way to describe the sonic environment at the '98 CES is: Imagine that the apocalypse took the form of a cocktail party. Male fans move through the fractal maze of booths in groups of three or more. Their expressions tend to be those of junior-high boys at a peephole, an expression that looks pretty surreal on a face with jowls and no hairline. Some among them are video retailers; most are not. Most are just hard-core fans, the industry's breath and bread. A lot of them not only recognize but seem to know the names, stage names, and curricula vitae of almost all the female performers.

It takes an average of two hours and twelve minutes to traverse the Adult CES expo, counting an average of four delays for getting lost after a chicane turn or some baroque ceiling-high cheval glass designed to double the visual exposure of Heatwave Video's display for *Texas Dildo Masquerade* gets you all turned around. Your corre-spondents are accompanied by Harold Hecuba and Dick Filth, who have very generously offered to act as guides and docents, and here is a random spatter of the things we see the first time we come in:

A second-tier Arrow Video starlet in a G-string poses for a photo, forked dorsally over the knee of a morbidly obese cellphone retailer from suburban Philadelphia. The guy taking the picture,

whose CES nametag says Hi and that his name is Sherm, addresses
the starlet as "babe" and asks her to readjust so as to "give us a little
more bush down there." An Elegant Angel starlet with polyresin
wings attached to her back is eating a Milky Way bar while she signs
video boxes. Actor Steven St. Croix is standing near the Caballero
Home Video booth, saying to no one in particular "Let me out
of here, I can't wait to get out of here."[6] Adult-video stores all have
a distinctive smell — a mix of cheap magnetic tape and disinfec-
tant — and the Sands' former parking garage is rank with it. Asian
businessmen move through the aisles in dense graceful packs and
are assiduously cheery and polite. A young guy in a full-color
Frankenstein T-shirt is spraypainting cartoon flames on an actress's
breasts at the Sin City booth. The actress — an obscure one, not
even Filth and Hecuba know her name — has normal-size breasts,
and there's not much of an audience. Producer/director Max
Hardcore draws a way bigger crowd at the MAXWORLD booth,
where one of his girls is squatting on the countertop masturbating
with the butt of a riding crop. Max's videos' promotional posters
have him carrying a girl in minishorts over his shoulder against the
backdrop of various city skylines; the pitches at the bottom say
"SEE PRETTY GIRLS SODOMIZED IN MANNERS MOST FOUL! SEE CUM-
SPLATTERED GIRLS TOO STUPID TO KNOW BETTER!" Max is a story all
to himself, according to Harold Hecuba. D. Filth and a porn executive dressed entirely in Campbell Nightwatch plaid are smoking
cigars and keep holding their cigars up together and comparing
the ash to see which one has the cleanest burn. A lot of the industry
males and even some of the starlets are also smoking cigars. 1998
is definitely the Year of the Cigar. The starlets are all in either extremely formal cocktail dresses or else abbreviated latex/vinyl/
Lycra ensembles. Heels are uniformly sharp and ultrahigh. Some
of the starlets are so heavily made up they look embalmed. They

---

[6] St. Croix's background is that he apprenticed as a mason but then couldn't get union
work. He's got great dark satanic-looking eyebrows and has won several AVN Awards.

tend to have complexly coiffed hair that looks really good from 20 feet away but on closer inspection is dry and dead. Someone who is either sometime-performer Jeff Marton or "Bizarro-Sleaze" filmmaker Gregory Dark is doing sleight-of-hand tricks with his trademark fedora.[7] Whoever he is, he has a goatee. Harold Hecuba also has a goatee; Dick Filth has more like a soul patch. H.H. and D.F., longtime industry journalists, know everybody here and keep getting stopped and drawn into conversations. (These delays, during which yr. corresps. sort of stand there awkwardly at the edge of the conversation and try to look around as if they too know people here and are waiting only to spot them in the crowd before they go off and get into their own involved conversations, have not been included in the 132-minute Adult CES–traversal average.) This year, a good 75 percent of the males in and around the porn industry appear to be sporting variants of the goatee.[8]

Next to the Outlaw Video booth, a starlet in a gold lamé spaghetti-strap gown, chewing gum and blowing large blue bubbles, is being videotaped by a disabled fan whose camera and parabolic mike are bolted to the arm of his wheelchair; the starlet is pointing to the tattoos on her left arm and appears to be explaining the origin and context of each one. At the Vivid Video multibooth complex,[9] Ms. Taylor Hayes has what is probably the longest autograph-and-flesh-press line in the entire Sands garage. Taylor is major-league pretty — she looks like a slightly debauched Cindy Crawford — and an oversize monitor suspended from the ceiling over the Vivid area plays clips of her scantily clad and dancing amid dry-ice fumes. There's a berm of boxed videos on the floor by the counter and a huge man with a visor and handheld credit card machine on Taylor's right flank as she greets each fan like a long-

---

[7] (meaning both men habitually wear fedoras)

[8] Dick Filth reports that a couple years ago the big industry trend was Heavy Metal and that everyone at the Adult CES had very long hair and wore black tanktops and iron crosses, etc.

[9] Vivid is one of the industry's great powers, a company famous for having billboards that sometimes cause traffic accidents in downtown LA.

lost relative. According to Dick Filth, Taylor is both a genuinely nice person and a consummate pro.

The booth for XPlor Media — a company known for its "Southern Belles" video series and ORGY FOR WORLD PEACE Website — is arresting because all the execs at XPlor seem to be under 25 and the booth's atmosphere is that of a fraternity party in its third straight day. One young bald guy is unconscious in a fetal position on the counter, and some wag has glued all sorts of feathers and flaccid plastic two-headed dildoish things to his skull. XPlor's owner-auteurs are two brothers, trust-fund babies from a Connecticut suburb of NYC. Their names are Farrel and Moffitt Timlake. Farrel, who wears twelve-hole Doc Martens and cargo pants and what's either a very light parka or very heavy sweatshirt with a hood that stays up at all times, is a particular cause célèbre at the '98 CES because he's apparently a friend of the two guys who do *South Park,* and these guys are rumored to be in Vegas and to possess tickets to Saturday's Awards banquet.[10]

---

[10] Here, if you're interested, is D. Filth's out-loud on-site peripatetic expansion re the camaraderie between XPlor and *South Park:*

XPlor is a kind of an anomaly type of thing in the porn business. By and large the industry is still run by these dim grim cigar-smoking numbnutses who'll just stare blankly at you if you should ever even like attempt a bonmot [pronounced as one consonant-intensive word] or whatnot. You get me? In contrast to how XPlor are more of your hippieish dope-smoking bunch of Gen Xers who are always up for a good gag. Like, after Trey [Parker, the Groening-type figure behind *South Park*] and Farrel [Timlake] became pals [via Parker's hanging out at XPlor to do research for his and Matt (Stone, Parker's partner on *South Park*)'s *Orgazmo,* an upcoming movie about which your correspondents know nothing], XPlor was doing a video shoot at Buck Henry's place [?!? Explanatory details unavailable — everyone simply acts as though Buck Henry's place being available for hard-core porn shoots were a matter of wide and public knowledge]. Richard Dreyfuss and I think Carrie Fisher also were at the shoot [?!? But no kidding, according to Filth, who yr. corresps. rather hope has a good attorney], and, as a goof, Trey and Farrel decide to switch identities, get it? So Trey pretends to direct, doing it in like big drama-queen persona — *"I want more ASS shots, goddammit!"* type of thing — while Farrel hung back and pretended to take notes. Get it? Then later at one point Trey orders Farrel, as Trey, to perform — because, oh, Farrel performs sometimes too, under the name Tim Lake, *Tim Lake,* get it? — and Farrel does, did, puts down the notebook and phone and dis, like, robes and dives right in, which you can understand this completely freaks out the assembled legit showbiz types [!?], like, they're like "I can't believe the guy from *South Park* is having sex in front of a camera!" Then at one point Trey gives the video rig to Carrie Fisher [?!] and tells her to try and do the close-ups as they're getting close to money [see below for defs. of industry jargon]. Get me? What a couple of yucks. [End of expansion.]

Everyone without exception is sweating. At all but a few of the booths, contract starlets treat the fans with the same absent, rigid-faced courtesy that flight attendants and restaurant hostesses tend to use. You can tell how bored the performers are by the way their faces light up when they see someone they know. Well over half of the industry's current superstars are in this huge room.[11] The infamous T.T. Boy is here, standing alone with his trademark glower, the Boy who is rumored to bring a semiautomatic pistol with him to the set and who was featured in a 1995 *New Yorker* article that was full of lines like "A porn shoot is an intricately delineated ecology." Mr. Vince Vouyer (*sic*) is on hand, as are Seth Gecko, Jake Steed, Serenity, Missy, and Nick East. Here is the ageless Randy West, who looks just the way a surfer would look if that surfer were also a Mob enforcer, with his perennial tan and hair like frozen surf. Mr. Jon Dough — winner of *AVN*'s coveted Best Actor/Video statuette in both '96 and '97 — alternates between various booths, wearing his customary expression of having psychologically evolved to the point where he's so incredibly cool and detached that life is one long yawn. Here also is Mark Davis, far and away the most hand-some of the current males, a near-double for Gregory Harrison of the old *Trapper John* series except for Davis's ultrashort psych-patient haircut (plus goatee).

And 20-year veteran Joey Silvera is at this year's CES, though mostly in his capacity as an auteur: Silvera now directs Evil Angel's popular "Butt Row" video series.[12] Following the lead of pioneers like John Leslie and Paul Thomas, most of today's top male stars now also direct (and, per the store boxes, "Present") their own line of videos, e.g. "Tom Byron's Cumback Pussy" series, "Jon Dough's

---

[11] The average professional lifespan of a female performer is two years. Males, though lower paid, tend to last much longer in the business — sometimes decades.

[12] Silvera, who broke in way back in the '70s at Times Square's old Show World, looks like a curly-haired and extremely fit praying mantis; he's even weirder-looking now that his curls are mostly gray. He's also famous for always showing up on the set with a small duffel bag filled with exotic vitamins and herbal and other supplements, all self-prescribed.

Dirty Stories," the eye-popping Rocco Siffredi's "[Various European Cities] By Night" line, etc. The So-and-So Presents series seems to be an industry trend, like cigars and goatees.

It is difficult to describe how it feels to gaze at living human beings whom you've seen perform in hard-core porn. To shake the hand of a man whose precise erectile size, angle, and vasculature are known to you. That strange I-think-we've-met-before sensation one feels upon seeing any celebrity in the flesh is here both intensified and twisted. It feels intensely twisted to see reigning industry queen Jenna Jameson chilling out at the Vivid booth in Jordaches and a latex bustier and to know already that she has a tattoo of a sundered valentine with the tagline HEART BREAKER on her right buttock and a tiny hairless mole just left of her anus. To watch Peter North try to get a cigar lit and to have that sight backlit by memories of his artilleryesque ejaculations.[13] To have seen these strangers' faces in orgasm — that most unguarded and purely neural of expressions, the one so vulnerable that for centuries you basically had to marry a person to get to see it.[14] This weirdness may

---

[13] What's maybe even weirder is that you can then scuttle back to your hotel, if you wish, and watch Jameson and North have hard-core gymnastic sex in *The Wicked One* on pay-per-view for $9.95.

[14] Mr. Harold Hecuba, whose magazine job entails reviewing dozens of adult releases every month, has an interesting vignette about a Los Angeles Police Dept. detective he met once when H.H.'s car got broken into and a whole box of Elegant Angel Inc. videotapes was stolen (a box with H.H.'s name and work address right on it) and subsequently recovered by the LAPD. A detective brought the box back to Hecuba personally, a gesture that H.H. remembered thinking was unusually thoughtful and conscientious until it emerged that the detective had really just used the box's return as an excuse to meet Hecuba, whose critical work he appeared to know, and to discuss the ins and outs of the adult-video industry. It turned out that this detective — 60, happily married, a grandpa, shy, polite, clearly a decent guy — was a hard-core fan. He and Hecuba ended up over coffee, and when H.H. finally cleared his throat and asked the cop why such an obviously decent fellow squarely on the side of law and civic virtue was a porn fan, the detective confessed that what drew him to the films was "the faces," i.e. the actresses' faces, i.e. those rare moments in orgasm or accidental tenderness when the starlets dropped their stylized "fuck-me-I'm-a-nasty-girl" sneer and became, suddenly, real people. "Sometimes — and you never know when, is the thing — sometimes all of a sudden they'll kind of reveal themselves" was the detective's way of putting it. "Their what-do-you-call . . . humanness." It turned out that the LAPD detective found adult films *moving*, in fact far more so than most mainstream Hollywood movies, in which latter films actors — sometimes very gifted actors — go about feigning genuine humanity, i.e.: "In real movies, it's all on purpose. I suppose what I like in porno is the accident of it."

account for some of the complex emotional intercourse taking place between the performers and fans at the Adult CES. The patrons may leer and elbow one another at a distance, but by the time the men get to the front of the line and face the living incarnation of their VCR's fantasy-babe, most of them turn into quivering goggle-eyed schoolboys, sheepish and salivaless and damp. The same thing evidently happens at the hundreds of strip clubs all over the country where porn starlets appear as Featured Dancers (for five figures a week, according to Filth) and do photos and autographs after the show:

"Most of these guys become incredibly nervous when I come up to them," veteran starlet Shane has explained. "I'll put my arms around a guy and his whole body will be trembling. They pretty much do whatever I tell them to do." The whole industry, now, has this oddly reversed equation — the consumers are the ones who seem ashamed or shy, while the performers are cocky and smooth and 100 percent pro.

*   *   *

(14, CONTINUED)

Hecuba's detective's explanation is intriguing, at least to yr. corresps., because it helps explain part of the deep appeal of hard-core films, films that are supposed to be "naked" and "explicit" but in truth are some of the most aloof, unrevealing footage for sale anywhere. Much of the cold, dead, mechanical* quality of adult films is attributable, really, to the performers' faces. These are faces that usually appear bored or blank or workmanlike but are in fact simply *hidden*, the self locked away someplace far behind the eyes. Surely this hiddenness is the way a human being who's giving away the very most private parts of himself preserves some sense of dignity and autonomy — he denies us true expression. (You can see this very particular bored, hard, dead look in strippers, prostitutes, and porn performers of all locales and genders.)

But it's also true that occasionally, in a hard-core scene, the hidden self appears. It's sort of the opposite of acting. You can see the porn performer's whole face change as self-consciousness (in most females) or crazed blankness (in most males) yields to some genuinely felt erotic joy in what's going on; the sighs and moans change from automatic to expressive. It happens only once in a while, but the detective is right: The effect on the viewer is electric. And the adult performers who can do this a lot — allow themselves to feel and enjoy what's taking place, cameras or no — become huge, legendary stars. The 1980s' Ginger Lynn and Keisha could do this, and now sometimes Jill Kelly and Rocco Siffredi can. Jenna Jameson and T.T. Boy cannot. They remain just bodies.

---

*N.B. Of those friends and intimates of your correspondents who happen to dislike porn, a large majority of them report disliking it not so much for moral or religious or political reasons but because they find it boring, and a lot of them seem to use robotic/mechanical/industrial metaphors to try to characterize the boredom, e.g.: "[Hard-core sex is usually] just organs going in and out of other organs, in and out, like watching an oil rig go up and down all day."

It is no longer the 1980s, and the Meese Commission mentality that led to a major crackdown on video porn is long gone. Federal task forces and PTA outrage are now focused on the Internet and kiddie porn. But today's adult industry is still hypersensitive about what it perceives as fascist attacks on its First Amendment freedoms. A specially prepared trailer now runs before many higher-end adult videos, right between the legal disclaimer on the product's compliance with or exemption from 18 U.S.C §2257 and ads for phone services like 900-666-FUCK. Against shots of flowing flags and the Lincoln Memorial, a voiceover says stuff like:

> Censorship goes against our Bill of Rights and the founding principles of this country. It is an attempt on the part of the government to legislate morality and to stifle free expression.[15] This new, "legal" morality is dangerous to all Americans. Vote for those who believe in limiting government intrusion into your personal affairs. Vote against government control of your life and home. Vote against censorship. Only you, the People, can keep the American ideal intact.

These trailers always say they're sponsored by either the Adult Video Association or something called the Free Speech Coalition. Both organizations (and the extent to which the two are separate is unclear) are basically industry PACs. Porn, in other words, has taken the political lessons of the '80s to heart; it is now a hard-lobbying political force no less than GM or RJR Nabisco.

Feminists of all different stripe oppose the adult industry for reasons having to do with pornography's putative effects on women. Their arguments are well-known and in some respects persuasive. But certain antiporn arguments in the 1990s are now centered on adult entertainment's alleged effects on the men who consume it. Some "masculists" believe that a lot of men get addicted to video

---

[15] Whether the framers of the US Constitution might, in their very wildest imaginations, have been able to foresee things like *Anal Virgins VIII* or 900-666-FUCK when they were thinking of expression they wanted to protect is obviously a thorny question and outside this article's purview.

porn in a way that causes grievous psychic harm. Example: An essayist named David Mura has a little book called *A Male Grief: Notes on Pornography and Addiction,* which is a bit New Agey but interesting in places, e.g.:

> At the essence of pornography is the image of flesh used as a drug, a way of numbing psychic pain. But this drug lasts only as long as the man stares at the image. . . . In pornographic perception, each gesture, each word, each image, is read first and foremost through sexuality. Love or tenderness, pity or compassion, become subsumed by, and are made subservient to, a "greater" deity, a more powerful force. . . . The addict to pornography desires to be blinded, to live in a dream. Those in the thrall of pornography try to eliminate from their consciousness the world outside pornography, and this includes everything from their family and friends or last Sunday's sermon to the political situation in the Middle East. In engaging in such elimination the viewer reduces himself. He becomes stupid.

This kind of stuff might sound a little out-there, maybe, until one observes the eerie similarity between the eyes of males in strip clubs or stroke parlors and the eyes of people in their fifth hour of pumping silver dollars into the slot machines of the Sands' casino, or maybe until one's seen firsthand the odd kind of shock on the faces of CES patrons seeing performers now "in the flesh," complete with chewing gum and chin-pimples and all the human stuff you never see — never want to see — in films.

Maybe just a little bit more here on the whole scene at the Adult CES, which is a lot more of a rub-elbows-type venue than the stylized Awards ceremony is going to end up being. . . . Mr. Harold Hecuba is deep in conversation with a marginal porn producer about one of his performers' being sidelined with something called a "prolapsed sphincter," which condition yr. corresps. decline to follow up on in any way. We are standing just west of a staff writer for *Digital Horizons* who's dropped by to scope out the legendary scene in here again this year and is telling two presumed other tech writers that being around porn people always makes him feel like he's been somehow astrally projected onto a cocktail napkin. It is also roughly now that Ms. Jasmin St. Claire is making an appearance at the Impressive Media booth in order to spell the starlet behind the counter, who is limping to the booth's rear area; she (i.e., the limping starlet) has (reportedly) had to be sprayed with silicon to fit into her pants. The crowd at the Impressive Media venue immediately starts to enlarge. Jasmin St. Claire is wearing a red vinyl jacket-and-miniskirt ensemble. A porn starlet entering any kind of room or area has a distinctive energy about her — you turn your head to look even if you don't seem to want to. It's like watching a figure from a pinball machine illustration or high-concept comic book step out into 3-D and head your way. It turns out really to be possible to feel as though your eyeballs are protruding slightly from their sockets. What makes the whole thing so weird is that Jasmin St. Claire isn't even all that pretty, at least not today. Her hair is dyed black in that cheap unreal Goth way, and she is so incredibly heavily made up that she looks like a crow. (She is also somewhat knock-kneed, plus of course has the requisite Howitzer-grade bust.) Ms. St. Claire is being escorted to the Impressive booth by two large men whose expressions are describable only as mug-shottish. This is another thing about porn starlets — they're never alone. They're always accompanied by at least one and sometimes as many as four flinty-eyed males. The impression is that of a very expensive thoroughbred being led onto the track under a silk blanket.

FYI, Ms. Jasmin St. Claire's cult-celebrity status at the '98 CES stems from her having broken the "World Gang Bang Record"[16] by taking on 300 men in a row in Amazing Pictures' 1996 *World's Biggest Gang Bang 2*. Since most of these 300 men were amateur porn-fans who'd had only to fill out an application and produce an HIV all-clear from the DPH, she now enjoys an almost legendary

---

16 (set previously in 1994, by one Amber Chang, at 251 males)

populist appeal — "the People's Porn Star" — and an enormous serpentine line of fans with cameras and autographable memorabilia has formed at the Impressive booth, which line Ms. St. Claire appears for the moment to be ignoring, because she and H. Hecuba, having exchanged double-cheek kisses, are now deep into some kind of tête-à-tête above the sockless Docksiders of the unconscious bald kid, who's (the kid has) evidently been carried or trundled by pranksters unknown from the XPlor counter (right next door) to this one. Dick Filth — after your correspondents have remarked on how it's kind of heartwarming that everyone in the porn industry all seem to be friends, even critics and performers — dishes an involved anecdote about how Jasmin St. Claire apparently once actually tried to *strangle* Harold Hecuba at an industry soirée a couple years ago, an anecdote which, if you're interested, appears as FN 17 just below. Twenty feet away, over at

---

[17] According to Dick Filth, the imbroglio started when Hecuba crashed the party and was spotted by Ms. Nici Sterling, about whom Mr. Hecuba had said in a recent film review that it was "unclear whether she'd win any beauty contests, but she sure could suck cock." It was apparently the beauty contest crack that had hurt Ms. Sterling's feelings, and on seeing H.H., and suffering the relaxation of social inhibitions for which entertainment parties of all kinds are famous, the starlet made a beeline for Hecuba, uttered two high-volume expletives, and attempted to strike the print journalist with an open-handed right cross, whereupon H.H. had the presence of mind (aided perhaps by the six-inch heels that made Ms. Sterling's balance precarious and forced her to telegraph the blow) to grab her hand before it could knock his trifocals off. Whereupon in turn Ms. Jasmin St. Claire, seeing Harold Hecuba clutching the upraised hand of an agitated and off-balance Nici Sterling, performed a set-pick off the three-foot width of Ron ("the Hedgehog") Jeremy and leapt on Hecuba's back and deployed what Filth averred was a pretty authentic- and impressive-looking LAPD-style chokehold, prompting Hecuba to whirl 360° in an effort to dislodge Ms. St. Claire while he still had the cerebral oxygen to do so, inadvertently whipcracking Ms. Sterling into Randy West and mussing Mr. West's coiffure for the first time in industry memory and (to the best of Filth's recollection) simultaneously dislodging H.H.'s special autotint trifocals and sending them out in an arc across the room and into the forbidding décolletage of Ms. Christy Canyon, never to be recovered (the glasses) or even seen ever again.

Filth also reports that the Sterling Incident had been just either the iceberg's tip or the camel's straw so far as Jasmin St. Claire and Harold Hecuba were concerned. H. Hecuba had evidently also conducted a recent interview with J. St. C. in which she had confided that she was taking the rather staggering amount of $ she was making from *World's Biggest Gang Bang 2* and investing it in a (pretty dubious-sounding) string of pornographic gumball machines all up and down the CA coast, and Hecuba had chosen

XPlor, Mr. Farrel Timlake has meanwhile produced what is alleged to be the prototype and world's only authorized Kenny® Action Figure from the upcoming *South Park* merchandising line — fourteen inches tall, kind of heavy for a doll, w/ hood up and face obscured (not unlike F. Timlake's own hood and face) — and is entertaining some of the IM crowd's spillover by manipulating the doll's limbs to simulate its "tok[ing] a bone."

Not unlike urban gangs, police, carnival workers, and certain other culturally marginalized guilds, the US porn industry is occluded and insular in a way that makes it seem like high school. There are cliques, anticliques, alliances, betrayals, conflagratory rumors, legendary enmities, and public bloodlettings, plus involved hierarchies of popularity and influence. You're either In or you're not. Performers, being the industry's fissile core, are of course In. Despite their financial power, studio execs and producers are not very In, and directors (especially those who've never undergone the initiation of having on-camera sex themselves) are less In than the performers. Film reviewers and industry journalists are even less In than execs; and nonindustry journalists are way, way non-In,

---

(17, CONTINUED)
to include this confidence in the published interview, and Ms. St. Claire was reportedly furious that Hecuba had publicized her "secret investment strategy," believing that now everyone and his brother were going to want to get into adult-themed-gumball-vending and it would glut the market, and so Jasmin St. Claire had had it in for Harold Hecuba for some time, and may well have viewed the Sterling Incident more as a convenient excuse than as the rescue of what appeared to be an endangered colleague — D. Filth says that debate over the motives behind the Chokehold-360°-Hair-Cleavage fiasco has been vigorous and multiform for 20 months now.

Dick Filth also appends, "apropos nada," that Ms. Jasmin St. Claire happens in real life to be the granddaughter of late NYC *capo di tutti capo* Paul Castellano, who was assassinated in the 1980s at least partly because of his opposition to the Mob's involvement in "immoral enterprises" like narcotics and porn, and who thus has to have been doing a good 180 rpm in his grave ever since *WBGB2.*

PLUS APPARENTLY COMING SOON TO AN ADULT RETAILER NEAR YOU: Ms. Jasmin St. Claire, in a bid to retain and even enhance her cult status, allows butane gas to be pumped via PVC into her lower colon and set afire on expulsion, resulting in a 3.5-foot anal blowtorch for Cream Productions' 1998 *Blow It Out Your Ass.*

almost as low-caste as the great mass of porn fans themselves (for which fans the Insider term is: *mook*[18]).

The foregoing is meant to help explain how exactly your correspondents ended up in porn titan Max Hardcore's personal suite at the Sahara and got to hang out in the suite's living room with Max, certain of his crew, porn starlets Alex Dane and Caressa Savage, and two B-girls — which is to say that it was actually Harold Hecuba and Dick Filth who were invited to hang out in the suite on Friday afternoon, but yr. corresps. clung almost like papooses to their backs, and the burly MAXWORLD Production Assistant wasn't quick enough about slamming the door.

So yr. corresps. were, for a couple hours, at least logistically speaking, In.

For a regular civilian male, hanging out in a hotel suite with porn starlets is a tense and emotionally convoluted affair. There is,

---

[18] *Mook* means roughly what *rube* used to mean among carnies. Like all psychically walled communities, the adult industry is rife with code and jargon. *Wood* is a camera-ready erection; *woodman* is a dependably potent male performer; and *waiting for wood* is a discreet way of explaining what everybody else in the cast and crew is doing when a male performer is experiencing *wood trouble*, which latter term is self-evident. *SS* means a sex scene; a *DP* is a Double Penetration, wherein a starlet's vagina and rectum are simultaneously accessed by two woodmen — q.v. 1996's semiclassic *NYDP Blue*. (Certain especially stoic and/or capacious actresses are apparently available for *Triple* Penetrations, but these performers are rare and so, thankfully, are TPs.) *Tush 'n' Bush* denotes a film with both anal and vaginal SSs. *Skeet* (*n/v*) is a term used for both the act of male orgasm (*v*) and the material thereby emitted (*n*). (N.B., however, that both H. Hecuba and D. Filth aver that one of their big challenges as reviewers is to keep coming up with lively and evocative synonyms for semen.) *Money* — short for *money shot* — is a successfully filmed male orgasm, which of course 100 percent of the time takes place external to the female partner; e.g. a *facial* is a money whose skeet is directed onto the partner's cheek or forehead. *Girl-Girl* signifies a sapphic SS, which every single hetero film seems to require at least one of. *Beam* denotes a straight-on deep-focus view of a dilated and wood-ready orifice. A *B-girl* is a second- or third-tier porn actress who's lower paid than a starlet and is usually available for more perverse, degrading, or painful SSs. *Fluff* (*v*) is unfilmed oral activity designed to induce, maintain, or enhance a woodman's wood (and high-end porn films used to employ what were actually called *fluff girls*, who were usually B-girls in waiting).
  EXERCISE: Use at least eight (8) of the prenominate adult-industry terms in a well-formed English sentence.
  SAMPLE SOLUTION: "After a kind of long wait for wood, a B-girl fluffed the rookie woodman into a state where he could take part in a DP SS whose frequent beams required maximum wood, and after a shaky start the SS ended up a spectacular double-facial in which the starlet really displayed her professionalism by managing to stay enthusiastic even though some of the skeet went in her right eye."

first, the matter of having seen the various intimate activities and anatomical parts of these starlets in videos heretofore and thus (weirdly) feeling shy about meeting them. But there is also a complex erotic tension. Because porn films' worlds are so sexualized, with everybody seemingly teetering right on the edge of coitus all the time and it taking only the slightest nudge or excuse — a stalled elevator, an unlocked door, a cocked eyebrow, a firm handshake — to send everyone tumbling into a tangled mass of limbs and orifices, there's a bizarre unconscious expectation/dread/hope that this is what might happen in Max Hardcore's hotel room. Yr. corresps. here find it impossible to overemphasize the fact that this is a *delusion*. In fact, of course, the unconscious expectation/dread/hope makes no more sense than it would make to be hanging out with doctors at a medical convention and to expect that at the slightest provocation everyone in the room would tumble into a frenzy of MRIs and epidurals. Nevertheless the tension persists, despite the fact that the actresses are obviously tired and disassociated from the day's CES,[19] plus, it emerges, somewhat sore — it turns out that Max Hardcore is shooting one of his "Gonzo" porn spectaculars right here at the 1998 Consumer Electronics Show, using the CES as a hook and backdrop, and the girls have been alternating CES booth-duty and riding-crop shenanigans with a tight and SS-intensive filming schedule. (Max, being a firm believer in the fait accompli method of filmmaking, has not yet gotten around to chatting with the CES's administration about his featuring the world's biggest consumer-tech tradeshow by name in a "SEE PRETTY GIRLS SODOMIZED IN MANNERS MOST FOUL" video.)

---

[19] The female performers seem, in truth, not just uncommunicative but downright surly. How much of this is tradeshow fatigue and how much is the stony demeanor of Insiders toward all Outsiders is anyone's guess. The actresses are all in post-CES mufti — baggy jeans and cotton halters and big fuzzy slippers, etc. Without their makeup and appurtenances, Savage and Dane look even prettier; the B-girls do not. They all spend most of the time on the suite's long vinyl couch watching a syndicated *Seinfeld* triple-header.

Mr. Max Hardcore — a.k.a. Max Steiner, a.k.a. Paul Steiner, né Paul Little — is 5'6" and a very fit 135. He is somewhere between 40 and 60 years old and resembles more than anything a mesomorphic and borderline-psycho Henry Gibson. He is wearing a black cowboy hat and what has to be one of the very few long-sleeved Hawaiian shirts in existence anywhere. Once the PA guarding the door mellows out and introductions are made (H.H. managing to drop the name of this magazine several times in one sentence), Max reveals himself to be a genial and garrulous host and offers everybody disposable plastic cups of vodka before settling in with yr. corresps. to discuss what for Max are the most pressing and relevant issues at this year's AVN Awards, which issues are the career, reputation, personal history, and overall life philosophy of Mr. Max Hardcore.

Pioneered (depending whom you talk to) by either Max Hardcore or John ("Buttman") Stagliano, "Gonzo" has become one of this decade's most popular and profitable genres of adult video. It's more or less a cross between an MTV documentary and the Hell panel from Bosch's *Garden of Earthly Delights*. A Gonzo film is always set at some distinctive locale or occasion — Daytona Beach at spring break, the Cannes Film Festival, etc. There's always a randy and salivous "host" talking directly to a handheld camera: "Well and we're here at the Cannes Film Festival, and it looks like there's going to be lots of excitement, John Travolta and Sigourney Weaver are supposed to both be in town, and there's also the world-famous beach, and I'm told there's always some real seriously good-looking little girls at the beach, so let's us head on down." (That's the approximate lead-in to a recent Max-at-Cannes Gonzo, a type of signature lead-in that Max refers to with a 56-tooth grin as "always mercifully brief" — and please note the "*little girls* at the beach" thing, because this is another of Max's professional signatures, the infantilization of his videos' females as dramatic foils for his own film persona, which is always that of a sort of degenerate uncle or stepdad.) Then the shaky but ever-focused camera heads on down to the ocean or mall or CES or whatever, scoping out attractive women[20] while the host moans and chews his knuckle in lust. Then pretty soon host and camera start actually coming up to the women they've been looking at and engaging them in little cameo "interviews" full of sideways leers and salacious entendres. Some of the interviewees are actual civilians, but some are always what Max refers to as "ringers," meaning professional porn actresses. And so the viewer is treated to the classic frathouse fantasy of moving, via just a couple of singles-bar "Hey there babe" lines, from scoping out an attractive woman to having wild and anatomically diverse sex with her, all while one of his buddies captures the whole thing on tape.[21]

The issue of who exactly invented Gonzo being impossibly vexed and so notwithstanding, it is true that Max Hardcore is famous as a director for several things: (1) Being incredibly disciplined about budgets and tactical logistics, right down to forcing his crew and staff to wear identical jumpsuits of scarlet nylon so that they look like a national ski team — Max's shoots are described (by Max) as "almost military operations"; (2) Not only employing ringers but actually sometimes being able to talk real live civilian "little girls" on the beach or in the mall into coming on back to the special MAXWORLD RV and having anal sex on camera;[22] (3) Being the first in "mainstream" (meaning nonfetish)

---

[20] (especially their bottoms, it seems, in the Gonzos of Max, Buttman, Mr. Ben Dover, and "Butt Row's" J. Silvera)

[21] So let's observe that whereas traditional, quote-unquote dramatic porn videos *simulate* the 100 percent sexualization of real life (viz. by creating a kind of alternative real world in which everyone from secretaries to firemen to dental hygienists is always just one prompt away from frantic intercourse), Gonzo videos push the envelope by offering the apparent sexualization of *actual* real life (by, for instance, combining real footage of babes on the Cannes beach with scripted footage of seduction and explicit sex). Gonzo thus obviously seems like the porn equivalent of the mainstream trend in Docudramas, *COPS, Real-Life Adventures of 3rd-Shift Trauma Surgeons*, etc.

[22] This is not a rumor. It is documented as fact. No theories on this phenomenon or on the civilian females' possible motives/susceptibilities will even be attempted here — the relevant questions are just too huge and stupefying.

adult video to perpetrate on women levels of violation and degradation that would have been unthinkable even a few years ago. W/r/t item (3), Max, after detailing for yr. correspondents the vo- and avocations that led him into the adult industry (a tale too literally incredible even to think about factchecking and trying to print), informs us that he is and always has been adult video's "cutting-edge blade," and that other less bold and original filmmakers have systematically stolen and used his, Max's, degradations of women as a blueprint for their own subsequent shabby and derivative films' degradations.[23] (Harold Hecuba and Dick Filth, by

---

[23] Max is here referring not only to Silvera and Byron and the rest of the Gonzo-come-latelies, but to directors like Gregory Dark and Rob Black, who are the spearheads of a certain other hot '90s genre called (by Dick Filth, in print) "Bizarro-Sleaze." Gregory Dark's recent *Snakepit* and *The Shocking Truth* do things like seat a starlet in an interview chair and then have an off-camera inquisitor ask her, e.g., whether she thinks she's a slut and whether she thinks she's eventually going to go to hell for her insatiable sluttiness and how she felt about the sexual attentions of her piggish stepfather, which example then segues into an SS where four men dressed stepfatherishly in bowties and cardigans and all with plastic pig-snouts strapped onto their faces gang-bang her into a stupor. Whereas Mr. Rob Black — compared to whom Gregory Dark is Frank Capra — offers entertainment like gang bangs of paraplegic women, women being made to eat Ritz crackers that have been skeeted on, and men taking turns spitting in women's faces.*

Your correspondents elect here to submit an opinion. Dark's and Black's movies are not for men who want to be aroused and maybe masturbate. They are for men who have problems with women and want to see them humiliated. Whether Bizarro-Sleaze might conceivably help armchair misogynists "work out" some of their anger at females is irrelevant. Catharsis is not these films' intent. Their intent is to capitalize on a market-demand that quite clearly exists — these directors' products, like Max Hardcore's, are near-constant presences in *Adult Video News*'s Top Sellers and Renters lists.

Dark's and Black's movies are vile. They are meant to be. And the truth is that in-your-face vileness is part of the schizoid direction porn's been moving in all decade. For just as adult entertainment has become more "mainstream" — meaning more widely available, more acceptable, more lucrative, more chic: *Boogie Nights* — it has become also more "extreme," and not just on the Bizarro margins. In nearly all hetero porn now there is a new emphasis on anal sex, painful penetrations, degrading tableaux, and the (at least) psychological abuse of women. In certain respects, this extremism may simply be porn's tracing Hollywood entertainment's own arc: It's hardly news that TV and legit film have also gotten more violent and explicit and raw in the last decade. So maybe. And yet there's something else.

The psychodynamics of porn seem always to have involved a certain real degree of shame, self-loathing, perception of "sin," etc. This has held both on the performing end — "I'm a nasty girl," "I'm a little fuckhole" — and on the consumption end — recall, or get someone to tell you about, the embarrassment of being seen at the ticket window of an adult theater, or the haunted faces of trenchcoated men in Times Square, Boston's Combat Zone, SF's Tenderloin. We note, though, that the faces of today's fans at the Adult CES seem different, the affect more complex. An observer gets the odd

---

*N.B. here in advance that Mr. Rob Black will win Best Director/Video at Saturday night's Awards gala.

the way, have heard Max hold forth many times before and are now outside the circle of discourse — D.F. in the bathroom for what seems like a peculiarly long time, H.H. on the couch with the actresses hashing out the implications of Seinfeld's retirement for NBC's '98 lineup.)

Alone and in a place of conspicuous honor on a wood-finish shelf above the suite's minibar is an actual AVN Awards statuette. The trophy resembles an Oscar/Emmy/Clio except that the figurine's arms are up and out (making it also look a bit like Richard Nixon at the climax of the '68 GOP convention), and something slightly blurry about the casting gives it a sort of cubic-zirconium aspect. Whether the statuette is heavy and solid vs. hollow and Little Leaguish remains unknown — there is no invitation to touch or heft it. One of the B-girls on the couch is now either laughing or weeping into her hands at something Harold Hecuba has said; her bare shoulders heave. It would be totally fantastic if the *Seinfeld* rerun on the huge TV were the episode about everybody trying to refrain from masturbating, but it isn't.

(23, CONTINUED)
sense that the average fan here feels slightly ashamed of being slightly ashamed of his enthusiasm for porn, since the performers and directors now appear to have abandoned shame in favor of the steely-eyed exultation that always attends success in the great US market. Wherever else it is, porn is no longer in the shadows and slums. As Max's scarlet-clad crewman put it, "In a way, it's kind of a drag. Now everybody's watching it. We used to be rebels. Now we're fucking *businessmen.*"†

The thing to recognize is that the adult industry's new respectability creates a paradox. The more acceptable in modern culture it becomes, the farther porn will have to go in order to preserve the sense of *un*acceptability that's so essential to its appeal. As should be evident, the industry's already gone pretty far; and with reenacted child abuse and barely disguised gang rapes now selling briskly, it is not hard to see where porn is eventually going to have to go in order to retain its edge of disrepute. Whether or not it ever actually gets there, it's clear that the real horizon late-'90s porn is heading toward is the Snuff Film. It's also clear — w/ all moral and cultural issues totally aside — that this is an extremely dangerous direction for the adult-film industry to have to keep moving in. It seems only a matter of time before another conservative pol sees in mainstream porn an outrage sufficient to hang his public ambitions on. The AVA, after all, is not the only powerful lobby with an interest in social norms. At this point, anyway, porn's own internal contradictions (e.g., constantly offending mainstream values ——→ the billions of $ that attend mainstream popularity) look to be the industry's most dangerous enemy.

† (Max's response to this crew member's analysis, accompanied by a thumbs-up: "God bless America, kid.")

Asked by one of yr. corresps. what he won this AVN Award on the shelf for, Max Hardcore slaps his knee: "I fucking *stole* it." It's now that hard middle-distance inspection reveals that the MAX HARDCORE on the metal strip at the trophy's base has been scratched in by someone who is not a professional engraver. It looks done with a screwdriver, in fact. Max expands on the statuette caper: Shut inexplicably out of the Awards for years, he last year, upon exiting the stage (he's always a presenter every year, which he regards as the AVNAs' way of twisting the emotional blade), espied in the wings a large cardboard box filled with blank and unused AVN Award statuettes.[24] Whereupon he thought, as he now puts it, "What the fuck, I fucking *deserve* it" and snagged one, hiding it in his enormous Stetson and deriving no little satisfaction from attending various post-Awards parties with an illicit statuette under his hat. Max's crew all laugh very hard at this anecdote, though the actresses don't.

Alex Dane is now telling Harold Hecuba about a stray dog she found and has decided to keep. She is excited as she describes the dog and for a moment seems about fourteen; the impression lasts only a second or two and is heartbreaking. One of the B-girls, meanwhile, is explaining that she has just gotten a pair of cutting-edge breast implants that she can actually adjust the size of by adding or draining fluid via small valves under her armpits, and then — perhaps mistaking your correspondents' expressions for ones of disbelief — she raises her arms to display the valves. There really are what appear to be valves.

So much about today's adult industry seems like an undeft parody of Hollywood and the nation writ large. The top performers are comic-book caricatures of sexual allure. The prosthetic breasts and lifted buttocks and (no kidding) artificial cheekbones are nothing

---

[24] (Here yr. corresps.' suspicion that the AVNA statuettes are bought in bulk, possibly hot, feels somehow confirmed.)

more than accentuations of a mentality that yields huge liposuction and collagen industries. The gynecologically explicit sexuality of Jenna, Jasmin, et al. seems more than anything like a *Mad* magazine spoof of the "smoldering" sexuality of Sharon Stone and Madonna and so many other mainstream iconettes.[25] Not to mention the fact that the adult industry takes many of the psychological deformities that Hollywood is famous for — the vanity, the vulgarity, the rank commercialism — and not only makes them overt and grotesque but seems then to *revel* in that grotesquerie.

Good old Max Hardcore, for instance, is a total psychopath — that's part of his on-screen Gonzo persona — but so is the real Max/Paul Steiner. You'd almost have to have been there in that suite. Max sits holding court in his hat and pointy boots, looking at once magisterial and mindless, while his red-suited acolytes laugh on cue and a jr. high dropout shows off her valves. In truth, the first ten minutes of the impromptu interview in the Sahara are spent passing around a copy of something called *Icon* magazine, which Max has told us is doing a profile on him — we are expected to leaf through the magazine and comment favorably on its content and layout while Max watches us in the same hyperexpectant way that parents watch you when you're looking at a snapshot of their kid that they've taken out uninvited and pressed on you. This is the actual chronology. There then follows a torrent of autobiography and background that yr. corresps. have decided to deny Max the satisfaction of seeing reproduced here. After which is a kind of Max 101–like survey of personal philosophy and Gonzo theory and the statuette anecdote. The vodka is top-shelf and the plastic cups dusty. Then one of the starlets decides that she's hungry, and Max insists on escorting her down to the Sahara's restaurant and wants everybody else to come along, which eventually results in the B-girls

---

[25] . . . and of the ubiquitous smolder that's so much a part of '90s commercial culture. Mr. H. Hecuba, for instance, during one of the marathon screenings of Award-nominated videos referenced above in FN 3, pointed out that the relation between a Calvin Klein ad and a hard-core adult film is essentially the same as the relation between a funny joke and an explanation of what's funny about that joke.

and crewmen and yr. corresps.[26] all standing there awkwardly at the maître d's podium while Max personally conducts the starlet to her table and pulls out her chair and tucks a serviette into her cleavage and pulls out a platinum-plated money clip and announces in a voice audible to everyone in the restaurant and foyer that he "want[s] to take care of the little girl's damages in advance" and shoves bills into the hanky-pocket of the maître d's tuxedo and then leaves her there by herself and herds us all back out and into the elevator and jabs impatiently at the button for his suite's floor, almost jumping up and down with fury at the elevator's delay; and we're all rushed back up to the suite because it's occurred to Max that he wants to show your corresps. something from this week's filming that he thinks will sum up his particular porn genius better than any amount of exposition could . . . and then, reseated, he starts flipping through a notebook to find something.

"What it is is we got this one little girl back in the [infamous MAXWORLD] trailer, and after some face-fucking[27] and reaming her asshole and, like, your standard depravities, we get her to stick a pen — no, a what-do-you-call . . ."

Crewman: "Magic Marker."

Max: ". . . Magic Marker, stick it up her asshole and write all this . . . this *stuff*," holding up the notebook, opened to a page; again he has us pass it around:

I'm a little fuck hole

---

[26] Hecuba and Filth, being both familiar with Max and financially independent of him, elect to remain in the suite under the beady and seemingly lidless eye of the Production Asst. (who, by the way, is not wearing a fire-colored MAXWORLD jumpsuit but has evidently been promised one if he completes his probationary employment period in good standing).

[27] = fellatio? = very energetic French kissing?

is thereon written in a hand[28] that seems impressively legible, considering. Dick Filth makes a waggish inquiry about future film plans involving this girl and a typewriter, but Max doesn't laugh (we noticed that Max never laughs at a joke he hasn't told), and so neither does anyone else.

Doubtless most of this is going to get cut by *Premiere*, but it's worth also observing — when this magazine's assigned photographer (who's also gotten in here with us this afternoon on H.H. and D.F.'s coattails) begins wondering aloud about the possibility of getting some good portraits at the Awards of winners holding their statuettes — the way Max right away jumps in with his idea of the perfect photo for the title page of this very article. The proposed shot is to be of Max Hardcore, holding several of the AVN Awards trophies he pledges either to win straight up or to gain possession of in other ways, seated in some kind of imperial-looking and really nice chair that is itself set up on the palm-studded boulevard of the famous Las Vegas Strip — so the photographer'll get lots of smeary neon and appropriately phallic bldgs. in the background — with a retinue of scantily clad starlets either draped swoonily over him or prostrate at his feet, or both. It is important to note that there are no audible scare-quotes, no irony or embarrassment or self-awareness of any sort on Max's face as he sketches this photo's tableau for us; he's in the kind of earnest that one imagines Irving Thalberg was always in.[29] Your correspondents immediately begin to lobby hard

---

[28] (so to speak)
[29] Yes, this is it: What's so unbelievable is not the extent or relentlessness of porn people's egotism (Jasmin St. Claire's way of greeting a journalist is to offer him a personally autographed photo; Tom Byron, who is 36 and has precisely one attribute, affects the air of a Mafia don at the Sands' bar's nightly porn parties, extending his hand knuckles-up as if for obeisance, etc. etc.). It's the *obtuseness* of it. Take, for just one other instance, the 29-year-old Mr. Scotty Schwartz, with whom through the good offices of Harold Hecuba your correspondents had a working supper that ended up being a whole Russian novel in itself. Young Mr. Schwartz, maybe 5'0" in low gravity and platform shoes, is a former Hollywood child star whose performances in Richard Pryor's *The Toy* and Darren McGavin's *A Christmas Story* were the zenith of a career the abrupt decline of which led — through a flux of circumstances too tortuous to even take notes on — to an acquaintance with the ubiquitous Ron Jeremy and an entrée to the insular social nexus of adult video. Either desperate or deranged or both, Scotty Schwartz evidently decided that the "controversy" of his appearance in a hard-core film would jump-start his legit career (kind of like a rehab or arrest, is Scotty's analogy; he repeatedly gnashes his teeth over the fact that his old rival Corey Feldman's career survived a rehab). And the adult industry, only too

(29, CONTINUED)
happy to cash in on the novelty of Scotty's mainstream celebrity (recall 1994's *John Wayne Bobbitt Uncut*, after all), starred Schwartz in Wicked Pictures' 1996 *Scotty's X-Rated Adventure*, a production beset by near-crippling anxiety and epic waits for wood, all of which psychic travails Scotty recounts in a detail that inspires pure empathic horror in yr. male corresps. (FYI, Mr. Bobbitt's porn debut, too, was marred by serious wood issues — impotence apparently being the Achilles' heel of nearly all nonprofessional woodmen [the term *performance anxiety* must take on a whole new hideous resonance in the magnesium glare of a working porn shoot] — but Bobbitt finally submitted to a penile injection of prostaglandin [known in the industry as "instant wood"], whereas Schwartz bravely/cravenly chose to limp through *S.'s X-R.A.* without medical assistance.)

... The thrust of the whole long story being that Schwartz, though (understandably) no longer a hard-core performer, has abandoned mainstream ambitions for the adult vortex and is now a budding Gonzo-genre director, and is even this week guiding something called *Scotty's Behind the Anal Door at the C.E.S.* (which presumably Max Hardcore doesn't know about) through a hectic series of Tush 'n' Bush shoots.

Anyway, the point is that yr. corresps. were on Thursday night lured to this supper meeting by Hecuba's reports that S. Schwartz had become sort of the unofficial mascot of the adult industry, and knew absolutely *everybody*, and was a near-manic chatterbox: We figured that he'd be a good source of background and context and gossip. H.H. had already prepared us for Schwartz's personal manner (which is ticcy and breathless and neurally irritating in the same way a musical note held much too long is neurally irritating), but what Hecuba neglected to mention was that Scotty Schwartz is also totally incapable of talking about anything other than himself. Two courses and half an hour are spent on Scotty's mainstream résumé and the fucking-over he got from fate's fickle finger (alliteration and anatomically mixed metaphor Schwartz's) and the comparative injustice of the arcs of his and C. Feldman's careers, then another 20 minutes on Schwartz's budding and allegedly platonic relationship with a born-again Christian girl he met on the Internet (during which whole initial 50 minutes one of yr. corresps. kept having to put his napkin in his mouth). Nor did Schwartz seem able or disposed to tell any story of which he himself was not the hero. Here — as close to verbatim as stupefaction permitted — is Scotty's tale of his introduction to Mr. Russ Hampshire, head of VCA Inc. and what Scotty terms "a very very big fish: like *this* if you know what I'm saying to you here" in the adult industry:

"So I'm at this party and hanging and schmoozing up the girls and there across the room is Russ Hampshire and Russ catches my like eye if you know what I'm saying and and goes, like, you know, 'Hey kid, c'mere' and so I do I go over I mean this is Russ fucking Hampshire you know what I'm saying here and I do I like go on over to where Russ is at and Russ comes over to me and goes, 'Scotty, I been watching you. I like your style. I'm a good judge of people, and Scotty, you're good people. I never heard one person say one bad thing about you.' [Keep in mind that this is Scotty telling this story. Note how verbatim he gets Hampshire's dialogue. Note the altered timbre and perfectly timed delivery. Note the way it never even *occurs* to Schwartz that a normal US citizen might be bored or repelled by Scotty's lengthy recitation of someone else's praise of him. Schwartz knows only that this interchange occurred and that it signifies that a big fish approves of him and that it redounds to Scotty's credit and that he wants it widely, widely known.] 'Kid, I just want you to know you're fucking OK in my book, and if there's anything I can do to, you know, help you, anything at all, I just want you to say the word.'"

... End of vignette, and now Scotty — like Max, like Jasmin, like Jenna and Randy and Tom and Caressa — looks around the table, examining his auditors' faces for the admiration that cannot possibly fail to appear. What is the socially appropriate response to an anecdote like this — a contextless anecdote, apropos nothing, with its smugly unsubtle (and yet not unmoving, finally, in its naked insecurity) agenda of getting you to admire the teller? The few seconds after, with the vignette hanging there and Scotty's eyes on your correspondents' faces like fingers, were the first of countless such moments over the AAVNA's weekend. How is one expected to respond? It was very uncomfortable. One of yr. corresps. opted for "Gosh. Wow." The other pretended to have had a brussels sprout go down the wrong way.

for Max's idea, figuring that the photo would make a great illustration for the story of Max's proposing this very photo — i.e., that it would point up the megalomania far more powerfully than mere reportage — but the *Premiere* photographer, who is no actor, does such a poor job of disguising his repulsion at Max's self-regard that the atmosphere of the whole suite gets stilted and complexly hostile, and the rest of the interview is kind of a fizzle-yield, and overall Dick Filth said that we failed, in his phrase, to "penetrate to the core of the essence of what it is to be Max Hardcore."[30]

The 15th Annual AVN Awards are actually split over two consecutive nights, a tactic that Max H. thought the legit Oscars would do well to emulate: "Get all the bullshit out of the way the first night — best packaging, marketing, best gay, shit like that. Who wants to sit through that shit?"

Held in a different, slightly smaller Caesars Palace ballroom, Friday's Awards show is indeed brisk. The ephemeral categories include Best Videography, Best Screenplay, Best Art Direction, Best Music. Each category's nominees are listed in the program, but only the winners are announced onstage, and they're announced four at a time, and applause is discouraged, and the master of ceremonies keeps telling the quartets of winners that "If you'll come on up quickly and help keep things moving it'll help us out a lot." Friday's only food is big wheels of vegetables and dip near the cash bar. The emcee is not headliner Robert Schimmel but a hypomanic guy named Dave Tyree, whose interpolated banter is 78 rpm and consists of stuff like "If God didn't want us to jerk off he would've made our arms shorter." There are maybe 1,000 people in attendance, most only slightly dressed up, and there are no assigned

---

[30] (Apparent pun accidental . . . although one of your corresps., on receiving Filth's overall review in the fleeing taxi, responded that surely we had penetrated as far into the core of Max as any sentient organism could ever want to penetrate. Filth's subsequent rebuttal, which consisted mainly of a long string of unsubstantiatable Max Hardcore stories, is, for basic legal reasons, here omitted.)

tables, and everybody in the ballroom is moving around and chattering and treating the onstage proceedings the way people in a cocktail lounge treat the piano player.

Q. $4,000,000,000 and 8,000 new releases a year — why is adult video so popular in this country?

A. Director and AVN-Hall-of-Fame inductee F. J. Lincoln: "It's always a little funny how it's called *adult*. What it really is, you get to be a kid again. You roll around and get dirty. It's the adult sandbox."

A. Veteran woodman Joey Silvera: "Dudes, let's face it — America wants to jerk off."

A. Industry journalist Harold Hecuba: "It's the new Barnum. Nobody ever goes broke overestimating the rage and misogyny of the average American male."

A. Porn starlet Jacklyn Lick: "I think a lot of fans are very lonely people."

Q. There don't seem to be a whole lot of condoms used in hardcore scenes.

A. Harold Hecuba: "Never have been. They're viewed as a turn-off. This business is about engineering fantasies."

Q. But even just venerially — all these anal shenanigans and everything. Is there much worry in the industry about HIV?

A. Harold Hecuba: "There's not as much worry about AIDS now. Everybody gets tested on a schedule."

Q. What about herpes?

A. H.H.: "I think it's rampant."

Last year's Best-Sex-Scene-in-a-Film winner Vince Vouyer's real name turns out to be John LaForme. Rhetorical Q.: How, if one's real name was John LaForme, could that person possibly feel the need for a nom de guerre?

Mr. Tom Byron describes being able to tumesce and ejaculate more or less on demand as an exercise in "control, like meditation or surfing. It's like a gymnast staying on the balance beam. You practice enough, you can do anything."[31]

Former woodman and current auteur Paul Thomas was a member of the original Broadway cast of *Jesus Christ Superstar.*

The tall, crazed-looking, and ever-rampant Mike Horner, three-time Best Actor winner and a member of the AVN Hall of Fame,[32] is actually a classically trained opera singer.

Deceased starlet Nancy Kelly's real name was Kelly Van Dyke. She was the daughter of TV's Jerry Van Dyke and so, of course, the niece of Dick.

Exotic rookie actress Midori, one of the nominees in the '98 AVNAs' Best New Starlet category, is the sister of '80s pop star Jodi Whatley. Midori has stated publicly that she views upscale contemporary porn as a stepping-stone to a mainstream career, not unlike becoming Miss America or doing a couple seasons on *SNL.* Harold Hecuba characterizes Midori's career strategy as "grievously ill-advised."

Adult Video News VP and Executive Editor Gene Ross, presenting the aforementioned 1998 AVN Award for Best Director/Video to *Miscreants'* Rob Black, will hail Mr. Black as "a guy who can take buttholes, midgets, and fried fish, and make a love story."[33]

From *The New Yorker*'s 1995 article on the psychosexual plight of the adult industry's woodman: "The Cal Jammers who are part of this feminization feel they have stormed the walls of female

---

[31] Mr. Tom Byron, by the way, who broke into the industry in the mid-'80s as a young man whose adolescent skinniness and Howdy-Doodyish mien were as compelling and distinctive as his penis, is now having the same weird thing happen to his face that Christopher Walken seemed to have happen to his face sometime after *The Dead Zone.* It's not just that Byron's freckles are now gone or that his eyes have taken on a dead menace — the actual skin of his face has become shiny and sort of plasticized-looking, overtaut in the way a death mask is overtaut. For anyone who remembers what Byron looked like as a kid fresh out of the University of Houston, his face now after thirteen years at the top of his trade is a chilling contradiction of the industry's claim that it's all about pleasure and unfettered play.

[32] (physical location of this Hall, if any, is unknown)

[33] [Laughter, cheers.]

ornament to reclaim male prerogative, only to find themselves lost in a garden of gender irony."

Mr. John "Buttman" Stagliano — CEO of Evil Angel Inc., a man described by *US News & World Report* as "the nation's leading director of hard-core videos" — not only has publicly announced testing positive for HIV but has identified the infection's vector as a transsexual prostitute in São Paulo with whom Stagliano had unprotected anal intercourse in 1995. He's anxious that people not get the wrong idea: "I am not particularly interested in guys, but I am interested in dicks. Forbidden taboos lead to all sorts of neurotic behavior, which leads to me being fucked in the ass without a rubber."

Are the AVN Awards possibly rigged? Max Hardcore (he of the purloined statuette, keep in mind) calls the Awards "a total conflict of interests." After all, he explains, *Adult Video News* is heavily ad-dependent,[34] and they're under "pressure from the big hitters like Vivid and VCA to like, you know, give the nod."

---

[34] Let us note that the slick, full-color 15th AAVNA Official Program is itself an advertiser-sponsored document, its lists of categories and nominees scattered among full-page production-company ads hyping the nominated films themselves. This doesn't seem beyond the pale — certainly *Variety* does the same sort of thing at Oscartime. Other ads in the AAVNA Program are for things like Wet Platinum–brand lubricant —

> STAYS SLICK EVEN UNDER WATER . . .
> NEVER DRIES . . . WILL NOT HARM LATEX!

— plus several from California Exotic Novelties Corp., maker of the RAMROD Penile Pump, of Doc Joc's Incredible Jack-Off Device, and of the "Anne Malle Facsimile Fullsize KNEELING DOLL":

> • KNEELING POSITION — READY TO BE TAKEN
> • EXCITING ANAL PENETRATION
> • RIPE LUSCIOUS SQUEEZABLE BREASTS
> • VIBRATING ACTION
> • BEAUTIFUL BLACK HAIR
> BEND OVER and TAKE ME NOW!!!

Whether these ads are niche-directed at industry Insiders (doubtful, although they're pretty much the only ones who are going to see the Programs), at retailers, or at plain old mooks is unclear.

38 DAVID FOSTER WALLACE

Ms. Ellen Thompson, *AVN* Associate Editor and an Awards judge who votes under the n.d.g. Ida Slapter:[35] "We've heard this for years. I hear this complaining also goes on in the mainstream. I don't like insulting anybody, but sometimes there's sour grapes. What are we supposed to say? Vivid and VCA put out good product. We truly, honestly do vote fairly."

Mr. Dick Filth: "The best perception, backed up by tons of anecdotal evidence, is that they are totally, totally fixed and rigged."

Saturday's the big night. The banquet, the onstage entertainment, the headline Awards. See & be seen. Gamblers and conventioneers and mooks of all ilk are massed at the Caesars cabstand to watch the starlets arrive. There are camcorders and flashbulbs but no paparazzi per se. Some of the performers come in limos, others in shiny penile sports cars; others seem to mysteriously just suddenly appear. There are even more starlets here than there were at the CES, and they are seriously dolled up. There are cerise halters and pear-colored Lycra bodysuits with open-toed pumps of burgundy suede. There are platinum lamé gowns slit all the way to the tenth rib. Bottoms less covered than shellacked look like they by all rights should have panty- or at least thong lines but do not have such lines. There are lime-green vinyl leotards and toile bellbottoms and fishscale bustiers and miniskirts the same texture and length as a tutu's ruffle. Garter straps flash and Merry Widow bodices shade

---

[35] There are 45 official voters listed in the Awards Program. Here are some of their names: Avie Chute, Rich C. Leather, Marlon Brandeis, Roland Tuggonit, Stroker Palmer, S. Andrew Roberts & Slave Girl (so actually there are either 45 or 44 official voters, depending on whether Slave Girl gets her own vote or is just along to rubber-stamp S. Andrew Roberts's vote). Oddly, Ms. Ellen Thompson appears on the list both as Ida Slapter and as Ellen Thompson, so one sort of wonders just how many ontologically distinct voters there actually are. Nor does an independent Big 6 accounting firm tally the ballots in secret under armed guard or any of that Oscar-type security. According to Slapter/Thompson, the Awards voting is "secret," but the completed ballots are all turned in to Paul Fishbein and Gene Ross, who are the Publisher and VP (and Fishbein a co-owner) of *Adult Video News*, and who thus have an obvious interest in happy sponsors and healthy ad revenues. The whole thing inspires something less than rock-solid confidence.

the interiors of translucent blouses. Several of the outfits defy very basic precepts of modern physics. Coiffures are towering and complex. The starlets are all on the arms of men, but none of these escorts are male porn performers. Average heel-height is 4"+. A loud-voiced civilian in the cabstand crowd actually utters the phrase "Va Va Voom," which yr. correspondents had never before heard anywhere outside a Sinatra movie. Breasts are uniformly zeppelinesque and in various perilous stages of semiconfinement. Max Hardcore is under a Stetson the color of weak chocolate milk, and his adjustable B-girl — arrayed in a type of scarlet cowboy suit that's mostly fringe — has inflated her breasts to what's got to be maximum capacity.

Woodman-wise, black is clearly In at the 15th Annual AVNAs. A lot of the men are in black tuxedos and black ties *and* black dress shirts. One is wearing a paisley suit of either serge or some kind of upholstery material. Another has silver platform shoes and a silver vest w/ no shirt underneath. The XPlor boys are in Klein sweatshirts and urban-camouflage fatigues, and there's a large contingent with them that may or may not include the *South Park* brain trust. A guy on the arm of Ms. Morgan Fairlane has an immense and razorous violet mohawk à la British punks of the late 1970s.

Inside the hotel, a kind of impromptu cocktail party forms in the broad marble hall outside Caesars Palace's largest and reportedly classiest ballroom, which is called Caesars Forum. Burly casino staffers stand taking tickets and being very discouraging about anybody trying to bum-rush the show. The crush of bodies out here entails a degree of physical contact that CES mooks never even dreamed of. There are pockets of klieg-glare as cable TV reporters interview various performers about (*sic:*) the air of keen excitement in the air. Mysterious bundles of co-ax emerge from under the Forum doors and go all the way up the length of the hallway and disappear around the corner. A suspicion that we'd had all week but decided was unverifiable is now instantly verified when one of yr. corresps. gets accidentally shoved against a starlet and is jabbed in the side by her breasts and it *hurts*. A lot of people are holding drinks in plastic glasses and it's unknown where they got them. The starlets take turns getting interviewed re atmospheric excitement while the woodmen all avoid the cameras like mafiosi. The TV lights are not doing anyone's skin tone any good at all. In their all-black tuxes, several of the male Insiders — including e.g. John Leslie and Tony Tedeschi — are so pallid and sallow as to appear diseased. Mr. Nick East devotes a full 5.5 minutes of rapt concentration to the cuticle of his left thumb. A slight surprise is that a lot of the industry's elite woodmen are short — 5'6", 5'7"[36] — and most of their companions tower over them. Dick Filth confirms that the contemporary industry's 5'6" standard helps a prodigious male organ look even more prodigious on videotape, a medium that apparently does all kinds of strange things to perspective.

Tickets for Saturday's main event are $195 per, in advance. It's unclear whether any Insiders' tickets are comped, but journalists pay full retail. Our tickets designate our table as #189. Twenty-five hundred tickets have been sold, and since it's highly doubtful that anybody got past the flinty-eyed casino guys outside without a ticket, tonight's attendance can confidently be fixed at 2,500.

The Caesars Forum ballroom itself is a huge L-shape with the stage at the — as it were — joint; thus half of the 15th Annual AVN Awards' audience is geometrically invisible to the other half. This problem is addressed via six sail-sized video screens that hang from the ceiling at strategic points throughout the auditorium. During the nearly two hours[37] between when the doors open and the Awards show actually starts, the screens alternate quick clips from porn classics[38] (recall that the theme of the 15th AAVNAs is "The

---

[36] What many of the top woodmen resemble most are gymnasts. They're compact and muscular and move with the liquid economy of athletes, as if equipped with internal gyroscopes. Little of their physical grace is ever visible on tape.
[37] We are not kidding — the Oscars are brisk and minimalist compared to the AVNAs.
[38] (e.g. *Debbie Does Dallas, Behind the Green Door,* something ill-lit with John Holmes in it, *The Devil in Miss Jones,* etc. — nothing identifiable from *Deep Throat,* though, and definitely nothing involving the statutorily infamous Traci Lords . . .)

History of Adult") with live shots of various people making their entrances and mugging for the remote cameras *AVN* has got circling the room.

Both Harold Hecuba and Dick Filth have come equipped with binoculars (H.H.'s in a very official-looking Audubon Society case), which seems mysterious until we all arrive at Table 189, which is at the very, very back of the ballroom's L's northern leg, hundreds of yards from even the nearest video screen. "They always put the print guys out in mookland," Hecuba explains. This fact is unpleasant surprise #1. Unpleasant surprise #2 is the supper the $195 includes, which turns out to be buffet-steam-table-style and might best be described by inviting you to imagine a very cosmopolitan and multiethnic hospital cafeteria.[39] Several of the male Insiders, we now notice, have brought in their own picnic hampers.

Now moving w/ laden plate to a table near us is a man in a full-body leopardskin suit whose way of acknowledging people he knows is to point at them rather than wave at them. On his arm is a B-girl in a body stocking made of what appears to be a densely woven net. Two Astral Ocean Cinema contract starlets have on identical copper-colored beaded gowns with myriad lengthwise slits in the skirt parts' fronts and backs and sides, so that as they walk to their table their upper halves look normal and their lower halves seem to be passing through an infinity of bead curtains. Obviously, the whole scene is overwhelming. The average American rarely gets to see aerobic legwarmers with 4" spike heels. The Caesars Forum ceiling is the color of rancid meringue; it has 24 chandeliers that are designed to look like concentric opened fans but actually look more like labia or very well-organized fungus. Mr. Joey Buttafuoco is in the house, accompanying[40] Al Goldstein of *Screw*, who is here to receive a Special AVN Achievement Award for His Lifelong

---

[39] There is something deeply surreal about standing behind a female performer in hot-pink peau de soie, a woman whose clitoris and perineum you have priorly seen, and watching her try to get a microwaved egg roll onto her plate with a cocktail fork.
[40] (platonically)

Defense of the First Amendment. Black is so resoundingly In this year that even the starched linen napkins at everyone's place settings are black. The wineglasses all have little frosted cameos of J. Caesar on them. Humorless men with walkie-talkies stand guard at each of the ballroom's fire doors — apparently last year there were some problems with unauthorized Caesars Palace employees sneaking in to watch the gala. The video screens are now showing the climactic scene of *Debbie Does Dallas,* the one where the nebbishy little stand-in for all mooks everywhere finally has sex with Bambi Woods and then the screen flashes *"NEXT?"* The *South Park* boys are indeed in attendance, up at Table 37 w/ Farrel and the XPlor coterie. There are also rumors that *Boogie Nights* auteur Paul Thomas Anderson possesses a ticket to the gala and might show up.[41]

The closest thing to any kind of Insider table near ours is #182, which according to its black table-tent is reserved for Anabolic Video (not an industry force) and is currently occupied by a spiriferously coiffed and sullenly chewing Dina Jewel (who declines to return Harold Hecuba's blown kiss) and her escort, a young fellow whom one can easily envision head-butting somebody in a mosh pit. D. Filth confides that this Anabolic guy is a close friend of woodman Vince Vouyer (again, *sic*), who himself is not up for many '98 Awards because he spent a good part of the past year in court and/or detention for helping operate an escort service which authorities alleged was not a bona fide escort service at all.

It turns out that Hecuba and Filth have kept from yr. correspondents as unpleasant surprise #3 the single chintziest thing about the $195-a-head 15th AAVNAs banquet & gala: Beverages are not compris. And not just alcohol, either; even a lousy club soda w/ lime[42] is $6.00. Worse, it turns out you can't run any sort of tab —

---

[41] Despite the fact that the movie presents everybody in porn as cretinous, pathetic, or both, the adult industry has evidently embraced *Boogie Nights* the same way the music industry embraced *This Is Spinal Tap,* and the Anderson rumor (which never comes to anything — if P. T. Anderson ever shows, it's deeply incognito) generates the least cynical enthusiasm of the evening.

[42] (We're on duty.)

you have to pay the waiter in cash when you order the lousy club soda w/ lime, and he (theoretically) brings your change back with the beverage. Thus a separate and memory-intensive transaction is required for each drink that each of the six-to-eight persons at each of the appr. 375 tables in the auditorium might order, with additional complications if certain people are buying drinks for certain tablemates but not for certain other tablemates, etc.[43] The whole unfree-drink situation is incredibly annoying, not only because of the outlandish ticket price but because the ballroom's 100 percent Middle Eastern waiters (decent and hardworking fellows all, to be sure, who are taking some serious abuse about the pay-as-you-go beverage policy from mooks with cigars at the nearby tables, despite the fact that the waiters don't make the rules and must surely find having to remember and make change for six to eight different customers per table a piercing pain in the ass[44]) have only rudimentary ESL skills and tend to confuse both drink orders and currency denominations. Dick Filth leans over and shouts: "Now you can maybe see why this is a multibillion-a-year industry — they're tight as a duck's butt!"[45]

The crowd lingers over hypersucrotic cake and coffee and $9.00 cordials and howls conversation at itself for 90 more minutes before the house lights dim and the 15th Annual AVN Awards gala starts. What follows thereon is a kaleidoscopic flux of stilted acceptances and blue one-liners and epileptic strobes and spotlights following winners' serpentine and high five–studded paths to the stage, of everything from generic Awards Show schmaltz to moments of near-Periclean eloquence, as in e.g.:

---

[43] For instance, H. Hecuba has strictly enjoined us from buying any sort of distilled beverage for Dick Filth, for reasons that become clear as the evening wears on.

[44] (The waiters' special 15th AAVNAs fringe benefit, which sharply reduced yr. corresps.' empathy with them, wasn't revealed until the gala concluded — see below.)

[45] Filth is shouting because between the screens' clips' audio and the stage band warming atonally up and the ambient conversational roar it's close to deafening in here. When the Awards Show starts, the audio techs will have the amplifiers turned all the way up to Shattering, which, even though it will tend to cause mussed hair and spilled drinks in both directions' front rows, those of us way back in mookland appreciate.

"Fellow MENSA members and aficionados of Shakespeare!" intones Al Goldstein of *Screw,* 62 and obese and white-bearded and crazy-haired and dressed in a sportcoat whose lapels are two different primary colors, looking pretty much exactly like that one certain old guy in the neighborhood your mom warned you never to try to sell Cub Scout chocolate mints to, and glorying in a Special AVN Achievement Award he confesses to feeling he's long deserved. "I want to thank my mother, who spread her legs and made all this possible." Large sections of the crowd are on their feet — Goldstein is a porn icon. He was distributing NYC's *Screw* on photostat when most of the people in this room were still playing with their toes. He's been a First Amendment ninja. He drinks in the applause and loves it and is hard not to sort of almost actually like. He's clearly an avatar of contemporary porn's *unabashedness,* its modern Yeah-OK-I'm-Scum-but-Underneath-All-Your-Hypocrisy-So-Are-You-and-at-Least-I-Have-the-Guts-to-Admit-It-and-Have-a-Good-Time persona:

"I salute the women with eleven-IQs and the men with eleven-inch cocks. The real heroes are the cocks and pussies who fuck on-screen. They're the real heroes." Goldstein is less conducted than borne back to his seat.

This has followed Robert Schimmel's intro and a 20-minute "Musical Salute to the History of Adult," in which topless dancing girls do a medley of disco, new wave, and so on.[46] The stage band is ragged and unevenly amplified, and they all have flared collars and tight perms — it's like watching *The Brady Bunch*'s final season through borrowed binoculars. The stage is lit by autotrack spotlights whose colors alternate w/o discernible scheme.

The whole 15th AAVNAs Show lasts 3.5 hours and resembles nothing so much as an obscene and extremely well-funded high

---

[46] As both the screens' preliminary clips and the Musical Salute indicate, *Adult Video News* appears to believe that the History of Adult begins circa 1975, when in fact this is merely the year when the locus of US porn moved from New York to California.

school assembly. The mix of garish self-congratulation[47] and clumsy choreography is often so weird as to be endearing. There are never fewer than six presenters for each award, and they never seem to know whose turn it is to announce a nominee, and there are always a couple who don't get close enough to the mike to be audible and a couple others who get *too* close to the mike and produce a jolt of feedback that sends people and cocktails flying out of chairs in the first rows of tables. Wicked Pictures' *Satyr,* a multiple-category nominee, gets repeatedly pronounced *"Satter."* Winners are supposed to exit stage-left after their acceptance speeches, but even people who've won and been through the process several times in recent years keep forgetting and trying to exit stage-right and colliding with the hostesses who are there to escort them leftward. Some presenters insert brief rote antidrug messages into their intros, while around them twitch and sniff other presenters — not many, but some — who are obviously coked to the gills.

Probably the most neutral and economical thing to say is that large parts of the ceremony are unintentionally funny. Winning woodmen extend earnest thanks to directors and execs for giving them "an opening" or "a shot" or "my big shot" and seem wholly unaware of the carnal entendres involved. Back at the journalists' table with us is a 40ish woman in two-piece Armani who's doing a spot on the Awards for ABC Radio; she spends most of the evening hunched over with her head in her hand and her tape recorder not even on. Dick Filth spends the show's whole second hour trying to track down a waiter who owes him beverage change. *AVN*'s Gene Ross pays tribute to '98's Male Performer of the Year by saying: "You haven't lived until you've seen Tom Byron's wrinkled nuts on a seventy-inch TV screen." Rob Black's *Miscreants* keeps getting nominated in category after category, and time and again there's a frantic caucus at the podium about the correct pronunciation of

---

[47] E. just one g.: *AVN* head Paul Fishbein takes a moment out from his welcoming remarks to announce that his proud parents are in the audience tonight . . . and they *are.*

miscreant, complete with a couple of presenters audibly whispering what in the fuck is the word even supposed to mean.[48]

To be fair, some of the nominated products' titles are genuinely confusing. *Triple Penetration Debutante Sluts 4* is up for Most Outrageous Sex Scene — along with *Wild Bananas on Butt Row* and *87 and Still Bangin'* — but loses out to a scene the Program entitles "Anal Food Express"[49] from a video called *My Girlfriend's Girlfriend.* Paul Thomas's *Bad Wives* wins Best Film. Evil Angel's *Buda* wins Best Shot-on-Video Feature. The Best Foreign Release statuette goes to something European called *President By Day, Hooker By Night. Bad Wives* also wins Best Actress/Film for Dyanna Lauren, Best Supporting Actress/Film for Melissa Hill, and Best Anal Sex Scene/Film[50] for Lauren and Steven St. Croix. Best Compilation Tape honors go to *The Voyeur's Favorite Blow Jobs & Anals.* David Cronenberg's mainstream *Crash* comes out of absolutely nowhere to win something called Best Alternative Adult Feature Film. Ms. Stephanie Swift wins Best Actress/Video and tells the crowd: "Thanks, everybody. My gang bang was a blast."[51]

Max Hardcore, to Table 189's immense and unkind delight, doesn't win one single thing.

An actor named Jim Buck wins *AVN*'s Gay Performer of the Year Award, and you better believe yr. corresps. sit bolt upright when the person who appears onstage to accept the award is a pink

---

[48] (Nobody mispronounces *Sodomania,* though, we notice.)

[49] There is no will left to inquire about this (much less about the gynecological logistics of a Triple Penetration); by this time yr. corresps. are slumped in opposite directions in their chairs, only slightly less fried than the lady from ABC Radio.

[50] Yes — it's a real category. There's also Best Anal Sex Scene/Video, Best Group Sex Scene/F & /V, Best All-Girl Sex Scene, Best Gay Sex Scene, Best Foreign Sex Scene, Best Tease Performance, and something called Best Solo Sex Scene. Etc. etc. Hence the Awards Show's extreme and numbing length: There's a total 104 categories overall, plus three Special Achievement Awards, an AVN Breakthrough Award, and sixteen new inductees to the already engorged AVN Hall of Fame.

[51] Though Ms. Swift won for *Miscreants,* she is here actually alluding to her and director R. Black's real breakthrough video in 1997, *Gangbang Angels,* which is essentially a one-woman show and features the year's most infamous scene: Twelve woodmen line up and do an about-face, and S. Swift performs analingus on each in turn; she then kneels and assumes a prayerful/compliant posture as the twelve men all do a right-face and form a moving line and take turns hawking and spitting in her face.

and leptosomatic 4'10" and is wearing an Eton collar and appears, even under 125X binoculation, to be a twelve-year-old boy. And it turns out it *is* a twelve-year-old boy: It's Jim Buck's little brother. "Jim can't be here tonight because he's performing in a Shakespeare festival in New Orleans," the little boy says (correspondential expressions of bug-eyed inquiry at Hecuba and Filth — Shakespeare festival? sending a prepubescent relative to collect your excellence-in-filmed-sodomy prize? — are met with bemused shrugs), "but I'm here to thank you on his behalf, and to say that I taught Jim everything he knows." [Enormous audience laugh and ovation, single spasmodic shudder from hunched ABC Radio lady.]

A strange and traumatic experience which one of yr. corrs. will not even try to describe consists of standing at a men's room urinal between professional woodmen Alex Sanders and Dave Hardman. Suffice it to say that the urge to look over/down at their penises is powerful and the motives behind this urge so complex as to cause anuresis (which in turn ups the trauma). Be informed that male porn stars create around themselves the exact same opaque affective privacy-bubble that all men at urinals everywhere create. The whole Caesars Forum's men's room's urinal area is an angst festival; take it from us. The sink-and-mirror-and-towelette area, however, turns out to be a priceless mash of Insider jargon and shoptalk, all made extra-resonant by echolalic tile and a surfeit of six-dollar drinks. One performer-turned-auteur is telling a colleague about an exciting new project:

"Found this Russian, this chick like nineteen, can't speak a word of English, which for this [= for the exciting project] is perfect."

"You going to get in there? Just for maybe like one scene?"

"Nah. That's the whole point. I'm the *director.* This is my *package* now."

"Oh man though but you got to get in there. Just one scene. Nineteen, no English. Probably got a butthole about this big" [illustrative gesture unseen because auditor is still standing complexly traumatized at urinal].

"Well, we'll see." [Mutual laughter replete w/ warmth of genuine friendship, fellow-feeling; exeunt.]

The Awards Show's planners have obviously studied at the Oscars' feet. Not only are the high-profile AVNAs held to the end — though with occasional teasers like Best Supporting thrown into the first two-thirds to keep people attentive[52] — but the endless lists of categories and nominees are interspersed with little entr'actes of musical entertainment. Ms. Dyanna Lauren, for instance, appears between Best-Selling Tape and Best Foreign Release to sing her original composition "Psycho Magnet," a hard-rock ballad about being a porn star and getting constantly stalked and harassed by mentally ill mooks. The song's argumentation strikes yr. corresps. as a bit uneven, but Ms. Lauren struts and contorts and punctuates her phrasing with uppercuts to the air like a genuine MTV diva. The downside is that vocally, even with heavy amplification and digital synthesis, Dyanna Lauren sounds like a scalded cat, although Dick Filth points out that so does Alanis Morissette, and H. Hecuba chimes in by shouting: "Say whatever you want about the song-and-dance numbers here, they sure beat what Wahlberg and Reilly were coming up with in *Boogie Nights!*"

Hecuba's claim seems unassailable until right before the Best Boxcover Concept category, when suddenly a piano is wheeled out for a chinless middle-aged man in the same sort of undersize porkpie that Art Carney always wore in *The Honeymooners*. This entertainer, who is introduced as "Doctor Dirty — the Dirtiest Musician in the History of Music," proceeds to belt out obscene parodies of popular ditties that put Table 189 in mind of *Mad* magazine if everyone at *Mad* somehow all lost their mind at the same time. "Just got home from prison./My asshole is fizzin'./Goo goo goo drippin' out

---

[52] (Meaning people in the live audience. *Adult Video News* is taping the whole Awards Show, and they're going to distribute the tape for sale/rent; and in the taped version, clips from various winning scenes are going to get spliced in, which seems clearly designed to mitigate at-home boredom.)

my back door" is the only snatch of actual lyrics that persists in memory, though titles like "Sit on a Happy Face" and "It's a Small Dick After All" have proved maddeningly hard to forget. Nobody at or around our table has ever heard of Doctor Dirty before, but almost everyone agrees that he's the '98 gala's low point and a credible rival for Scotty Schwartz's 1997 seminude rendition of "Thank Heaven for Little Girls" as the most repellent AVNA interlude in modern memory. There's also the '98 ceremony's climax, in which Midori[53] and two other starlets take the stage as "the Spicy Girls" and do a rappish 4/4 number that ends with pretty much every female porn performer in the crowd[54] up on stage dancing lasciviously and blowing kisses at the *AVN* cameras. This climactic distaff shindig apparently caps the Awards every year.

Something else happens every year. It's never part of *AVN*'s videotape of the gala, but it's a tradition that finally explains why the ballroom's poor waiters are willing to spend five hours enduring beverage abuse and scuttling around to find change. After the Awards Show is over and the lights go up, some of the starlets always pose for obscene snapshots with the Forum's waiters. A lot of this year's picture-taking happens at the back, right near our table. One waiter stands with his arm around the shoulders of Leanna Hart, who pulls down the starboard side of her strapless taffeta and allows the waiter to cup her right breast while Table 189's own personal waiter[55] snaps the photo. Another waiter goes around behind Ms. Ann Amoré — a very personable black lady with a 50-inch bust and gang tattoos all down both arms — and hunches over behind her as she bends forward and releases her breasts from confinement, and the waiter paws them and tries to look like he's having intercourse with her from behind as his friend's flash goes off. What the waiters are going to do with these photos is unguessable, but they're visibly thrilled, and the starlets are patient and obliging

---

[53] (who is no J. Whatley but at least doesn't screech)

[54] No woodmen are invited to join in, or at any rate none try to.

[55] (whom D. Filth is still hectoring for $13.00 in alleged Grand Marnier change)

with them in the same blank, distant way that they were with the mooks at the Adult CES.

Trying to leave after the AAVNAs gala is another slow process, because the broad hallway outside the ballroom is again filled with industry people with Caesar-cameo'd glasses they've somehow forgotten to leave at their tables, all standing in clumps and congratulating one another and making plans for various Insider parties later. But the slowest, scariest egressive part is traversing the long glass vestibule to the hotel's side exit. A mass of fans and Caesars Palace custodians and assorted other civilians are there, and the crowd parts slightly to allow a narrow passage for the Awards' attendees, who must run this gauntlet nearly single file. It's late, and everyone's tired, and this crowd has none of the awestruck reticence of the cabstand's spectators earlier. Now it's like every mook has his own special high-volume comment for the passing stars, and there's a weird mix of adulation and derision:

"Love you, Brittany!"

"How'd you get that dress on, baby?"

"Look over here!"

"Does your mother know where you're at right now?"

One florid 30ish man holding a plastic cup of beer now reaches out from the crowd and very deliberately pinches the breast of the B-girl walking just in front of us. She slaps his hand away without breaking stride. Because we cannot see her face, we don't know whether there is any reaction there at all. We have an informed guess, though.

Mr. Dick Filth is behind us with one hand on each of yr. corresps.' shoulders (we're basically supporting him out). Everyone's ears are still ringing, and Filth knows enough to almost shout:

"You know," he says, "we've also got the XRCO Awards in February. X-Rated Critics Organization Awards — you get me? They're not in Vegas, and they're not rigged. And yet they manage to be just as ridiculous."

1998

CERTAINLY THE END OF *SOMETHING* OR OTHER, ONE WOULD SORT OF HAVE TO THINK

(Re John Updike's *Toward the End of Time*)

Of nothing but me . . . I sing, lacking another song.
— J. UPDIKE, *MIDPOINT*, CANTO I, 1969

MAILER, UPDIKE, ROTH — the Great Male Narcissists* who've dominated postwar American fiction are now in their senescence, and it must seem to them no coincidence that the prospect of their own deaths appears backlit by the approaching millennium and online predictions of the death of the novel as we know it. When a solipsist dies, after all, everything goes with him. And no US novelist has mapped the inner terrain of the solipsist better than John Updike, whose rise in the 1960s and '70s established him as both chronicler and voice of probably the single most self-absorbed generation since Louis XIV. As were Freud's, Updike's big preoccupations have always been with death and sex (not necessarily in that order), and the fact that his books' mood has gotten more wintry in recent years is understandable — Updike has always written mainly

---

* Hereafter, GMNs.

about himself, and since the surprisingly moving *Rabbit at Rest* he's been exploring, more and more overtly, the apocalyptic prospect of his own death.

Toward the End of Time concerns an extremely erudite, successful, narcissistic, and sex-obsessed retired guy who's keeping a one-year journal in which he explores the apocalyptic prospect of his own death. *Toward the End of Time* is also, of the let's say two dozen Updike books I've read, far and away the worst, a novel so clunky and self-indulgent that it's hard to believe the author let it be published in this kind of shape.

I'm afraid the preceding sentence is this review's upshot, and most of the remainder here will consist simply of presenting evidence/justification for such a disrespectful assessment. First, though, if I may poke the critical head into the frame for just one moment, I'd like to offer assurances that your reviewer is not one of these spleen-venting spittle-spattering Updike haters one often encounters among literary readers under forty. The fact is that I am probably classifiable as one of the very few actual subforty Updike *fans*. Not as rabid a fan as, say, Nicholson Baker, but I do believe that *The Poorhouse Fair, Of the Farm,* and *The Centaur* are all great books, maybe classics. And even since '81's *Rabbit Is Rich* — as his characters seemed to become more and more repellent, and without any corresponding sign that the author understood that they were repellent — I've continued to read Updike's novels and to admire the sheer gorgeousness of his descriptive prose.

Most of the literary readers I know personally are under forty, and a fair number are female, and none of them are big admirers of the postwar GMNs. But it's John Updike in particular that a lot of them seem to hate. And not merely his books, for some reason — mention the poor man *himself* and you have to jump back:

"Just a penis with a thesaurus."

"Has the son of a bitch ever had one unpublished thought?"

"Makes misogyny seem literary the same way Rush makes fascism seem funny."

And trust me: these are actual quotations, and I've heard even worse ones, and they're all usually accompanied by the sort of facial expression where you can tell there's not going to be any profit in appealing to the intentional fallacy or talking about the sheer aesthetic pleasure of Updike's prose. None of the other famous phallocrats of Updike's generation — not Mailer, not Exley or Roth or even Bukowski — excites such violent dislike.

There are, of course, some obvious explanations for part of this dislike — jealousy, iconoclasm, PC backlash, and the fact that many of our parents revere Updike and it's easy to revile what your parents revere. But I think the deep reason so many of my generation dislike Updike and the other GMNs has to do with these writers' radical self-absorption, and with their uncritical celebration of this self-absorption both in themselves and in their characters.

John Updike, for example, has for decades been constructing protagonists who are basically all the same guy (see for instance Rabbit Angstrom, Dick Maple, Piet Hanema, Henry Bech, Rev. Tom Marshfield, *Roger's Version*'s "Uncle Nunc") and who are all clearly stand-ins for Updike himself. They always live in either Pennsylvania or New England, are either unhappily married or divorced, are roughly Updike's age. Always either the narrator or the point-of-view character, they tend all to have the author's astounding perceptual gifts; they think and speak in the same effortlessly lush, synesthetic way that Updike does. They are also always incorrigibly narcissistic, philandering, self-contemptuous, self-pitying . . . and deeply alone, alone the way only an emotional solipsist can be alone. They never seem to belong to any sort of larger unit or community or cause. Though usually family men, they never really love anybody — and, though always heterosexual to the point of satyriasis, they especially don't love women.* The

---

* Unless, of course, you consider delivering long encomiums to a woman's "sacred several-lipped gateway" or saying things like "It is true, the sight of her plump lips obediently distended around my swollen member, her eyelids lowered demurely, afflicts me with a religious peace" to be the same as loving her.

very world around them, as gorgeously as they see and describe it, tends to exist for them only insofar as it evokes impressions and associations and emotions and desires inside the great self.

I'm guessing that for the young educated adults of the sixties and seventies, for whom the ultimate horror was the hypocritical conformity and repression of their own parents' generation, Updike's evection of the libidinous self appeared refreshing and even heroic. But young adults of the nineties — many of whom are, of course, the children of all the impassioned infidelities and divorces Updike wrote about so beautifully, and who got to watch all this brave new individualism and sexual freedom deteriorate into the joyless and anomic self-indulgence of the Me Generation — today's subforties have very different horrors, prominent among which are anomie and solipsism and a peculiarly American loneliness: the prospect of dying without even once having loved something more than yourself. Ben Turnbull, the narrator of Updike's latest novel, is sixty-six years old and heading for just such a death, and he's shitlessly scared. Like so many of Updike's protagonists, though, Turnbull seems scared of all the wrong things.

Toward the End of Time is being marketed by its publisher as an ambitious departure for Updike, his foray into the futuristic-dystopic tradition of Huxley and Ballard and soft sci-fi. The year is AD 2020, and time has as they say not been kind. A Sino-American nuclear war has killed millions and ended centralized government as we know it. The dollar's gone; Massachusetts now uses scrip named for Bill Weld. There are no more taxes; local toughs now charge fees to protect the well-to-do from other local toughs. AIDS has been cured, the Midwest is depopulated, and parts of Boston are bombed out and (presumably?) irradiated. An abandoned low-orbit space station hangs in the night sky like a junior moon. There are tiny but rapacious "metallobioforms" that have somehow mutated from toxic waste and go around eating electricity and the occasional human. Mexico has reappropriated the US Southwest and is threatening wholesale invasion even as thousands of young

Americans are sneaking south across the Rio Grande in search of a better life. America, in short, is getting ready to die.

The novel's futuristic elements are sometimes cool, and verily they would represent an ambitious departure for Updike if they weren't all so sketchy and tangential, mostly tossed off as subordinate clauses in the narrator's endless descriptions of every tree, plant, flower, and shrub around his home. What 95 percent of *Toward the End of Time* actually consists in is Ben Turnbull describing the prenominate flora (over and over again as each season passes) and his brittle, castrating wife Gloria, and remembering the ex-wife who divorced him for adultery, and rhapsodizing about a young prostitute he moves into the house when Gloria's away on a trip. It's also got a lot of pages of Turnbull brooding about senescence, mortality, and the tragedy of the human condition, and even more pages of Turnbull talking about sex and the imperiousness of the sexual urge, and detailing how he lusts after assorted prostitutes and secretaries and neighbors and bridge partners and daughters-in-law and a girl who's part of the group of young toughs he pays for protection, a thirteen-year-old whose breasts — "shallow taut cones tipped with honeysuckle-berry nipples" — Turnbull finally gets to fondle in the woods behind his house when his wife's not looking.

In case that summary sounds too harsh, here is some hard statistical evidence of just how much a "departure" from Updike's regular MO this novel really is:

Total # of pages about Sino-American war — causes, duration, casualties: 0.75

Total # of pages about deadly mutant metallobioforms: 1.5

Total # of pages about flora around Turnbull's New England home, plus fauna, weather, and how his ocean view looks in different seasons: 86

Total # of pages about Mexican repossession of US Southwest: 0.1

Total # of pages about Ben Turnbull's penis and his various thoughts and feelings about it: 10.5

Total # of pages about what life's like in Boston proper without municipal services or police, plus whether the war's nuclear exchanges have caused fallout or radiation sickness: 0.0

Total # of pages about prostitute's body, w/ particular attention to sexual loci: 8.5

Total # of pages about golf: 15

Total # of pages of Ben Turnbull saying things like "I want women to be dirty" and "She was a choice cut of meat and I hoped she held out for a fair price" and the quoted stuff at the bottom of p. 53 and "The sexual parts are fiends, sacrificing everything to that aching point of contact" and "ferocious female nagging is the price men pay for our much-lamented prerogatives, the power and the mobility and the penis": 36.5

Toward the End of Time's best parts are a half-dozen little set pieces where Turnbull imagines himself inhabiting different historical figures — a tomb robber in ancient Egypt, Saint Mark, a guard at a Nazi death camp, etc. They're gems, and the reader wishes there were more of them. The problem is that they don't have much of a function other than to remind us that Updike can write really great little imaginative set pieces when he's in the mood. Their plot justification stems from the fact that the narrator is a science fan (the novel has minilectures on astrophysics and quantum mechanics, nicely written but evincing a roughly *Newsweek*-level comprehension). Turnbull is particularly keen on subatomic physics and something he calls the "Theory of Many Worlds" — a real theory, by the way, which was proposed in the fifties as a solution to certain quantum paradoxes entailed by the Principles of Indeterminacy and Complementarity, and which in truth is wildly complex and technical, but which Turnbull seems to believe is basically the same as the Theory of Past-Life Channeling, thereby explaining the set pieces where Turnbull is somebody else. The whole quantum setup ends up being embarrassing in the special way something pretentious is embarrassing when it's also wrong.

Better, and more convincingly futuristic, are the narrator's soliloquies on the blue-to-red shift and the eventual implosion of the known universe near the book's end; and these would be among the novel's highlights, too, if it weren't for the fact that Ben Turnbull is interested in cosmic apocalypse all and only because it serves as a grand metaphor for his own personal death. Likewise all the Housmanesque descriptions of the Beautiful But Achingly Transient flowers in his yard, and the optometrically significant year 2020, and the book's final, heavy description of "small pale moths [that] have mistakenly hatched" on a late-autumn day and "flip and flutter a foot or two above the asphalt as if trapped in a narrow wedge of space-time beneath the obliterating imminence of winter."

The clunky bathos of this novel seems to have infected even the line-by-line prose, Updike's great strength for almost forty years. *Toward the End of Time* does have flashes of beautiful writing — deer described as "tender-faced ruminants," leaves as "chewed to lace by Japanese beetles," a car's tight turn as a "slur" and its departure as a "dismissive acceleration down the driveway." But a horrific percentage of the book consists of stuff like "Why indeed do women weep? They weep, it seemed to my wandering mind, for the world itself, in its beauty and waste, its mingled cruelty and tenderness" and "How much of summer is over before it begins! Its beginning marks its end, as our birth entails our death" and "This development seems remote, however, among the many more urgent issues of survival on our blasted, depopulated planet." Not to mention whole reams of sentences with so many modifiers — "The insouciance and innocence of our independence twinkled like a kind of sweat from their bare and freckled or honey-colored or mahogany limbs" — and so much subordination — "As our species, having given itself a hard hit, staggers, the others, all but counted out, move in" — and such heavy alliteration —

"the broad sea blares a blue I would not have believed obtainable without a tinted filter" — that they seem less like John Updike than like somebody doing a mean parody of John Updike.

Besides distracting us with worries about whether Updike might be injured or ill, the turgidity of the prose here also ups our dislike of the novel's narrator. (It's hard to like somebody whose way of saying that his wife doesn't like going to bed before him is "She hated it when I crept into bed and disturbed in her the fragile chain of steps whereby consciousness dissolves" or who refers to his grandchildren as "this evidence that my pending oblivion had been hedged, my seed had taken root.") And this dislike pretty much torpedoes *Toward the End of Time*, a novel whose tragic climax is a prostate operation that leaves Turnbull impotent and extremely bummed. It is made clear that the author expects us to sympathize with or even share Turnbull's grief at "the pathetic shrunken wreck the procedures [have] made of my beloved genitals." These demands on our compassion echo the major crisis of the book's first half, described in a flashback, where we are supposed to empathize not only with the rather textbookish existential dread that hits Turnbull at thirty as he's in his basement building a dollhouse for his daughter — "I would die, but also the little girl I was making this for would die. . . . There was no God, each detail of the rusting, moldering cellar made clear, just Nature, which would consume my life as carelessly and relentlessly as it would a dung-beetle corpse in a compost pile" — but also with Turnbull's relief at discovering a remedy for this dread — "an affair, my first. Its colorful weave of carnal revelation and intoxicating risk and craven guilt eclipsed the devouring gray sensation of time."

Maybe the one thing that the reader ends up appreciating about Ben Turnbull is that he's such a broad caricature of an Updike protagonist that he helps clarify what's been so unpleasant and frustrating about this author's recent characters. It's not that Turnbull is stupid: he can quote Pascal and Kierkegaard on angst, discourse on the death of Schubert, distinguish between a sinistrorse and a dextrorse *Polygonum* vine, etc. It's that he persists in the bizarre, adolescent belief that getting to have sex with whomever one wants whenever one wants to is a cure for human despair. And *Toward the End of Time*'s author, so far as I can figure out, believes it too. Updike makes it plain that he views the narrator's final impotence as catastrophic, as the ultimate symbol of death itself, and he clearly wants us to mourn it as much as Turnbull does. I am not shocked or offended by this attitude; I mostly just don't get it. Rampant or flaccid, Ben Turnbull's unhappiness is obvious right from the novel's first page. It never once occurs to him, though, that the reason he's so unhappy is that he's an asshole.

1998

SOME REMARKS ON KAFKA'S FUNNINESS FROM WHICH PROBABLY NOT ENOUGH HAS BEEN REMOVED

ONE REASON for my willingness to speak publicly on a subject for which I am direly underqualified is that it affords me a chance to declaim for you a short story of Kafka's that I have given up teaching in literature classes and miss getting to read aloud. Its English title is "A Little Fable":

> "Alas," said the mouse, "the world is growing smaller every day. At the beginning it was so big that I was afraid, I kept running and running, and I was glad when at last I saw walls far away to the right and left, but these long walls have narrowed so quickly that I am in the last chamber already, and there in the corner stands the trap that I must run into." "You only need to change your direction," said the cat, and ate it up.

For me, a signal frustration in trying to read Kafka with college students is that it is next to impossible to get them to see that Kafka is funny. Nor to appreciate the way funniness is bound up with the power of his stories. Because, of course, great short stories and great jokes have a lot in common. Both depend on what communications theorists sometimes call *exformation,* which is a certain quantity of vital information removed from but evoked by a communication in such a way as to cause a kind of explosion of associative connections within the recipient.[1] This is probably why the effect of both short stories and jokes often feels sudden and percussive, like the venting of a long-stuck valve. It's not for nothing that Kafka spoke of literature as "a hatchet with which we chop at the frozen seas inside us." Nor is it an accident that the technical achievement of great short stories is often called *compression* — for both the pressure and the release are already inside the reader. What Kafka seems able to do better than just about anyone else is to orchestrate the pressure's increase in such a way that it becomes intolerable at the precise instant it is released.

The psychology of jokes helps account for part of the problem in teaching Kafka. We all know that there is no quicker way to empty a joke of its peculiar magic than to try to explain it — to point out, for example, that Lou Costello is mistaking the proper name *Who* for the interrogative pronoun *who,* and so on. And we all know the weird antipathy such explanations arouse in us, a feeling of not so much boredom as offense, as if something has been blasphemed. This is a lot like the teacher's feelings at running a Kafka story through the gears of your standard undergrad critical analysis — plot to chart, symbols to decode, themes to exfoliate, etc. Kafka, of course, would be in a unique position to appreciate the irony of submitting his short stories to this kind of high-efficiency critical machine, the literary equivalent of tearing the

---

[1] Compare e.g. in this regard the whole "What was the old man in despair about?"– "Nothing" interchange in the opening pages of Hemingway's "A Clean, Well-Lighted Place" with water-cooler zingers like "The big difference between a White House intern and a Cadillac is that not everybody's been in a Cadillac." Or consider the single word "Goodbye" at the end of Vonnegut's "Report on the Barnhouse Effect" vs. the function of "The fish!" as a response to "How many surrealists does it take to screw in a lightbulb?"

petals off and grinding them up and running the goo through a spectrometer to explain why a rose smells so pretty. Franz Kafka, after all, is the story writer whose "Poseidon" imagines a sea god so overwhelmed with administrative paperwork that he never gets to sail or swim, and whose "In the Penal Colony" conceives description as punishment and torture as edification and the ultimate critic as a needled harrow whose coup de grâce is a spike through the forehead.

Another handicap, even for gifted students, is that — unlike, say, those of Joyce or Pound — the exformative associations that Kafka's work creates are not intertextual or even historical. Kafka's evocations are, rather, unconscious and almost sort of sub-archetypal, the primordial little-kid stuff from which myths derive; this is why we tend to call even his weirdest stories *nightmarish* rather than *surreal.* The exformative associations in Kafka are also both simple and extremely rich, often just about impossible to be discursive about: imagine, for instance, asking a student to unpack and organize the various signification networks behind *mouse, world, running, walls, narrowed, chamber, trap, cat,* and *cat eats mouse.*

Not to mention that the particular kind of funniness Kafka deploys is deeply alien to students whose neural resonances are American.[2] The fact is that Kafka's humor has almost none of the particular forms and codes of contemporary US amusement. There's no recursive wordplay or verbal stunt-pilotry, little in the way of wisecracks or mordant lampoon. There is no body-function humor in Kafka, nor sexual entendre, nor stylized attempts to rebel by offending convention. No Pynchonian slapstick with banana peels or rogue adenoids. No Rothish priapism or Barthish meta-

---

[2] I'm not referring to lost-in-translation stuff here. Tonight's whole occasion[*] notwithstanding, I have to confess that I have very little German, and the Kafka I know and teach is Mr. and Mrs. Muir's Kafka, and though Lord only knows how much more I'm missing, the funniness I'm talking about is funniness that's right there in the good old Muirs' English version.

* [= a PEN American Center event concerning a big new translation of *The Castle* by a man from I think Princeton. In case it's not obvious, that's what this whole document is — the text of a very quick speech.]

parody or Woody Allen–type kvetching. There are none of the ba-bing ba-bang reversals of modern sitcoms; nor are there preco-cious children or profane grandparents or cynically insurgent coworkers. Perhaps most alien of all, Kafka's authority figures are never just hollow buffoons to be ridiculed, but are always absurd and scary and sad all at once, like "In the Penal Colony"'s Lieu-tenant.

My point is not that his wit is too subtle for US students. In fact, the only halfway effective strategy I've come up with for exploring Kafka's funniness in class involves suggesting to students that much of his humor is actually sort of unsubtle — or rather anti-subtle. The claim is that Kafka's funniness depends on some kind of radi-cal literalization of truths we tend to treat as metaphorical. I opine to them that some of our most profound collective intuitions seem to be expressible only as figures of speech, that that's why we call these figures of speech *expressions*. With respect to "The Metamor-phosis," then, I might invite students to consider what is really being expressed when we refer to someone as *creepy* or *gross* or say that he is forced to *take shit* as part of his job. Or to reread "In the Penal Colony" in light of expressions like *tongue-lashing* or *tore him a new asshole* or the gnomic "By middle age, everyone's got the face they deserve." Or to approach "A Hunger Artist" in terms of tropes like *starved for attention* or *love-starved* or the double entendre in the term *self-denial,* or even as innocent a factoid as that the etymologi-cal root of *anorexia* happens to be the Greek word for longing.

The students usually end up engaged here, which is great; but the teacher still sort of writhes with guilt, because the comedy-as-literalization-of-metaphor tactic doesn't begin to countenance the deeper alchemy by which Kafka's comedy is always also tragedy, and this tragedy always also an immense and reverent joy. This usually leads to an excruciating hour during which I backpedal and hedge and warn students that, for all their wit and exformative voltage, Kafka's stories are *not* fundamentally jokes, and that the rather simple and lugubrious gallows humor that marks so many of

Kafka's personal statements — stuff like "There is hope, but not for us" — is not what his stories have got going on.

What Kafka's stories have, rather, is a grotesque, gorgeous, and thoroughly modern complexity, an ambivalence that becomes the multivalent Both/And logic of the, quote, "unconscious," which I personally think is just a fancy word for soul. Kafka's humor — not only not neurotic but *anti*-neurotic, heroically sane — is, finally, a religious humor, but religious in the manner of Kierkegaard and Rilke and the Psalms, a harrowing spirituality against which even Ms. O'Connor's bloody grace seems a little bit easy, the souls at stake pre-made.

And it is this, I think, that makes Kafka's wit inaccessible to children whom our culture has trained to see jokes as entertainment and entertainment as reassurance.[3] It's not that students don't "get" Kafka's humor but that we've taught them to see humor as something you *get* — the same way we've taught them that a self is something you just *have*. No wonder they cannot appreciate the really central Kafka joke: that the horrific struggle to establish a human self results in a self whose humanity is inseparable from that horrific struggle. That our endless and impossible journey toward

---

[3] There are probably whole Johns Hopkins U. Press books to be written on the lallating function that humor serves in today's US psyche. A crude way to put the whole thing is that our present culture is, both developmentally and historically, adolescent. And since adolescence is acknowledged to be the single most stressful and frightening period of human development — the stage when the adulthood we claim to crave begins to present itself as a real and narrowing system of responsibilities and limitations (taxes, death) and when we yearn inside for a return to the same childish oblivion we pretend to scorn* — it's not difficult to see why we as a culture are so susceptible to art and entertainment whose primary function is *escape*, i.e. fantasy, adrenaline, spectacle, romance, etc. Jokes are a kind of art, and because most of us Americans come to art now essentially to escape ourselves — to pretend for a while that we're not mice and walls are parallel and the cat can be outrun — it's understandable that most of us are going to view "A Little Fable" as not all that funny, or maybe even see it as a repulsive instance of the exact sort of downer-type death-and-taxes reality for which "real" humor serves as a respite.

*(Do you think it's a coincidence that college is when many Americans do their most serious fucking and falling-down drinking and generally ecstatic Dionysian-type reveling? It's not. College students are adolescents, and they're terrified, and they're dealing with their terror in a distinctively US way. Those naked boys hanging upside-down out of their frat house's windows on Friday night are simply trying to buy a few hours' escape from the grim adult stuff that any decent school has forced them to think about all week.)

home is in fact our home. It's hard to put into words, up at the blackboard, believe me. You can tell them that maybe it's good they don't "get" Kafka. You can ask them to imagine his stories as all about a kind of door. To envision us approaching and pounding on this door, increasingly hard, pounding and pounding, not just wanting admission but needing it; we don't know what it is but we can feel it, this total desperation to enter, pounding and ramming and kicking. That, finally, the door opens . . . and it opens *outward* — we've been inside what we wanted all along. Das ist komisch.

1999

"Save up to 50%, and More!" Between you and I. On accident. Somewhat of a. Kustom Kar Kare Autowash. "The cause was due to numerous factors." "Orange Crush — A Taste That's All It's Own." "Vigorex: Helping men conquer sexual issues." "Equal numbers of both men and women opposed the amendment." Feedback. "As drinking water becomes more and more in short supply." "IMATION — Borne of 3M Innovation." Point in time. Time frame. "At this point in time, the individual in question was observed, and subsequently apprehended by authorities." Here for you, there for you. *Fail to comply with* for *violate.* Comprised of. From whence. *Quote* for *quotation. Nauseous* for *nauseated.* Besides the point. To mentor, to parent. To partner. To critique. *Indicated* for *said. Parameters* for *limits* and *options* for *choices* and *viable options* for *options* and *workable solution* for *solution.* In point of fact. Prior to this time. As of this point in the time frame. Serves to. Tends to be. *Convince* for *persuade, portion* for *part.* Commence to, cease to. Expedite. *Request* for *ask. Eventuate* for *happen.* Subsequent to this time. Facilitate. "Author's Forward." Aid in. Utilize. Detrimental. Equates with. In regards to. "It has now made its way into the mainstream of verbal discourse." Tragic, tragedy. *Grow* as non-ag. transitive. *Keep* for *stay.* "To demonstrate the power of Epson's New Stylus Color Inkjet Printer with 1440 d.p.i., just listen:" Could care less. Personal issues, core issues. Fellow colleagues. Goal-orientated. Resources. To share. Feelings. Nurture, empower, recover. *Valid* for *true.* Authentic. Productive, unproductive. "I choose to view my opponent's negative attacks as unproductive to the real issues facing the citizens of this campaign." Incumbent upon. Mandate. Plurality. *Per anum.* Conjunctive adverbs in general. Instantaneous. *Quality* as adj. Proactive. Proactive Mission Statement. Positive feedback. A positive role model. Compensation. Validation. As for example. True facts are often impactful. "Call now for your free gift!" I only wish. Not too good of a. *Potentiality* for *potential.* Pay the consequences of. Obligated. At this juncture. To reference. To process. Process. The process of. The healing process. The grieving process. "Processing of feelings is a major component of the grieving process." To transition. Commensurant. "Till the stars fall from the sky/For you and I." Working together. Efficacious, effectual. Lifestyle. This phenomena, these criterion. Irregardless. *If* for *whether. As* for *because.* "Both sides are working together to achieve a workable consensus." Dysfunctional family of origin. S.O. To nest. Support. Relate to. Merge together. KEEP IN OWN LANE. For whomever wants it. "My wife and myself wish to express our gratitude and thanks to you for being there to support us at this difficult time in our life." Diversity. Quality time. Values, family values. To conference. "French provincial twin bed with canape and box spring, $150." Take a wait-and-see attitude. Cum-N-Go Quik Mart. Travelodge. Self-confessed. Precise estimate. More correct. Very possible, very unique. "Travel times on the expressways are reflective of its still being bad out there." Budgetel. More and more inevitable. EZPAY. RENT2OWN. MENS' ROOM. LADY'S ROOM. *Individual* for *person. Whom* for *who, that* for *who.* "The accident equated to a lot of damage." *Ipse dixie.* Falderol. "'Waiting on' is a dialectical locution on the rise and splitting its meaning." Staunch the flow. AM in the morning. *Forte* as "*for*tay." Advisement. Most especially. Sum total. Final totals. Complete dearth. "You can donate your used car or truck in any condition." At present. At the present time. *Challenge* for *problem, challenging* for *hard.* Closure. Judgement. Nortorious. Miniscule. Mischievious. "Both died in an apartment Dr. Kevorkian was leasing after inhaling carbon monoxide." Bald-faced. "No obligation required!" ☺

AUTHORITY AND AMERICAN USAGE*

Acknowledgements. To give off the impression. Instrumentality. Suffice to say. "The third-leading cause of death of both American men and women." *Positive* for *good.* Alright. "This begs the question, why are our elected leaders silent on this issue?" To reference. To privilege, to gender. "DiBlasi's work shows how sex can bring people together and pull them apart." "Come in and take advantage of our knowledgeable staff!" "We get the job done, not make excuses." In so far as. "Chances of rain are prevalent." NO TRUCK'S. Beyond the pail. National Highway Traffic Safety Administration Rule and Regulation Amendment Task Force. *Further* for *farther.* "The Fred Pryor Seminar has opened my eyes to better time management techniques. Also it has given real life situations and how to deal with them effectively." Hands-on, can-do. "Each of the variants indicated in boldface type count as an entry." Visualize, visualization. "Insert and tighten metric calibrated hexscrews (K) into arc (C) comprised of intersecting vertical pieces (A) along transverse section of Structure." Creativity, creative. To message, to send a message, to bring our message to. To reach out to. Context. A factor, a major factor, a decisive factor. Myriads of decisive factors. "It is a federal requirement to comply with all safety regulations on this flight." In this context, of this context. On a frequent basis. From the standpoint of. Contextualization. Within the parameters of this context. Decontextualization. Defamiliarization. Disorientated. "The artist's employment of a radical visual idiom serves to decontextualize both conventional modes of representation and the patriarchal contexts on which such traditional hegemonic notions as representation, tradition, and even conventional contextualization have come to be seen as depending for their canonical privileging as aestheto-interpretive mechanisms." I don't feel well but expect to recoup. "As parents, the responsibility of talking to your kids about drugs is up to you." Who would of thought? Last and final call. Achieve. Achievement. Excellence. Pursuit of a standard of total excellence. Partial completion. An astute observance. *Misrepresent* for *lie.* A long-standing tradition of achievement in the arena of excellence. "All dry cleaners are not the same." Visible to the eye. *Which* for *that, I* for *me.* That which. With regards to this issue. *Data* as singular, *media* as singular, *graffiti* as singular. *Remain* for *stay.* On-task. *Escalate* as transitive. Community. "Iran must realize that it cannot flaunt with impunity the expressed will and law of the world community." Community support. Community-based. Broad appeal. Rally support. Outpourings of support. "Tried to lay the cause at the feet of Congress." Epidemic proportions. Proportionate response. Feasibility. "This anguishing national ordeal." Bipartisan, nonpartisan. Widespread outbreaks. Constructive dialogue. To appeal for. To impact. Hew and cry. From this aspect. Hayday. Appropriate, inappropriate. Contingency. Contingent upon. Every foreseeable contingency. Audible to the ear. *As* for *since.* Palpably quiet. "The enormity of this administration's accomplishments." Frigid temperatures. Loud volume. "Surrounded on all sides, my workable options at this time are few in number." Chaise lounge, nucular, deep-seeded, bedroom suit, reek havoc. "Her ten-year rein atop the competition? The reason why is because she still continues to hue to the basic fundamentals." Ouster. Lucrative salaries, expensive prices. *Forgo* for *forego* and vice versa. Breech of conduct. Award for meretricious service. Substantiate, unsubstantiated, substantial. Re-elected to another term. Fulsome praise. Service. Public service. "A tradition of servicing your needs." "A commitment to accountability in a lifetime of public service." I thought to myself. As best as we can. WAVE ALL INTEREST FOR 90 DAYS. "But I also want to have — be the president that protects the rights of, of people to, to have arms. And that — so you don't go so far that the legitimate rights on some legislation are, are, you know, impinged on." "Dr. Charles Frieses' theories." Conflict. Conflict-resolution. The mutual advantage of both sides in this widespread conflict. "We will make a determination in terms of an appropriate response." Impact, to impact. Future plans. Don't go there! PLEASE WAIT HERE UNTIL NEXT AVAILABLE CLERK. Fellow countrymen. *Misappropriate* for *steal.* Off of. I'll be there momentarily. At some later point in time. I'm not adverse to that. Have a good one. Luv ya. Alot.

* (or, "POLITICS AND THE ENGLISH LANGUAGE" IS REDUNDANT)

Dilige et quod vis fac.
— AUGUSTINE

———————

DID YOU KNOW that probing the seamy underbelly of US lexicography reveals ideological strife and controversy and intrigue and nastiness and fervor on a near-Lewinskian scale?

For instance, did you know that some modern dictionaries are notoriously liberal and others notoriously conservative, and that certain conservative dictionaries were actually conceived and designed as corrective responses to the "corruption" and "permissiveness" of certain liberal dictionaries? That the oligarchic device of having a special "Distinguished Usage Panel . . . of outstanding professional speakers and writers" is some dictionaries' attempt at a compromise between the forces of egalitarianism and traditionalism in English, but that most linguistic liberals dismiss the Usage Panel device as mere sham-populism, as in e.g. "Calling upon the opinions of the elite, it claims to be a democratic guide"?

Did you know that US lexicography even *had* a seamy underbelly?

The occasion for this article is Oxford University Press's recent release of Mr. Bryan A. Garner's *A Dictionary of Modern American Usage*, a book that Oxford is marketing aggressively and that it is my assigned function to review. It turns out to be a complicated assignment. In today's US, a typical book review is driven by market logic and implicitly casts the reader in the role of consumer. Rhetorically, its whole project is informed by a question that's too crass ever to mention up front: "Should you buy this book?" And because Bryan A. Garner's usage dictionary belongs to a particular subgenre of a reference genre that is itself highly specialized and particular, and because at least a dozen major usage guides have been published in the last couple years and some of them have been quite good indeed,[1] the central unmentionable question here appends the prepositional comparative ". . . rather than *that* book?" to the main clause and so entails a discussion of whether and how *ADMAU* is different from other recent specialty-products of its kind.

The fact of the matter is that Garner's dictionary is extremely good, certainly the most comprehensive usage guide since E. W. Gilman's *Webster's Dictionary of English Usage,* now a decade out of date.[2] But the really salient and ingenious features of *A Dictionary of Modern American Usage* involve issues of rhetoric and ideology and style, and it is impossible to describe why these issues are important and why Garner's management of them borders on genius without talking about the historical context[3] in which *ADMAU* appears, and

---

[1] (the best and most substantial of these being *The American Heritage Book of English Usage,* Jean Eggenschwiler's *Writing: Grammar, Usage, and Style,* and Oxford/Clarendon's own *The New Fowler's Modern English Usage*)

[2] *The New Fowler's* is also extremely comprehensive and fine, but its emphasis is on British usage.

[3] Sorry about this phrase; I hate this phrase, too. This happens to be one of those very rare times when "historical context" is the phrase to use and there is no equivalent phrase that isn't even worse (I actually tried "lexico-temporal backdrop" in one of the middle drafts, which I think you'll agree is not preferable).

INTERPOLATION

The above ¶ is motivated by the fact that this reviewer nearly always sneers and/or winces when he sees a phrase like "historical context" deployed in a piece of writing and thus hopes to head off any potential sneers/winces from the reader here, especially in an article about felicitous usage. One of the little personal lessons I've learned in working on this essay is that being chronically inclined to sneer/wince at other people's usage tends to make me chronically anxious about other people's sneering/wincing at my usage. It is, of course, possible that this bivalence is news to nobody but me; it may be just a straightforward instance of Matt. 7:1's thing about "Judge not lest ye be judged." In any case, the anxiety seems worth acknowledging up front.

this context turns out to be a veritable hurricane of controversies involving everything from technical linguistics and public education to political ideology,[4] and these controversies take a certain amount of time to unpack before their relation to what makes Garner's dictionary so eminently worth your hard-earned reference-book dollar can even be established; and in fact there's no way even to begin the whole harrowing polymeric discussion without first taking a moment to establish and define the highly colloquial term *SNOOT*.

From one perspective, a certain irony attends the publication of any good new book on American usage. It is that the people who are going to be interested in such a book are also the people who are least going to need it — i.e., that offering counsel on the finer points of US English is preaching to the choir. The relevant choir here comprises that small percentage of American citizens who actually care about the current status of double modals and ergative verbs. The same sorts of people who watched *The Story of English* on PBS (twice) and read Safire's column with their half-caff every Sunday. The sorts of people who feel that special blend of wincing despair and sneering superiority when they see EXPRESS LANE — 10 ITEMS OR LESS or hear *dialogue* used as a verb or realize that the founders of the Super 8 Motel chain must surely have been ignorant of the meaning of *suppurate*. There are lots of epithets for people like this — Grammar Nazis, Usage Nerds, Syntax Snobs, the Grammar Battalion, the Language Police. The term I was raised with is *SNOOT*.[5] The word might be slightly self-mocking, but those

---

[4] One of the claim-clusters I'm going to spend a lot of both our time arguing for is that issues of English usage are fundamentally and inescapably political, and that putatively disinterested linguistic authorities like dictionaries are always the products of certain ideologies, and that as authorities they are accountable to the same basic standards of sanity and honesty and fairness as our political authorities.

[5] SNOOT (n) (*highly colloq*) is this reviewer's nuclear family's nickname à clef for a really extreme usage fanatic, the sort of person whose idea of Sunday fun is to hunt for mistakes in the very prose of Safire's column. This reviewer's family is roughly 70 percent SNOOT, which term itself derives from an acronym, with the big historical family joke being that whether S.N.O.O.T. stood for "Sprachgefühl Necessitates Our Ongoing Tendance" or "Syntax Nudniks Of Our Time" depended on whether or not you were one.

other terms are outright dysphemisms. A SNOOT can be loosely defined as somebody who knows what *dysphemism* means and doesn't mind letting you know it.

I submit that we SNOOTs are just about the last remaining kind of truly elitist nerd. There are, granted, plenty of nerd-species in today's America, and some of these are elitist within their own nerdy purview (e.g., the skinny, carbuncular, semi-autistic Computer Nerd moves instantly up on the totem pole of status when your screen freezes and now you need his help, and the bland condescension with which he performs the two occult keystrokes that unfreeze your screen is both elitist and situationally valid). But the SNOOT's purview is interhuman life itself. You don't, after all (despite withering cultural pressure), have to use a computer, but you can't escape language: language is everything and everywhere; it's what lets us have anything to do with one another; it's what separates us from animals; Genesis 11:7–10 and so on. And we SNOOTs know when and how to hyphenate phrasal adjectives and to keep participles from dangling, and we know that we know, and we know how very few other Americans know this stuff or even care, and we judge them accordingly.

In ways that certain of us are uncomfortable with, SNOOTs' attitudes about contemporary usage resemble religious/political conservatives' attitudes about contemporary culture.[6] We combine a

---

[6] This is true in my own case, at any rate — plus also the "uncomfortable" part. I teach college English part-time. Mostly Lit, not Composition. But I am so pathologically obsessed with usage that every semester the same thing happens: once I've had to read my students' first set of papers, we immediately abandon the regular Lit syllabus and have a three-week Emergency Remedial Usage and Grammar Unit, during which my demeanor is basically that of somebody teaching HIV prevention to intravenous-drug users. When it emerges (as it does, every term) that 95 percent of these intelligent upscale college students have never been taught, e.g., what a clause is or why a misplaced *only* can make a sentence confusing or why you don't just automatically stick in a comma after a long noun phrase, I all but pound my head on the blackboard; I get angry and self-righteous; I tell them they should sue their hometown school boards, and mean it. The kids end up scared, both of me and for me. Every August I vow silently to *chill about usage* this year, and then by Labor Day there's foam on my chin. I can't seem to help it. The truth is that I'm not even an especially good or dedicated teacher; I don't have this kind of fervor in class about anything else, and I know it's not a very productive fervor, nor a healthy one — it's got elements of fanaticism and rage to it, plus a snobbishness that I know I'd be mortified to display about anything else.

missionary zeal and a near-neural faith in our beliefs' importance with a curmudgeonly hell-in-a-handbasket despair at the way English is routinely defiled by supposedly literate adults.[7] Plus a dash of the elitism of, say, Billy Zane in *Titanic* — a fellow SNOOT I know likes to say that listening to most people's public English feels like watching somebody use a Stradivarius to pound nails. We[8] are the Few, the Proud, the More or Less Constantly Appalled at Everyone Else.

*   *   *

---

[7] N.B. that this article's own title page features blocks of the typical sorts of contemporary boners and clunkers and oxymorons and solecistic howlers and bursts of voguish linguistic methane that tend to make a SNOOT's cheek twitch and forehead darken. (N.B. further that it took only about a week of semi-attentive listening and note-taking to assemble these blocks — the Evil is all around us.)

[8] Please note that the strategically repeated 1-P pronoun is meant to iterate and emphasize that this reviewer is very much one too, a SNOOT, plus to connote the nuclear family mentioned *supra*. SNOOTitude runs in families. In *ADMAU*'s preface, Bryan Garner mentions both his father and grandfather and actually uses the word *genetic*, and it's probably true: 90 percent of the SNOOTs I know have at least one parent who is, by profession or temperament or both, a SNOOT. In my own case, my mom is a Comp teacher and has written remedial usage books and is a SNOOT of the most rabid and intractable sort. At least part of the reason I am a SNOOT is that for years my mom brainwashed us in all sorts of subtle ways. Here's an example. Family suppers often involved a game: if one of us children made a usage error, Mom would pretend to have a coughing fit that would go on and on until the relevant child had identified the relevant error and corrected it. It was all very self-ironic and lighthearted; but still, looking back, it seems a bit excessive to pretend that your small child is actually *denying you oxygen* by speaking incorrectly. The really chilling thing, though, is that I now sometimes find myself playing this same "game" with my own students, complete with pretend pertussion.

INTERPOLATION

As something I'm all but sure *Harper's* will excise, I will also insert that we even had a fun but retrospectively chilling little family *song* that Mom and we little SNOOTlets would sing in the car on long trips while Dad silently rolled his eyes and drove (you have to remember the theme to *Underdog* in order to follow the song):

> *When idiots in this world appear*
> *And fail to be concise or clear*
> *And solecisms rend the ear*
> *The cry goes up both far and near*
> *for Blunderdog*
> *Blunderdog*
> *Blunderdog*
> *Blunderdog*
> *Pen of iron, tongue of fire*
> *Tightening the wid'ning gyre*
> *Blunderdo-O-O-O-O-O . . .*
> *[etc.]**

*(Since this'll almost surely get cut, I'll admit that, yes, I, as a kid, was in fact the author of this song. But by this time I'd been thoroughly brainwashed. It was sort of our family's version of "100 Bottles . . . Wall." My mother was the one responsible for the "wid'ning gyre" line in the refrain, which after much debate was finally substituted for a supposedly "forced" rhyme for *fire* in my own original lyrics — and again, years later, when I actually understood the apocalyptic thrust of that Yeats line I was, retrospectively, a bit chilled.)

THESIS STATEMENT FOR WHOLE ARTICLE

Issues of tradition vs. egalitarianism in US English are at root political issues and can be effectively addressed only in what this article
hereby terms a "Democratic Spirit." A Democratic Spirit is one that
combines rigor and humility, i.e., passionate conviction plus a sedulous respect for the convictions of others. As any American knows,
this is a difficult spirit to cultivate and maintain, particularly when
it comes to issues you feel strongly about. Equally tough is a DS's
criterion of 100 percent intellectual integrity — you have to be willing to look honestly at yourself and at your motives for believing
what you believe, and to do it more or less continually.

This kind of stuff is advanced US citizenship. A true Democratic
Spirit is up there with religious faith and emotional maturity and
all those other top-of-the-Maslow-Pyramid-type qualities that people
spend their whole lives working on. A Democratic Spirit's constituent
rigor and humility and self-honesty are, in fact, so hard to maintain on
certain issues that it's almost irresistibly tempting to fall in with some
established dogmatic camp and to follow that camp's line on the issue
and to let your position harden within the camp and become inflexible and to believe that the other camps[9] are either evil or insane and
to spend all your time and energy trying to shout over them.

I submit, then, that it is indisputably easier to be Dogmatic than
Democratic, especially about issues that are both vexed and highly
charged. I submit further that the issues surrounding "correctness"
in contemporary American usage are both vexed and highly
charged, and that the fundamental questions they involve are ones
whose answers have to be literally *worked out* instead of merely found.

A distinctive feature of *ADMAU* is that its author is willing to
acknowledge that a usage dictionary is not a bible or even a textbook but rather just the record of one bright person's attempts to
work out answers to certain very difficult questions. This willingness appears to me to be informed by a Democratic Spirit. The big

---

[9] (It seems to be a natural law that camps form only in opposition to other camps and
that there are always at least two w/r/t any difficult issue.)

question is whether such a spirit compromises Bryan Garner's ability to present himself as a genuine "authority" on issues of usage. Assessing Garner's book, then, requires us to trace out the very weird and complicated relationship between Authority and Democracy in what we as a culture have decided is English. That relationship is, as many educated Americans would say, still in process at this time.

A *Dictionary of Modern American Usage* has no Editorial Staff or Distinguished Panel. It's been conceived, researched, and written *ab ovo usque ad mala* by Mr. Bryan A. Garner. This Garner is an interesting guy. He's both a lawyer and a usage expert (which seems a bit like being both a narcotics wholesaler and a DEA agent). His 1987 *A Dictionary of Modern Legal Usage* is already a minor classic; and now, instead of practicing law anymore, he goes around conducting writing seminars for JDs and doing prose-consulting for various judicial bodies. Garner's also the founder of something called the H. W. Fowler Society,[10] a worldwide group of usage Trekkies who like to send one another linguistic boners clipped from different periodicals. You get the idea. This Garner is one serious and very hard-core SNOOT.

The lucid, engaging, and extremely sneaky preface to *ADMAU* serves to confirm Garner's SNOOTitude in fact while undercutting it in tone. For one thing, whereas the traditional usage pundit cultivates a remote and imperial persona — the kind who uses *one* or *we* to refer to himself — Garner gives us an almost Waltonishly endearing sketch of his own background:

> I realized early — at the age of 15[11] — that my primary intellectual interest was the use of the English language. . . . It became an

---

[10] If Samuel Johnson is the Shakespeare of English usage, think of Henry Watson Fowler as the Eliot or Joyce. His 1926 *A Dictionary of Modern English Usage* is the granddaddy of modern usage guides, and its dust-dry wit and blushless imperiousness have been models for every subsequent classic in the field, from Eric Partridge's *Usage and Abusage* to Theodore Bernstein's *The Careful Writer* to Wilson Follett's *Modern American Usage* to Gilman's '89 *Webster's*.

[11] (Garner prescribes spelling out only numbers under ten. I was taught that this rule applies just to Business Writing and that in all other modes you spell out one through nineteen and start using cardinals at 20. *De gustibus non est disputandum*.)

all-consuming passion. . . . I read everything I could find on the subject. Then, on a wintry evening while visiting New Mexico at the age
of 16, I discovered Eric Partridge's *Usage and Abusage.* I was enthralled.
Never had I held a more exciting book. . . . Suffice it to say that by the
time I was 18, I had committed to memory most of Fowler, Partridge,
and their successors.

Although this reviewer regrets the bio-sketch's failure to mention the rather significant social costs of being an adolescent whose
overriding passion is English usage,[12] the critical hat is off to yet
another personable preface-section, one that Garner entitles "First
Principles": "Before going any further, I should explain my approach. That's an unusual thing for the author of a usage dictionary to do — unprecedented, as far as I know. But a guide to good
writing is only as good as the principles on which it's based. And
users should be naturally interested in those principles. So, in the
interests of full disclosure . . ."[13]

The "unprecedented" and "full disclosure" here are actually
good-natured digs at Garner's Fowlerite predecessors, and a slight
nod to one camp in the wars that have raged in both lexicography
and education ever since the notoriously liberal *Webster's Third New
International Dictionary* came out in 1961 and included terms like
heighth and *irregardless* without any monitory labels on them. You
can think of *Webster's Third* as sort of the Fort Sumter of the contemporary Usage Wars. These wars are both the context and the
target of a very subtle rhetorical strategy in *A Dictionary of Modern*

---

[12] From personal experience, I can assure you that any kid like this is going to be at best
marginalized and at worst savagely and repeatedly Wedgied — see *sub.*
[13] What follow in the preface are "the ten critical points that, after years of working on
usage problems, I've settled on." These points are too involved to treat separately, but a
couple of them are slippery in the extreme — e.g., "10. **Actual Usage.** In the end, the
actual usage of educated speakers and writers is the overarching criterion for correctness,"
of which both "educated" and "actual" would really require several pages of abstract clarification and qualification to shore up against Usage Wars–related attacks, but which Garner rather ingeniously elects to define and defend via their application in his dictionary
itself. Garner's ability not only to stay out of certain arguments but to render them irrelevant ends up being very important — see much *sub.*

American Usage, and without talking about them it's impossible to explain why Garner's book is both so good and so sneaky.

We regular citizens tend to go to The Dictionary for authoritative guidance.[14] Rarely, however, do we ask ourselves who exactly decides what gets in The Dictionary or what words or spellings or pronunciations get deemed substandard or incorrect. Whence the authority of dictionary-makers to decide what's OK and what isn't? Nobody elected them, after all. And simply appealing to precedent or tradition won't work, because what's considered correct changes over time. In the 1600s, for instance, the second-singular took a singular conjugation — "You is." Earlier still, the standard 2-S pronoun wasn't *you* but *thou.* Huge numbers of now-acceptable words like *clever, fun, banter,* and *prestigious* entered English as what usage authorities considered errors or egregious slang. And not just usage conventions but English itself changes over time; if it didn't, we'd all still be talking like Chaucer. Who's to say which changes are natural and good and which are corruptions? And when Bryan Garner or E. Ward Gilman do in fact presume to say, why should we believe them?

These sorts of questions are not new, but they do now have a certain urgency. America is in the midst of a protracted Crisis of Authority in matters of language. In brief, the same sorts of political upheavals that produced everything from Kent State to Independent Counsels have produced an influential contra-SNOOT school for whom normative standards of English grammar and usage are functions of nothing but custom and the ovine docility of a populace that lets self-appointed language experts boss them around. See for example MIT's Steven Pinker in a famous *New Republic* article — "Once introduced, a prescriptive rule is very hard to eradicate, no matter how ridiculous. Inside the writing

---

[14] There's no better indication of The Dictionary's authority than that we use it to settle wagers. My own father is still to this day living down the outcome of a high-stakes bet on the correct spelling of *meringue,* a bet made on 14 September 1978.

establishment, the rules survive by the same dynamic that perpetuates ritual genital mutilations" — or, at a somewhat lower emotional pitch, Bill Bryson in *Mother Tongue: English and How It Got That Way:*

> Who sets down all those rules that we know about from childhood — the idea that we must never end a sentence with a preposition or begin one with a conjunction, that we must use *each other* for two things and *one another* for more than two . . . ? The answer, surprisingly often, is that no one does, that when you look into the background of these "rules" there is often little basis for them.

In *ADMAU*'s preface, Garner himself addresses the Authority question with a Trumanesque simplicity and candor that simultaneously disguise the author's cunning and exemplify it:

> As you might already suspect, I don't shy away from making judgments. I can't imagine that most readers would want me to. Linguists don't like it, of course, because judgment involves subjectivity.[15] It isn't scientific. But rhetoric and usage, in the view of most professional writers,[16]

---

[15] This is a clever half-truth. Linguists compose only one part of the anti-judgment camp, and their objections to usage judgments involve way more than just "subjectivity."

[16] Notice, please, the subtle appeal here to the same "writing establishment" that Steven Pinker scorns. This isn't accidental; it's rhetorical.* What's crafty is that this is one of several places where Garner uses professional writers and editors as support for his claims, but in the preface he also treats these language pros as the primary *audience* for *ADMAU*, as in e.g. "The problem for professional writers and editors is that they can't wait idly to see what direction the language takes. Writers and editors, in fact, influence that direction: they must make decisions. . . . That has traditionally been the job of the usage dictionary: to help writers and editors solve editorial predicaments."

This is the same basic rhetorical move that President R. W. Reagan perfected in his televised Going-Over-Congress's-Head-to-the-People addresses, one that smart politicians ever since have imitated. It consists in citing the very audience you're addressing as the source of support for your proposals: "I'm pleased to announce tonight that we are taking the first steps toward implementing the policies that you elected me to implement," etc. The tactic is crafty because it (1) flatters the audience, (2) disguises the fact that the rhetor's purpose here is actually to persuade and rally support, not to inform or celebrate, and (3) preempts charges from the loyal opposition that the actual policy proposed is in any way contrary to the interests of the audience. I'm not suggesting that Bryan Garner has any particular political agenda. I'm simply pointing out that *ADMAU*'s preface is fundamentally rhetorical in the same way that Reagan's little Chats With America were.

* (In case it's not totally obvious, be advised that this article is using the word *rhetoric* in its strict traditional sense, something like "the persuasive use of language to influence the thoughts and actions of an audience.")

aren't scientific endeavors. You[17] don't want dispassionate descriptions; you want sound guidance. And that requires judgment.

Whole monographs could be written just on the masterful rhetoric of this passage. Besides the FN 16 stuff, note for example the ingenious equivocation of *judgment,* which in "I don't shy away from making judgments" means actual rulings (and thus invites questions about Authority), but in "And that requires judgment" refers instead to perspicacity, discernment, reason. As the body of *ADMAU* makes clear, part of Garner's overall strategy is to collapse these two different senses of *judgment,* or rather to use the second sense as a justification for the first. The big things to recognize here are (1) that Garner wouldn't be doing any of this if he weren't *keenly* aware of the Authority Crisis in modern usage, and (2) that his response to this crisis is — in the best Democratic Spirit — rhetorical.

So . . .

COROLLARY TO THESIS STATEMENT FOR WHOLE ARTICLE
The most salient and timely feature of Bryan A. Garner's dictionary is that its project is both lexicographical and rhetorical. Its main strategy involves what is known in classical rhetoric as the Ethical Appeal. Here the adjective, derived from the Greek *ēthos,* doesn't mean quite what we usually mean by *ethical.* But there are affinities. What the Ethical Appeal amounts to is a complex and sophisticated "Trust me." It's the boldest, most ambitious, and also most democratic of rhetorical Appeals because it requires the rhetor to convince us not just of his intellectual acuity or technical competence but of his basic decency and fairness and sensitivity to the audience's own hopes and fears.[18]

These latter are not qualities one associates with the traditional SNOOT usage-authority, a figure who for many Americans exemplifies snobbishness and anality, and one whose modern image is

---

[17] See?

[18] In this last respect, recall for example W. J. Clinton's "I feel your pain," which was a blatant if not especially deft Ethical Appeal.

not helped by stuff like *The American Heritage Dictionary*'s Distinguished Usage Panelist Morris Bishop's "The arrant solecisms of the ignoramus are here often omitted entirely, 'irregardless' of how he may feel about this neglect" or critic John Simon's "The English language is being treated nowadays exactly as slave traders once handled their merchandise." Compare those lines' authorial personas with Garner's in, e.g., "English usage is so challenging that even experienced writers need guidance now and then."

The thrust here is going to be that *A Dictionary of Modern American Usage* earns Garner pretty much all the trust his Ethical Appeal asks us for. What's interesting is that this trust derives not so much from the book's lexicographical quality as from the authorial persona and spirit it cultivates. *ADMAU* is a feel-good usage dictionary in the very best sense of *feel-good*. The book's spirit marries rigor and humility in such a way as to let Garner be extremely prescriptive without any appearance of evangelism or elitist put-down. This is an extraordinary accomplishment. Understanding why it's basically a *rhetorical* accomplishment, and why this is both historically significant and (in this reviewer's opinion) politically redemptive, requires a more detailed look at the Usage Wars.

You'd definitely know that lexicography had an underbelly if you read the different little introductory essays in modern dictionaries — pieces like *Webster's DEU*'s "A Brief History of English Usage" or *Webster's Third*'s "Linguistic Advances and Lexicography" or *AHD-2*'s "Good Usage, Bad Usage, and Usage" or *AHD-3*'s "Usage in the Dictionary: The Place of Criticism." But almost nobody ever bothers with these little intros, and it's not just their six-point type or the fact that dictionaries tend to be hard on the lap. It's that these intros aren't actually written for you or me or the average citizen who goes to The Dictionary just to see how to spell (for instance) *meringue*. They're written for other lexicographers and critics; and in fact they're not really introductory at all, but polemical. They're salvos in the Usage Wars that have been under way ever since editor

Philip Gove first sought to apply the value-neutral principles of structural linguistics to lexicography in *Webster's Third*. Gove's now-famous response to conservatives who howled[19] when *W3* endorsed *OK* and described *ain't* as "used colloquially by educated speakers in many regions of the United States" was this: "A dictionary should have no truck with artificial notions of correctness or superiority. It should be descriptive and not prescriptive." Gove's terms stuck and turned epithetic, and linguistic conservatives are now formally known as Prescriptivists and linguistic liberals as Descriptivists.

The former are better known, though not because of dictionaries' prologues or scholarly Fowlerites. When you read the columns of William Safire or Morton Freeman or books like Edwin Newman's *Strictly Speaking* or John Simon's *Paradigms Lost*, you're actually reading Popular Prescriptivism, a genre sideline of certain journalists (mostly older males, the majority of whom actually do wear bow ties[20]) whose bemused irony often masks a Colonel Blimp's rage at the way the beloved English of their youth is being trashed in the decadent present. Some Pop Prescriptivism is funny and smart, though much of it just sounds like old men grumbling about the vulgarity of modern mores.[21] And some PP is offensively small-minded and knuckle-dragging, such as *Paradigms Lost's* simplistic dismissal of Standard Black English: "As for 'I be,' 'you be,' 'he be,' etc., which should give us all the heebie-jeebies, these may

---

[19] Really, *howled:* Blistering reviews and outraged editorials from across the country — from the *Times* and *The New Yorker* and the *National Review* and good old *Life*, or see e.g. this from the January '62 *Atlantic Monthly:* "We have seen a novel dictionary formula improvised, in great part, out of snap judgments and the sort of theoretical improvement that in practice impairs; and we have seen the gates propped wide open in enthusiastic hospitality to miscellaneous confusions and corruptions. In fine, the anxiously awaited* work that was to have crowned cisatlantic linguistic scholarship with a particular glory turns out to be a scandal and a disaster."

   *(Sic — should obviously be "eagerly awaited." *Nemo mortalium omnibus horis sapit.*)

[20] It's true: Newman, Simon, Freeman, James J. Kilpatrick . . . can George F. Will's bestseller on usage be long in coming?

[21] Even Edwin Newman, the most thoughtful and least hemorrhoidal of the pop SNOOTs, sometimes lets his Colonel B. poke out, as in e.g. "I have no wish to dress as many younger people do nowadays. . . . I have no wish to impair my hearing by listening to their music, and a communication gap between an electronic rock group and me is something I devotedly cherish and would hate to see disappear."

indeed be comprehensible, but they go against all accepted classical and modern grammars and are the product not of a language
with its roots in history but of ignorance of how a language works."
But what's really interesting is that the plutocratic tone and styptic
wit of Newman and Safire and the best of the Pop Prescriptivists are
modeled after the mandarin-Brit personas of Eric Partridge and
H. W. Fowler, the same twin towers of scholarly Prescriptivism whom
Garner talks about revering as a kid.[22]

Descriptivists, on the other hand, don't have weekly columns
in the *Times*. These guys tend to be hard-core academics, mostly linguists or Comp theorists. Loosely organized under the banner of
structural (or "descriptive") linguistics, they are doctrinaire posi-
tivists who have their intellectual roots in Comte and Saussure and
L. Bloomfield[23] and their ideological roots firmly in the US Sixties.
The brief explicit mention Garner's preface gives this crew —

> Somewhere along the line, though, usage dictionaries got hijacked
> by the descriptive linguists,[24] who observe language scientifically.
> For the pure descriptivist, it's impermissible to say that one form of

---

[22] Note for instance the mordant pith (and royal *we*) of this random snippet from
Partridge's *Usage and Abusage:*

> **anxious of.** 'I am not hopeless of our future. But I am profoundly anxious of it,'
> Beverley Nichols, *News of England,* 1938: which made us profoundly anxious *for*
> (or *about*) — not *of* — Mr. Nichols's literary future.

Or observe the near-Himalayan condescension of Fowler, here on some people's habit of
using words like *viable* or *verbal* to mean things the words don't really mean:

> **slipshod extension** . . . is especially likely to occur when some accident gives currency
> among the uneducated to words of learned origin, & the more if they are isolated
> or have few relatives in the vernacular. . . . The original meaning of *feasible* is simply
> doable (L. *facere* do); but to the unlearned it is a mere token, of which he has to
> infer the value from the contexts in which he hears it used, because such relatives
> as it has in English — *feat, feature, faction,* &c. — either fail to show the obvious
> family likeness to which he is accustomed among families of indigenous words,
> or are (like *malfeasance*) outside his range.

[23] FYI, Leonard Bloomfield's 1933 *Language* pretty much founded descriptive linguistics
by claiming that the proper object of study was not language but something called
"language behavior."
[24] Utter bushwa: As *ADMAU*'s body makes clear, Garner knows precisely where along the
line the Descriptivists started influencing usage guides.

language is any better than another: as long as a native speaker says it, it's OK — and anyone who takes a contrary stand is a dunderhead. . . . Essentially, descriptivists and prescriptivists are approaching different problems. Descriptivists want to record language as it's actually used, and they perform a useful function — although their audience is generally limited to those willing to pore through vast tomes of dry-as-dust research.[25]

— is disingenuous in the extreme, especially the "approaching different problems" part, because it vastly underplays the Descriptivists' influence on US culture. For one thing, Descriptivism so quickly and thoroughly took over English education in this country that just about everybody who started junior high after c. 1970 has been taught to write Descriptively — via "freewriting," "brainstorming," "journaling"—a view of writing as self-exploratory and -expressive rather than as communicative, an abandonment of systematic grammar, usage, semantics, rhetoric, etymology. For another thing, the very language in which today's socialist, feminist, minority, gay, and environmental movements frame their sides of political debates is informed by the Descriptivist belief that traditional English is conceived and perpetuated by Privileged WASP Males[26] and is thus inherently capitalist, sexist, racist, xenophobic, homophobic, elitist: unfair. Think Ebonics. Think Proposition 227. Think of the involved contortions people undergo to avoid using *he* as a generic pronoun, or of the tense, deliberate way white males now adjust their

---

[25] His SNOOTier sentiments about linguists' prose emerge in Garner's preface via his recollection of studying under certain eminent Descriptivists in college: "The most bothersome thing was that they didn't write well: their offerings were dreary gruel. If you doubt this, go pick up any journal of linguistics. Ask yourself whether the articles are well-written. If you haven't looked at one in a while, you'll be shocked."

INTERPOLATION

Garner's aside about linguists' writing has wider applications, though *ADMAU* mostly keeps them implicit. The truth is that most US academic prose is appalling — pompous, abstruse, claustral, inflated, euphuistic, pleonastic, solecistic, sesquipidelian, Heliogabaline, occluded, obscure, jargon-ridden, empty: resplendently dead. See textual INTERPOLATION much below.

[26] (which is in fact true)

vocabularies around non-w.m.'s. Think of the modern ubiquity of spin or of today's endless rows over just the *names* of things — "Affirmative Action" vs. "Reverse Discrimination," "Pro-Life" vs. "Pro-Choice,"* "Undocumented Worker" vs. "Illegal Alien," "Perjury" vs. "Peccadillo," and so on.

*INTERPOLATION
EXAMPLE OF THE APPLICATION OF WHAT THIS ARTICLE'S
THESIS STATEMENT CALLS A DEMOCRATIC SPIRIT TO A
HIGHLY CHARGED POLITICAL ISSUE, WHICH EXAMPLE
IS MORE RELEVANT TO GARNER'S *ADMAU* THAN IT
MAY INITIALLY APPEAR

In this reviewer's opinion, the only really coherent position on the abortion issue is one that is both Pro-Life *and* Pro-Choice.

Argument: As of 4 March 1999, the question of defining human life *in utero* is hopelessly vexed. That is, given our best present medical and philosophical understandings of what makes something not just a living organism but a person, there is no way to establish at just what point during gestation a fertilized ovum becomes a human being. This conundrum, together with the basically inarguable soundness of the principle "When in irresolvable doubt about whether something is a human being or not, it is better not to kill it," appears to me to require any reasonable American to be Pro-Life. At the same time, however, the principle "When in irresolvable doubt about something, I have neither the legal nor the moral right to tell another person what to do about it, especially if that person feels that s/he is *not* in doubt" is an unassailable part of the Democratic pact we Americans all make with one another, a pact in which each adult citizen gets to be an autonomous moral agent; and this principle appears to me to require any reasonable American to be Pro-Choice.

This reviewer is thus, as a private citizen and an autonomous agent, both Pro-Life and Pro-Choice. It is not an easy or comfortable position to maintain. Every time someone I know decides to terminate a pregnancy, I am required to believe simultaneously that she is doing the wrong thing and that she has every right to do it. Plus, of course, I have both to believe that a Pro-Life + Pro-Choice stance is the only really coherent one *and* to restrain myself from trying to force that position on other people whose ideological or religious convictions seem (to me) to override reason and yield a (in my opinion) wacko dogmatic position. This restraint has to be maintained even when somebody's (to me) wacko dogmatic position appears (to me) to reject the very Democratic tolerance that is keeping me from trying to force my position on him/her; it requires me not to press or argue or retaliate even when somebody calls me Satan's Minion or Just Another Shithead Male, which forbearance represents the really outer and tooth-grinding limits of my own personal Democratic Spirit.

Wacko name-calling notwithstanding, I have encountered only one serious kind of objection to this Pro-Life + Pro-Choice position. But it's a powerful objection. It concerns not my position per se but certain facts about me, the person who's developed and maintained it. If this sounds to you both murky and extremely remote from anything having to do with American usage, I promise that it becomes almost excruciatingly clear and relevant below.

The Descriptivist revolution takes a little time to unpack, but it's worth it. The structural linguists' rejection of conventional usage rules in English depends on two main kinds of argument. The first is academic and methodological. In this age of technology, some Descriptivists contend, it's the scientific method — clinically objective, value-neutral, based on direct observation and demonstrable hypothesis — that should determine both the content of dictionaries and the standards of "correct" English. Because language is constantly evolving, such standards will always be fluid. Philip Gove's now-classic introduction to *Webster's Third* outlines this type of Descriptivism's five basic edicts: "1 — Language changes constantly; 2 — Change is normal; 3 — Spoken language *is* the language; 4 — Correctness rests upon usage; 5 — All usage is relative."

These principles look prima facie OK — simple, commonsensical, and couched in the bland s.-v.-o. prose of dispassionate science — but in fact they're vague and muddled and it takes about three seconds to think of reasonable replies to each one of them, viz.:

1 — All right, but how much and how fast?

2 — Same thing. Is Hericlitean flux as normal or desirable as gradual change? Do some changes serve the language's overall pizzazz better than others? And how many people have to deviate from how many conventions before we say the language has actu-

ally changed? Fifty percent? Ten percent? Where do you draw the line? Who draws the line?

3 — This is an old claim, at least as old as Plato's *Phaedrus*. And it's specious. If Derrida and the infamous Deconstructionists have done nothing else, they've successfully debunked the idea that speech is language's primary instantiation.[27] Plus consider the weird arrogance of Gove's (3) with respect to correctness. Only the most mullah-like Prescriptivists care all that much about spoken English; most Prescriptive usage guides concern Standard *Written* English.[28]

4 — Fine, but whose usage? Gove's (4) begs the whole question. What he wants to suggest here, I think, is a reversal of the traditional entailment-relation between abstract rules and concrete usage: instead of usage's ideally corresponding to a rigid set of regulations, the regulations ought to correspond to the way real people are actually using the language. Again, fine, but which people? Urban Latinos? Boston Brahmins? Rural Midwesterners? Appalachian Neogaelics?

5 — *Huh*? If this means what it seems to mean, then it ends up biting Gove's whole argument in the ass. Principle (5) appears to imply that the correct answer to the above "which people?" is: All of them. And it's easy to show why this will not stand up as a lexicographical principle. The most obvious problem with it is that not everything can go in The Dictionary. Why not? Well, because you can't actually observe and record every last bit of every last native

---

[27] (Q.v. the "Pharmakon" stuff in Derrida's *La dissémination* — but you'd probably be better off just trusting me.)

[28] Standard Written English (SWE) is sometimes called Standard English (SE) or Educated English, but the basic inditement-emphasis is the same. See for example *The Little, Brown Handbook*'s definition of Standard English as "the English normally expected and used by educated readers and writers."

SEMI-INTERPOLATION

Plus let's note that Garner's preface explicitly characterizes his dictionary's intended audience as "writers and editors." And even the recent ads for *ADMAU* in organs like the *New York Review of Books* are built around the slogan "If you like to WRITE . . . **Refer to us.**"*

* (Your SNOOT reviewer cannot help observing, w/r/t this ad, that the opening *r* in its **Refer** shouldn't be capitalized after a dependent clause + ellipsis. *Quandoque bonus dormitat Homerus*.)

speaker's "language behavior," and even if you could, the resultant dictionary would weigh four million pounds and need to be updated hourly.[29] The fact is that any real lexicographer is going to have to make choices about what gets in and what doesn't. And these choices are based on . . . what? And so we're right back where we started.

It is true that, as a SNOOT, I am naturally predisposed to look for flaws in Gove et al.'s methodological argument. But these flaws still seem awfully easy to find. Probably the biggest one is that the Descriptivists' "scientific lexicography" — under which, keep in mind, the ideal English dictionary is basically number-crunching: you somehow observe every linguistic act by every native/naturalized speaker of English and put the sum of all these acts between two covers and call it The Dictionary — involves an incredibly crude and outdated understanding of what *scientific* means. It requires a naive belief in scientific Objectivity, for one thing. Even in the physical sciences, everything from quantum mechanics to Information Theory has shown that an act of observation is itself part of the phenomenon observed and is analytically inseparable from it.

If you remember your old college English classes, there's an analogy here that points up the trouble scholars get into when they confuse observation with interpretation. It's the New Critics.[30] Recall their belief that literary criticism was best conceived as a "scientific" endeavor: the critic was a neutral, careful, unbiased, highly trained observer whose job was to find and objectively describe meanings that were right there, literally inside pieces of literature. Whether you know what happened to New Criticism's reputation

---

[29] Granted, some sort of 100 percent compendious real-time Megadictionary might conceivably be possible online, though it would take a small army of lexical webmasters and a much larger army of *in situ* actual-use reporters and surveillance techs; plus it'd be GNP-level expensive (. . . plus what would be the point?).

[30] *New Criticism* refers to T. S. Eliot and I. A. Richards and F. R. Leavis and Cleanth Brooks and Wimsatt & Beardsley and the whole autotelic Close Reading school that dominated literary criticism from the Thirties to well into the Seventies.

depends on whether you took college English after c. 1975; suffice it to say that its star has dimmed. The New Critics had the same basic problem as Gove's Methodological Descriptivists: they believed that there was such a thing as unbiased observation. And that linguistic meanings could exist "Objectively," separate from any interpretive act.

The point of the analogy is that claims to Objectivity in language study are now the stuff of jokes and shudders. The positivist assumptions that underlie Methodological Descriptivism have been thoroughly confuted and displaced — in Lit by the rise of post-structuralism, Reader-Response Criticism, and Jaussian Reception Theory, in linguistics by the rise of Pragmatics — and it's now pretty much universally accepted that (a) meaning is inseparable from some act of interpretation and (b) an act of interpretation is always somewhat biased, i.e., informed by the interpreter's particular ideology. And the consequence of (a)+(b) is that there's no way around it — decisions about what to put in The Dictionary and what to exclude are going to be based on a lexicographer's ideology. And every lexicographer's got one. To presume that dictionary-making can somehow avoid or transcend ideology is simply to subscribe to a particular ideology, one that might aptly be called Unbelievably Naive Positivism.

There's an even more important way Descriptivists are wrong in thinking that the scientific method developed for use in chemistry and physics is equally appropriate to the study of language. This one doesn't depend on stuff about quantum uncertainty or any kind of postmodern relativism. Even if, as a thought experiment, we assume a kind of 19th-century scientific realism — in which, even though some scientists' interpretations of natural phenomena might be biased,[31] the natural phenomena themselves can be supposed to exist wholly independent of either observation or interpretation — it's still true that no such realist supposition can

---

[31] ("EVIDENCE OF CANCER LINK REFUTED BY TOBACCO INSTITUTE RESEARCHERS")

be made about "language behavior," because such behavior is both *human* and fundamentally *normative*.

To understand why this is important, you have only to accept the proposition that language is by its very nature public — i.e., that there is no such thing as a private language[32] — and then to observe the way Descriptivists seem either ignorant of this fact or

---

[32] This proposition is in fact true, as is interpolatively demonstrated just below, and although the demonstration is persuasive it is also, as you can see from the size of this FN, lengthy and involved and rather, umm, dense, so that once again you'd maybe be better off simply granting the truth of the proposition and forging on with the main text.

INTERPOLATIVE DEMONSTRATION OF THE FACT THAT THERE IS NO SUCH THING AS A PRIVATE LANGUAGE

It is sometimes tempting to imagine that there can be such a thing as a private language. Many of us are prone to lay-philosophizing about the weird privacy of our own mental states, for example; and from the fact that when my knee hurts only I can feel it, it's tempting to conclude that for me the word *pain* has a very subjective internal meaning that only I can truly understand. This line of thinking is sort of like the adolescent pot-smoker's terror that his own inner experience is both private and unverifiable, a syndrome that is technically known as Cannabic Solipsism. Eating Chips Ahoy! and staring very intently at the television's network PGA event, for instance, the adolescent pot-smoker is struck by the ghastly possibility that, e.g., what he sees as the color green and what other people call "the color green" may in fact not be the same color-experiences at all: the fact that both he and someone else call Pebble Beach's fairways green and a stoplight's GO signal green appears to guarantee only that there is a similar consistency in their color-experiences of fairways and GO lights, not that the actual subjective quality of those color-experiences is the same; it could be that what the ad. pot-smoker experiences as green everyone else actually experiences as blue, and that what we "mean" by the word *blue* is what he "means" by *green*, etc. etc., until the whole line of thinking gets so vexed and exhausting that the a. p.-s. ends up slumped crumb-strewn and paralyzed in his chair.

The point here is that the idea of a private language, like private colors and most of the other solipsistic conceits with which this reviewer has at various times been afflicted, is both deluded and demonstrably false.

In the case of private language, the delusion is usually based on the belief that a word like *pain* or *tree* has the meaning it does because it is somehow "connected" to a feeling in my knee or to a picture of a tree in my head. But as Mr. L. Wittgenstein's *Philosophical Investigations* proved in the 1950s, words actually have the meanings they do because of certain rules and verification tests that are imposed on us from outside our own subjectivities, viz., by the community in which we have to get along and communicate with other people. Wittgenstein's argument centers on the fact that a word like *tree* means what it does for me because of the way the community I'm part of has tacitly agreed to use *tree*. What makes this observation so powerful is that Wittgenstein can prove that it holds true even if I am an angst-ridden adolescent pot-smoker who believes that there's no way I can verify that what I mean by *tree* is what anybody else means by *tree*. Wittgenstein's argument is very technical but goes something like:

(1) A word has no meaning apart from how it is actually used, and even if

(2) "The question of whether my use agrees with others has been given up as a bad job,"* still,

(3) The only way a word can be used meaningfully even to myself is if I use it "correctly," with

(32, CONTINUED)

(4) *Correctly* here meaning "consistently with my own definition" (that is, if I use *tree* one time to mean a tree and then the next time turn around and use *tree* to mean a golf ball and then the next time willy-nilly use *tree* to mean a certain brand of high-cal corporate cookie, etc., then, even in my own little solipsistic universe, *tree* has ceased really to "mean" anything at all), but

(5) The criterion of consistency-with-my-own-definition is satisfiable only if there exist certain rules that are independent of any one individual language-user (viz., in this case, me). Without the existence of these external rules, there is no difference between the statement "I am in fact using *tree* consistently with my own definition" and the statement "I happen to be under the impression that I am using *tree* consistently with my own definition." Wittgenstein's basic way of putting it is:

> Now how is it to be decided whether I have used the [privately defined] word consistently? What will be the difference between my having used it consistently and its *seeming* to me that I have? Or has this distinction vanished? . . . If the distinction between 'correct' and 'seems correct' has disappeared, then so has the concept *correct*. It follows that the 'rules' of my private language are only *impressions* of rules. My impression that I follow a rule does not confirm that I follow the rule, unless there can be something that will prove my impression correct. "And that something cannot be another impression — for this would be as if someone were to buy several copies of the morning paper to assure himself that what it said was true."

Step (5) is the real kicker; step (5) is what shows that even if the involuted adolescent decides that he has his own special private definition of *tree,* he himself cannot make up the "rules of consistency" via which he confirms that he's using *tree* the way he privately defined it — i.e., "The proof that I am following a rule must appeal to something *independent* of my impression that I am."

If you are thinking that all this seems not just hideously abstract but also irrelevant to the Usage Wars or to anything you have any interest in at all, I submit that you are mistaken. If words' and phrases' meanings depend on transpersonal rules and these rules on community consensus,[†] then language is not only non-private but also irreducibly *public, political,* and *ideological.* This means that questions about our national consensus on grammar and usage are actually bound up with every last social issue that millennial America's about — class, race, sex, morality, tolerance, pluralism, cohesion, equality, fairness, money: you name it.

And if you at least provisionally grant that meaning is use and language public and communication impossible without consensus and rules, you're going to see that the Descriptivist argument is open to the objection that its ultimate aim — the abandonment of "artificial" linguistic rules and conventions — would make language itself impossible. As in Genesis 11:1–10–grade impossible, a literal Babel. There have to be *some* rules and conventions, no? We have to agree that *tree* takes *e*'s and not *u*'s and denotes a large woody thing with branches and not a small plastic thing with dimples and TITLEIST on it, right? And won't this agreement automatically be "artificial," since it's human beings making it? Once you accept that at least some artificial conventions are necessary, then you can get to the really hard and interesting questions: which conventions are necessary? and when? and where? and who gets to decide? and whence their authority to do so? And because these are the very questions that Gove's crew believes Dispassionate Science can transcend, their argument appears guilty of both *petitio principii* and *ignoratio elenchi,* and can pretty much be dismissed out of hand.

---

*Because *The Investigations*' prose is extremely gnomic and opaque and consists largely of Wittgenstein having weird little imaginary dialogues with himself, the quotations here are actually from Norman Malcolm's definitive paraphrase of L.W.'s argument, in which paraphrase Dr. Malcolm uses single quotation marks for tone quotes and double quotation marks for when he's actually quoting Wittgenstein — which, when I myself am quoting Malcolm quoting Wittgenstein's tone quotes, makes for a rather irksome surfeit of quotation marks, admittedly; but using Malcolm's exegesis allows this interpolative demonstration to be about 60 percent shorter than it would be if we were to grapple with Wittgenstein directly.

† There's a whole argument for this, but intuitively you can see that it makes sense: if the rules can't be subjective, and if they're not actually "out there" floating around in some kind of metaphysical hyperreality (a floating hyperreality that you can believe in if you wish, but you should know that people with beliefs like this usually get forced to take medication), then community consensus is really the only plausible option left.

oblivious to its consequences, as in for example one Dr. Charles Fries's introduction to an epigone of *Webster's Third* called *The American College Dictionary:*

> A dictionary can be an "authority" only in the sense in which a book of chemistry or physics or of botany can be an "authority" — by the accuracy and the completeness of its record of the observed facts of the field examined, in accord with the latest principles and techniques of the particular science.

This is so stupid it practically drools. An "authoritative" physics text presents the results of *physicists'* observations and *physicists'* theories about those observations. If a physics textbook operated on Descriptivist principles, the fact that some Americans believe electricity flows better downhill (based on the observed fact that power lines tend to run high above the homes they serve) would require the Electricity Flows Better Downhill Hypothesis to be included as a "valid" theory in the textbook — just as, for Dr. Fries, if some Americans use *infer* for *imply* or *aspect* for *perspective,* these usages become *ipso facto* "valid" parts of the language. The truth is that structural linguists like Gove and Fries are not scientists at all; they're pollsters who misconstrue the importance of the "facts" they are recording. It isn't scientific phenomena they're observing and tabulating, but rather a set of human behaviors, and a lot of human behaviors are — to be blunt — moronic. Try, for instance, to imagine an "authoritative" ethics textbook whose principles were based on what most people actually *do.*

Grammar and usage conventions are, as it happens, a lot more like ethical principles than like scientific theories. The reason the Descriptivists can't see this is the same reason they choose to regard the English language as the sum of all English utterances: they confuse mere regularities with *norms.*

Norms aren't quite the same as rules, but they're close. A norm can be defined here simply as something that people have agreed on as the optimal way to do things for certain purposes. Let's keep in mind that language didn't come into being because our hairy ancestors were sitting around the veldt with nothing better to do. Language was invented to serve certain very specific purposes — "That mushroom is poisonous"; "Knock these two rocks together and you can start a fire"; "This shelter is mine!" and so on. Clearly, as linguistic communities evolve over time, they discover that some ways of using language are better than others — not better *a priori*, but better with respect to the community's purposes. If we assume that one such purpose might be communicating which kinds of food are safe to eat, then we can see how, for example, a misplaced modifier could violate an important norm: "People who eat that kind of mushroom often get sick" confuses the message's recipient about whether he'll get sick only if he eats the mushroom frequently or whether he stands a good chance of getting sick the very first time he eats it. In other words, the fungiphagic community has a vested practical interest in excluding this kind of misplaced modifier from acceptable usage; and, given the purposes the community uses language for, the fact that a certain percentage of tribesmen screw up and use misplaced modifiers to talk about food safety does not *eo ipso* make m.m.'s a good idea.

Maybe now the analogy between usage and ethics is clearer. Just because people sometimes lie, cheat on their taxes, or scream at their kids, this doesn't mean that they think those things are "good."[33] The whole point of establishing norms is to help us evaluate our actions (including utterances) according to what we as a community have decided our real interests and purposes are. Granted, this analysis is oversimplified; in practice it's incredibly hard to arrive at norms and to keep them at least minimally fair or sometimes even to agree on what they are (see e.g. today's Culture

---

[33] In fact, the Methodological Descriptivists' reasoning is known in social philosophy as the "Well, Everybody Does It" fallacy — i.e., if a lot of people cheat on their taxes, that means it's somehow morally OK to cheat on your taxes. Ethics-wise, it takes only two or three deductive steps to get from there to the sort of State of Nature where everybody's hitting each other over the head and stealing their groceries.

Wars). But the Descriptivists' assumption that all usage norms are arbitrary and dispensable leads to — well, have a mushroom.

The different connotations of *arbitrary* here are tricky, though — and this sort of segues into the second main kind of Descriptivist argument. There is a sense in which specific linguistic conventions really *are* arbitrary. For instance, there's no particular metaphysical reason why our word for a four-legged mammal that gives milk and goes moo is *cow* and not, say, *prtlmpf.* The uptown term for this is "the arbitrariness of the linguistic sign,"[34] and it's used, along with certain principles of cognitive science and generative grammar, in a more philosophically sophisticated version of Descriptivism that holds the conventions of SWE to be more like the niceties of fashion than like actual norms. This "Philosophical Descriptivism" doesn't care much about dictionaries or method; its target is the standard SNOOT claim that prescriptive rules have their ultimate justification in the community's need to make its language meaningful and clear.

Steven Pinker's 1994 *The Language Instinct* is a good and fairly literate example of this second kind of Descriptivist argument, which, like the Gove-et-al. version, tends to deploy a jr.-high-filmstrip SCIENCE: POINTING THE WAY TO A BRIGHTER TOMORROW–type tone:

> [T]he words "rule" and "grammar" have very different meanings to a scientist and a layperson. The rules people learn (or, more likely, fail to learn) in school are called "prescriptive" rules, prescribing how one *ought* to talk. Scientists studying language propose "descriptive"

---

[34] This phrase is attributable to Ferdinand de Saussure, the Swiss philologist who more or less invented modern technical linguistics, separating the study of language as an abstract formal system from the historical and comparative emphases of 19th-century philology. Suffice it to say that the Descriptivists like Saussure a *lot.* Suffice it also to say that they tend to misread him and take him out of context and distort his theories in all kinds of embarrassing ways — e.g., Saussure's "arbitrariness of the linguistic sign" means something other and far more complicated than just "There's no ultimate necessity to English speakers' saying *cow.*" (Similarly, the structural linguists' distinction between "language behavior" and "language" is based on a simplistic misreading of Saussure's distinction between *"parole"* and *"langue."*)

rules, describing how people *do* talk. Prescriptive and descriptive grammar are simply different things.[35]

The point of this version of Descriptivism is to show that the descriptive rules are more fundamental and way more important than the prescriptive rules. The argument goes like this. An English sentence's being *meaningful* is not the same as its being *grammatical.* That is, such clearly ill-formed constructions as "Did you seen the car keys of me?" or "The show was looked by many people" are nevertheless comprehensible; the sentences do, more or less, communicate the information they're trying to get across. Add to this the fact that nobody who isn't damaged in some profound Oliver Sacksish way actually ever makes these sorts of very deep syntactic errors[36] and you get the basic proposition of N. Chomsky's generative linguistics, which is that there exists a Universal Grammar beneath and common to all languages, plus that there is probably an actual part of the human brain that's imprinted with this Universal Grammar the same way birds' brains are imprinted with Fly South and dogs' with Sniff Genitals. There's all kinds of compelling evidence and support for these ideas, not least of which are the advances that linguists and cognitive scientists and AI researchers have been able to make with them, and the theories have a lot of credibility, and they are adduced by the Philosophical Descriptivists to show that since the really *important* rules of language are at birth already hardwired into people's neocortex, SWE prescriptions against dangling participles or mixed metaphors are basically the linguistic equivalent of whalebone corsets and short forks for salad. As Steven Pinker puts it, "When a scientist considers all the high-

---

[35] (If that last line of Pinker's pourparler reminds you of Garner's "Essentially, descriptivists and prescriptivists are approaching different problems," be advised that the similarity is neither coincidence nor plagiarism. One of the many cunning things about *ADMAU's* preface is that Garner likes to take bits of Descriptivist rhetoric and use them for very different ends.)

[36] Pinker puts it this way: "No one, not even a valley girl, has to be told not to say *Apples the eat boy* or *The child seems sleeping* or *Who did you meet John and?* or the vast, vast majority of the millions of trillions of mathematically possible combinations of words."

tech mental machinery needed to order words into everyday sentences, prescriptive rules are, at best, inconsequential decorations."

This argument is not the barrel of drugged trout that Methodological Descriptivism was, but it's still vulnerable to objections. The first one is easy. Even if it's true that we're all wired with a Universal Grammar, it doesn't follow that *all* prescriptive rules are superfluous. Some of these rules really do seem to serve clarity and precision. The injunction against two-way adverbs ("People who eat this often get sick") is an obvious example, as are rules about other kinds of misplaced modifiers ("There are many reasons why lawyers lie, some better than others") and about relative pronouns' proximity to the nouns they modify ("She's the mother of an infant daughter who works twelve hours a day").

Granted, the Philosophical Descriptivist can question just how absolutely necessary these rules are: it's quite likely that a recipient of clauses like the above could figure out what they mean from the sentences on either side or from the overall context or whatever.[37] A listener can usually figure out what I really mean when I misuse *infer* for *imply* or say *indicate* for *say*, too. But many of these solecisms — or even just clunky redundancies like "The door was rectangular in shape" — require at least a couple extra nanoseconds of cognitive effort, a kind of rapid sift-and-discard process, before the recipient gets it. Extra work. It's debatable just how much extra work, but it seems indisputable that we put *some* extra interpretive burden on the recipient when we fail to honor certain conventions. W/r/t confusing clauses like the above, it simply seems more "considerate" to follow the rules of correct English . . . just as it's more "considerate" to de-slob your home before entertaining guests or to brush your teeth before picking up a date. Not just more considerate but more *respectful* somehow — both of your listener/reader and of what you're trying to get across. As we sometimes also say

---

[37] (FYI, there happens to be a whole subdiscipline of linguistics called Pragmatics that essentially studies the way statements' meanings are created by various contexts.)

about elements of fashion and etiquette, the way you use English "makes a statement" or "sends a message" — even though these statements/messages often have nothing to do with the actual information you're trying to communicate.

We've now sort of bled into a more serious rejoinder to Philosophical Descriptivism: from the fact that linguistic communication is not strictly dependent on usage and grammar it does *not* necessarily follow that the traditional rules of usage and grammar are nothing but "inconsequential decorations." Another way to state this objection is that something's being "decorative" does not necessarily make it "inconsequential." Rhetoric-wise, Pinker's flip dismissal is very bad tactics, for it invites precisely the question it's begging: inconsequential *to whom?*

A key point here is that the resemblance between usage rules and certain conventions of etiquette or fashion is closer than the Philosophical Descriptivists know and far more important than they understand. Take, for example, the Descriptivist claim that so-called correct English usages like *brought* rather than *brung* and *felt* rather than *feeled* are arbitrary and restrictive and unfair and are supported only by custom and are (like irregular verbs in general) archaic and incommodious and an all-around pain in the ass. Let us concede for the moment that these claims are 100 percent reasonable. Then let's talk about pants. Trousers, slacks. I suggest to you that having the so-called correct subthoracic clothing for US males be pants instead of skirts is arbitrary (lots of other cultures let men wear skirts), restrictive and unfair (US females get to wear either skirts or pants), based solely on archaic custom (I think it's got to do with certain traditions about gender and leg-position, the same reasons women were supposed to ride sidesaddle and girls' bikes don't have a crossbar), and in certain ways not only incommodious but illogical (skirts are more comfortable than pants;[38] pants ride up; pants are hot; pants can squish the 'nads and reduce

---

[38] (presumably)

fertility; over time pants chafe and erode irregular sections of men's leg-hair and give older men hideous half-denuded legs; etc. etc.). Let us grant — as a thought experiment if nothing else — that these are all sensible and compelling objections to pants as an androsartorial norm. Let us, in fact, in our minds and hearts say yes — *shout* yes — to the skirt, the kilt, the toga, the sarong, the jupe. Let us dream of or even in our spare time work toward an America where nobody lays any arbitrary sumptuary prescriptions on anyone else and we can all go around as comfortable and aerated and unchafed and motile as we want.

And yet the fact remains that in the broad cultural mainstream of millennial America, men do not wear skirts. If you, the reader, are a US male, and even if you share my personal objections to pants and dream as I do of a cool and genitally unsquishy American Tomorrow, the odds are still 99.9 percent that in 100 percent of public situations you wear pants/slacks/shorts/trunks. More to the point, if you are a US male and also have a US male child, and if that child might happen to come to you one evening and announce his desire/intention to wear a skirt rather than pants to school the next day, I am 100 percent confident that you are going to discourage him from doing so. *Strongly* discourage him. You could be a Molotov-tossing anti-pants radical or a kilt manufacturer or Dr. Steven Pinker himself — you're going to stand over your kid and be prescriptive about an arbitrary, archaic, uncomfortable, and inconsequentially decorative piece of clothing. Why? Well, because in modern America any little boy who comes to school in a skirt (even, say, a modest all-season midi) is going to get stared at and shunned and beaten up and called a total geekoid by a whole lot of people whose approval and acceptance are important to him.[39] In

---

[39] In the case of little Steve Pinker Jr., these people are the boy's peers and teachers and crossing guards. In the case of adult cross-dressers and drag queens who have jobs in the straight world and wear pants to those jobs, it's bosses and coworkers and customers and people on the subway. For the die-hard slob who nevertheless wears a coat and tie to work, it's mostly his boss, who doesn't want his employees' clothes to send clients "the wrong message." But it's all basically the same thing.

our present culture, in other words, a boy who wears a skirt is "making a statement" that is going to have all kinds of gruesome social and emotional consequences for him.

You can probably see where this is headed. I'm going to describe the intended point of the pants analogy in terms that I'm sure are simplistic — doubtless there are whole books in Pragmatics or psycholinguistics or something devoted to unpacking this point. The weird thing is that I've seen neither Descriptivists nor SNOOTs deploy it in the Wars.[40, 41]

When I say or write something, there are actually a whole lot of different things I am communicating. The propositional content (i.e., the verbal information I'm trying to convey) is only one part of it. Another part is stuff about me, the communicator. Everyone knows this. It's a function of the fact that there are so many different well-formed ways to say the same basic thing, from e.g. "I was attacked by a bear!" to "Goddamn bear tried to kill me!" to "That ursine juggernaut did essay to sup upon my person!" and so on. Add the Saussurian/Chomskian consideration that many grammatically ill-formed sentences can also get the propositional content across — "Bear attack Tonto, Tonto heap scared!" — and the number of subliminal options we're scanning/sorting/interpreting as we communicate with one another goes transfinite very quickly. And different levels of diction and formality are only the simplest kinds of distinction; things get way more complicated in the sorts of interpersonal communication where social relations and feelings and moods come into play. Here's a familiar kind of example. Suppose that you and I are acquaintances and we're in my apart-

---

[40] Even Garner scarcely mentions it, and just once in his dictionary's miniessay on CLASS DISTINCTIONS: "[M]any linguistic pratfalls can be seen as class indicators — even in a so-called classless society such as the United States." And when Bryan A. Garner uses a clunky passive like "can be seen" as to distance himself from an issue, you know something's in the air.
[41] In fact, pretty much the only time one ever hears the issue made wholly explicit is in radio ads for tapes that promise to improve people's vocabularies. These ads tend to be extremely ominous and intimidating and always start out with "DID YOU KNOW PEOPLE JUDGE YOU BY THE WORDS YOU USE?"

ment having a conversation and that at some point I want to terminate the conversation and not have you be in my apartment anymore. Very delicate social moment. Think of all the different ways I
can try to handle it: "Wow, look at the time"; "Could we finish this
up later?"; "Could you please leave now?"; "Go"; "Get out"; "Get the
hell out of here"; "Didn't you say you had to be someplace?"; "Time
for you to hit the dusty trail, my friend"; "Off you go then, love"; or
that sly old telephone-conversation-ender: "Well, I'm going to let
you go now"; etc. etc." And then think of all the different factors
and implications of each option.[42]

The point here is obvious. It concerns a phenomenon that
SNOOTs blindly reinforce and that Descriptivists badly underestimate and that scary vocab-tape ads try to exploit. People really do
judge one another according to their use of language. Constantly.
Of course, people are constantly judging one another on the basis
of all kinds of things — height, weight, scent, physiognomy, accent,
occupation, make of vehicle[43] — and, again, doubtless it's all terribly complicated and occupies whole battalions of sociolinguists.
But it's clear that at least one component of all this interpersonal
semantic judging involves *acceptance*, meaning not some touchy-
feely emotional affirmation but actual acceptance or rejection of
someone's bid to be regarded as a peer, a member of somebody
else's collective or community or Group. Another way to come at
this is to acknowledge something that in the Usage Wars gets mentioned only in very abstract terms: "correct" English usage is, as a

---

[42] To be honest, the example here has a special personal resonance for this reviewer
because in real life I always seem to have a hard time winding up a conversation or asking
somebody to leave, and sometimes the moment becomes so delicate and fraught with
social complexity that I'll get overwhelmed trying to sort out all the different possible
ways of saying it and all the different implications of each option and will just sort of
blank out and do it totally straight — "I want to terminate the conversation and not have
you be in my apartment anymore" — which evidently makes me look either as if I'm very
rude and abrupt or as if I'm semi-autistic and have no sense of how to wind up a conversation gracefully. Somehow, in other words, my reducing the statement to its bare propositional content "sends a message" that is itself scanned, sifted, interpreted, and judged
by my auditor, who then sometimes never comes back. I've actually lost friends this way.
[43] (. . . not to mention color, gender, ethnicity — you can see how fraught and charged
all this is going to get)

practical matter, a function of whom you're talking to and of how you want that person to respond — not just to your utterance but also to *you*. In other words, a large part of the project of any communication is rhetorical and depends on what some rhet-scholars call "Audience" or "Discourse Community."[44] It is the present existence in the United States of an enormous number of different Discourse Communities, plus the fact that both people's use of English and their interpretations of others' use are influenced by rhetorical assumptions, that are central to understanding why the Usage Wars are so politically charged and to appreciating why Bryan Garner's *ADMAU* is so totally sneaky and brilliant and modern.

Fact: There are all sorts of cultural/geographical dialects of American English — Black English, Latino English, Rural Southern, Urban Southern, Standard Upper-Midwest, Maine Yankee, East-Texas Bayou, Boston Blue-Collar, on and on. Everybody knows this. What not everyone knows — especially not certain Prescriptivists — is that many of these non-SWE-type dialects have their own highly developed and internally consistent grammars, and that some of these dialects' usage norms actually make more linguistic/aesthetic sense than do their Standard counterparts.* Plus, of course, there are also innumerable sub- and subsubdialects[45] based on all sorts of things that have nothing to do with locale or ethnicity — Medical-School English, Twelve-Year-Old-Males-Whose-Worldview-Is-Deeply-Informed-by-*South-Park* English — that are nearly incomprehensible to anyone who isn't inside their very tight and

---

[44] *Discourse Community* is a rare example of academic jargon that's actually a valuable addition to SWE because it captures something at once very complex and very specific that no other English term quite can.*

   * (The above, while true, is an obvious attempt to preempt readerly sneers/winces at the term's continued deployment in this article.)

[45] Just how tiny and restricted a subdialect can get and still be called a subdialect isn't clear; there might be very firm linguistic definitions of what's a dialect and what's a subdialect and what's a subsub-, etc. Because I don't know any better and am betting you don't either, I'm going to use *subdialect* in a loose inclusive way that covers idiolects as distinctive as Peorians-Who-Follow-Pro-Wrestling-Closely or Geneticists-Who-Specialize-in-Hardy-Weinberg-Equilibrium. *Dialect* should probably be reserved for major players like Standard Black English et al.

specific Discourse Community (which of course is part of their function[46]).

*INTERPOLATION
POTENTIALLY DESCRIPTIVIST-LOOKING EXAMPLE OF SOME GRAMMATICAL ADVANTAGES OF A NON-STANDARD DIALECT THAT THIS REVIEWER ACTUALLY KNOWS ABOUT FIRSTHAND

I happen to have two native English dialects — the SWE of my hyper-educated parents and the hard-earned Rural Midwestern of most of my peers. When I'm talking to RMs, I tend to use constructions like "Where's it at?" for "Where is it?" and sometimes "He don't" instead of "He doesn't." Part of this is a naked desire to fit in and not get rejected as an egghead or fag (see *sub*). But another part is that I, SNOOT or no, believe that these RMisms are in certain ways superior to their Standard equivalents.

For a dogmatic Prescriptivist, "Where's it at?" is double-damned as a sentence that not only ends with a preposition but whose final preposition forms a redundancy with *where* that's similar to the re-dundancy in "the reason is because" (which latter usage I'll admit makes me dig my nails into my palms). Rejoinder: First off, the avoid-terminal-prepositions rule is the invention of one Fr. R. Lowth, an 18th-century British preacher and indurate pedant who did things like spend scores of pages arguing for *hath* over the trendy and degenerate *has*. The a.-t.-p. rule is antiquated and stupid and only the most ayotolloid SNOOT takes it seriously. Garner himself calls the rule "stuffy" and lists all kinds of useful constructions like "a person I have great respect for" and "the man I was listening to" that we'd have to discard or distort if we really enforced it.

Plus, the apparent redundancy of "Where's it at?"[47] is offset by its metrical logic: what the *at* really does is license the contraction of *is* after the interrogative adverb. You can't say "Where's it?" So the choice is between "Where is it?" and "Where's it at?", and the latter, a strong anapest, is prettier and trips off the tongue better than "Where is it?", whose meter is either a clunky monosyllabic-foot + trochee or it's nothing at all.

---

[46] (Plus it's true that whether something gets called a "subdialect" or "jargon" seems to de-pend on how much it annoys people outside its Discourse Community. Garner himself has miniessays on AIRPLANESE, COMPUTERESE, LEGALESE, and BUREAUCRATESE, and he more or less calls all of them jargon. There is no *ADMAU* miniessay on DIALECTS, but there is one on JARGON, in which such is Garner's self-restraint that you can almost hear his tendons straining, as in "[Jargon] arises from the urge to save time and space — and occasionally to conceal meaning from the uninitiated.")

[47] (a redundancy that's a bit arbitrary, since "Where's it *from*?" isn't redundant [mainly because *whence* has receded into semi-archaism])

Using "He don't" makes me a little more uncomfortable; I admit that its logic isn't quite as compelling. Nevertheless, a clear trend in the evolution of English from Middle to Modern has been the gradual regularizing of irregular present-tense verbs,[48] a trend justified by the fact that irregulars are hard to learn and to keep straight and have nothing but history going for them. By this reasoning, Standard Black English is way out on the cutting edge of English with its abandonment of the 3-S present in *to do* and *to go* and *to say* and its marvelously streamlined six identical present-tense inflections of *to be*. (Granted, the conjugation "he be" always sounds odd to me, but then SBE is not one of my dialects.)

This is probably the place for your SNOOT reviewer openly to concede that a certain number of traditional prescriptive rules really are stupid and that people who insist on them (like the legendary assistant to Margaret Thatcher who refused to read any memo with a split infinitive in it, or the jr.-high teacher I had who automatically graded you down if you started a sentence with *Hopefully*) are that very most contemptible and dangerous kind of SNOOT, the SNOOT Who Is Wrong. The injunction against split infinitives, for instance, is a consequence of the weird fact that English grammar is modeled on Latin even though Latin is a synthetic language and English is an analytic language.[49] Latin infinitives consist of one word and are impossible to as it were split, and the earliest English Prescriptivists — so enthralled with Latin that their English usage guides were actually *written* in Latin[50] — decided that English infinitives shouldn't be split either. Garner himself takes out after the s.i. rule in his mini-essays on both SPLIT INFINITIVES and SUPERSTITIONS.[51] And *Hopefully* at the beginning of a sentence, as a certain cheeky eighth-grader once (to his everlasting social cost) pointed out in class, actually functions

---

[48] E.g., for a long time English had a special 2-S present conjugation — "thou lovest," "thou sayest" — that now survives only in certain past tenses (and in the present of *to be*, where it consists simply in giving the 2-S a plural inflection).
[49] A synthetic language uses grammatical inflections to dictate syntax, whereas an analytic languages uses word order. Latin, German, and Russian are synthetic; English and Chinese are analytic.
[50] (Q.v. for example Sir Thomas Smith's cortex-withering *De Recta et Emendata Linguae Anglicae Scriptione Dialogus* of 1568.)
[51] N.B., though, that he's sane about it. Some split infinitives really are clunky and hard to parse, especially when there are a lot of words between *to* and the verb ("We will attempt to swiftly and to the best of our ability respond to these charges"), which Garner calls "wide splits" and sensibly discourages. His overall verdict on split infinitives — which is that some are "perfectly proper" and some iffy and some just totally bad news, and that no one wide tidy dogmatic ukase can handle all s.i. cases, and thus that "knowing when to split an infinitive requires a good ear and a keen eye" — is a fine example of the way Garner distinguishes sound and helpful Descriptivist objections from wacko or dogmatic objections and then incorporates the sound objections into a smarter and more flexible Prescriptivism.

not as a misplaced modal auxiliary or as a manner adverb like *quickly* or *angrily* but as a sentence adverb (i.e., as a special kind of "veiled reflexive" that indicates the speaker's attitude about the state of affairs described by the rest of the sentence — examples of perfectly OK sentence adverbs are *clearly, basically, luckily*), and only SNOOTs educated in the high-pedantic years 1940–1960 blindly proscribe it or grade it down.

The cases of split infinitives and *Hopefully* are in fact often trotted out by dogmatic Descriptivists as evidence that all SWE usage rules are arbitrary and dumb (which is a bit like pointing to Pat Buchanan as evidence that all Republicans are maniacs). FYI, Garner rejects *Hopefully*'s knee-jerk proscription, too, albeit grudgingly, saying "the battle is lost" and including the adverb in his miniessay on SKUNKED TERMS, which is his phrase for a usage that is "hotly disputed . . . any use of it is likely to distract some readers." (Garner also points out something I'd never quite realized, which is that *hopefully*, if misplaced/ mispunctuated in the body of a sentence, can create some of the same two-way ambiguities as other adverbs, as in e.g. "I will borrow your book and hopefully read it soon."

Whether we're conscious of it or not, most of us are fluent in more than one major English dialect and in several subdialects and are probably at least passable in countless others. Which dialect you choose to use depends, of course, on whom you're addressing. More to the point, I submit that the dialect you use depends mostly on what sort of Group your listener is part of and on whether you wish to present yourself as a fellow member of that Group. An obvious example is that traditional upper-class English has certain dialectal differences from lower-class English and that schools used to have courses in elocution whose whole *raison* was to teach people how to speak in an upper-class way. But usage-as-inclusion is about much more than class. Try another sort of thought experiment: A bunch of US teenagers in clothes that look several sizes too large for them are sitting together in the local mall's food court, and imagine that a 53-year-old man with jowls, a comb-over, and clothes that fit perfectly comes over to them and says he was scoping them and thinks they're totally rad and/or phat and asks is it cool if he just kicks it and chills with them here at their table. The kids' reaction is going to be either scorn or embarrassment for the guy — most likely a mix of both. Q: Why? Or imagine that two hard-core young urban black guys are standing there talking and I, who am resoundingly and in all ways white, come up and greet them with "Yo" and address one or both as "Brother" and ask "s'up, s'goin' on," pronouncing *on* with that NYCish o͞o-ŏ diphthong that Young Urban Black English deploys for a standard o. Either these guys are going to think that I am mocking them and be offended or they are going to think I am simply out of my mind. No other reaction is remotely foreseeable. Q: Why?

Why: A dialect of English is learned and used either because it's your native vernacular or because it's the dialect of a Group by which you wish (with some degree of plausibility) to be accepted. And although it is a major and vitally important one, SWE is only one dialect. And it is never, or at least hardly ever,[52] anybody's only dialect. This is because there are — as you and I both know and yet no one in the Usage Wars ever seems to mention — situations in which faultlessly correct SWE is *not* the appropriate dialect.

Childhood is full of such situations. This is one reason why SNOOTlets tend to have such a hard social time of it in school. A SNOOTlet is a little kid who's wildly, precociously fluent in SWE (he is often, recall, the offspring of SNOOTs). Just about every class has a SNOOTlet, so I know you've seen them — these are the sorts of six-to-twelve-year-olds who use *whom* correctly and whose response to striking out in T-ball is to shout "How incalculably dreadful!" The elementary-school SNOOTlet is one of the earliest identifiable species of academic geekoid and is duly despised by his peers and praised by his teachers. These teachers usually don't see the incredible amounts of punishment the SNOOTlet is receiving from his classmates, or if they do see it they blame the classmates and shake their heads sadly at the vicious and arbitrary cruelty of which children are capable.

---

[52] (It is, admittedly, difficult to imagine William F. Buckley using or perhaps even being aware of anything besides SWE.)

Teachers who do this are dumb. The truth is that his peers' punishment of the SNOOTlet is not arbitrary at all. There are important things at stake. Little kids in school are learning about Group-inclusion and -exclusion and about the respective rewards and penalties of same and about the use of dialect and syntax and slang as signals of affinity and inclusion. They're learning about Discourse Communities. Little kids learn this stuff not in Language Arts or Social Studies but on the playground and the bus and at lunch. When his peers are ostracizing the SNOOTlet or giving him monstrous quadruple Wedgies or holding him down and taking turns spitting on him, there's serious learning going on. Everybody here is learning except the little SNOOT[53] — in fact, what the SNOOTlet is being punished for is precisely his *failure* to learn. And his Language Arts teacher — whose own Elementary Education training prizes "linguistic facility" as one of the "social skills"

---

[53]   AMATEUR DEVELOPMENTAL-SOCIOLINGUISTIC INTERPOLATION #1
The SNOOTlet is, as it happens, an indispensable part of the other children's playground education. School and peers are kids' first socialization outside the family. In learning about Groups and Group tectonics, the kids are naturally learning that a Group's identity depends as much on exclusion as inclusion. They are, in other words, starting to learn about Us and Them, and about how an Us always needs a Them because being not-Them is essential to being Us. Because they're little children and it's school, the obvious Them is the teachers and all the values and appurtenances of the teacher-world.*
This teacher-Them helps the kids see how to start to be an Us, but the SNOOTlet completes the puzzle by providing a kind of missing link: he is the traitor, the Us who is in fact not Us but *Them*. The SNOOTlet, who at first appears to be one of Us because like Us he's three feet tall and runny-nosed and eats paste, nevertheless speaks an erudite SWE that signals membership not in Us but in Them, which since Us is defined as not-Them is equivalent to a rejection of Us that is also a *betrayal* of Us precisely because the SNOOTlet is a kid, i.e., one of Us.
Point: The SNOOTlet is teaching his peers that the criteria for membership in Us are not just age, height, paste-ingestion, etc., that in fact Us is primarily a state of mind and a set of sensibilities. An ideology. The SNOOTlet is also teaching the kids that Us has to be *extremely vigilant* about persons who may at first appear to be Us but are in truth *not* Us and may need to be identified and excluded *at a moment's notice*. The SNOOTlet is not the only type of child who can serve as traitor: the Teacher's Pet, the Tattletale, the Brown-Noser, and the Mama's Boy can also do nicely . . . just as the Damaged and Deformed and Fat and Generally Troubled children all help the nascent mainstream Us-Groups refine the criteria for in- and exclusion.
In these crude and fluid formations of ideological Groupthink lies American kids' real socialization. We all learn early that community and Discourse Community are the same thing, and a fearsome thing indeed. It helps to know where We come from.
    *(Plus, because the teacher-Them are tall humorless punishers/rewarders, they come to stand for all adults and — in a shadowy, inchoate way — for the Parents, whose gradual shift from composing Us to defining Them is probably the biggest ideological adjustment of childhood.)

that ensure children's "developmentally appropriate peer rapport,"[54] but who does not or cannot consider the possibility that linguistic facility might involve more than lapidary SWE — is unable to see that her beloved SNOOTlet is actually *deficient* in Language Arts. He has only one dialect. He cannot alter his vocabulary, usage, or grammar, cannot use slang or vulgarity; and it's these abilities that are really required for "peer rapport," which is just a fancy academic term for being accepted by the second-most-important Group in the little kid's life.[55] If he is sufficiently in thrall to his teachers and those teachers are sufficiently clueless, it may take years and unbelievable amounts of punishment before the SNOOTlet learns that you need more than one dialect to get along in school.

This reviewer acknowledges that there seems to be some, umm, personal stuff getting dredged up and worked out here;[56] but the stuff is germane. The point is that the little A+ SNOOTlet is actually in the same dialectal position as the class's "slow" kid who can't learn to stop using *ain't* or *bringed*. Exactly the same position. One is punished in class, the other on the playground, but both are deficient in the same linguistic skill — viz., the ability to move between various dialects and levels of "correctness," the ability to communicate one way with peers and another way with teachers and another with family and another with T-ball coaches and so on. Most of these dialectal adjustments are made below the level of conscious awareness, and our ability to make them seems part

---

[54] (Elementary Ed professors really do talk this way.)

[55]   AMATEUR DEVELOPMENTAL-SOCIOLINGUISTIC INTERPOLATION #2
And by the time the SNOOTlet hits adolescence it'll have supplanted the family to become the *most* important Group. And it will be a Group that depends for its definition on a rejection of traditional Authority.* And because it is the recognized dialect of mainstream adult society, there is no better symbol of traditional Authority than SWE. It is not an accident that adolescence is the time when slang and code and subdialects of subdialects explode all over the place and parents begin to complain that they can hardly even understand their kids' language. Nor are lyrics like "I can't get no / Satisfaction" an accident or any kind of sad commentary on the British educational system. Jagger et al. aren't stupid; they're rhetoricians, and they know their audience.
    *(That is, the teacher-/parent-Them becomes the Establishment, Society — Them becomes THEM.)

[56] (The skirt-in-school scenario was not personal stuff, though, FYI.)

psychological and part something else — perhaps something hard-wired into the same motherboard as Universal Grammar — and in truth this ability is a much better indicator of a kid's raw "verbal IQ" than test scores or grades, since US English classes do far more to retard dialectal talent than to cultivate it.

EXAMPLE OF HOW CONCEPTS OF RHETORIC AND DIALECT AND GROUP-INCLUSION CAN HELP MAKE SENSE OF SOME OF THE USAGE WARS' CONSTITUENT BATTLES

Well-known fact: In neither K–12 nor college English are systematic SWE grammar and usage much taught anymore. It's been this way for more than 20 years, and the phenomenon drives Prescriptivists nuts; it's one of the big things they cite as evidence of America's gradual murder of English. Descriptivists and English-Ed specialists counter that grammar and usage have been abandoned because scientific research has proved that studying SWE conventions doesn't help make kids better writers.[57] Each side in the debate tends to regard the other as mentally ill or/and blinded by ideology. Neither camp appears ever to have considered whether maybe the *way* prescriptive SWE was traditionally taught had something to do with its inutility.

By *"way"* here I'm referring not so much to actual method as to spirit or attitude. Most traditional teachers of English grammar have, of course, been dogmatic SNOOTs, and like most dogmatists they've been extremely stupid about the rhetoric they used and the audience they were addressing. I refer specifically to these teachers'[58] assumption that SWE is the sole appropriate English dialect and that the only reasons anyone could fail to see this are ignorance or amentia or grave deficiencies in character. As rhetoric,

---

[57] There is a respectable body of English-Ed research to back up this claim, the best known being the Harris, Bateman-Zidonis, and Mellon studies of the 1960s.

[58] There are still some of them around, at least here in the Midwest. You know the type: lipless, tweedy, cancrine — old maids of both genders. If you ever had one (as I did, 1976–77), you surely remember him.

this sort of attitude works only in sermons to the choir, and as pedagogy it's disastrous, and in terms of teaching writing it's especially
bad because it commits precisely the error that most Freshman
Composition classes spend all semester trying to keep kids from
making — the error of *presuming* the very audience-agreement that
it is really their rhetorical job to *earn*.[59] The reality is that an average US student is going to take the trouble to master the difficult
conventions of SWE only if he sees SWE's relevant Group or Discourse Community as one he'd like to be part of. And in the
absence of any sort of argument for why the correct-SWE Group is
a good or desirable one (an argument that, recall, the traditional
teacher hasn't given, because he's such a dogmatic SNOOT he sees
no need to), the student is going to be reduced to evaluating the
desirability of the SWE Group based on the one obvious member
of that Group he's encountered, namely the SNOOTy teacher
himself. And what right-thinking average kid would want to be
part of a Group represented by so smug, narrow, self-righteous,

---

[59]   INTERPOLATIVE BUT RELEVANT, IF ONLY BECAUSE THE ERROR HERE
         IS ONE THAT GARNER'S *ADMAU* MANAGES NEVER ONCE TO MAKE
This kind of mistake results more from a habit of mind than from any particular false
premise — it is a function not of fallacy or ignorance but of self-absorption. It also happens to be the most persistent and damaging error that most college writers make, and
one so deeply rooted that it often takes several essays and conferences and revisions to
get them to even see what the problem is. Helping them eliminate the error involves
drumming into student writers two big injunctions: (1) Do not presume that the reader
can read your mind — anything that you want the reader to visualize or consider or conclude, you must provide; (2) Do not presume that the reader feels the same way that you
do about a given experience or issue — your argument cannot just assume as true the
very things you're trying to argue for.
     Because (1) and (2) seem so simple and obvious, it may surprise you to know that
they are actually *incredibly hard* to get students to understand in such a way that the principles inform their writing. The reason for the difficulty is that, in the abstract, (1) and
(2) are intellectual, whereas in practice they are more things of the spirit. The injunctions require of the student both the imagination to conceive of the reader as a separate
human being and the empathy to realize that this separate person has preferences and
confusions and beliefs of her own, p/c/b's that are just as deserving of respectful consideration as the writer's. More, (1) and (2) require of students the humility to distinguish
between a universal truth ("This is the way things are, and only an idiot would disagree")
and something that the writer merely opines ("My reasons for recommending this are as
follows:"). These sorts of requirements are, of course, also the elements of a Democratic
Spirit. I therefore submit that the hoary cliché "Teaching the student to write is teaching
the student to think" sells the enterprise way short. Thinking isn't even half of it.

condescending, utterly uncool a personage as the traditional Prescriptivist teacher?

I'm not trying to suggest here that an effective SWE pedagogy would require teachers to wear sunglasses and call students Dude. What I am suggesting is that the rhetorical situation of a US English class — a class composed wholly of young people whose Group identity is rooted in defiance of Adult Establishment values, plus also composed partly of minorities whose primary dialects are different from SWE — requires the teacher to come up with overt, honest, and compelling arguments for why SWE is a dialect worth learning.

These arguments are hard to make. Hard not intellectually but emotionally, politically. Because they are baldly elitist.[60] The real truth, of course, is that SWE is the dialect of the American elite. That it was invented, codified, and promulgated by Privileged WASP Males and is perpetuated as "Standard" by same. That it is the shibboleth of the Establishment, and that it is an instrument of political power and class division and racial discrimination and all manner of social inequity. These are shall we say rather *delicate* subjects to bring up in an English class, especially in the service of a pro-SWE argument, and *extra*-especially if you yourself are both a Privileged WASP Male and the teacher and thus pretty much a walking symbol of the Adult Establishment. This reviewer's opinion, though, is that both students and SWE are way better served if the teacher makes his premises explicit and his argument overt — plus it obviously helps his rhetorical credibility if the teacher presents himself as an advocate of SWE's utility rather than as some sort of prophet of its innate superiority.

Because the argument for SWE is both most delicate and (I believe) most important with respect to students of color, here is a condensed version of the spiel I've given in private conferences[61]

---

[60] (Or rather the arguments require us openly to acknowledge and talk about elitism, whereas a traditional dogmatic SNOOT's pedagogy is merely elitism in action.)

[61] (I'm not a total idiot.)

with certain black students who were (a) bright and inquisitive as
hell and (b) deficient in what US higher education considers written
English facility:

> I don't know whether anybody's told you this or not, but when you're
> in a college English class you're basically studying a foreign dialect.
> This dialect is called Standard Written English. [Brief overview of
> major US dialects à la page 98.] From talking with you and reading
> your first couple essays, I've concluded that your own primary dialect
> is [one of three variants of SBE common to our region]. Now, let me
> spell something out in my official teacher-voice: the SBE you're flu-
> ent in is different from SWE in all kinds of important ways. Some of
> these differences are grammatical — for example, double negatives
> are OK in Standard Black English but not in SWE, and SBE and SWE
> conjugate certain verbs in totally different ways. Other differences
> have more to do with style — for instance, Standard Written English
> tends to use a lot more subordinate clauses in the early parts of sen-
> tences, and it sets off most of these early subordinates with commas,
> and under SWE rules, writing that doesn't do this tends to look
> "choppy." There are tons of differences like that. How much of this
> stuff do you already know? [STANDARD RESPONSE = some variation
> on "I know from the grades and comments on my papers that the
> English profs here don't think I'm a good writer."] Well, I've got
> good news and bad news. There are some otherwise smart English
> profs who aren't very aware that there are real dialects of English
> other than SWE, so when they're marking up your papers they'll put,
> like, "Incorrect conjugation" or "Comma needed" instead of "SWE
> conjugates this verb differently" or "SWE calls for a comma here."
> That's the good news — it's not that you're a bad writer, it's that you
> haven't learned the special rules of the dialect they want you to write
> in. Maybe that's not such good news, that they've been grading you
> down for mistakes in a foreign language you didn't even know was a
> foreign language. That they won't let you write in SBE. Maybe it
> seems unfair. If it does, you're probably not going to like this other
> news: I'm not going to let you write in SBE either. In my class, you
> have to learn and write in SWE. If you want to study your own pri-
> mary dialect and its rules and history and how it's different from
> SWE, fine — there are some great books by scholars of Black English,
> and I'll help you find some and talk about them with you if you want.
> But that will be outside class. In class — in my English class — you
> will have to master and write in Standard Written English, which we
> might just as well call "Standard White English" because it was devel-

oped by white people and is used by white people, especially educated, powerful white people. [RESPONSES at this point vary too widely to standardize.] I'm respecting you enough here to give you what I believe is the straight truth. In this country, SWE is perceived as the dialect of education and intelligence and power and prestige, and anybody of any race, ethnicity, religion, or gender who wants to succeed in American culture has got to be able to use SWE. This is just How It Is. You can be glad about it or sad about it or deeply pissed off. You can believe it's racist and unfair and decide right here and now to spend every waking minute of your adult life arguing against it, and maybe you should, but I'll tell you something — if you ever want those arguments to get listened to and taken seriously, you're going to have to communicate them in SWE, because SWE is the dialect our nation uses to talk to itself. African-Americans who've become successful and important in US culture know this; that's why King's and X's and Jackson's speeches are in SWE, and why Morrison's and Angelou's and Baldwin's and Wideman's and Gates's and West's books are full of totally ass-kicking SWE, and why black judges and politicians and journalists and doctors and teachers communicate professionally in SWE. Some of these people grew up in homes and communities where SWE was the native dialect, and these black people had it much easier in school, but the ones who didn't grow up with SWE realized at some point that they had to learn it and become able to write fluently in it, and so they did. And [STUDENT'S NAME], you're going to learn to use it, too, because I am going to make you.

I should note here that a couple of the students I've said this stuff to were offended — one lodged an Official Complaint — and that I have had more than one colleague profess to find my spiel "racially insensitive." Perhaps you do, too. This reviewer's own humble opinion is that some of the cultural and political realities of American life are themselves racially insensitive and elitist and offensive and unfair, and that pussyfooting around these realities with euphemistic doublespeak is not only hypocritical but toxic to the project of ever really changing them.

*   *   *

ANOTHER KIND OF USAGE WARS–RELATED EXAMPLE, THIS ONE WITH A PARTICULAR EMPHASIS ON DIALECT AS A VECTOR OF SELF-PRESENTATION VIA POLITENESS [62]

Traditionally, Prescriptivists tend to be political conservatives and Descriptivists tend to be liberals. But today's most powerful influence on the norms of public English is actually a stern and exacting form of liberal Prescriptivism. I refer here to Politically Correct English (PCE), under whose conventions failing students become "high-potential" students and poor people "economically disadvantaged" and people in wheelchairs "differently abled" and a sentence like "White English and Black English are different, and you better learn White English or you're not going to get good grades" is not blunt but "insensitive." Although it's common to make jokes about PCE (referring to ugly people as "aesthetically challenged" and so on), be advised that Politically Correct English's various pre- and proscriptions are taken very seriously *indeed* by colleges and corporations and government agencies, whose institutional dialects now evolve under the beady scrutiny of a whole new kind of Language Police.

From one perspective, the rise of PCE evinces a kind of Lenin-to-Stalinesque irony. That is, the same ideological principles that informed the original Descriptivist revolution — namely, the rejections of traditional authority (born of Vietnam) and of traditional inequality (born of the civil rights movement) — have now actually produced a far more inflexible Prescriptivism, one largely unencumbered by tradition or complexity and backed by the threat of real-world sanctions (termination, litigation) for those who fail to conform. This is funny in a dark way, maybe, and it's true that most

---

[62]   ESPECIALLY GOOD EPIGRAPHS FOR THIS SECTION
"Passive voice verbs, in particular, may deny female agency."
— DR. MARILYN SCHWARTZ AND THE TASK FORCE ON
BIAS-FREE LANGUAGE OF THE ASSOCIATION OF
AMERICAN UNIVERSITY PRESSES

"He raised his voice suddenly, and shouted for dinner. Servants shouted back that it was ready. They meant that they wished it was ready, and were so understood, for nobody moved."
— E. M. FORSTER

criticisms of PCE seem to consist in making fun of its trendiness or vapidity. This reviewer's own opinion is that prescriptive PCE is not just silly but ideologically confused and harmful to its own cause.

Here is my argument for that opinion. Usage is always political, but it's complexly political. With respect, for instance, to political change, usage conventions can function in two ways: on the one hand they can be a *reflection* of political change, and on the other they can be an *instrument* of political change. What's important is that these two functions are different and have to be kept straight. Confusing them — in particular, mistaking for political efficacy what is really just a language's political symbolism — enables the bizarre conviction that America ceases to be elitist or unfair simply because Americans stop using certain vocabulary that is historically associated with elitism and unfairness. This is PCE's core fallacy — that a society's mode of expression is productive of its attitudes rather than a product of those attitudes[63] — and of course it's nothing but the obverse of the politically conservative SNOOT's delusion that social change can be retarded by restricting change in standard usage.[64]

Forget Stalinization or Logic 101–level equivocations, though. There's a grosser irony about Politically Correct English. This is that PCE purports to be the dialect of progressive reform but is in fact — in its Orwellian substitution of the euphemisms of social equality for social equality itself — of vastly more help to conservatives and the US status quo than traditional SNOOT prescriptions ever were. Were I, for instance, a political conservative who opposed using taxation as a means of redistributing national wealth, I would be delighted to watch PC progressives spend their time and energy arguing over whether a poor person should be described as "low-income" or "economically disadvantaged" or "pre-prosperous" rather than constructing effective public arguments for redistribu-

---

[63] (A pithier way to put this is that *politeness* is not the same as *fairness*.)
[64] E.g., this is the reasoning behind Pop Prescriptivists' complaint that shoddy usage signifies the Decline of Western Civilization.

tive legislation or higher marginal tax rates. (Not to mention that strict codes of egalitarian euphemism serve to burke the sorts of painful, unpretty, and sometimes offensive discourse that in a pluralistic democracy lead to actual political change rather than symbolic political change. In other words, PCE acts as a form of censorship, and censorship always serves the status quo.)

As a practical matter, I strongly doubt whether a guy who has four small kids and makes $12,000 a year feels more empowered or less ill-used by a society that carefully refers to him as "economically disadvantaged" rather than "poor." Were I he, in fact, I'd probably find the PCE term insulting — not just because it's patronizing (which it is) but because it's hypocritical and self-serving in a way that oft-patronized people tend to have really good subliminal antennae for. The basic hypocrisy about usages like "economically disadvantaged" and "differently abled" is that PCE advocates believe the beneficiaries of these terms' compassion and generosity to be poor people and people in wheelchairs, which again omits something that everyone knows but nobody except the scary vocabulary-tape ads' announcer ever mentions — that part of any speaker's motive for using a certain vocabulary is always the desire to communicate stuff about himself. Like many forms of Vogue Usage,[65] PCE functions primarily to signal and congratulate certain virtues in the speaker — scrupulous egalitarianism, concern for the dig-

---

[65] *A Dictionary of Modern American Usage* includes a miniessay on VOGUE WORDS, but it's a disappointing one in which Garner does little more than list VWs that bug him and say that "vogue words have such a grip on the popular mind that they come to be used in contexts in which they serve little purpose." This is one of the rare places in *ADMAU* where Garner is simply wrong. The real problem is that every sentence blends and balances at least two different communicative functions — one the transmission of raw info, the other the transmission of certain stuff about the speaker — and Vogue Usage throws this balance off. Garner's "serve little purpose" is exactly incorrect: vogue words serve *too much* the purpose of presenting the speaker in a certain light (even if this is merely as with-it or hip), and people's odd little subliminal BS-antennae pick this imbalance up, and that's why even nonSNOOTs often find Vogue Usages irritating and creepy. It's the same phenomenon as when somebody goes out of her way to be incredibly solicitous and complimentary and nice to you and after a while you begin to find her solicitude creepy: you are sensing that a disproportionately large part of this person's agenda consists in trying to present herself as Nice.

nity of all people, sophistication about the political implications of language — and so serves the self-regarding interests of the PC far more than it serves any of the persons or groups renamed.*†

*INTERPOLATION

The unpleasant truth is that the same self-serving hypocrisy that informs PCE tends to infect and undermine the US Left's rhetoric in almost every debate over social policy. Take the ideological battle over wealth-redistribution via taxes, quotas, Welfare, enterprise zones, AFDC/TANF, you name it. As long as redistribution is conceived as a form of charity or compassion (and the Bleeding Left appears to buy this conception every bit as much as the Heartless Right), then the whole debate centers on utility — "Does Welfare help poor people get on their feet or does it foster passive dependence?" "Is government's bloated social-services bureaucracy an effective way to dispense charity?" and so on — and both camps have their arguments and preferred statistics, and the whole thing goes around and around. . . .

Opinion: The mistake here lies in both sides' assumption that the real motives for redistributing wealth are charitable or unselfish. The conservatives' mistake (if it is a mistake) is wholly conceptual, but for the Left the assumption is also a serious tactical error. Progressive liberals seem incapable of stating the obvious truth: that we who are well off should be willing to share more of what we have with poor people not for the poor people's sake but for our own; i.e., we should share what we have in order to become less narrow and frightened and lonely and self-centered people. No one ever seems willing to acknowledge aloud the thoroughgoing *self-interest* that underlies all impulses toward economic equality — especially not US progressives, who seem so invested in an image of themselves as Uniquely Generous and Compassionate and Not Like Those Selfish Conservatives Over There that they allow the conservatives to frame the debate in terms of charity and utility, terms under which redistribution seems far less obviously a good thing.

I'm talking about this example in such a general, simplistic way because it helps show why the type of leftist vanity that informs PCE is actually inimical to the Left's own causes. For in refusing to abandon the idea of themselves as Uniquely Generous and Compassionate (i.e., as morally superior), progressives lose the chance to frame their redistributive arguments in terms that are both realistic and realpolitikal. One such argument would involve a complex, sophisticated analysis of what we really mean by *self-interest,* particularly the distinctions between short-term financial self-interest and longer-term moral or social self-interest. As it is, though, liberals' vanity tends to grant conservatives a monopoly on appeals to self-interest, enabling the conservatives to depict progressives as pie-in-the-sky idealists and themselves as real-world back-pocket pragmatists. In short, leftists' big mistake here is not conceptual or ideological but spiritual and rhetorical — their narcissistic attachment to assumptions that maximize their own appearance of virtue tends to cost them both the theater and the war.

†INTERPOLATION
EXAMPLE OF A SNOOT-RELATED ISSUE IN THE FACE OF WHOSE MALIGNANCY THIS REVIEWER'S DEMOCRATIC SPIRIT GIVES OUT ALTOGETHER, ADMITTEDLY

This issue is Academic English, a verbal cancer that has metastasized now to afflict both scholarly writing —

> If such a sublime cyborg would insinuate the future as post-Fordist subject, his palpably masochistic locations as ecstatic agent of the sublime superstate need to be decoded as the "now all-but-unreadable DNA" of the fast industrializing Detroit, just as his Robocop-like strategy of carceral negotiation and street control remains the tirelessly American one of inflicting regeneration through violence upon the racially heteroglassic wilds and others of the inner city.[66]

— and prose as mainstream as the *Village Voice*'s —

> At first encounter, the poems' distanced cerebral surfaces can be daunting, evading physical location or straightforward emotional arc. But this seeming remoteness quickly reveals a very real passion, centered in the speaker's struggle to define his evolving self-construction.

Maybe it's a combination of my SNOOTitude and the fact that I end up having to read a lot of it for my job, but I'm afraid I regard Academic English not as a dialectal variation but as a grotesque debasement of SWE, and loathe it even more than the stilted incoherences of Presidential English ("This is the best and only way to uncover, destroy, and prevent Iraq from reengineering weapons of mass destruction") or the mangled pieties of BusinessSpeak ("Our Mission: to proactively search and provide the optimum networking skills and resources to service the needs of your growing business"); and in support of this total contempt and intolerance I cite no less an authority than Mr. G. Orwell, who 50 years ago had AE pegged as a "mixture of vagueness and sheer incompetence" in which "it is normal to

---

[66] FYI, this snippet, which appears in *ADMAU*'s miniessay on OBSCURITY, is quoted from a 1997 *Sacramento Bee* article entitled "No Contest: English Professors Are Worst Writers on Campus."

come across long passages which are almost completely lacking in meaning."[67]

It probably isn't the whole explanation, but as with the voguish hypocrisy of PCE, the obscurity and pretension of Academic English can be attributed in part to a disruption in the delicate rhetorical balance between language as a vector of meaning and language as a vector of the writer's own résumé. In other words, it is when a scholar's vanity/insecurity leads him to write *primarily* to communicate and reinforce his own status as an Intellectual that his English is deformed by pleonasm and pretentious diction (whose function is to signal the writer's erudition) and by opaque abstraction (whose function is to keep anybody from pinning the writer down to a definite assertion that can maybe be refuted or shown to be silly). The latter characteristic, a level of obscurity that often makes it just about impossible to figure out what an AE sentence is really saying,[68] so closely resembles political and corporate doublespeak ("revenue enhancement," "downsizing," "proactive resource-allocation restructuring")

---

[67] This was in his 1946 "Politics and the English Language," an essay that despite its date (and the basic redundancy of its title) remains the definitive SNOOT statement on Academese. Orwell's famous AE translation of the gorgeous "I saw under the sun that the race is not to the swift" part of Ecclesiastes as "Objective consideration of contemporary phenomena compels the conclusion that success or failure in competitive activities exhibits no tendency to be commensurate with innate capacity, but that a considerable element of the unpredictable must invariably be taken into account" should be tattooed on the left wrist of every grad student in the anglophone world.

[68] If you still think assertions like that are just SNOOT hyperbole, see also e.g. Dr. Fredric Jameson, author of *The Geopolitical Aesthetic* and *The Prison-House of Language*, whom *The Johns Hopkins Guide to Literary Theory and Criticism* calls "one of the foremost contemporary Marxist literary critics writing in English." Specifically, have a look at the first sentence of Dr. Jameson's 1992 *Signatures of the Visible* —

> The visual is *essentially* pornographic, which is to say that it has its end in rapt, mindless fascination; thinking about its attributes becomes an adjunct to that, if it is unwilling to betray its object; while the most austere films necessarily draw their energy from the attempt to repress their own excess (rather than from the thankless effort to discipline the viewer).

— in which not only is each of its three main independent clauses totally obscure and full of predicates without evident subjects and pronouns without clear antecedents, but whatever connection between those clauses justifies stringing them together into one long semicolonic sentence is anyone's guess at all.

Please be advised (a) that the above sentence won 1997's First Prize in the World's Worst Writing Contest held annually at Canterbury University in New Zealand, a competition in which American academics regularly sweep the field, and (b) that F. Jameson was and is an extremely powerful and influential and oft-cited figure in US literary scholarship, which means (c) that if you have kids in college, there's a good chance that they are being taught how to write by high-paid adults for whom the above sentence is a model of erudite English prose.

that it's tempting to think AE's real purpose is concealment and its real motivation fear.[69]

The insecurities that drive PCE, AE, and vocab-tape ads are far from groundless, though. These are tense linguistic times. Blame it on Heisenbergian uncertainty or postmodern relativism or Image Over Substance or the ubiquity of advertising and PR or the rise of Identity Politics or whatever you will — we live in an era of terrible preoccupation with presentation and interpretation, one in which the relations between who someone is and what he believes and how he "expresses himself"[70] have been thrown into big-time flux. In rhetorical terms, certain long-held distinctions between the Ethical Appeal, Logical Appeal (= an argument's plausibility or soundness, from *logos*), and Pathetic Appeal (= an argument's emotional impact, from *pathos*) have now pretty much collapsed — or rather the different sorts of Appeals now affect and are affected by one another in ways that make it nearly impossible to advance an argument on "reason" alone.

A vividly concrete illustration here concerns the Official Complaint that a certain black undergraduate filed against me after one of my little *in camera* spiels described on pages 108–109. The complainant was (I opine) wrong, but she was not crazy or stupid; and I was able later to see that I did bear some responsibility for the whole nasty administrative swivet. My culpability lay in gross rhetorical naïveté. I'd seen my speech's primary Appeal as Logical: the aim was to make a conspicuously blunt, honest argument for SWE's utility. It wasn't pretty, maybe, but it was true, plus so manifestly bullshit-free that I think I expected not just acquiescence but gratitude for my candor.[71] The problem I failed to see, of course, lay not

---

[69] Even in Freshman Comp, bad student essays are far, far more often the products of fear than of laziness or incompetence. In fact, it often takes so long to identify and help with students' fear that the Freshman Comp teacher never gets to find out whether they might have other problems, too.

[70] (Notice the idiom's syntax — it's never "expresses his beliefs" or "expresses his ideas.")

[71] (Please just don't even say it.)

with the argument per se but with the person making it — namely me, a Privileged WASP Male in a position of power, thus someone whose statements about the primacy and utility of the Privileged WASP Male dialect appeared not candid/hortatory/authoritative/ true but elitist/high-handed/authoritarian/racist. Rhetoric-wise, what happened was that I allowed the substance and style of my Logical Appeal to completely torpedo my Ethical Appeal: what the student heard was just another PWM rationalizing why his Group and his English were top dog and ought "logically" to stay that way (plus, worse, trying to use his academic power over her to coerce her assent[72]).

If for any reason you happen to find yourself sharing this particular student's perceptions and reaction,[73] I would ask that you bracket your feelings just long enough to recognize that the PWM instructor's very modern rhetorical dilemma in that office was not much different from the dilemma faced by any male who makes a Pro-Life argument, or any atheist who argues against creation science, or any caucasian who opposes Affirmative Action, or any African-American who decries racial profiling, or anyone over eighteen who tries to make a case for raising the legal driving age to eighteen, etc. The dilemma has nothing to do with whether the arguments themselves are plausible or right or even sane, because the debate rarely gets that far — any opponent with sufficiently strong feelings or a dogmatic bent can discredit the argument and pretty much foreclose all further discussion with a rejoinder we Americans have come to know well: "Of course *you'd* say that"; "Easy for *you* to say"; "What right do *you* have to . . . ?"

Now (still bracketing) consider the situation of any reasonably intelligent and well-meaning SNOOT who sits down to prepare a

---

[72] (The student professed to have been especially traumatized by the climactic "I am going to make you," which was indeed a rhetorical boner.)

[73] FYI, the dept. chair and dean did not, at the Complaint hearing, share her reaction . . . though it would be disingenuous not to tell you that they happened also to be PWMs, which fact was also remarked on by the complainant, such that the whole proceeding got pretty darn tense indeed, before it was over.

prescriptive usage guide. It's the millennium, post-everything: whence the authority to make any sort of credible Appeal for SWE at all?

ARTICLE'S CRUX: WHY BRYAN A. GARNER IS A GENIUS (I)

It isn't that *A Dictionary of Modern American Usage* is perfect. It doesn't seem to cover *conversant in* vs. *conversant with,* for example, or *abstruse* vs. *obtuse,* or to have anything on *hereby* and *herewith* (which I tend to use interchangeably but always have the uneasy feeling I'm screwing up). Garner's got a good discussion of *used to* but nothing on *supposed to.* Nor does he give any examples to help explain irregular participles and transitivity ("The light shone" vs. "I shined the light," etc.), and these would seem to be more important than, say, the correct spelling of *huzzah* or the plural of *animalculum,* both of which get discussed. In other words, a rock-ribbed SNOOT is going to be able to find stuff to kvetch about in any usage dictionary, and *ADMAU* is no exception.

But it's still really, really good. Except for the VOGUE WORDS snafu and the absence of a pronunciation entry on *trough,*[74] the above were pretty much the only quibbles this reviewer could find. *ADMAU* is thorough and timely and solid, as good as Follett's and Gilman's and the handful of other great American usage guides of the century. Their format — which was Fowler's — is *ADMAU*'s, too: concise entries on individual words and phrases and expository cap-titled MINIESSAYS on any issue broad enough to warrant more general discussion. Because of both his Fowler Society and the advent of online databases, though, Garner has access to many more examples of actual published SWE than did Gilman nine

---

[74] To be honest, I noticed this omission only because midway through working on this article I happened to use the word *trough* in front of the same SNOOT friend who compares public English to violin-hammering, and he fell sideways out of his chair, and it emerged that I have somehow all my life misheard *trough* as ending with a *th* instead of an *f* and thus have publicly mispronounced it God only knows how many scores of times, and I all but burned rubber getting home to see whether perhaps the error was so common and human and understandable that *ADMAU* had a good-natured entry on it — but no such luck, which in fairness I don't suppose I can really blame Garner for.

years ago, and he uses them to great, if lengthy, effect. But none of this is why Bryan Garner is a genius.

ADMAU is a collection of judgments and so is in no way Descriptivist, but Garner structures his judgments very carefully to avoid the elitism and anality of traditional SNOOTitude. He does not deploy irony or scorn or caustic wit, nor tropes or colloquialisms or contractions . . . or really any sort of verbal style at all. In fact, even though Garner talks openly about himself and uses the 1-S pronoun throughout the whole dictionary, his personality is oddly effaced, neutralized. It's like he's so bland he's barely there. For instance, as this reviewer was finishing the book's final entry,[75] it struck me that I had no idea whether Bryan A. Garner was black or white, gay or straight, Democrat or Dittohead. What was even more striking was that I hadn't once wondered about any of this up to now; something about Garner's lexical persona kept me from ever asking where the guy was coming from or what particular agendas or ideologies were informing what he had admitted right up front were "value judgments." This seemed very odd indeed. Bland people can have axes to grind, too, so I decided that *bland* probably wasn't the right word to describe Garner's *ADMAU* persona. The right word was probably more like *objective,* but with a little *o,* as in "disinterested," "reasonable." Then something kind of obvious occurred to me, but in an unobvious way — this small-*o* kind of objectivity was very different from the metaphysical, capital *O*–type Objectivity whose postmodern loss had destroyed (I'd pretty much concluded) any possibility of genuine Authority in issues of usage.

Then it occurred to me that if *Objectivity* still had a lowercase sense unaffected by modern relativism, maybe *Authority* did as well. So, just as I'd done w/r/t Garner's use of *judgment,* I went to my trusty conservative *American Heritage Dictionary* and looked up *authority.*

---

[75] (on *zwieback* vs. *zweiback*)

Does any of this make sense? Because this was how I discovered that Bryan Garner is a genius.

WHY BRYAN A. GARNER IS A GENIUS (II)

Bryan Garner is a genius because *A Dictionary of Modern American Usage* just about completely resolves the Usage Wars' problem of Authority. The book's solution is both semantic and rhetorical. Garner manages to collapse the definitions of certain key terms and to control the compresence of rhetorical Appeals so cleverly that he is able to transcend both Usage Wars camps and simply tell the truth, and to tell the truth in a way that does not torpedo his own credibility but actually enhances it. His argumentative strategy is totally brilliant and totally sneaky, and part of both qualities is that it usually doesn't seem like there's even an argument going on at all.

WHY BRYAN A. GARNER IS A GENIUS (III)

Rhetorically, traditional Prescriptivists depend almost entirely on the Logical Appeal. One reason they are such inviting targets for liberal scorn is their arrogance, and their arrogance is based on their utter disdain for considerations of persona or persuasion. This is not an exaggeration. Doctrinaire Prescriptivists conceive of themselves not as advocates of correct English but as avatars of it. The truth of what they prescribe is itself their "authority" for prescribing it; and because they hold the truth of these prescriptions to be self-evident, they regard those Americans who reject or ignore the prescriptions as "ignoramuses" who are pretty much beneath notice except as evidence for the general deterioration of US culture.

Since the only true audience for it is the Prescriptivists themselves, it really doesn't matter that their argument is almost Euthyphrotically circular — "It's the truth because we say so, and we say so because it's the truth." This is dogmatism of a purity you don't often see in this country, and it's no accident that hard-core Prescriptivists are just a tiny fringe-type element of today's culture. The American Conversation is an argument, after all, and way worse than our fear of error or anarchy or Gomorrahl decadence is our fear of theocracy or autocracy or any ideology whose project is not to argue or persuade but to adjourn the whole debate *sine die.*[76]

The hard-line Descriptivists, for all their calm scientism and avowed preference for fact over value, rely mostly on rhetorical *pathos,* the visceral emotional Appeal. As mentioned, the relevant emotions here are Sixtiesish in origin and leftist in temperament — an antipathy for conventional Authority and elitist put-downs and uptight restrictions and casuistries and androcaucasian bias and snobbery and overt smugness of any sort . . . i.e., for the very attitudes embodied in the prim glare of the grammarian and the languid honk of Buckley-type elites, which happen to be the two most visible species of SNOOT still around. Whether Methodological or Philosophical or pseudo-progressive, Descriptivists are, all and essentially, demagogues; and dogmatic Prescriptivists are actually their most valuable asset, since Americans' visceral distaste for dogmatism and elitist fatuity gives Descriptivism a ready audience for its Pathetic Appeal.

What the Descriptivists haven't got is logic. The Dictionary can't sanction everything, and the very possibility of language depends on rules and conventions, and Descriptivism offers no *logos* for determining which rules and conventions are useful and which are pointless/oppressive, nor any arguments for how and by whom such determinations are to be made. In short, the Descriptivists don't have any kind of Appeal that's going to persuade anyone who doesn't already have an EAT THE RICH–type hatred of Authority per se. Homiletically speaking, the only difference between the Prescriptivists and the Descriptivists is that the latter's got a bigger choir.

Mr. Bryan A. Garner recognizes something that neither of these camps appears to get: given 40 years of the Usage Wars, "authority" is no longer something a lexicographer can just presume *ex officio.*

---

[76] It's this logic (and perhaps this alone) that keeps protofascism or royalism or Maoism or any sort of really dire extremism from achieving mainstream legitimacy in US politics — how does one vote for No More Voting?

In fact, a large part of the project of any contemporary usage dictionary will consist in *establishing* this authority. If that seems rather obvious, be apprised that nobody before Garner seems to have figured it out — that the lexicographer's challenge now is to be not just accurate and comprehensive but *credible*. That in the absence of unquestioned, capital-A Authority in language, the reader must now be moved or persuaded to grant a dictionary its authority, freely and for what appear to be good reasons.

Garner's *A Dictionary of Modern American Usage* is thus both a collection of information and a piece of Democratic[77] rhetoric. Its primary Appeal is Ethical, and its goal is to recast the Prescriptivist's persona: the author presents himself not as a cop or a judge but as more like a doctor or lawyer. This is an ingenious tactic. In the same sort of move we can see him make w/r/t *judgment* and *objective*, Garner here alters the relevant *AHD* definitions of *authority* from (1) "The right and power to command, enforce laws, exact obedience, determine, or judge" / "A person or group invested with this power" to (2) "Power to influence or persuade resulting from knowledge or experience" / "An accepted source of expert information or advice." *ADMAU*'s Garner, in other words, casts himself as an authority not in an *autocratic* sense but in a *technocratic* sense. And the technocrat is not only a thoroughly modern and palatable image of authority but also immune to the charges of elitism/classism that have hobbled traditional Prescriptivism. After all, do we call a doctor or lawyer "elitist" when he presumes to tell us what we should eat or how we should do our taxes?

Of course, Garner really *is* a technocrat. He's an attorney, recall, and in *ADMAU* he cultivates just the sort of persona good jurists project: knowledgeable, reasonable, dispassionate, fair. His judgments about usage tend to be rendered like legal opinions — exhaustive citation of precedent (other dictionaries' judgments, published examples of actual usage) combined with clear, logical

---

[77] (meaning *literally* Democratic — it Wants Your Vote)

reasoning that's always informed by the larger consensual purposes SWE is meant to serve.

Also technocratic is Garner's approach to the whole issue of whether anybody's even going to be interested in his 700 pages of fine-pointed counsel. Like any mature specialist, he simply assumes that there are good practical reasons why some people choose to concern themselves with his area of expertise; and his attitude about the fact that most Americans "could care less" about SWE usage isn't scorn or disapproval but the phlegmatic resignation of a professional who realizes that he can give good advice but can't make you take it:

> The reality I care about most is that some people still want to use the language well.[78] They want to write effectively; they want to speak effectively. They want their language to be graceful at times and powerful at times. They want to understand how to use words well, how to manipulate sentences, and how to move about in the language without seeming to flail. They want good grammar, but they want more: they want rhetoric[79] in the traditional sense. That is, they want to use the language deftly so that it's fit for their purposes.

It's now possible to see that all the autobiographical stuff in *ADMAU*'s preface does more than just humanize Mr. Bryan A. Garner. It also serves to detail the early and enduring passion that helps make someone a credible technocrat — we tend to like and trust experts whose expertise is born of a real love for their specialty instead of just a desire to be expert at something. In fact, it turns out that *ADMAU*'s preface quietly and steadily invests Garner with every single qualification of modern technocratic authority: passionate devotion, reason and accountability (recall "in the interests of full disclosure, here are the ten critical points . . ."), experience (". . . that, after years of working on usage problems, I've settled on"), exhaustive and tech-savvy research ("For contemporary usage, the

---

[78] The last two words of this sentence, of course, are what the Usage Wars are all about — whose "language" and whose "well"? The most remarkable thing about the sentence is that coming from Garner it doesn't sound naive or obnoxious but just . . . reasonable.
[79] (Did you think I was kidding?)

files of our greatest dictionary makers pale in comparison with the full-text search capabilities now provided by NEXIS and WESTLAW"[80]), an even and judicious temperament (see e.g. this from his HYPERCORRECTION: "Sometimes people strive to abide by the strictest etiquette, but in the process behave inappropriately"[81]), and the sort of humble integrity (for instance, including in one of the entries a past published usage-error of his own) that not only renders Garner likable but transmits the kind of reverence for English that good jurists have for the law, both of which are bigger and more important than any one person.

Probably the most ingenious and attractive thing about his dictionary's Ethical Appeal, though, is Garner's scrupulousness about considering the reader's own hopes and fears and reasons for caring enough about usage to bother with something like *ADMAU* at all. These reasons, as Garner makes clear, tend to derive from a reader's concern about his/her *own* linguistic authority and rhetorical persona and ability to convince an audience that he/she cares. Again and again, Garner frames his prescriptions in rhetorical terms: "To the writer or speaker for whom credibility is important, it's a good idea to avoid distracting *any* readers or listeners"; "Whatever you do, if you use *data* in a context in which its number becomes known, you'll bother some of your readers." *A Dictionary of Modern American Usage*'s real thesis, in other words, is that the purposes of the expert authority and the purposes of the lay reader are identical, and identically rhetorical — which I submit is about as Democratic these days as you're going to get.

---

[80] Cunning — what is in effect Garner's blowing his own archival horn is cast as humble gratitude for the resources made available by modern technology. Plus notice also Garner's implication here that he's once again absorbed the sane parts of Descriptivism's cast-a-wide-net method: "Thus, the prescriptive approach here is leavened by a thorough canvassing of actual usage in modern edited prose."

[81] (Here, this reviewer's indwelling and ever-vigilant SNOOT can't help but question Garner's deployment of a comma before the conjunction in this sentence, since what follows the conjunction is neither an independent clause nor any sort of plausible complement for "strive to." But respectful disagreement between people of goodwill is of course Democratically natural and healthy and, when you come right down to it, kind of fun.)

BONUS FULL-DISCLOSURE INFO ON THE SOURCES OF CERTAIN STUFF THAT DOES OR SHOULD APPEAR INSIDE QUOTATION MARKS IN THIS ARTICLE

p. 67 "Distinguished Usage Panel . . ." = Morris Bishop, "Good Usage, Bad Usage, and Usage," an intro to the 1976 New College Edition of *The American Heritage Dictionary of the English Language*, published by Houghton Mifflin Co.

p. 67 "Calling upon the opinions of the elite . . ." = John Ottenhoff, "The Perils of Prescriptivism: Usage Notes and *The American Heritage Dictionary*," *American Speech*, v. 31 #3, 1996, p. 274.

p. 73–74 "I realized early . . ." = *ADMAU*, preface, pp. xiv–xv.

p. 74 "Before going any . . ." = *Ibid.*, p. x.

p. 74 FN 13 "the ten critical points . . . " = *Ibid.*, pp. x–xi.

p. 75–76 "Once introduced, a prescriptive . . ." = Steven Pinker, "Grammar Puss" (excerpted from ch. 12 of Pinker's book *The Language Instinct*, Morrow, 1994), which appeared in the *New Republic* on 31 Jan. '94 (p. 20). Some of the subsequent Pinker quotations are from the *NR* excerpt because they tend to be more compact.

p. 76 "Who sets down . . . ?" = p. 141 of Bryson's *Mother Tongue* (Avon, 1990).

pp. 76–77 "As you might already . . ." = *ADMAU*, preface, p. xiii.

p. 76 FN 16 "The problem for professional . . ." = *Ibid.*, p. xi; plus the traditional-type definition of *rhetoric* is adapted from p. 1114 of the 1976 *AHD*.

p. 78 "The arrant solecisms . . ." = Bishop, 1976 *AHD* intro, p. xxiii.

p. 78 "The English language is being . . ." = John Simon, *Paradigms Lost: Reflections on Literacy and Its Decline* (Crown, 1980), p. 106.

p. 79 FN 19 "We have seen a novel . . ." = Wilson Follett, "Sabotage in Springfield," the *Atlantic Monthly*, January '62, p. 73.

p. 79 "A dictionary should have no . . ." = P. Gove in a letter to the *New York Times* replying to their howling editorial, said letter reprinted in Sledd and Ebbitt, eds., *Dictionaries and That Dictionary* (Scott, Foresman, 1962), p. 88.

p. 79 FN 21 Newman's "I have no wish . . ." = *Strictly Speaking: Will America Be the Death of English?* (Bobbs-Merrill, 1974), p. 10.

pp. 79–80 Simon's "As for 'I be,' . . ." = *Paradigms Lost*, pp. 165–166.

p. 80 FN 22 The Partridge quotation is from p. 36 of *Usage and Abusage* (Hamish Hamilton, 1947). The Fowler snippet is from *A Dictionary of Modern English Usage* (Oxford, 1927), pp. 540–541.

pp. 80–81 "Somewhere along the line . . ." = *ADMAU*, preface, p. xi.

p. 81 FN 25 "The most bothersome . . ." = *Ibid.*, preface, p. xv.

p. 83 "1 — Language changes . . ." = Philip Gove, "Linguistic Advances and Lexicography," Introduction to *Webster's Third*. Reprinted in Sledd and Ebbitt; Gove's axioms appear therein on p. 67.

p. 84 FN 28 "the English normally expected . . ." = p. 459 of *The Little, Brown Handbook*, Fourth Edition (Scott, Foresman, 1989).

pp. 87–88 FN 32 Norman Malcolm's exegesis of Wittgenstein's private-language argument (which argument occupies sections 258–265 of the *Philosophical Investigations*) appears in Malcolm's *Knowledge and Certainty* (Prentice-Hall, 1963), pp. 98–99.

p. 89 "A dictionary can be . . ." = "Usage Levels and Dialect Distribution," intro to the *American College Dictionary* (Random House, 1962), p. xxv; reprinted in Gove's letter to the *NYT*.

pp. 91–92 "[T]he words 'rule' . . ." = S. Pinker, *The Language Instinct*, p. 371. The chunk also appears in Pinker's "Grammar Puss" *New Republic* article, p. 19.

p. 92 FN 36 "No one, not even . . ." = *The Language Instinct*, p. 372.

pp. 92–93 "When a scientist . . ." = "Grammar Puss," p. 19.

p. 96 FN 40 Garner's CLASS DISTINCTIONS miniessay is on *ADMAU*'s pp. 124–126.

p. 99 FN 46 "[Jargon] arises from . . ." = *ADMAU*, p. 390.

p. 100 FN 51 "knowing when to split . . ." = *Ibid.*, pp. 616–617.

p. 101 "hotly disputed . . ." = *ADMAU*'s SKUNKED TERMS miniessay, which is on pp. 603–604.

p. 105 FN 57 A concise overview of these studies can be found in Janice Neuleib's "The Relation of Formal Grammar to Composition," *College Composition and Communication,* October '77.

p. 110 FN 62 Dr. Schwartz and the Task Force are listed as the authors of *Guidelines for Bias-Free Writing* (Indiana U. Press, 1995), in which the quoted sentence appears on p. 28. The Forster snippet is from the opening chapter of *A Passage to India.*

p. 112 FN 65 "vogue words have such a grip . . ." = *ADMAU,* p. 682.

p. 114 "At first encounter . . ." = Karen Volkman's review of Michael Palmer's *The Lion Bridge: Selected Poems* in the *Village Voice Literary Supplement,* October '98, p. 6.

p. 114 FN 66 The OBSCURITY miniessay is on p. 462 of *ADMAU.*

p. 114 "This is the best and only way . . ." = President Clinton verbatim in mid-November '98.

pp. 114–115 & p. 115 FN 67 Quoted bits of Orwell's "Politics and the English Language" are from the essay as it appears in, e.g., Hunt and Perry, eds., *The Dolphin Reader,* Fifth Edition (Houghton Mifflin, 1999), pp. 670–682.

p. 115 FN 68 The Jameson sentence also appears in *ADMAU*'s miniessay on OBSCURITY, p. 462; plus it appears in the same *Sacramento Bee* article mentioned in FN 66.

p. 122 The various quoted definitions of *authority* here come from *The American Heritage Dictionary,* Third Edition (Houghton Mifflin, 1992), p. 124.

p. 123 "The reality I care about . . ." = *ADMAU,* preface, pp. ix–x. The next five quotation-snippets — on pp. 123–124 and in FN 80 — are also from the preface.

p. 124 "Sometimes people strive to . . ." = *ADMAU,* p. 345.

p. 124 "To the writer or speaker for whom . . ." = *Ibid.,* p. 604.

p. 124 "Whatever you do . . ." = *Ibid.,* p. 186.

THE VIEW FROM
MRS. THOMPSON'S

LOCATION: BLOOMINGTON, ILLINOIS
DATES: 11–13 SEPTEMBER 2001
SUBJECT: OBVIOUS

SYNECDOCHE In true Midwest fashion, people in Bloomington aren't unfriendly but do tend to be reserved. A stranger will smile warmly at you, but there normally won't be any of that strangerly chitchat in waiting areas or checkout lines. But now, thanks to the Horror, there's something to talk about that overrides all inhibition, as if we were somehow all standing right there and just saw the same traffic accident. Example: Overheard in the checkout line at Burwell Oil (which is sort of the Neiman Marcus of gas station/ convenience store plazas — centrally located athwart both one-way main drags, and with the best tobacco prices in town, it's a municipal treasure) between a lady in an Osco cashier's smock and a man in a dungaree jacket cut off at the shoulders to make a sort of homemade vest: "With my boys they thought it was all some movie like that *Independence Day*, till then they started to notice how it was the same movie on all the channels." (The lady didn't say how old her boys were.)

WEDNESDAY Everyone has flags out. Homes, businesses. It's odd: you never see anybody putting out a flag, but by Wednesday morning there they all are. Big flags, small, regular flag-sized flags. A lot of homeowners here have those special angled flag-holders by their front door, the kind whose brace takes four Phillips screws. Plus thousands of the little handheld flags-on-a-stick you normally see at parades — some yards have dozens of these stuck in the ground all over, as if they'd somehow all just sprouted overnight. Rural-road people attach the little flags to their mailboxes out by the street. A good number of vehicles have them wedged in their grille or attached to the antenna. Some upscale people have actual poles; their flags are at half-mast. More than a few large homes around Franklin Park or out on the east side even have enormous multistory flags hanging gonfalon-style down over their facades. It's a total mystery where people can buy flags this big or how they got them up there, or when.

My own next-door neighbor, a retired bookkeeper and USAF vet whose home- and lawn-care are nothing short of phenomenal, has a regulation-size anodized flagpole secured in eighteen inches of reinforced cement that none of the other neighbors like very much because they feel it draws lightning. He says there's a very particular etiquette to having your flag at half-mast: you're supposed to first run it all the way up to the finial at the top and *then* bring it halfway down. Otherwise it's some kind of insult. His flag is out straight and popping smartly in the wind. It's far and away the biggest flag on our street. You can also hear the wind in the cornfields just south; it sounds roughly the way light surf sounds when you're two dunes back from the shore. Mr. N——'s pole's halyard has metal elements that clank against the pole when it's windy, which is something else the neighbors don't much care for. His driveway and mine are almost right together, and he's out here on a stepladder polishing his pole with some kind of special ointment and a chamois cloth — I shit you not — although in the morning sun it's true that his metal pole does shine like God's own wrath.

"Hell of a nice flag and display apparatus, Mr. N——."

"Ought to be. Cost enough."

"Seen all the other flags out everywhere this morning?"

This gets him to look down and smile, if a bit grimly. "Something, isn't it." Mr. N—— is not what you'd call the friendliest next-door neighbor. I really only know him because his church and mine are in the same softball league, for which he serves with great seriousness and precision as his team's statistician. We are not close. Nevertheless he's the first one I ask:

"Say, Mr. N——, suppose somebody like a foreign person or a TV reporter or something were to come by and ask you what the purpose of all these flags after what happened yesterday was, exactly — what do you think you'd say?"

"Why" (after a little moment of him giving me the same sort of look he usually gives my lawn), "to show our support towards what's going on, as Americans."*

The overall point being that on Wednesday here there's a weird accretive pressure to have a flag out. If the purpose of displaying a flag is to make a statement, it seems like at a certain point of density of flags you're making more of a statement if you *don't* have a flag out. It's not totally clear what statement this would be, though. What if you just don't happen to have a flag? Where has

---

* Plus: Selected other responses from various times during the day's flag-hunt when circumstances permitted the question to be asked without one seeming like a smartass or loon:

"To show we're Americans and we're not going to bow down to nobody";

"It's a classic pseudo-archetype, a reflexive semion designed to preempt and negate the critical function" (grad student);

"For pride."

"What they do is symbolize unity and that we're all together behind the victims in this war and they've fucked with the wrong people this time, amigo."

everyone gotten these flags, especially the little ones you can fasten to your mailbox? Are they all from the Fourth of July and people just save them, like Christmas ornaments? How do they know to do this? There's nothing in the Yellow Pages under *Flag*. At some point there starts to be actual tension. Nobody walks by or stops their car and says, "Hey, how come your house doesn't have a flag?," but it gets easier and easier to imagine them thinking it. Even a sort of half-collapsed house down the street that everybody thought was abandoned has one of the little flags on a stick in the weeds by the driveway. None of Bloomington's grocery stores turn out to stock flags. The big novelty shop downtown has nothing but Halloween stuff. Only a few businesses are actually open, but even the closed ones are now displaying some sort of flag. It's almost surreal. The VFW hall is obviously a good bet, but it can't open until noon if at all (it has a bar). The counter lady at Burwell Oil references a certain hideous KWIK-N-EZ convenience store out by I-55 at which she's pretty sure she recalls seeing some little plastic flags back in the racks with all the bandannas and NASCAR caps, but by the time I get down there they all turn out to be gone, snapped up by parties unknown. The cold reality is that there is not a flag to be had in this town. Stealing one out of somebody's yard is clearly just out of the question. I'm standing in a fluorescent-lit KWIK-N-EZ afraid to go home. All those people dead, and I'm sent to the edge by a plastic flag. It doesn't get really bad until people come over and ask if I'm OK and I have to lie and say it's a Benadryl reaction (which in fact can happen).

. . . And so on until, in one more of the Horror's weird twists of fate and circumstance, it's the KWIK-N-EZ proprietor himself (a Pakistani, by the way) who offers solace and a shoulder and a strange kind of unspoken understanding, and who lets me go back and sit in the stockroom amid every conceivable petty vice and indulgence America has to offer and compose myself, and who only slightly later, over styrofoam cups of a strange kind of per-fumey tea with a great deal of milk in it, suggests construction paper and "Magical Markers," which explains my now-beloved and proudly displayed homemade flag.

AERIAL & GROUND VIEWS   Everyone here gets the local news organ, the *Pantagraph,* which is roundly loathed by most of the natives I know. Imagine, let's say, a well-funded college newspaper co-edited by Bill O'Reilly and Martha Stewart. Wednesday's headline is: **ATTACKED!** After two pages of AP stuff, you get to the real *Pantagraph.* Everything to follow is *sic.* Wednesday's big local headers are: STUNNED CITIZENS RUN THROUGH MANY EMOTIONS; CLERGY OPEN ARMS TO HELP PEOPLE DEAL WITH TRAGEDY; ISU PROFESSOR: B-N NOT A LIKELY TARGET; PRICES ROCKET AT GAS PUMPS; AMPUTEE GIVES INSPIRATIONAL SPEECH. There's a half-page photo of a student at Bloomington Central Catholic HS saying the rosary in response to the Horror, which means that some staff photographer came in and popped a flash in the face of a traumatized kid at prayer. The Op-Ed column for 9/12 starts out: "The carnage we have seen through the eyes of lenses in New York City and Washington, D.C., still seems like an R-rated movie out of Hollywood."

Bloomington is a city of 65,000 in the central part of a state that is extremely, emphatically flat, so that you can see the town's salients from way far away. Three major interstates converge here, and several rail lines. The town's almost exactly halfway between Chicago and St. Louis, and its origins involve being an important train depot. Bloomington is the birthplace of Adlai Stevenson and the putative hometown of Colonel Blake on *M*A*S*H.* It has a smaller twin city, Normal, that's built around a public university and is a whole different story. Both towns together are like 110,000 people.

As Midwest cities go, the only remarkable thing about Bloomington is its prosperity. It is all but recession-proof. Some of this is due to the county's farmland, which is world-class fertile and so expensive per acre that a civilian can't even find out how much it costs. But Bloomington is also the national HQ for State Farm, which is the great dark god of US consumer insurance and for all practical purposes owns the town, and because of which Bloomington's east side is now all smoked-glass complexes and Build to Suit developments and a six-lane beltway of malls and franchises that's killing off the old downtown, plus an ever-wider split between the town's two basic classes and cultures, so well and truly symbolized by the SUV and the pickup truck, respectively.*

Winter here is a pitiless bitch, but in the warm months Bloomington is a lot like a seaside community except here the ocean is corn, which grows steroidically and stretches to the earth's curve in all directions. The town itself in summer is intensely green — streets bathed in tree-shade and homes' explosive gardens and dozens of manicured parks and ballfields and golf courses you almost need eye protection to look at, and broad weedless fertilized lawns all made to line up exactly flush to the sidewalk with special edging tools.† To be honest, it's all a little creepy, especially in high summer, when nobody's out and all that green just sits in the heat and seethes.

Like most Midwest towns, B-N is crammed with churches: four full pages in the phone book. Everything from Unitarian to bug-eyed Pentecostal. There's even a church for agnostics. But except for church — plus I guess your basic parades, fireworks, and a couple corn festivals — there isn't much public community. Everybody has his family and neighbors and tight little circle of friends. Folks keep to themselves (the native term for light conversation is *visit*). They basically all play softball or golf and grill out, and watch their kids play soccer, and sometimes go to mainstream movies . . .

. . . And they watch massive, staggering amounts of TV. I don't just mean the kids, either. Something that's obvious but important

---

* *Pace* some people's impression, the native accent around here isn't southern so much as just rural. The town's corporate transplants, on the other hand, have no accent at all — in Mrs. Bracero's phrase, State Farm people "sound like the folks on TV."
† People here are deeply, deeply into lawn-care; my own neighbors mow about as often as they shave.

to keep in mind re Bloomington and the Horror is that reality —
any felt sense of a larger world — is mainly televisual. New York's
skyline, for instance, is as recognizable here as anyplace else, but
what it's recognizable from is TV. TV's also a more social phenomenon than on the East Coast, where in my experience people are
almost constantly leaving home to go meet other people face-to-
face in public places. There don't really tend to be parties or mix-
ers per se so much here — what you do in Bloomington is all get
together at somebody's house and watch something.

In Bloomington, therefore, to have a home without a TV is to
become a kind of constant and Kramer-like presence in others'
homes, a perpetual guest of folks who can't quite understand why
somebody wouldn't own a TV but are totally respectful of your
need to watch TV, and who will offer you access to their TV in the
same instinctive way they'd bend to offer a hand if you fell down in
the street. This is especially true for some kind of must-see, crisis-
type situation like the 2000 election or this week's Horror. All you
have to do is call someone you know and say you don't have a TV:
"Well shoot, boy, get over here."

TUESDAY   There are maybe ten days a year when it's gorgeous in
Bloomington, and 11 September is one of them. The air is clear
and temperate and wonderfully dry after several weeks of what's
felt very much like living in someone's armpit. It's just before serious harvesting starts, when the region's pollen is at its worst, and a
good percentage of the city is stoned on Benadryl, which as you
probably know tends to give the early morning a kind of dreamy,
underwater quality. Time-wise, we're an hour behind the East
Coast. By 8:00, everybody with a job is at it, and just about everybody else is home drinking coffee and blowing their nose and
watching *Today* or one of the other network AM shows that all
broadcast (it goes without saying) from New York. At 8:00 on Tuesday I personally was in the shower, trying to listen to a Bears post-
mortem on WSCR Sports Radio in Chicago.

The church I belong to is on the south side of Bloomington, near where my house is. Most of the people I know well enough to ask if I can come over and watch their TV are members of my church. It's not one of those churches where people throw Jesus' name around a lot or talk about the End Times, but it's fairly serious, and people in the congregation get to know each other well and to be pretty tight. As far as I know, all the congregants are natives of the area. Most are working-class or retired from same. There are some small-business owners. A fair number are veterans and/or have kids in the military or — especially — in the Reserves, because for many of these families that's what you do to pay for college.

The house I end up sitting with shampoo in my hair watching most of the actual unfolding Horror at belongs to Mrs. Thompson, who is one of the world's cooler seventy-four-year-olds and exactly the kind of person who in an emergency even if her phone is busy you know you can just come on over. She lives about a mile away from me on the other side of a mobile-home park. The streets are not crowded, but they're also not as empty as they're going to get. Mrs. Thompson's is a tiny immaculate one-story home that on the West Coast would be called a bungalow and on the south side of Bloomington is called a house. Mrs. Thompson is a long-time member and a leader in the congregation, and her living room tends to be kind of a gathering place. She's also the mom of one of my very best friends here, F——, who was in the Rangers in Vietnam and got shot in the knee and now works for a contractor installing various kinds of franchise stores in malls. He's in the middle of a divorce (long story) and living with Mrs. T. while the court decides on the disposition of his house. F—— is one of those veterans who doesn't talk about the war or belong to the VFW but is sometimes preoccupied in a dark way, and goes quietly off to camp by himself over Memorial Day weekend, and you can tell that he carries some serious shit in his head. Like most people who work construction, he wakes up very early and was long gone by the time I got to his mom's, which happened to be just after the second plane hit the South Tower, meaning probably around 8:10.

In retrospect, the first sign of possible shock was the fact that I didn't ring the bell but just came on in, which normally here one would never do. Thanks in part to her son's trade connections, Mrs. T. has a forty-inch flat-panel Philips TV on which Dan Rather appears for a second in shirtsleeves with his hair slightly mussed. (People in Bloomington seem overwhelmingly to prefer CBS News; it's unclear why.) Several other ladies from church are already over here, but I don't know if I exchanged greetings with anyone because I remember when I came in everybody was staring transfixed at one of the very few pieces of video CBS never reran, which was a distant wide-angle shot of the North Tower and its top floors' exposed steel lattice in flames, and of dots detaching from the building and moving through smoke down the screen, which then a sudden jerky tightening of the shot revealed to be actual people in coats and ties and skirts with their shoes falling off as they fell, some hanging onto ledges or girders and then letting go, upside-down or wriggling as they fell and one couple almost seeming (unverifiable) to be hugging each other as they fell those several stories and shrank back to dots as the camera then all of a sudden pulled back to the long view — I have no idea how long the clip took — after which Dan Rather's mouth seemed to move for a second before any sound emerged, and everyone in the room sat back and looked at one another with expressions that seemed somehow both childlike and terribly old. I think one or two people made some sort of sound. I'm not sure what else to say. It seems grotesque to talk about being traumatized by a piece of video when the people in the video were dying. Something about the shoes also falling made it worse. I think the older ladies took it better than I did. Then the hideous beauty of the rerun clip of the second plane hitting the tower, the blue and silver and black and spectacular orange of it, as more little moving dots fell. Mrs. Thompson was in her chair, which is a rocker with floral cushions. The living room has two other chairs, and a huge corduroy sofa that F—— and I had had to take the front door off its hinges to get in the house. All the seats were occupied, meaning I think five or six other people, most women, all these over fifty, and there were more voices in the kitchen, one of which was very upset-sounding and belonged to the psychologically delicate Mrs. R——, who I don't know very well but is said to have once been a beauty of great local repute. Many of the people are Mrs. T.'s neighbors, and some are still in robes, and at various times people leave to go home and use the phone and come back, or leave altogether (one younger lady went to go take her children out of school), and other people came. At one point, around the time the South Tower was falling so perfectly-seeming down into itself (I remember thinking that it was falling the way an elegant lady faints, but it was Mrs. Bracero's normally pretty much useless and irritating son, Duane, who pointed out that what it really looked like is if you took some film of a NASA liftoff and ran it backward, which now after several re-viewings does seem dead on), there were at least a dozen people in the house. The living room was dim because in summer here everyone always keeps their drapes pulled.*

Is it normal not to remember things very well after only a couple days, or at any rate the order of things? I know at some point for a while there was the sound outside of some neighbor mowing his lawn, which seemed totally bizarre, but I don't remember if any-body remarked on it. Sometimes it seemed like nobody said any-thing and sometimes like everybody was talking at once. There was also a lot of telephonic activity. None of these women carry cell phones (Duane has a pager whose function is unclear), so it's just Mrs. T.'s old wall-mount in the kitchen. Not all the calls made

---

* Mrs. Thompson's living room is prototypical working-class Bloomington, too: double-pane windows, white Sears curtains w/ valence, catalogue clock with a background of mallards, woodgrain magazine rack with *CSM* and *Reader's Digest*, inset bookshelves used to display little collectible figurines and framed photos of relatives and their families. There are two knit samplers w/ the Desiderata and Prayer of St. Francis, antimacassars on every good chair, and wall-to-wall carpet so thick that you can't see your feet (people take their shoes off at the door — it's basic common courtesy).

rational sense. One side effect of the Horror was an overwhelming desire to call everyone you loved. It was established early on that you couldn't get New York — dialing 212 yielded only a weird whooping sound. People keep asking Mrs. T.'s permission until she tells them to knock it off and for heaven's sake just use the phone. Some of the ladies reach their husbands, who are apparently all gathered around TVs and radios at their various workplaces; for a while bosses are too shocked to think to send people home. Mrs. T. has coffee on, but another sign of crisis is that if you want some you have to go get it yourself — usually it just sort of appears. From the door to the kitchen I remember seeing the second tower fall and being confused about whether it was a replay of the first tower falling. Another thing about the hay fever is that you can't ever be totally sure someone's crying, but over the two hours of first-run Horror, with bonus reports of the crash in PA and Bush being moved into a SAC bunker and a car bomb that's gone off in Chicago (the latter then retracted), pretty much everybody either cries or comes very close, according to his or her relative abilities. Mrs. Thompson says less than almost anyone. I don't think she cries, but she doesn't rock in her chair as usual, either. Her first husband's death was apparently sudden and grisly, and I know at times during the war F—— would be out in the field and she wouldn't hear from him for weeks at a time and didn't know whether he was even alive. Duane Bracero's main contribution is to keep iterating how much like a movie it all seems. Duane, who's at least twenty-five but still lives at home while supposedly studying to be a welder, is one of these people who always wears camouflage T-shirts and paratrooper boots but would never dream of actually enlisting (as, to be fair, neither would I). He has also kept his hat, the front of which promotes something called SLIPKNOT, on his head indoors in Mrs. Thompson's house. It always seems to be important to have at least one person in the vicinity to hate.

It turns out the cause of poor tendony Mrs. R——'s meltdown in the kitchen is that she has either a grandniece or removed cousin who's doing some type of internship at Time, Inc., in the Time-Life Building or whatever it's called, about which Mrs. R—— and whoever she's managed to call know only that it's a vertiginously tall skyscraper someplace in New York City, and she's out of her mind with worry, and two other ladies have been out here the whole time holding both her hands and trying to decide whether they should call her doctor (Mrs. R—— has kind of a history), and I end up doing pretty much the only good I do all day by explaining to Mrs. R—— where midtown Manhattan is. It thereupon emerges that none of the people here I'm watching the Horror with — not even the couple ladies who'd gone to see *Cats* as part of some group tour thing through the church in 1991 — have even the vaguest notion of New York's layout and don't know, for example, how radically far south the Financial District and Statue of Liberty are; they have to be shown this via pointing out the ocean in the foreground of the skyline they all know so well (from TV).

The half-assed little geography lesson is the start of a feeling of alienation from these good people that builds in me all throughout the part of the Horror where people flee rubble and dust. These ladies are not stupid, or ignorant. Mrs. Thompson can read both Latin and Spanish, and Ms. Voigtlander is a certified speech therapist who once explained to me that the strange gulping sound that makes NBC's Tom Brokaw so distracting to listen to is an actual speech impediment called a *glottal L*. It was one of the ladies out in the kitchen supporting Mrs. R—— who pointed out that 11 September is the anniversary of the Camp David Accords, which was certainly news to me.

What these Bloomington ladies are, or start to seem to me, is innocent. There is what would strike many Americans as a marked, startling lack of cynicism in the room. It does not, for instance, occur to anyone here to remark on how it's maybe a little odd that *all three* network anchors are in shirtsleeves, or to consider the possibility that Dan Rather's hair's being mussed might not be wholly accidental, or that the constant rerunning of horrific footage might not be just in case some viewers were only now tuning in and hadn't seen it yet. None of the ladies seem to notice the president's odd little lightless eyes appear to get closer and closer together throughout his taped address, nor that some of his lines sound almost plagiaristically identical to those uttered by Bruce Willis (as a right-wing wacko, recall) in *The Siege* a couple years back. Nor that at least some of the sheer weirdness of watching the Horror unfold has been how closely various shots and scenes have mirrored the plots of everything from *Die Hard I–III* to *Air Force One*. Nobody's near hip enough to lodge the sick and obvious po-mo complaint: We've Seen This Before. Instead, what they do is all sit together and feel really bad, and pray. No one in Mrs. Thompson's crew would ever be so nauseous as to try to get everybody to pray aloud or form a prayer circle, but you can still tell what they're all doing.

Make no mistake, this is mostly a good thing. It forces you to think and do things you most likely wouldn't alone, like for instance while watching the address and eyes to pray, silently and fervently, that you're wrong about the president, that your view of him is maybe distorted and he's actually far smarter and more substantial than you believe, not just some soulless golem or nexus of corporate interests dressed up in a suit but a statesman of courage and probity and . . . and it's good, this is good to pray this way. It's just a bit lonely to have to. Truly decent, innocent people can be taxing to be around. I'm not for a moment trying to suggest that everyone I know in Bloomington is like Mrs. Thompson (e.g., her son F—— isn't, though he's an outstanding person). I'm trying, rather, to explain how some part of the horror of the Horror was knowing, deep in my heart, that whatever America the men in those planes hated so much was far more my America, and F——'s, and poor old loathsome Duane's, than it was these ladies'.

2001

HOW TRACY AUSTIN
BROKE MY HEART

❦

BECAUSE I AM a long-time rabid fan of tennis in general and Tracy Austin in particular, I've rarely looked forward to reading a sports memoir the way I looked forward to Ms. Austin's *Beyond Center Court: My Story*, ghosted by Christine Brennan and published by Morrow. This is a type of mass-market book — the sports-star-"with"-somebody autobiography — that I seem to have bought and read an awful lot of, with all sorts of ups and downs and ambivalence and embarrassment, usually putting these books under something more highbrow when I get to the register. I think Austin's memoir has maybe finally broken my jones for the genre, though.

Here's *Beyond Center Court*'s Austin on the first set of her final against Chris Evert at the 1979 US Open: "At 2–3, I broke Chris, then she broke me, and I broke her again, so we were at 4–4."

And on her epiphany after winning that final: "I immediately knew what I had done, which was to win the US Open, and I was thrilled."

Tracy Austin on the psychic rigors of pro competition: "Every professional athlete has to be so fine-tuned mentally."

Tracy Austin on her parents: "My mother and father never, ever pushed me."

Tracy Austin on Martina Navratilova: "She is a wonderful person, very sensitive and caring."

On Billie Jean King: "She also is incredibly charming and accommodating."

On Brooke Shields: "She was so sweet and bright and easy to talk to right away."

Tracy Austin meditating on excellence: "There is that little bit extra that some of us are willing to give and some of us aren't. Why is that? I think it's the challenge to be the best."

You get the idea. On the upside, though, this breathtakingly insipid autobiography can maybe help us understand both the seduction and the disappointment that seem to be built into the mass-market sports memoir. Almost uniformly poor as books, these athletic "My Story"s sell incredibly well; that's why there are so many of them. And they sell so well because athletes' stories seem to promise something more than the regular old name-dropping celebrity autobiography.

Here is a theory. Top athletes are compelling because they embody the comparison-based achievement we Americans revere — fast*est*, strong*est* — and because they do so in a totally unambiguous way. Questions of the best plumber or best managerial accountant are impossible even to define, whereas the best relief pitcher, free-throw shooter, or female tennis player is, at any given time, a matter of public statistical record. Top athletes fascinate us by appealing to our twin compulsions with competitive superiority and hard data.

Plus they're beautiful: Jordan hanging in midair like a Chagall bride, Sampras laying down a touch volley at an angle that defies Euclid. And they're inspiring. There is about world-class athletes carving out exemptions from physical laws a transcendent beauty that makes manifest God in man. So actually more than one theory, then. Great athletes are profundity in motion. They enable abstractions like *power* and *grace* and *control* to become not only incarnate but televisable. To be a top athlete, performing, is to be that exquisite hybrid of animal and angel that we average unbeautiful watchers have such a hard time seeing in ourselves.

So we want to know them, these gifted, driven physical achievers. We too, as audience, are driven: watching the performance is not enough. We want to get intimate with all that profundity. We want inside them; we want the Story. We want to hear about humble roots, privation, precocity, grim resolve, discouragement, persistence, team spirit, sacrifice, killer instinct, liniment and pain. We want to know how they did it. How many hours a night did the child Bird spend in his driveway hitting jumpers under home-strung floodlights? What ungodly time did Bjorn get up for practice every morning? What exact makes of cars did the Butkus boys work out by pushing up and down Chicago streets? What did Palmer and Brett and Payton and Evert have to give up? And of course, too, we want to know how it *feels*, inside, to be both beautiful and best ("How did it feel to win the big one?"). What combination of blankness and concentration is required to sink a putt or a free-throw for thousands of dollars in front of millions of unblinking eyes? What goes through their minds? Are these athletes real people? Are they even remotely like us? Is their Agony of Defeat anything like our little agonies of daily frustration? And of course what about the Thrill of Victory — what might it feel like to hold up that #1 finger and be able to actually *mean* it?

I am about the same age and played competitive tennis in the same junior ranks as Tracy Austin, half a country away and several plateaus below her. When we all heard, in 1977, that a California girl who'd just turned fourteen had won a professional tournament in Portland, we weren't so much jealous as agog. None of us could come close to testing even a top eighteen-year-old, much less pro-caliber adults. We started to hunt her up in tennis magazines, search out her matches on obscure cable channels. She was about four foot six and eighty-five pounds. She hit the hell out of the ball and never missed and never choked and had braces and pigtails that swung wildly around as she handed pros their asses. She was the first real child star in women's tennis, and in the late Seventies she was prodigious, beautiful, and inspiring. There was an incongruously adult genius about her game, all the more radiant for her little-girl giggle and silly hair. I remember meditating, with all the intensity a fifteen-year-old can summon, on the differences that kept this girl and me on our respective sides of the TV screen. She was a genius and I was not. How must it have felt? I had some serious questions to ask her. I wanted, very much, her side of it.

So the point, then, about these sports memoirs' market appeal: Because top athletes are profound, because they make a certain type of genius as carnally discernible as it ever can get, these ghost-written invitations inside their lives and their skulls are terribly seductive for book buyers. Explicitly or not, the memoirs make a promise — to let us penetrate the indefinable mystery of what makes some persons geniuses, semidivine, to share with us the secret and so both to reveal the difference between us and them and to erase it, a little, that difference . . . to give us the (we want, expect, only one, the master narrative, the key) Story.

However seductively they promise, though, these autobiographies rarely deliver. And *Beyond Center Court: My Story* is especially bad. The book fails not so much because it's poorly written (which it is — I don't know what ghostwriter Brennan's enhancing function was supposed to be here, but it's hard to see how Austin herself could have done any worse than two hundred dead pages of "Tennis took me like a magic carpet to all kinds of places and all kinds of people" enlivened only by wincers like "Injuries — the signature of the rest of my career — were about to take hold of me"), but because it commits what any college sophomore knows is the capital crime of expository prose: it forgets who it's supposed to be for.

Obviously, a good commercial memoir's first loyalty has got to be to the reader, the person who's spending money and time to access the consciousness of someone he wishes to know and will never meet. But none of *Beyond Center Court*'s loyalties are to the reader. The author's primary allegiance seems to be to her family and friends. Whole pages are given over to numbing Academy Award–style tributes to parents, siblings, coaches, trainers, and agents, plus little burbles of praise for pretty much every athlete and celebrity she's ever met. In particular, Austin's account of her own (extremely, transcendently interesting) competitive career keeps digressing into warm fuzzies on each opponent she faces. Typical example: Her third round at 1980's Wimbledon was against American Barbara Potter, who, we learn,

> is a really good person. Barbara was very nice to me through my injuries, sending me books, keeping in touch, and checking to see how I was doing. Barbara definitely was one of the smartest people on the tour; I've heard she's going to college now, which takes a lot of initiative for a woman our age. Knowing Barbara, I'm sure she's working harder than all her fellow students.

But there is also here an odd loyalty to and penchant for the very clichés with which we sports fans weave the veil of myth and mystery that these sports memoirs promise to part for us. It's almost as if Tracy Austin has structured her own sense of her life and career to accord with the formulas of the generic sports bio. We've got the sensitive and doting mother, the kindly dad, the mischievous siblings who treat famous Tracy like just another kid. We've got the ingenue heroine whose innocence is eroded by experience and transcended through sheer grit; we've got the gruff but tenderhearted coach and the coolly skeptical veterans who finally accept the heroine. We've got the wicked, backstabbing rival (in Pam Shriver, who receives the book's only unfulsome mention). We even get the myth-requisite humble roots. Austin, whose father is a corporate scientist and whose mother is one of those lean tan ladies who seem to spend all day every day at the country club tennis courts, tries to portray her childhood in posh Rolling Hills Estates CA as impoverished: "We had to be frugal in all kinds of ways . . . we cut expenses by drinking powdered milk . . . we didn't have bacon except on Christmas." Stuff like this seems way out of touch with reality until we realize that the kind of reality the author's chosen to be in touch with here is not just un- but anti-real.

In fact, as unrevealing of character as its press-release tone and generic-myth structure make this memoir, it's the narrator's clue-lessness that permits us our only glimpses of anything like a real and faceted life. That is, relief from the book's skewed loyalties can be found only in those places where the author seems unwittingly to betray them. She protests, for instance, repeatedly and with an almost Gertrudian fervor, that her mother "did not force" her into tennis at age three, it apparently never occurring to Tracy Austin that a three-year-old hasn't got enough awareness of choices to require any forcing. This was the child of a mom who'd spent the evening before Tracy's birth hitting tennis balls to the family's other four children, three of whom also ended up playing pro tennis. Many of the memoir's recollections of Mrs. Austin seem almost Viennese in their repression — "My mother always made sure I behaved on court, but I never even considered acting up" — and downright creepy are some of the details Austin chooses in order to evince "how nonintense my tennis background really was":

> Everyone thinks every young tennis player is very one-dimensional, which just wasn't true in my case. Until I was fourteen, I never played tennis on Monday. . . . My mother made sure I never put in seven straight days on the court. She didn't go to the club on Mondays, so we never went there.

It gets weirder. Later in the book's childhood section, Austin discusses her "wonderful friendship" with a man from their country club who "set up . . . matches for me against unsuspecting foes in later years and . . . won a lot of money from his friends" and, as a token of friendship, "bought me a necklace with a T hanging on it. The T had fourteen diamonds on it." She was apparently ten at this point. As the book's now fully adult Austin analyzes the relationship, "He was a very wealthy criminal lawyer, and I didn't have very much money. With all his gifts for me, he made me feel special." What a guy. Regarding her de facto employment in what is technically known as sports hustling: "It was all in good fun."

In the subsequent section, Austin recalls a 1978 pro tournament in Japan that she hadn't much wanted to enter:

> It was just too far from home and I was tired from the travel grind. They kept offering me more and more money for an appearance fee — well over a hundred thousand dollars — but I said no. Finally, they offered to fly my whole family over. That did it. We went, and I won easily.

Besides displaying an odd financial sense (she won't come for $100,000+, but will come if they add a couple thousand in airfare?), Tracy Austin seems here unaware of the fact that, in the late Seventies, any player who accepted a guaranteed payment just for entering a tournament was in violation of a serious tour rule. The backstory here is that both genders' player associations had outlawed these payments because they threatened both the real and the perceived integrity of pro tennis. A tournament that has paid some star player a hefty guarantee — wanting her in the draw because her celebrity will help increase ticket sales, corporate sponsorships, TV revenues, etc. — thereafter has an obvious stake in that player's survival in the tournament, and so has an equally obvious interest in keeping her from getting upset by some lesser-known player in the early rounds, which, since matches' linesmen and umpires are employed by the tournament, can lead to shady officiating. And has so led. Far stranger things than a marquee player's receiving a suspicious number of favorable line calls have happened . . . though apparently somehow not in Tracy Austin's experience.

The naïveté on display throughout this memoir is doubly confusing. On the one hand, there's little sign in this narrator of anything like the frontal-lobe activity required for outright deception. On the other, Austin's ignorance of her sport's grittier realities seems literally incredible. Random examples. When she sees a player "tank" a 1988 tournament match to make time for a lucrative appearance in a TV ad, Tracy "couldn't believe it. . . . I had never played with anyone who threw a match before, so it took me a set and a half to realize what was happening." This even though match-tanking had been widely and publicly reported as a dark consequence of skyrocketing exhibition and endorsement fees for at least the eleven years Austin had been in pro tennis. Or, drugs-wise, although problems with everything up to cocaine and heroin in pro tennis had been not only acknowledged but written about in the 1980s,* Austin manages to move the reader to both scorn and pity with pronouncements like "I assume players were experimenting with marijuana and certainly were drinking alcohol, but I don't know who or when or where. I wasn't invited to those parties, if they were happening at all. And I'm very glad I wasn't." And so on and so on.

Ultimately, though, what makes *Beyond Center Court* so especially disappointing is that it could have been much more than just another I-was-born-to-play sports memoir. The facts of Tracy Austin's life and its trajectory are almost classically tragic. She was the first of tennis's now-ubiquitous nymphet prodigies, and her rise was meteoric. Picked out of the crowd as a toddler by coaching guru Vic Braden, Austin was on the cover of *World Tennis* magazine at age four. She played her first junior tournament at seven, and by ten she had won the national girls' twelve-and-under championship both indoors and out- and was being invited to play public exhibitions. At thirteen she had won national titles in most junior

---

* AP reporter Michael Mewshaw's *Short Circuit* (Atheneum, 1983) is just one example of national-press stuff about drugs on the tour.

age-groups, been drafted as a professional by World Team Tennis, and appeared on the cover of *Sports Illustrated* under the teaser "A Star Is Born." At fourteen, having chewed up every female in US juniors, she entered the preliminary qualifiers for her first professional tournament and proceeded to win not just the qualifying event but the whole tourney — a feat roughly equivalent to someone who was ineligible for a DMV learner's permit winning the Indianapolis 500. She played Wimbledon at fourteen, turned pro as a ninth-grader, won the US Open at sixteen, and was ranked number one in the world at just seventeen, in 1980. This was the same year her body started to fall apart. She spent the next four years effectively crippled by injuries and bizarre accidents, playing sporadically and watching her ranking plummet, and was for all practical purposes retired from tennis at age twenty-one. In 1989, her one serious attempt at a comeback ended on the way to the US Open, when a speeder ran a red light and nearly killed her. She is now, as of this writing, a professional former sports star, running celebrity clinics for corporate sponsors and doing sad little bits of color commentary on some of the same cable channels I'd first seen her play on.

What's nearly Greek about her career's arc is that Tracy Austin's most conspicuous virtue, a relentless workaholic perfectionism that combined with raw talent to make her such a prodigious success, turned out to be also her flaw and bane. She was, even after puberty, a tiny person, and her obsessive practice regimen and uncompromising effort in every last match began to afflict her with what sports MDs now know to be simple consequences of hypertrophy and chronic wear: hamstring and hip flexor pulls, sciatica, scoliosis, tendinitis, stress fractures, plantar fasciitis. Then too, since woe classically breeds more woe, she was freak-accident-prone: coaches who fall on her while ice-skating and break her ankle, psychotic chiropractors who pull her spine out of alignment, waiters who splash her with scalding water, color-blind speeders on the JFK Parkway.

A successful Tracy Austin autobiography, then, could have afforded us plain old plumbers and accountants more than just access to the unquestioned genius of an athletic savant or her high-speed ascent to the top of a univocal, mathematically computed hierarchy. This book could actually have helped us to countenance the sports myth's dark side. The only thing Tracy Austin had ever known how to do, her art — what the tragic-savvy Greeks would have called her *technē*, that state in which Austin's mastery of craft facilitated a communion with the gods themselves — was removed from her at an age when most of us are just starting to think seriously about committing ourselves to some pursuit. This memoir could have been about both the seductive immortality of competitive success and the less seductive but way more significant fragility and impermanence of all the competitive venues in which mortal humans chase immortality. Austin's story could, since the predicament of a dedicated athletic prodigy washed up at twenty-one differs in nothing more than degree from that of a dedicated CPA and family man dying at sixty-two, have been profound. The book could, since having it all at seventeen and then losing it all by twenty-one because of stuff outside your control is just like death except you have to go on living afterward, have been truly inspirational. And the publisher's flap copy promises just this: "The inspirational story of Tracy Austin's long struggle to find a life beyond championship tennis."

But the publisher's flap copy lies, because it turns out that *inspirational* is being used on the book jacket only in its ad-cliché sense, one basically equivalent to *heartwarming* or *feel-good* or even (God forbid) *triumphant.* Like all good ad clichés, it manages to suggest everything and mean nothing. Honorably used, *to inspire* means, according to Mr. American Heritage, "to animate the mind or emotions of; to communicate by divine influence." Which is to say that *inspirational,* honorably used, describes precisely what a great athlete becomes when she's in the arena performing, sharing the particular divinity she's given her life for, letting people witness concrete, transient instantiations of a grace that for most of us remains abstract and immanent.

Transcendent as were Tracy Austin's achievements on a public court, her autobiography does not come anywhere close to honoring the promise of its flap copy's "inspirational." Because forget divine — there's not even a recognizable human being in here. And this isn't just because of clunky prose or luxated structure. The book is inanimate because it communicates no real feeling and so gives us no sense of a conscious person. There's nobody at the other end of the line. Every emotionally significant moment or event or development gets conveyed in either computeresque staccato or else a prepackaged PR-speak whose whole function is (think about it) to deaden feeling. See, for instance, Austin's account of the moment when she has just beaten a world-class adult to win her first professional tournament:

> It was a tough match and I simply outlasted her. I was beginning to get a reputation for doing that. When you play from the baseline, perseverance is everything. The prize money for first place was twenty-eight thousand dollars.[*]

Or check out the book's description of her career's tragic climax. After working for five years to make a comeback and then, literally on the way to Flushing Meadow's National Tennis Center, getting sideswiped by a van and having her leg shattered through sheer bad luck, Tracy Austin was now permanently finished as a world-class athlete, and had then to lie for weeks in traction and think about the end of the only life she'd ever known. In *Beyond Center Court,* Austin's inspirational prose-response to this consists of quoting Leo Buscaglia, reporting on her newfound enthusiasm for shopping, and then giving us an excruciating chapter-long list of every celebrity she's ever met.

---

[*] Or listen again to her report of how winning her first US Open felt: "I immediately knew what I had done, which was to win the US Open, and I was thrilled." This line haunts me; it's like the whole letdown of the book boiled down into one dead bite.

Of course, neither Austin nor her book is unique. It's hard not to notice the way this same air of robotic banality suffuses not only the sports-memoir genre but also the media rituals in which a top athlete is asked to describe the content or meaning of his *technē.* Turn on any post-contest TV interview: "Kenny, how did it feel to make that sensational game-winning shoestring catch in the end zone with absolutely no I mean *zero* time remaining on the clock?" "Well, Frank, I was just real pleased. I was real happy and also pleased. We've all worked hard and come a long way as a team, and it's always a good feeling to be able to contribute." "Mark, you've now homered in your last eight straight at-bats and lead both leagues in RBIs — any comment?" "Well, Bob, I'm just trying to take it one pitch at a time. I've been focusing on the fundamentals, you know, and trying to make a contribution, and all of us know we've got to take it one game at a time and hang in there and not look ahead and just basically do the best we can at all times." This stuff is stupefying, and yet it also seems to be inevitable, maybe even necessary. The baritones in network blazers keep coming up after games, demanding of physical geniuses these recombinant strings of dead clichés, strings that after a while start to sound like a strange kind of lullaby, and which of course no network would solicit and broadcast again and again if there weren't a large and serious audience out here who find the banalities right and good. As if the emptiness in these athletes' descriptions of their feelings confirmed something we need to believe.

All right, so the obvious point: Great athletes usually turn out to be stunningly inarticulate about just those qualities and experiences that constitute their fascination. For me, though, the important question is why this is always so bitterly disappointing. And why I keep buying these sports memoirs with expectations that my own experience with the genre should long ago have modified . . . and why I nearly always feel thwarted and pissed when I finish them. One sort of answer, of course, is that commercial autobiographies like these promise something they cannot deliver: personal and verbal access to an intrinsically public and performative kind of genius. The problem with this answer is that I and the rest of the US book market aren't that stupid — if impossible promises were all there was to it, we'd catch on after a while, and it would stop being so profitable for publishers to churn these memoirs out.

Maybe what keeps us buying in the face of constant disappointment is some deep compulsion both to experience genius in the concrete and to universalize genius in the abstract. Real indisputable genius is so impossible to define, and true *technē* so rarely visible (much less televisable), that maybe we automatically expect people who are geniuses as athletes to be geniuses also as speakers and writers, to be articulate, perceptive, truthful, profound. If it's just that we naively expect geniuses-in-motion to be also geniuses-in-reflection, then their failure to be that shouldn't really seem any crueler or more disillusioning than Kant's glass jaw or Eliot's inability to hit the curve.

For my part, though, I think there's something deeper, and scarier, that keeps my hope one step ahead of past experience as I make my way to the bookstore's register. It remains very hard for me to reconcile the vapidity of Austin's narrative mind, on the one hand, with the extraordinary mental powers that are required by world-class tennis, on the other. Anyone who buys the idea that great athletes are dim should have a close look at an NFL playbook, or at a basketball coach's diagram of a 3–2 zone trap . . . or at an archival film of Ms. Tracy Austin repeatedly putting a ball in a court's corner at high speed from seventy-eight feet away, with huge sums of money at stake and enormous crowds of people watching her do it. Ever try to concentrate on doing something difficult with a crowd of people watching? . . . worse, with a crowd of spectators maybe all vocally hoping you fail so that their favorite will beat you? In my own comparatively low-level junior matches, before audiences that rarely hit three digits, it used to be all I could do to manage my sphincter. I would drive myself crazy: ". . . but what if I double-fault here and go down a break with all these folks watching? . . . don't think about it . . . yeah but except if I'm consciously not thinking about it then doesn't part of me have to think about it in order for me to remember what I'm not supposed to think about? . . . shut *up*, quit thinking about it and serve the goddamn ball . . . except how can I even be talking to myself about not thinking about it unless I'm still aware of what it is I'm talking about not thinking about?" and so on. I'd get divided, paralyzed. As most ungreat athletes do. Freeze up, choke. Lose our focus. Become self-conscious. Cease to be wholly present in our wills and choices and movements.

It is not an accident that great athletes are often called "naturals," because they can, in performance, be totally present: they can proceed on instinct and muscle-memory and autonomic will such that agent and action are one. Great athletes can do this even — and, for the truly great ones like Borg and Bird and Nicklaus and Jordan and Austin, *especially* — under wilting pressure and scrutiny. They can withstand forces of distraction that would break a mind prone to self-conscious fear in two.

The real secret behind top athletes' genius, then, may be as esoteric and obvious and dull and profound as silence itself. The real, many-veiled answer to the question of just what goes through a great player's mind as he stands at the center of hostile crowd-noise and lines up the free-throw that will decide the game might well be: *nothing at all.*

How can great athletes shut off the Iago-like voice of the self? How can they bypass the head and simply and superbly act? How, at the critical moment, can they invoke for themselves a cliché as trite as "One ball at a time" or "Gotta concentrate here," and *mean* it, and then *do* it? Maybe it's because, for top athletes, clichés present themselves not as trite but simply as true, or perhaps not even as declarative expressions with qualities like depth or triteness or falsehood or truth but as simple imperatives that are either useful or not and, if useful, to be invoked and obeyed and that's all there is to it.

What if, when Tracy Austin writes that after her 1989 car crash, "I quickly accepted that there was nothing I could do about it," the statement is not only true but *exhaustively descriptive* of the entire acceptance process she went through? Is someone stupid or shallow because she can say to herself that there's nothing she can do about something bad and so she'd better accept it, and thereupon simply accept it with no more interior struggle? Or is that person maybe somehow natively wise and profound, enlightened in the childlike way some saints and monks are enlightened?

This is, for me, the real mystery — whether such a person is an idiot or a mystic or both and/or neither. The only certainty seems to be that such a person does not produce a very good prose memoir. That plain empirical fact may be the best way to explain how Tracy Austin's actual history can be so compelling and important and her verbal account of that history not even alive. It may also, in starting to address the differences in communicability between thinking and doing and between doing and being, yield the key to why top athletes' autobiographies are at once so seductive and so disappointing for us readers. As is so often SOP with the truth, there's a cruel paradox involved. It may well be that we spectators, who are not divinely gifted as athletes, are the only ones able truly to see, articulate, and animate the experience of the gift we are denied. And that those who receive and act out the gift of athletic genius must, perforce, be blind and dumb about it — and not because blindness and dumbness are the price of the gift, but because they are its essence.

1994

UP, SIMBA

Seven Days on the Trail of an Anticandidate

OPTIONAL FOREWORD
FROM THE AD 2000 INTRODUCTION TO THE
ELECTRONIC EDITION OF "UP, SIMBA," MANDATED
AND OVERSEEN BY THE (NOW-DEFUNCT) "I-PUBLISH"
DIVISION OF LITTLE, BROWN AND COMPANY, INC.

Dear Person Reading This:

Evidently I'm supposed to say something about what the following document is and where it came from.

From what I understand, in autumn 1999 the powers that be at *Rolling Stone* magazine decided they wanted to get four writers who were not political journalists to do articles on the four big presidential candidates and their day-to-day campaigns in the early primaries. My own résumé happens to have "NOT A POLITICAL JOURNALIST" right there at the very top, and *Rolling Stone* magazine called, and pitched the idea, and furthermore said I could pick whichever candidate I wanted (which of course was flattering, although in retrospect they probably told the other three writers the same thing — magazines are always very flattering and *carte blanche*ish when they're trying to get you to do something). The only candidate I could see trying to write about was Senator John McCain (R-AZ), whom I'd seen a recent tape of on *Charlie Rose* and had decided was either incredibly honest and forthright or else just insane. There were other reasons for wanting to write about McCain and party politics, too, all of which are explored in considerable detail in the document itself and so I don't see any reason to inflict them on you here.

The *Electronic Editor* (actual title, like on his office letterhead and everything) says I should insert here that I, the author, am not a Republican, and that actually I ended up voting for Sen. Bill Bradley (D-NJ) in the Illinois primary. I don't personally see how my own politics are anybody's business, but I'm guessing the point of the insertion is to make clear that there are no partisan motives or conservative agenda behind the article even though parts of it (i.e., of the upcoming article) might appear to be pro-McCain. It's not, though neither is it anti-; it's just meant to be the truth as one person saw it.

What else to tell you. At first I was supposed to follow McCain around in New Hampshire as he campaigned for 1 February's big primary there. Then, around Christmastime, *Rolling Stone* decided that they wanted to abort the assignment because Governor Bush was way ahead in the polls and outspending McCain ten to one and they thought McCain was going to get flattened in New Hampshire and that his campaign would be over by the time anything could come out in *Rolling Stone* and that they'd look stupid. Then on 1 February, when the early NH returns had McCain ahead, the magazine suddenly turned around and called again and said the article was a Go again but that now they wanted me to fly out to NH and start that very night, which (because I happen to have dogs with professionally diagnosed emotional problems who require special care, and it always takes me several days to recruit, interview, select, instruct, and field-test a dogsitter) was out of the question. Some of this is probably not too germane, but the point is that I ended up flying out the following week and riding with the McCain2000 traveling press corps from 7 to 13 February, which in retrospect was probably the most interesting and complicated week of the whole 2000 GOP race.

Especially the complicated part. For it turned out that the more interesting a campaign-related person or occurrence or intrigue or strategy or happenstance was, the more time and page-space it took to make sense of it, or, if it made no sense, to describe what it was and explain why it didn't make sense but was interesting anyway if viewed in a certain context that then itself had to be described, and so on. With the end result being that the actual document delivered per contract to *Rolling Stone* magazine turned out to be longer and more complicated than they'd asked for. Quite a bit longer, actually. In fact the article's editor pointed out that running the whole thing would take up most of *Rolling Stone*'s text-space and might even cut into the percentage of the magazine reserved for advertisements, which obviously would not do.* And so at least half the article got cut out, plus some of the more complicated stuff got way compressed and simplified, which was especially disappointing because, as previously mentioned, the most complicated stuff also tended to be the most interesting.

The point here is that what you've just now purchased the ability to download or have e-mailed to you or whatever (it's been explained to me several times, but I still don't totally understand it) is the original uncut document, the as it were director's cut, verbally complete and unoccluded by any lush photos of puffy-lipped girls with their Diesels half unzipped, etc.

There are only a couple changes. All typos and factual boners have now (hopefully) been fixed, for one thing. There were also certain places where the original article talked about the fact that it was appearing in *Rolling Stone* magazine and that whoever was reading it was sitting there actually holding a copy of *Rolling Stone,* etc., and many of these got changed because it just seemed too weird to keep telling you you were reading this in an actual 10" × 12" magazine when you now quite clearly are not. (Again, this was the Electronic Editor's suggestion.) You will note, though, that the author is usually still referred to in the document as *"Rolling Stone"* or *"RS."* I'm sorry if this looks strange to you, but I have declined to change it. Part of the reason is that I was absurdly proud of my *Rolling Stone* press badge and of the fact that most of the pencils and campaign staff referred to me as "the guy from *Rolling Stone.*" I will confess that I even borrowed a friend's battered old black leather jacket to wear on the Trail so I'd better project the kind of edgy, vaguely dangerous vibe I imagined an *RS* reporter ought to give off. (You have to understand that I hadn't read *Rolling Stone* in quite some time.) Plus, journalistically, my covering the campaign for this particular organ turned out to have a big effect on what I got to see and how various people conducted themselves when I was around. For example, it was the main reason why the McCain2000 High Command

---

* Here I should point out that this *RS* editor, whose name was Mr. Tonelli, delivered the length-and-space verdict with sympathy and good humor, and that he was pretty much a mensch through the whole radically ablative editorial process that followed, which process was itself unusually rushed and stressful because right in the middle of it (the process) came Super Tuesday's bloodbath, and McCain really did drop out — Mr. Tonelli was actually watching McCain's announcement on his office TV while we were doing the first round of cuts on the telephone — and apparently *Rolling Stone*'s top brass's fear of looking stupid came roaring back into their limbic system and they told poor Mr. Tonelli that the article had to be all of a sudden crammed into the very next issue of *RS,* even though that issue was scheduled to "close" and go to the printer in less than 48 hours, which, if you know anything about magazines' normally interminable editing and fact-checking and copyediting and typesetting and proofreading and retypesetting and layout and printing processes, you'll understand why Mr. Tonelli's good humor through the whole thing was noteworthy.

pretty much refused to have anything to do with me* but why the network techs were so friendly and forthcoming and let me hang around with them (the sound techs, in particular, were *Rolling Stone* fans from way back). Finally, the document itself is sort of rhetorically directed at voters of a particular age-range and attitude, and I'm figuring that the occasional *Rolling Stone* reference might help keep the reasons for some of this rhetoric clear.

The other thing I'd note is simply what the article's about, which turned out to be not so much the campaign of one impressive guy, but rather what McCain's candidacy and the brief weird excitement it generated might reveal about how millennial politics and all its packaging and marketing and strategy and media and spin and general sepsis actually makes us US voters feel, inside, and whether anyone running for anything can even be "real" anymore — whether what we actually want is something real or something else. Whether it works on your screen or Palm or not, for me the whole thing ended up relevant in ways far beyond any one man or magazine. If you don't agree, I imagine you'll have only to press a button or two to make it all go away.

---

* In particular I never got to talk to Mr. Mike Murphy, who if you read the document you'll understand why he'd be the one McCain staffer you'd just about give a nut to get three or four drinks into and then start probing. Despite sustained pestering and sleeve-tugging and pride-swallowing appeals to the Head Press Liaison for even just ten lousy minutes, though — and even after *RS*'s Mr. Tonelli himself called McCain2000 HQ in Virginia to bitch and wheedle — Mike Murphy avoided this reporter to the point of actually starting to duck around corners whenever he saw me coming. The unending pursuit of this one interview (what eventually in my notebook got called *"MurphyQuest 2000"*) actually turned into one of the great personal subdramas of the week, and there's a whole very lengthy and sordid story to tell here, including some embarrassing but probably in retrospect kind of funny attempts to corner the poor man in all sorts of awkward personal venues where I figured he'd have a hard time escaping . . . nevertheless the crux here is that Murphy's total inaccessibility to yrs. truly was not, I finally realized, anything personal, but rather a simple function of my being from *Rolling Stone*, a (let's face it) politically featherweight organ whose readership was clearly not part of any GOP demographic that was going to help Mike Murphy's candidate in SC or MI or any of the other upcoming sink-or-swim primaries. In fact, because the magazine was a biweekly with a long lead time — the Lebanese-Australian lady from the *Boston Globe* (see document) pointed all this out to yrs. truly after we'd just watched Murphy more or less fake an epileptic seizure to get out of riding in an elevator with me — even a droolingly pro-McCain *Rolling Stone* article wouldn't actually appear until after 7 March's Super Tuesday, by which time, she predicted (correctly), the nomination battle would effectively be over.

WHO CARES

All right so now yes yes *more* press attention for John S. McCain III, USN, POW, USC, GOP, 2000.com. The Rocky of Politics. The McCain Mutiny. The Real McCain. The Straight Talk Express. Internet fund-raiser. Media darling. Navy flier. Middle name Sidney. Son and grandson of admirals. And a serious hard-ass — a way-Right Republican senator from one of the most politically troglodytic states in the nation. A man who opposes *Roe v. Wade,* gun control, and funding for PBS, who supports the death penalty and defense buildups and constitutional amendments outlawing flag-burning and making school prayer OK. Who voted to convict at Clinton's impeachment trial, twice. And who, starting sometime last fall, has become the great populist hope of American politics. Who wants your vote but won't whore himself to get it, and wants you to vote for him *because* he won't whore. An anticandidate. Who cares.

Facts. The 1996 presidential election had the lowest Young Voter turnout in US history. The 2000 GOP primary in New Hampshire had the highest. And the experts agree that McCain drew most of them. He drew first-time and never-before voters; he drew Democrats and Independents, Libertarians and soft socialists and college kids and soccer moms and weird furtive guys whose affiliations sounded more like cells than parties, and won by 18 points, and nearly wiped the smirk off Bush$_2$'s face. McCain has spurned soft money and bundled money and still raised millions, much of it on the Internet and from people who've never given to a campaign before. On 7 Feb. '00 he's on the cover of all three major newsweeklies at once, and the Shrub is on the run. The next big vote is South Carolina, heart of the true knuckle-dragging Christian Right, where Dixie's flag flutters proud over the statehouse and the favorite sport is video poker and the state GOP is getting sued over its habit of not even opening polls in black areas on primary day; and when McCain's chartered plane lands here at 0300h on the night of his New Hampshire win, a good 500 South Carolina college students are waiting to greet him, cheering and waving signs and dancing and holding a weird kind of GOP rave. Think about this — 500 kids at 3:00 AM out of their minds with enthusiasm for . . . a politician. "It was as if," *Time* said, "[McCain] were on the cover of *Rolling Stone*," giving the rave all kinds of attention.

And of course attention breeds attention, as any marketer can tell you. And so now more attention, from the aforementioned ur-liberal *Rolling Stone* itself, whose editors send the least professional pencil they can find to spend a week on the campaign with McCain and *Time* and the *Times* and CNN and MSNBC and MTV and all the rest of this country's great digital engine of public fuss. Does John McCain deserve all this? Is the attention real attention, or just hype? Is there a difference? Can it help him get elected? Should it?

A better question: Do you even give a shit whether McCain can or ought to win. Since you're reading *Rolling Stone*, the chances are good that you are an American between say 18 and 35, which demographically makes you a Young Voter. And no generation of Young Voters has ever cared less about politics and politicians than yours. There's hard demographic and voter-pattern data backing this up . . . assuming you give a shit about data. In fact, even if you're reading other stuff in *RS*, the odds are probably only about 50-50 that you'll read this whole document once you've seen what it's really about — such is the enormous shuddering yawn that the political process tends to evoke in us now in this post-Watergate-post-Iran-Contra-post-Whitewater-post-Lewinsky era, an era in which politicians' statements of principle or vision are understood as self-serving ad copy and judged not for their truth or ability to inspire but for their tactical shrewdness, their marketability. And no generation has been marketed and spun and pitched to as relentlessly as today's demographic Young. So when Senator John McCain says, in Michigan or SC, "I run for president not to Be Somebody, but to Do Something," it's hard to hear it as anything more than a marketing tactic, especially when he says it as he's going around surrounded by cameras and reporters and cheering crowds . . . in other words, Being Somebody.

And when Senator John McCain also says — constantly, thumping it hard at the start and end of every speech and Town Hall Meeting — that his goal as president will be "to inspire young Americans to devote themselves to causes greater than their own self-interest," it's hard not to hear it as just one more piece of the carefully scripted bullshit that presidential candidates hand us as they go about the self-interested business of trying to become the most powerful, important, and talked-about human being on earth, which is of course their real "cause," a cause to which they appear to be so deeply devoted that they can swallow and spew whole mountains of noble-sounding bullshit and convince even themselves they mean it. Cynical as that may sound, polls show it's how most of us feel. And we're beyond not believing the bullshit; mostly we don't even *hear* it now, dismissing it at the same deep level, below attention, where we also block out billboards and Muzak.

One of the things that makes John McCain's "causes greater than self-interest" line harder to dismiss, though, is that this guy also sometimes says things that are manifestly true but which no other mainstream candidate will say. Such as that special-interest money, billions of dollars of it, controls Washington and that all this "reforming politics" and "cleaning up Washington" stuff that every candidate talks about will remain impossible until certain well-known campaign-finance scams like soft money and bundles are outlawed. All Congress's talk about health-care reform and a Patients' Bill of Rights, for example, McCain has said publicly is total bullshit because the GOP is in the pocket of pharmaceutical and HMO lobbies and the Democrats are funded by trial lawyers' lobbies, and it is in these backers' self-interest to see that the current insane US health-care system stays just the way it is.

But health-care reform is politics, and so are marginal tax rates and defense procurement and Social Security, and politics is boring — complex, abstract, dry, the province of policy wonks and Rush Limbaugh and nerdy little guys on PBS, and basically who cares.

Except there's something underneath politics here, something riveting and unspinnable and true. It has to do with McCain's military background and Vietnam combat and the 5+ years he spent in a North Vietnamese prison, mostly in solitary, in a box-sized cell, getting tortured and starved. And with the unbelievable honor and balls he showed there. It's very easy to gloss over the POW thing, partly because we've all heard so much about it and partly because it's so off-the-charts dramatic, like something in a movie instead of a man's real life. But it's worth considering for a minute, carefully, because it's what makes McCain's "causes greater than self-interest" thing easier to maybe swallow.

Here's what happened. In October of '67 McCain was himself still a Young Voter and was flying his 26th Vietnam combat mission and his A-4 Skyhawk plane got shot down over Hanoi, and he had to eject, which basically means setting off an explosive charge that blows your seat out of the plane, and the ejection broke both McCain's arms and one leg and gave him a concussion and he started falling out of the skies over Hanoi. Try to imagine for a second how much this would hurt and how scared you'd be, three limbs broken and falling toward the enemy capital you just tried to bomb. His chute opened late and he landed hard in a little lake in a park right in the middle of downtown Hanoi. (There is still an NV statue of McCain by this lake today, showing him on his knees with his hands up and eyes scared and on the pediment the inscription "McCan — famous air pirate" [*sic*].) Imagine treading water with broken arms and trying to pull the life vest's toggle with your teeth as a crowd of North Vietnamese men all swim out toward you (there's film of this, somebody had a home-movie camera and the NV government released it, though it's grainy and McCain's face is hard to see). The crowd pulled him out and then just about killed him. Bomber pilots were especially hated, for obvious reasons. McCain got bayoneted in the groin; a soldier broke his shoulder apart with a rifle butt. Plus by this time his right knee was bent 90 degrees to the side, with the bone sticking out. This is all public record. Try to imagine it. He finally got tossed on a jeep and taken only about five blocks to the infamous Hoa Lo prison — a.k.a. the Hanoi Hilton, of much movie fame — where for a week they made him beg for a doctor and finally set a couple of the fractures without anesthetic and let two other fractures and the groin wound (imagine: *groin wound*) go untreated. Then they threw him in a cell. Try for a moment to feel this. The media profiles all talk about how McCain still can't lift his arms over his head to comb his hair, which is true. But try to imagine it at the time, yourself in his place, because it's important. Think about how *diametrically* opposed to your own self-interest getting knifed in the nuts and having fractures set without a general would be, and then about getting thrown in a cell to just lie there and hurt, which is what happened. He was mostly delirious with pain for weeks, and his weight dropped to 100 pounds, and the other POWs were sure he would die; and then, after he'd hung on like that for several months and his bones had mostly knitted and he could sort of stand up, the prison people came and brought him to the commandant's office and closed the door and out of nowhere offered to let him go. They said he could just . . . leave. It turned out that US Admiral John S. McCain II had just been made head of all naval forces in the Pacific, meaning also Vietnam, and the North Vietnamese wanted the PR coup of mercifully releasing his son, the baby-killer. And John S. McCain III, 100 pounds and barely able to stand, refused the offer. The US military's Code of Conduct for Prisoners of War apparently said that POWs had to be released in the order they were captured, and there were others who'd been in Hoa Lo a much longer time, and McCain refused to violate the Code. The prison commandant, not at all pleased, right there in his office had guards break McCain's ribs, rebreak his arm, knock his teeth out. McCain still refused to leave without the other POWs. Forget how many movies stuff like this happens in and try to imagine it as real: a man without teeth refusing release. McCain spent four more years in Hoa Lo like this, much of the time in solitary, in the dark, in a special closet-sized box called a "punishment cell." Maybe you've heard all this before; it's been in umpteen different media profiles of McCain this year. It's overexposed, true. Still, though, take a second or two to do some creative visualization and imagine the moment between John McCain's first getting offered early release and his turning it down. Try to imagine it was you. Imagine how loudly your most basic, primal self-interest would cry out to you in that moment, and all the ways you could rationalize accepting the offer: What difference would one less POW make? Plus maybe it'd give the other POWs hope and keep them going, and I mean 100 pounds and expected to die and surely the Code of Conduct doesn't apply to you if you need a doctor or else you're going to die, plus if you could stay alive by getting out you could make a promise to God to do nothing but Total Good from now on and make the world better and so your accepting would be better for the world than your refusing, and maybe if Dad wasn't worried about the Vietnamese retaliating against you here in prison he could prosecute the war more aggressively and end it sooner and actually save lives so yes maybe you could actually *save lives* if you took the offer and got out versus what real purpose gets served by you staying here in a box and getting beaten to death, and by the way oh Jesus imagine it a real doctor and real surgery with pain-killers and clean sheets and a chance to heal and not be in agony and to see your kids again, your wife, to smell your wife's hair. . . . Can you hear it? What would be happening inside your head? Would you have refused the offer? *Could* you have? You can't know for sure. None of us can. It's hard even to imagine the levels of pain and fear and want in that moment, much less to know how we'd react. None of us can know.

But, see, we *do* know how this man reacted. That he chose to spend four more years there, mostly in a dark box, alone, tapping messages on the walls to the others, rather than violate a Code. Maybe he was nuts. But the point is that with McCain it feels like we *know*, for a proven fact, that he is capable of devotion to something other, more, than his own self-interest. So that when he says the line in speeches now you can feel like maybe it's not just more candidate bullshit, that with this guy it's maybe the truth. Or maybe both the truth *and* bullshit — the man does want your vote, after all.

But so that moment in the Hoa Lo office in '68 — right before John McCain refused, with all his basic primal human self-interest howling at him — that moment is hard to blow off. For the whole week, through Michigan and South Carolina and all the tedium and cynicism and paradox of the campaign, that moment seems to underlie McCain's "greater than self-interest" line, moor it, give it a deep sort of reverb that's hard to ignore. The fact is that John McCain is a genuine hero of maybe the only kind Vietnam has to offer us, a hero because of not what he did but what he suffered — voluntarily, for a Code. This gives him the moral authority both to utter lines about causes beyond self-interest and to expect us, even in this age of spin and lawyerly cunning, to believe he means them. And yes, literally: "moral authority," that old cliché, like so many other clichés — "service," "honor," "duty" — that have become now just mostly words, slogans invoked by men in nice suits who want something from us. The John McCain of recent seasons, though — arguing for his doomed campaign-finance bill on the Senate floor in '98, calling his colleagues crooks to their faces on C-SPAN, talking openly about a bought-and-paid-for government on *Charlie Rose* in July '99, unpretentious and bright as hell in the Iowa debates and New Hampshire THMs — something about him made a lot of us feel that the guy wanted something different from us, something more than votes or dollars, something old and maybe corny but with a weird achy pull to it like a smell from childhood or a name on the tip of your tongue, something that would make us hear clichés as more than just clichés and start us trying to think about what terms like "service" and "sacrifice" and "honor" might really refer to, like whether the words actually *stand* for something. To think about whether anything past well-spun self-interest might be real, was ever real, and if so then what happened? These, for the most part, are not lines of thinking that our culture has encouraged Young Voters to pursue. Why do you suppose that is?

GLOSSARY OF RELEVANT CAMPAIGN TRAIL VOCAB, MOSTLY COURTESY OF JIM C. AND THE NETWORK NEWS TECHS

22.5 = The press corps' shorthand for McCain's opening remarks at *THMs* (see *THM*), which remarks are always the same and always take exactly 22½ minutes.

B-film = Innocuous little audio-free shots of McCain doing public stuff — shaking hands, signing books, getting *scrummed* (see *Scrum*), etc. — for use behind a TV voice-over report on the day's campaigning, as in "The reason the *techs* [see *Tech*] have to *feed* [see *Feed*] so much irrelevant and repetitive daily footage is that they never know what the network wants to use for *B-film*."

Baggage Call = The grotesquely early AM time, listed on the next day's schedule (N.B.: the last vital media-task of the day is making sure to get the next day's schedule from Travis), by which you have to get your suitcase back in the bus's bowels and have a seat staked out and be ready to go or else you get left behind and have to try to wheedle a ride to the first *THM* (see *THM*) from FoxNews, which is a drag in all kinds of ways.

Bundled Money = A way to get around the Federal Election Commission's $1,000 limit for individual campaign contributions. A wealthy donor can give $1,000 for himself, then he can say that yet another $1,000 comes from his wife, and another $1,000 from his kid, and another from his Aunt Edna, etc. The *Shrub*'s (see *Shrub*) favorite trick is to designate CEOs and other top corporate executives as "Pioneers," each of whom pledges to raise $100,000 for Bush2000 — $1,000 comes from them individually, and the other 99 one-grand contributions come "voluntarily" from their employees. McCain makes a point of accepting neither b*undled money* nor s*oft money* (see *Soft Money*).

Cabbage (v) = To beg, divert, or outright steal food from one of the many suppertime campaign events at which McCain's audience all sit at tables and get supper and the press corps has to stand around foodless at the back of the room.

DT = Drive Time, the slots in the daily schedule set aside for caravanning from one campaign event to another.

F&F = An hour or two in the afternoon when the campaign provides downtime and an *F&F* Room for the press corps to *file* and *feed* (see *File* and *Feed*).

File and *Feed* = What print and broadcast press, respectively, have to do every day, i.e., print reporters have to finish their daily stories and *file* them via fax or e-mail to their newspapers, while the *techs* (see *Tech*) and field producers have to find a satellite or *Gunner* (see *Gunner*) and *feed* their film, *B-film, stand-ups* (see *Stand-up*), and anything else their bosses might want to the network HQ. (For alternate meaning of *feed*, see *Pool*.)

Gunner = A portable satellite-uplink rig that the networks use to *feed* on-scene from some campaign events. Gunner is the company that makes and/or rents out these rigs, which consist of a blinding white van with a boat-trailerish thing on which is an eight-foot satellite dish angled 40 degrees upward at the southwest sky and emblazoned in fiery blue caps **GUNNER GLOBAL UPLINKING FOR NEWS, NETWORKING, ENTER-TAINMENT.**

Head = Local or network TV correspondent (see also *Talent*).

ODT = Optimistic Drive Time, which refers to the daily schedule's nag-ging habit of underestimating the amount of time it takes to get from one event to another, causing the Straight Talk Express driver to speed like a maniac and thereby to incur the rabid dislike of Jay and the Bullshit 2 driver. (On the night of 9 February, one BS2 driver actually quit on the spot after an especially hair-rising ride from Greenville to Clemson U, and an emergency replacement driver [who wore a brown cowboy hat with two NRA pins on the brim and was so obsessed with fuel economy that he refused ever to turn on BS2's generator, causing all BS2 press who needed working AC outlets to crowd onto BS1 and turning BS2 into a veritable moving tomb used only for *OTC*s] had to be flown in from Cincinnati, which is apparently the bus company's HQ.)

OTC = Opportunity to Crash, meaning a chance to grab a nap on the bus (placement and posture variable).

OTS = Opportunity to Smoke.

Pencil = A member of the Trail's print press.

Pool (v) = Refers to occasions when, because of space restrictions or McCain2000 fiat, only one network camera-and-sound team is allowed into an event, and by convention all the other networks get to *feed* (meaning, in this case, *pool*) that one team's tape.

Press-Avail (or just *Avail*) = Brief scheduled opportunity for traveling press corps to interface as one body w/ McCain or staff High Command, often deployed for *Reacts* (see *React*). An *Avail* is less formal than a press conference, which latter usually draws extra local *pencils* and *heads* and is uncancelable, whereas *Avails* are often bagged because of *ODT*'s and related snafus.

React (n) = McCain's or McCain2000 High Command's on-record response to a sudden major development in the campaign, usually some tactical move or allegation from the *Shrub* (see *Shrub*).

Scrum (n) = The moving 360-degree ring of *techs* (see *Tech*) and *heads* around a candidate as he makes his way from the Straight Talk Express into an event or vice versa; *(v)* = to gather around a moving candidate in such a ring.

Shrub = GOP presidential candidate George W. Bush (also sometimes referred to as Dubya or Bush$_2$).

Soft Money = The best-known way to finesse the FEC's limit on campaign contributions. Enormous sums are here given to a certain candidate's political party instead of to the candidate, but the party then by some strange coincidence ends up disbursing those enormous sums to exactly the candidate the donor had wanted to give to in the first place.

Stand-up = A *head* doing a remote report from some event McCain's at.

Stick = A sound *tech's* (see *Tech*) black telescoping polymer rod (full extension = 9'7") with a boom microphone at the end, used mostly for *scrums* and always the most distinctive visible feature thereof because of the way a fully extended *stick* wobbles and boings when the sound *tech* (which, again, see *Tech*) walks with it.

Talent = A marquee network *head* who flies in for just one day, gets briefed by a field producer, and does a *stand-up* on the campaign, as in "We got *talent* coming in tomorrow, so I need to get all this *B-film* archived." Recognizable *talent* this week includes Bob Schieffer of CBS, David Bloom of NBC, and Judy Woodruff of CNN.

Tech = A TV news camera or sound technician. (N.B.: In the McCain corps this week, all the *techs* are male, while over 80 percent of the field producers are female. No credible explanation ever obtained.)

THM = Town Hall Meeting, McCain2000's signature campaign event, where the *22.5* is followed by an hour-long unscreened Q&A with the audience.

The Twelve Monkeys (or *12M*) = The *techs'* private code-name for the most elite and least popular *pencils* in the McCain press corps, who on *DTs* are almost always allowed into the red-intensive salon at the very back of the Straight Talk Express to interface with McCain and political consultant Mike Murphy. The *12M* are a dozen high-end journalists and political-analysis guys from important papers and weeklies and news services (e.g. Copley, *W. Post, WSJ, Newsweek,* UPI, *Ch. Tribune, National Review, Atlanta Constitution,* etc.) and tend to be so totally identical in dress and demeanor as to be almost surreal — twelve immaculate and wrinkle-free navy-blue blazers, half-Windsored ties, pleated chinos, oxfordcloth shirts that even when the jackets come off stay 100 percent buttoned at collar and sleeves, Cole Haan loafers, and tortoiseshell specs they love to take off and nibble the arm of, plus a uniform self-seriousness that reminds you of every over-achieving dweeb you ever wanted to kick the ass of in school. The *Twelve Monkeys* never smoke or drink, and always move in a pack, and always cut to the front of every *scrum* and *Press-Avail* and line for continental breakfast in the hotel lobby before *Baggage Call*, and whenever any of them are rotated briefly back onto Bullshit 1 they always sit together identically huffy and pigeon-toed with their attaché cases in their laps and always end up discussing esoteric books on political theory and public policy in voices that are all the exact same plummy Ivy League honk. The *techs* (who wear old jeans and surplus-store parkas and also all tend to hang in a pack) pretty much try to ignore the *Twelve Monkeys,* who in turn treat the *techs* the way someone in an executive washroom treats the attendant. As you might already have gathered, *Rolling Stone* dislikes the *12M* intensely, for all the above reasons, plus the fact that they're tight as the bark on a tree when it comes to sharing even very basic general-knowledge political information that might help somebody write a slightly better article, plus the issue of two separate occasions at late-night hotel check-ins when one or more of the *Twelve Monkeys* just out of nowhere turned and handed *Rolling Stone* their suitcases to carry, as if *Rolling Stone* were a bellboy or gofer instead of a hardworking journalist just like them even if he didn't have a portable Paul Stuart steamer for his slacks.

Weasel = The weird gray fuzzy thing that sound *techs* put over their *sticks'* mikes at *scrums* to keep annoying wind-noise off the audio. It looks like a large floppy mouse-colored version of a certain popular kind of fuzzy bathroom slipper. (N.B.: *Weasels,* which are also sometimes worn by sound *techs* as headgear during *OTS*s when it's really cold, are thus sometimes also known as *tech toupees.*)

SUBSTANTIALLY FARTHER BEHIND THE SCENES THAN YOU'RE APT TO WANT TO BE

It's now precisely 1330h on Tuesday, 8 February 2000, on Bullshit 1, proceeding southeast on I-26 back toward Charleston SC. There's now so much press and staff and techs and stringers and field producers and photographers and heads and pencils and political columnists and hosts of political radio shows and local media covering John McCain and the McCain2000 phenomenon that there's more than one campaign bus. Here in South Carolina there are three, a veritable convoy of Straight Talk, plus FoxNews's green SUV and the MTV crew's sprightly red Corvette and two much-antenna'd local TV vans (one of which has muffler trouble). On DTs like this, McCain's always in his personal red recliner next to pol. consultant Mike Murphy's red recliner in the little press salon he and Murphy have in the back of the lead bus, the well-known Straight Talk Express, which is up ahead and already drawing away. The Straight Talk Express's driver is a leadfoot and the other drivers hate him. Bullshit 1 is the caravan's second bus, a luxury Grumman with good current and workable phone jacks, and a lot of the national pencils use it to pound out copy on their laptops and send faxes and e-mail stuff to their editors. The campaign's logistics are dizzyingly complex, and one of the things the McCain-2000 staff has to do is rent different buses and decorate the nicest one with STRAIGHT TALK EXPRESS and McCAIN2000.COM in each new state. In Michigan yesterday there was just the STE plus one bus for non-elite press, which had powder-gray faux-leather couches and gleaming brushed-steel fixtures and a mirrored ceiling from front to back; it creeped everyone out and was christened the Pimpmobile. The two press buses in South Carolina are known as Bullshit 1 and Bullshit 2, names conceived as usual by the extremely cool and laid-back NBC News cameraman Jim C. and — to their credit — immediately seized on and used with great glee at every opportunity by McCain's younger Press Liaisons, who are themselves so cool and unpretentious it's tempting to suspect that they are *professionally* cool and unpretentious.

Right now Bullshit 1's Press Liaison, Travis — 23, late of Georgetown U and a six-month backpack tour of Southeast Asia during which he says he came to like fried bugs — is again employing his single most important and impressive skill as a McCain2000 staffer, which is the ability to sleep anywhere, anytime, and in any position for ten-to-fifteen-minute intervals, with a composed face and no unpleasant sounds or fluids, and then to come instantly and unfuzzily awake the moment he's needed. It's not clear whether he thinks people can't tell he's sleeping or what. Travis, who wears wide-wale corduroys and a sweater from Structure and seems to subsist entirely on Starburst Fruit Chews, tends to speak with the same deprecatory irony that is the whole staff's style, introducing himself to new media today as either "Your press lackey" or "The Hervé Villechaize of Bullshit 1," or both. His latest trick is to go up to the front of the bus and hook his arm over the little brushed-steel safety bar above the driver's head and to lean against it so that from behind it looks as if he's having an involved navigational conversation with the driver, and to go to sleep, and the driver — a 6'7" bald black gentleman named Jay, whose way of saying goodnight to a journalist at the end of the day is "Go on and get you a woman, boy!" — knows exactly what's going on and takes extra care not to change lanes or brake hard, and Travis, whose day starts at 0500 and ends after midnight just like all the other staffers, lives this way.

McCain just got done giving a Major Policy Address on crime and punishment at the South Carolina Criminal Justice Academy in Columbia, which is where the caravan is heading back to Charleston from. It was a resoundingly scary speech, delivered in a large airless cinderblock auditorium surrounded by razor wire and guard towers (the SCCJA adjoined a penal institution so closely that it wasn't clear where one left off and the other began) and introduced by some kind of very high-ranking Highway Patrol officer whose big hanging gut and face the color of rare steak seemed right out of southern-law-enforcement central casting and who spoke approvingly and at some length about Senator McCain's military background and his 100 percent conservative voting record on crime, punishment, firearms, and the war on drugs. This wasn't a Town Meeting Q&A–type thing; it was a Major Policy Address, one of three this week prompted by Bush2000's charges that McCain is fuzzy on policy, that he's image over substance. The speech's putative audience was 350 neckless young men and women sitting at attention (if that's possible) in arrow-straight rows of folding chairs, with another couple hundred law enforcement pros in Highway Patrol hats and mirrored shades standing at parade-rest behind them, and then behind and around them the media — the real audience for the speech — including NBC's Jim C. and his soundman Frank C. (no relation) and the rest of the network techs on the ever-present fiberboard riser facing the stage and filming McCain, who as is SOP first thanks a whole lot of local people nobody's heard of and then w/o ado jumps right into what's far and away the most frightening speech of the week, backed as always by a 30' × 50' American flag so that when you see B-film of these things on TV it's McCain and the flag, the flag and McCain, a visual conjunction all the candidates try to hammer home. The seated cadets — none of whom fidget or scratch or move in any way except to blink in what looks like perfect sync — wear identical dark-brown khakis and junior models of the same round big-brimmed hats their elders wear, so that they look like ten perfect rows of brutal and extremely attentive forest rangers. McCain, who does not ever perspire, is wearing a dark suit and wide tie and has the only dry forehead in the hall. US congressmen Lindsey Graham (R-SC, of impeachment-trial fame) and Mark Sanford (R-SC, rated the single most fiscally conservative member of the '98–'00 Congress) are up there onstage behind McCain, as is also SOP; they're sort of his living letters of introduction down here this week. Graham, as usual, looks like he slept in his suit, whereas Sanford is tan and urbane in a V-neck sweater and Guccis whose shine you could read by. Mrs. Cindy McCain is up there too, brittly composed and smiling at the air in front of her and thinking about God knows what. Half the buses' press don't listen to the speech; most of them are at different spots at the very back of the auditorium, walking in little unconscious circles with their cellular phones. (You should be apprised up front that national reporters spend an enormous amount of time either on their cell phones or waiting for their cell phones to ring. It is not an exaggeration to say that when somebody's cell phone breaks they almost have to be sedated.) The techs for CBS, NBC, CNN, ABC, and Fox will film the whole speech plus any remarks afterward, then they'll unbolt their cameras from the tripods and go mobile and scrum McCain's exit and the brief Press-Avail at the door to the Straight Talk

Express, and then the field producers will call network HQ and summarize the highlights and HQ will decide which five- or ten-second snippet gets used for their news's nightly bit on the GOP campaign.

It helps to conceive a campaign week's events in terms of boxes, boxes inside other boxes, etc. The national voting audience is the great huge outer box, then the SC-electorate audience, mediated respectively by the inner layers of national and local press, just inside which lie the insulating boxes of McCain's staff's High Command who plan and stage events and spin stuff for the layers of press to interpret for the layers of audience, and the Press Liaisons who shepherd the pencils and heads and mediate their access to the High Command and control which media get rotated onto the ST Express (which is itself a box in motion) and then decide (the Liaisons do) which of these chosen media then get to move all the way into the extreme rear's salon to interface with McCain himself, who is the campaign's narrator and narrative at once, a candidate whose biggest draw of course is that he's an anticandidate, someone who's open and accessible and "thinks outside the box," but who is in fact the campaign's Chinese boxes' central and inscrutable core box, and whose own intracranial thoughts on all these boxes and layers and lenses and on whether this new kind of enclosure is anything like Hoa Lo's dark box are pretty much anyone in the media's guess, since all he'll talk about is politics.

Plus Bullshit 1 is also a box, of course, just the way anything you can't exit till somebody else lets you out is, and right now there are 27 members of the national political media on board, halfway to Charleston. A certain percentage of them aren't worth introducing you to because they'll get rotated back off the Trail tonight and be gone tomorrow, replaced by others you'll just be starting to recognize by the time they too rotate out. That's what these pros call it, the Trail, the same way musicians talk about the Road. The schedule is fascist: wake-up call and backup alarm at 0600h, express check-out, Baggage Call at 0700 to throw bags and techs' gear under the bus, haul ass to McCain's first THM at 0800, then another, then another, maybe an hour off to F&F someplace if ODTs permit, then usually two big evening events, plus hours of dead highway DT between functions, finally getting into that night's Marriott or Hampton Inn at like 2300 just when room service closes so that you're begging rides from FoxNews to find a restaurant still open, then an hour at the hotel bar to try to shut your head off so you can hit the rack at 0130 and get up at 0600 and do it all again. Usually it's four to six days for the average pencil and then you go off home on a gurney and your editor rotates in fresh meat. The network techs, who are old hands at the Trail, stay on for months at a time. The McCain2000 staff have all been doing this full-time since Labor Day, and even the young ones look like the walking dead. Only McCain seems to thrive. He's 63 and practically Rockette-kicks onto the Express every morning. It's either inspiring or frightening.

Here's a quick behind-the-scenes tour of everything that's happening on BS1 at 1330h. A few of the press are slumped over sleeping, open-mouthed and twitching, using their topcoats for pillows. The CBS and NBC techs are in their usual place on the couches way up front, their cameras and sticks and boom mikes and boxes of tapes and big Duracells piled around them, discussing obscure stand-up comedians of the early 70s and trading press badges from New Hampshire and Iowa and Delaware, which badges are laminated and worn around the neck on nylon cords and apparently have value for collectors. Jim C., who looks like a chronically sleep-deprived Elliott Gould, is also watching Travis's leather bookbag swing metronomically by its over-shoulder strap as Travis leans against the safety bar and dozes. All the couches and padded chairs face in, perpendicular to BS1's length, instead of a regular bus's forward-facing seats. So everyone's legs are always out in the aisle, but there's none of the normal social anxiety about your leg maybe touching somebody else on a bus's leg because nobody can help it and everyone's too tired to care. Right behind each set of couches are small white plastic tables with recessed cup-receptacles and AC outlets that work if Jay can be induced to turn on the generator (which he will unless he's low on fuel); and the left side's table has two pencils and two field producers at it, and one of the pencils is Alison Mitchell, as in *the* Alison Mitchell, who is the *NY Times*'s daily eye on McCain and a very high-end journalist but not (refreshingly) one of the Twelve Monkeys, a slim calm kindly lady of maybe 45 who wears dark tights, pointy boots, a black sweater that looks home-crocheted, and a perpetual look of concerned puzzlement, as if life were one long request for clarification. Alison Mitchell is usually a regular up on the Straight Talk Express but today has a tight 1500h deadline and is using BS1's superior current to whip out the story on her Apple PowerBook. (Even from outside the bus it's easy to tell who's banging away on a laptop right then, because their window shades are always down against daytime glare, which is every laptop-journalist's great nemesis.) An ABC field producer across the table from A. Mitchell is trying to settle a credit card dispute on his distinctive cell phone, which is not a headset phone per se but consists of an earplug and a tiny hanging podular thing he holds to his mouth with two fingers to speak, a device that manages to make him look simultaneously deaf and schizophrenic. People in both seats behind the table are reading *USA Today* (and this might be worth noting — the only news daily read by every single member of the national campaign press is, believe it or not, *USA Today*, which always appears as if by dark magic under everybody's hotel door with their express check-out bill every morning, and is free, and media are as susceptible to shrewd marketing as anybody else). The local TV truck's muffler gets louder the farther back you go. About two-thirds of the way down the aisle is a little area that has the bus's refrigerator and the liquor cabinets (the latter unbelievably well stocked on yesterday's Pimpmobile, totally empty on BS1) and the bathroom with the hazardous door. There's also a little counter area piled with Krispy Kreme doughnut boxes, and a sink whose water nobody ever uses (for what turn out to be good reasons). Krispy Kremes are sort of the Deep South equivalent of Dunkin' Donuts, ubiquitous and cheap and great in a sort of what-am-I-doing-eating-dessert-for-breakfast way, and are a cornerstone of what Jim C. calls the Campaign Diet.

Behind the buses' digestive areas is another little lounge, which up on the Express serves as McCain's press salon but which on Bullshit 1 is just an elliptic table of beige plastic ringed with a couch it's just a bit too high for, plus a fax machine and multiple jacks and outlets, the whole area known to the Press Liaisons as the ERPP (=Extreme Rear Press Palace). Right now Mrs. McCain's personal assistant on the Trail, Wendy — who has electric-blue contact lenses and rigid blond hair and immaculate makeup and accessories and French nails and can perhaps best be described as a very Republican-looking young lady indeed — is back here at the beige table eating a large styrofoam cup of soup and using her cell phone to try to find someplace in downtown Charleston where Mrs. McCain can get her nails done. All three walls in the ERPP are mirrored, an unsettling echo of yesterday's reflective bus (except here the mirrors have weird little white ghostly shapes embedded in the plate, apparently as decorations), so that you can see not only everybody's reflections but all sorts of multi-angled reflections of those reflections, and so on, which on top of all the jouncing and swaying keeps most folks up front despite the ERPP's wealth of facilities. Just why Wendy is arranging for her mistress's manicure here on Bullshit 1 is unclear, but Mrs. McC.'s sedulous attention to her own person's dress and grooming is already a minor legend among the press corps, and some of the techs speculate that things like getting her nails and hair done, together with being almost Siametically attached to Ms. Lisa Graham Keegan (who is AZ's education superintendent and supposedly traveling with the senator as his "Advisor on Issues Affecting Education" but is quite plainly really along because she's Cindy McCain's friend and confidante and the one person in whose presence Mrs. McC. doesn't look like a jacklighted deer), are the only things keeping this extremely fragile person together on the Trail, where she's required to stand under hot lights next to McCain at every speech and THM and Press-Avail and stare cheerfully into the middle distance while her husband speaks to crowds and lenses — in fact some of the cable-network techs have a sort of running debate about what Cindy McCain's really looking at as she stands onstage being scrutinized but never getting to say anything . . . and anyway, everybody understands and respects the enormous pressure Wendy's under to help Mrs. McC. keep it together, and nobody makes fun of her for things like getting more and more stressed as it becomes obvious that there's some special Southeast idiom for manicure that Wendy doesn't know, because nobody she talks to on the cell phone seems to have any idea what she means by "manicure." Also back here, directly across from Wendy, is a ridiculously handsome guy in a green cotton turtleneck, a photographer for Reuters, sitting disconsolate in a complex nest of wires plugged into just about every jack in the ERPP; he's got digital photos of the Columbia speech in his Toshiba laptop and has his cell phone plugged into both the wall and the laptop (which is itself plugged into the wall) and is trying to file the pictures via some weird inter-Reuters e-mail, except his laptop has decided it doesn't like his cell phone anymore ("like" = his term), and he can't get it to file.

If this all seems really static and dull, by the way, then understand that you're getting a bona fide look at the reality of media life on the Trail, much of which consists of wandering around killing time on Bullshit 1 while you wait for the slight meaningful look from Travis that means he's gotten the word from his immediate superior, Todd (28 and so obviously a Harvard alum it wasn't ever worth asking), that after the next stop you're getting rotated up into the big leagues on the Express to sit squished and paralyzed on the crammed red press-couch in back and listen to John S. McCain

and Mike Murphy answer the Twelve Monkeys' questions, and to
look up-close and personal at McCain and the way he puts his
legs way out on the salon's floor and crosses them at the ankle and
sucks absently at his right bicuspid and swirls the coffee in his
McCain2000.com mug, and to try to penetrate the innermost box
of this man's thoughts on the enormous hope and enthusiasm he's
generating in press and voters alike . . . which you should be told
up front does not and cannot happen, this penetration, for two reasons. The smaller reason (1) is that when you are finally rotated up
into the Straight Talk salon you discover that most of the questions
the Twelve Monkeys ask back here are simply too vapid and obvious
for McCain to waste time on, and he lets Mike Murphy handle
them, and Murphy is so funny and dry and able to make such deli-
ciously cruel sport of the 12M —

MONKEY: If, say, you win here in South Carolina, what do you do
          then?
MURPHY: Fly to Michigan that night.
MONKEY: And what if hypothetically you, say, *lose* here in South
          Carolina?
MURPHY: Fly to Michigan that night win or lose.
MONKEY: Can you perhaps explain why?
MURPHY: 'Cause the plane's already paid for.
MONKEY: I think he means: can you explain why specifically
          Michigan?
MURPHY: 'Cause it's the next primary.
MONKEY: I think what we're trying to get you to elaborate on if
          you will, Mike, is: what will your goal be in Michigan?
MURPHY: To get a whole lot of votes. That's part of our secret strat-
          egy for winning the nomination.

— that it's often hard even to notice McCain's there or what his
face or feet are doing, because it takes almost all your concentration
not to start giggling like a maniac at Murphy and at the way the

12M all nod somberly and take down whatever he says in their identical steno notebooks. The bigger and more interesting reason (2) is that this also happens to be the week in which John S. McCain's anticandidate status threatens to dissolve before almost everyone's eyes and he becomes increasingly opaque and paradoxical and in certain ways indistinguishable as an entity from the Shrub and the GOP Establishment against which he'd defined himself and shone so in New Hampshire, which of course is a whole story unto itself.

What's hazardous about Bullshit 1's lavatory door is that it opens and closes laterally, sliding with a *Star Trek*-ish whoosh at the light touch of the DOOR button just inside — i.e., you go in, lightly push DOOR to close, attend to business, lightly push DOOR again to open: simple — except that the DOOR button's placement puts it only inches away from the left shoulder of any male journalist standing over the commode attending to business, a commode without rails or handles or anything to (as it were) hold on to, and even the slightest leftward lurch or lean makes said shoulder touch said button — which keep in mind this is a moving bus — causing the door to whoosh open while you're right there with business under way, and with the consequences of suddenly whirling to try to stab at the button to reclose the door while you're *in medias res* being too obviously horrid to detail, with the result that by 9 February the great unspoken rule among the regulars on Bullshit 1 is that when a male gets up and goes two-thirds of the way back into the lavatory anybody who's back there clears the area and makes sure they're not in the door's line of sight; and the way you can tell that a journalist is local or newly rotated onto the Trail and this is his first time on BS1 is the small strangled scream you always hear when he's in the lavatory and the door unexpectedly whooshes open, and usually the grizzled old *Charleston Post and Courier* pencil will smile and call out "Welcome to national politics!" as the new guy stabs frantically at the button, and Jay at the wheel will toot the horn lightly with the heel of his hand in mirth, taking these long and mostly mindless DTs' fun where he finds it.

Coming back up Bullshit 1's starboard side, no laptops are in play and few window shades pulled, and the cleanest set of windows is just past the fridge, and outside surely the sun is someplace up there but the February vista still seems lightless. The central-SC countryside looks blasted, lynched, the skies the color of low-grade steel, the land all dead sod and broomsedge, with scrub oak and pine leaning at angles, and you can almost hear the mosquitoes breathing in their baggy eggs awaiting spring. Winter down here is both chilly and muggy, and Jay ends up alternating the heater with the AC as various different people bitch about being hot or cold. Scraggly cabbage palms start mixing with the pine as you get farther south, and the mix of conifer and palm is dissonant in a bad-dream sort of way. A certain percentage of the passing trees are dead and hung with kudzu and a particular type of Spanish moss that resembles a kind of drier-lint from hell. Eighteen-wheelers and weird tall pickups are the buses' only company, and the pickups are rusted and all have gun racks and right-wing bumper stickers; some of them toot their horns in support. BS1's windows are high enough that you can see right into the big rigs' cabs. The highway itself is colorless and the sides of it look chewed on, and there's litter, and the median strip is withered grass with a whole lot of different tire tracks and skidmarks striping the sod for dozens of miles, as if from the mother of all multivehicle pileups sometime in I-26's past. Everything looks dead and not happy about it. Birds fly in circles with no place to go. There are also some weird smooth-barked luminous trees that might be pecan; no one seems to know. The techs keep their shades pulled even though they have no laptops. You can tell it must be spooky down here in the summer, all wet moss and bog-steam and dogs with visible ribs and everybody sweating through their hat. None of the media ever seem to look out the window. Everyone's used to being in motion all the time. Location is mentioned only on phones: the journalists and producers are always on their cell phones trying to reach somebody else's cell phone and saying "South Carolina! And where are you!" The other constant in most cell calls on a moving bus is "I'm losing you, can you hear me, should I call back!" A distinctive thing about the field producers is that they pull their cell phones' antennas all the way out with their teeth; journalists use their fingers, or else they have headset phones, which they talk on while they type.

Right now, in fact, most of the starboard side is people on cell phones. There are black cell phones and matte-gray cell phones; one MSNBC lady has a pink cell phone her fiancé got her from Hammacher Schlemmer. Some of the phones are so miniaturized that the mouthpiece barely clears the caller's earlobe and you wonder how they make themselves heard. There are headset cell phones of various makes and color schemes, some without antennas, plus the aforementioned earplug-and-hanging-podular-speaker cell phones. There are also pagers, beepers, vibrating beepers, voice-message pagers whose chips make all the voices sound distressed, and Palm Pilots that display CNN headlines and full-text messages from people's different 1-800 answering services, which all 27 of the media on BSl have (1-800 answering services) and often kill time comparing the virtues of and relating funny anecdotes about. A lot of the cell phones have specially customized rings, which in a confined area with this many phones in play probably makes sense. There's one "Twinkle Twinkle Little Star," a "Hail Hail the Gang's All Here," one that plays the opening to Beethoven's Symphony No. 5 op. 67 in a weird 3/4 up-tempo, and so on. The only fly in the ointment here is that a *US News and W. R.* photographer, a Copley News Service pencil, and a leggy CNN producer who always wears red hose and a scrunchie all have the same "William Tell Overture" ring, so there's always some confusion and three-way scrambling for phones when a "William Tell Overture" goes off in transit. The network techs' phones all have regular rings.

Jay, the official Bullshit 1 driver and one of only two regulars aboard without a cell phone (he uses Travis's big gray Nokia when he needs to call one of the other bus drivers, which happens a lot because as Jay will be the first to admit he's a little weak in some of your navigational-type areas), carries a small attaché case full of CDs, and on long DTs he listens to them on a Sony Discman with big padded studio-quality headphones (which actually might be illegal), but Jay refuses to speak on-record to *Rolling Stone* about what music he listens to. John S. McCain himself is said to favor 60s classics and to at least be able to abide Fatboy Slim, which seems broad-minded indeed. The only other person who listens to headphones is a 12M who's trying to learn conversational Cantonese and whenever he's off the Express sits way back on BS1's port side with his Cantonese-lesson tapes and repeats bursts of inscrutable screeching over and over at a volume his headphones prevent him from regulating very well, and this guy often has a whole large area to himself. Travis, now again awake and in cellular contact with Todd up ahead on the Express, is in his customary precarious position at the very edge of a seat occupied by a wild-haired and slightly mad older Brit from the *Economist* who likes to talk at great length about how absolutely enraptured the British reading public is with John McCain and the whole populist-Tory McCain phenomenon, and tends to bore the hell out of everyone, but is popular anyway because he's an extraordinarily talented cabbager of hot food at mealtime events, and shares. The *Miami Herald* pencil in the seat next to them is reorganizing his Palm Pilot's address-book function by hitting tiny keys with what looks like a small black swizzle stick. There's also an anecdote under way by a marvelously caustic and funny Lebanese lady from Australia (don't ask) who writes for the *Boston Globe,* and is drinking a vanilla Edensoy and telling Alison Mitchell and the ABC field producer w/ earplug-phone across the aisle about apparently checking in and going up to her assigned room at the North Augusta Radisson last night and finding it already occupied by a nude male — "Naked as a jaybob. In his altogether. Starkers" — with only a washcloth over his privates — "and not a large one either, I can tell you," referring (as Alison M. later said she construed) to the washcloth.

The only BS1 regulars not covered so far are at the starboard work-table that's just past the edge of the crowded couch and behind the gang of techs at the front. They are CNN correspondent Jonathan Karl and CNN field producer Jim McManus (both of whom look about eleven) and their sound tech, and they're doing something interesting enough to warrant standing awkwardly balanced to watch and ignoring the slightly mad *Economist* guy's irritated throat-clearings at having somebody's unlaundered bottom swaying in the aisle right next to his head. The CNN sound tech (Mark A., 29, from Atlanta, and after Jay the tallest person on the Trail, vertiginous to talk to, able to get a stick's boom mike directly over McCain's head from the back of even the thickest scrum) has brought out from a complexly padded case a Sony SX-Series Portable Digital Editor ($32,000 retail) and connected it to some headphones and to Jonathan Karl's Dell Latitudes laptop and cell phone, and the three of them are running the CNN videotape of this morning's South Carolina Criminal Justice Academy address, trying to find a certain place where Jonathan Karl's notes indicate that McCain said something like "Regardless of how Governor Bush and his surrogates have distorted my position on the death penalty . . ." A digital timer below the SX's thirteen-inch screen counts seconds and parts of seconds down to four decimal places and is mesmerizing to watch as they fast-forward and Mark A. listens to what must be unimaginable FF chipmunkspeak on his headphones, waiting to tell Karl to stop the tape when he comes to what McManus says are the speech's "fighting words," which CNN HQ wants fed to them immediately so they can juxtapose the bite with something vicious the Shrub apparently said about McCain this morning in Michigan and do a breaking story on what-all Negative stuff is being said in the campaign today.

There's a nice opportunity here for cynicism about the media's idea of "fighting words" as the CNN crew FFs through the speech, Jim McManus eating his fifth Krispy Kreme of the day and awaiting Mark A.'s signal, Jonathan Karl polishing his glasses on his tie, Mark A. leaning forward with his eyes closed in aural concentration; and just behind Mark's massive shoulder, at the rear edge of the front starboard couch, is NBC camera tech Jim C., who has a bad case of the Campaign Flu, pouring more blood-red tincture of elderberry into a bottle of water, his expression carefully stoic because the elderberry remedy's been provided by his wife, who happens to be the NBC crew's field producer and is right across the aisle on the port couch watching him closely to see that he drinks it, and it'll be fun to hear Jim C. crack wise about the elderberry later when she's not around. Cynical observation: The fact that John McCain in this morning's speech several times invoked a "moral poverty" in America, a "loss of shame" that he blamed on "the ceaseless assault of violence-driven entertainment that has lost its moral compass to greed" (McCain's metaphors tend to mix a bit when he gets excited), and made noises that sounded rather a lot like proposing possible federal regulation of all US entertainment, which would have dicey constitutional implications to say the least — this holds no immediate interest for CNN. Nor are they hunting for the hair-raising place in the speech where McCain declared that our next president should be considered "Commander in Chief of the war on drugs" and granted the authority to send both money and (it sounded like) *troops,* if necessary, into "nations that seem to need assistance controlling their exports of poisons that threaten our children." When you consider that state control of the media is one of the big evils we point to to distinguish liberal democracies from repressive regimes, and that sending troops to "assist" in the internal affairs of sovereign nations has gotten the US into some of its worst messes of the last half century, these parts of McCain's speech seem like the real "fighting words" that a mature democratic electorate might care to hear the news talk about. But we don't care, evidently, and so neither do the networks. In fact, it's possible to argue that a big reason why so many young Independents and Democrats are excited about McCain is that the campaign media focus so much attention on McCain's piss-and-vinegar candor and so little attention on the sometimes *extremely* scary right-wing stuff this candor drives him to say . . . but no matter, because what's really riveting here at BS1's starboard table right now is what happens to McCain's face on the Sony SX's screen as they fast-forward through the speech's dull specifics. McCain has white hair (premature, from Hoa Lo), and dark eyebrows, and a pink scalp under something that isn't quite a comb-over, and kind of chubby cheeks, and in a regular analog fast-forward you'd expect his face to look silly, the way everybody on film looks spastic and silly when they're FF'd. But CNN's tape and editing equipment are digital, so what happens on FF is that the shoulders-up view of McCain against eight of the big flag's stripes doesn't speed up and get silly but rather just kind of *explodes* into myriad little digital boxes and squares, and these pieces jumble wildly around and bulge and recede and collapse and whirl and rearrange themselves at a furious FF pace, and the resultant image is like something out of the very worst drug experience of all time, a physiognomic Rubik's Cube's constituent squares and boxes flying around and changing shape and sometimes seeming right on the verge of becoming a human face but never quite resolving into a face, on the high-speed screen.

WHO EVEN CARES WHO CARES

It's hard to get good answers to why Young Voters are so uninterested in politics. This is probably because it's next to impossible to get someone to think hard about why he's not interested in something. The boredom itself preempts inquiry; the fact of the feeling's enough. Surely one reason, though, is that politics is not cool. Or say rather that cool, interesting, alive people do not seem to be the ones who are drawn to the political process. Think back to the sort of kids in high school who were into running for student office: dweeby, overgroomed, obsequious to authority, ambitious in a sad way. Eager to play the Game. The kind of kids other kids would want to beat up if it didn't seem so pointless and dull. And now consider some of 2000's adult versions of these very same kids:

Al Gore, best described by CNN sound tech Mark A. as "amazingly lifelike"; Steve Forbes, with his wet forehead and loony giggle; G. W. Bush's patrician smirk and mangled cant; even Clinton himself, with his big red fake-friendly face and "I feel your pain." Men who aren't enough like human beings even to hate — what one feels when they loom into view is just an overwhelming lack of interest, the sort of deep disengagement that is often a defense against pain. Against sadness. In fact, the likeliest reason why so many of us care so little about politics is that modern politicians make us sad, hurt us deep down in ways that are hard even to name, much less talk about. It's way easier to roll your eyes and not give a shit. You probably don't want to hear about all this, even.

One reason a lot of the media on the Trail like John McCain is simply that he's a cool guy. Nondweeby. In school, Clinton was in student government and band, whereas McCain was a varsity jock and a hell-raiser whose talents for partying and getting laid are still spoken of with awe by former classmates, a guy who graduated near the bottom of his class at Annapolis and got in trouble for flying jets too low and cutting power lines and crashing all the time and generally being cool. At 63, he's witty, and smart, and he'll make fun of himself and his wife and staff and other pols and the Trail, and he'll tease the press and give them shit in a way they don't ever mind because it's the sort of shit that makes you feel that here's this very cool, important guy who's noticing you and liking you enough to give you shit. Sometimes he'll wink at you for no reason. If all that doesn't sound like a big deal, you have to remember that these pro reporters have to spend a lot of time around politicians, and most politicians are painful to be around. As one national pencil told *Rolling Stone* and another nonpro, "If you saw more of how the other candidates conduct themselves, you'd be way more impressed with [McCain]. It's that he acts somewhat in the ballpark of the way a real human being would act." And the grateful press on the Trail transmit — maybe even exaggerate — McCain's humanity to their huge audience, the electorate, which electorate in turn seems so paroxysmically thankful for a presidential candidate *somewhat in the ballpark of a real human being* that it has to make you stop and think about how starved voters are for just some minimal level of genuineness in the men who want to "lead" and "inspire" them.

There are, of course, some groups of Young Voters who are way, way into modern politics. There's Rowdy Ralph Reed's far-Right Christians for one, and then out at the other end of the spectrum there's ACT UP and the sensitive men and angry womyn of the PC Left. It is interesting, though, that what gives these small fringe blocs such disproportionate power is the simple failure of most mainstream Young Voters to get off their ass and vote. It's like we all learned in social studies back in junior high: If I vote and you don't, my vote counts double. And it's not just the fringes who benefit — the fact is that it is to some very powerful Establishments' advantage that most younger people hate politics and don't vote. This, too, deserves to be thought about, if you can stand it.

There's another thing John McCain always says. He makes sure he concludes every speech and THM with it, so the buses' press hear it about 100 times this week. He always pauses a second for effect and then says: "I'm going to tell you something. I may have said some things here today that maybe you don't agree with, and I might have said some things you hopefully do agree with. But I will always. Tell you. The truth." This is McCain's closer, his last big reverb on the six-string as it were. And the frenzied standing-O it always gets from his audience is something to see. But you have to wonder. Why do these crowds from Detroit to Charleston cheer so wildly at a simple promise not to lie?

Well, it's obvious why. When McCain says it, the people are cheering not for him so much as for how good it feels to believe him. They're cheering the loosening of a weird sort of knot in the electoral tummy. McCain's résumé and candor, in other words, promise not empathy with voters' pain but relief from it. Because we've been lied to and lied to, and it hurts to be lied to. It's ultimately just about that complicated: it hurts. We learn this at like age four — it's grownups' first explanation to us of why it's bad to lie ("How would *you* like it if . . . ?"). And we keep learning for years, from hard experience, that getting lied to sucks — that it diminishes you, denies you respect for yourself, for the liar, for the world. Especially if the lies are chronic, systemic, if experience seems to teach that everything you're supposed to believe in's really just a game based on lies. Young Voters have been taught well and thoroughly. You may not personally remember Vietnam or Watergate, but it's a good bet you remember "No new taxes" and "Out of the loop" and "No direct knowledge of any impropriety at this time" and "Did not inhale" and "Did not have sex with that Ms. Lewinsky" and etc. etc. It's painful to believe that the would-be "public servants" you're forced to choose between are all phonies whose only real concern is their own care and feeding and who will lie so outrageously and with such a straight face that you know they've just got to believe you're an idiot. So who wouldn't yawn and turn away, trade apathy and cynicism for the hurt of getting treated with contempt? And who wouldn't fall all over themselves for a top politician who actually seemed to talk to you like you were a person, an intelligent adult worthy of respect? A politician who all of a sudden out of nowhere comes on TV as this total long-shot candidate and says that Washington is paralyzed, that everybody there's been bought off, and that the only way to really "return government to the people" as all the other candidates claim they want to do is to outlaw huge unreported political contributions from corporations and lobbies and PACs . . . all of which are obvious truths that everybody knows but no recent politician anywhere's had the stones to say. Who wouldn't cheer, hearing stuff like this, especially from a guy we know chose to sit in a dark box for four years instead of violate a Code? Even in AD 2000, who among us is so cynical that he doesn't have some good old corny American hope way down deep in his heart, lying dormant like a spinster's ardor, not dead but just waiting for the right guy to give it to? That John S. McCain III opposed making Martin Luther King's birthday a holiday in Arizona, or that he thinks clear-cut logging is good for America, or that he feels our present gun laws are not clinically insane — this stuff counts for nothing with these Town Hall crowds, all on their feet, cheering their own ability to finally really fucking *cheer*.

And are these crowds all stupid, or naive, or all over 40? Look again. And if you still think Young Voters as a generation have lost the ability — or transcended the desire — to believe in a politician, take a good look at *Time* magazine's shots of the South Carolina rave, or at the wire photos of Young NH Voters on the night McCain won there.

But then look at the photos of McCain's own face that night. He's the only one not smiling. Why? Can you guess? It's because now he might possibly win. At the start, on PBS and C-SPAN, in his shitty little campaign van with just his wife and a couple aides, he was running about 3 percent in the polls. And it's easy (or at least comparatively easy) to tell the truth when there's nothing to lose. New Hampshire changed everything. The 7 Feb. issues of all three big newsmagazines have good shots of McCain's face right at the moment the NH results are being announced. It's worth looking hard at his eyes in these photos. Now there's something to lose, or to win. Now it gets complicated, the campaign and the chances and the strategy; and complication is dangerous, because the truth is rarely complicated. Complication usually has more to do with mixed motives, gray areas, compromise. On the news, the first ominous rumble of this new complication was McCain's bobbing and weaving around questions about South Carolina's Confederate flag. That was a couple days ago. Now everybody's watching. Don't think the Trail's press have nothing at stake in this. There are two big questions about McCain now, today, as everyone starts the two-week slog through SC. The easy question, the one all the pencils and heads spend their time on, is whether he'll win. The other — the one posed by those photos' eyes — is hard to even put into words.

* * *

NEGATIVITY

7 to 13 February is pitched to *Rolling Stone* as a real "down week" on the GOP Trail, an interval almost breathtaking in its political unsexiness. Last week was the NH shocker; next week is the mad dash to SC's 19 Feb. primary, which the Twelve Monkeys all believe could now make or break both McCain and the Shrub. This week is the trenches: flesh-pressing, fund-raising, traveling, poll-taking, strategizing, grinding out eight-event days in Michigan and Georgia and New York and SC. The Daily Press Schedule goes from twelve-point type to ten-. Warren MI Town Hall Meeting in Ukrainian Cultural Center. Saginaw County GOP Lincoln Day Dinner. Editorial Meeting w/ *Detroit News*. Press Conference at Weird Meth Lab–Looking Internet Company in Flint. Red-Eye to North Savannah on Chartered 707 with Faint *PanAm* Still Stenciled on Tail. Spartanburg SC Town Hall Meeting. Charleston Closed-Circuit TV Reception for McCain Supporters in Three States. AARP Town Forum. North Augusta THM. Live Town Hall Forum at Clemson U with Chris Matthews of MSNBC's *Hardball.* Goose Creek THM. Press Conference in Greenville. Door-to-Door Campaigning with Congressmen Lindsey Graham and Mark Sanford and Senator Fred Thompson (R-TN) and About 300 Media in Florence SC. NASCAR Tour and Test-Drive at Darlington Raceway. National Guard Armory THM in Fort Mill. Six Hours Flying for Two-Hour Fund-Raiser with NYC Supporters. Congressman Lindsey Graham Hosts Weird BBQ for a Lot of Flinty-Eyed Men in Down Vests and Trucker's Hats in Seneca SC. Book Signing at Chapter 11 Books in Atlanta. Taping of *Tim Russert Show* for CNBC. Greer THM. Cyber-Fund-Raiser in Charleston. *Larry King Live* with Larry King Looking Even More Like a Giant Bug than Usual. Press-Avail in Sumter. Walterboro THM. On and on. Breakfast a Krispy Kreme, lunch a sandwich in Saran and store-brand chips, supper anyone's guess. Everyone but McCain is grim and tired. "We're in maybe a little bit of a trough in terms of excitement," Travis concedes in his orientation for new pencils on Monday morning . . .

. . . Until that very day's big tactical shift, which catches the McCain press corps unawares and gets all sorts of stuff under way for midweek's dramatic tactical climax, the Chris Duren Incident, all of which is politically sexy and exciting as hell, though not quite in the kind of way you cheer for.

The big tactical shift starts in the F&F Room of something called the Riverfront Hotel in the almost unbelievably blighted and depressing Flint MI, where all the Express's and Pimpmobile's media are at 1500h on 7 February while McCain is huddled with the staff High Command in a suite upstairs. In the primary campaign there is no more definitive behind-the-scenes locale than an F&F Room, which is usually some hotel's little third-string banquet- or meeting room off the lobby that McCain2000 rents (at the media's expense, precisely prorated and tallied, just like each day's seat on the buses and plane and the continental breakfasts before Baggage Call and even the F&F Rooms' "catered lunches," which today are strange bright-red ham on Wonder Bread, Fritos, and coffee that tastes like hot water with a brown crayon in it, and the pencils all bitch about the McCain2000 food and wistfully recount rumors that the Bush2000 press lunches are supposedly hot and multi–food group and served on actual plates by unctuous men with white towels over their arm) so that those media with PM deadlines can finish their stories and file and feed. In Flint, the F&F Room is a 60' × 50' banquet room with fluorescent chandeliers and overpat- terned carpet and eight long tables with fax machines, outlets and jacks, and folding chairs (padded) for the corps to sit in and open notebooks and set up laptops and Sony SX- and DVS-Series Digital Editors and have at it. By 1515h, each chair is filled by a producer or pencil trying to eat and type and talk on the phone all at once, and there's an enormous bespectacled kid of unknown origin and status going around with NoGlare™ Computer Screen Light Filters and Power Strip™ Anti-Surge Eight-Slot Adapters and offering tech- nical support for people whose laptops or phones are screwing up, and Travis and Todd and the other Press Liaisons are handing out reams of daily press releases, and the whole F&F Room is up and running and alive with the quadruple-ding of Windows booting up, the honk and static of modem connections, the multiphase clicking of 40+ keyboards, the needly screech of fax gear saying hi to New York and Atlanta, and the murmur of people on headset phones doing the same. The Twelve Monkeys have their own long table and are seated there in some very precise hierarchical order known only to them, each positioned exactly the same with his ankles crossed under his chair and a steno notebook and towering bottle of Evian at his left hand.

Everyone seems very touchy about anybody looking over their shoulder to see what they're working on.

Those McCain2000 media without any sort of daily deadline — meaning the techs, a very young guy from one of those weeklies that people can pick up free at Detroit supermarkets, and (after having no luck wandering around the tables trying to look over people's shoulders) *Rolling Stone* — are at the back of the F&F Room on a sort of very long makeshift ottoman composed of coats and luggage and non-hard cases of electronic gear. Even the network techs, practically Zen masters at waiting around and killing time, are bored out of their minds at today's F&F, where after racing back and forth to get all their gear off the bus in this bad neighborhood and making a chaise of it (the gear) here in the back there's nothing to do but they also can't really go anywhere because their field producer might suddenly need help feeding tape. The way the techs handle deep boredom is to become extremely sluggish and torpid, so that lined up on the ottoman they look like an exhibit of lizards whose tank isn't hot enough. Nobody reads. Pulse rates are about 40. The ABC cameraman lets his eyes almost close and naps in an unrestful way. The CBS and CNN techs, who like cards, today are not even bothering to play cards but are instead recounting memorable card games they've been in in the past. When *Rolling Stone* rejoins the techs here in the back there's a brief and not unkind discussion of deadline-journalism's privations and tensions and why looking over reporters' shoulders when they're typing is a faux pas. There are a lot of undistributed Power Strip adapters lying around, and for a while the techs do a gentle snipe hunting–type put-on of the Detroit-free-weekly kid involving plugging in a whole lot of multi-outlet Power Strips and playing something they claim is called Death Cribbage, complete with rules and fake anecdotes about games of Death Cribbage in past F&F Rooms, until Jim C. finally explains that they're just kidding and says the kid (who's extremely nervous-seeming and eager to please) might as well put all the Power Strips back.

It's taken less than a day to learn that the network techs — most of whom, granted, look and dress like aging roadies but are nevertheless 100 percent pro when it comes time to scrum or film a THM — are exponentially better to hang out with and listen to than anybody else on the Trail. It's true that McCain's younger staff and Press Liaisons are all very cool and laid-back and funny, with a very likable sort of Ivy League–frathouse camaraderie between them (their big thing this week is to come up to each other and pantomime karate-chopping the person's neck and yell "Hiiii-*ya!*" so loudly that it annoys the Twelve Monkeys), but their camaraderie is insular, sort of like a military unit that's been through combat together, and they're markedly cautious and reserved around pencils, and even off-record won't talk very much about themselves or the campaign, clearly warned by the High Command to avoid diverting attention from their candidate or letting something slip that could hurt him in the press.

Even the techs can be guarded if you come on too strong. Here at the Flint F&F, one of the sound guys recounts an unverified and almost incredible incident involving some older tech friends of his actually *smoking dope* in the lavatory of then-candidate Jimmy Carter's campaign plane in Feb. '76 — "There was some real wild shit went on back then, a lot more, like, you know, relaxed than the Trail is now" — but when he's asked for these older friends' names and phone numbers (another serious faux pas, Jim C. explains later) the sound guy's face clouds and he refuses both the names and permission to put the narrative in the *RS* notebook under any attribution less general than "one of the sound guys," so the incident is mentioned here only as unverified, and for the rest of the week this particular sound guy clams up completely whenever he sees *Rolling Stone* anyplace around, which feels both sad and kind of flattering.

"OTS" is, as previously mentioned, Trailese for "Opportunity to Smoke," which with very few exceptions only the techs seem to do — and do a *lot* — and which is prohibited on the buses even if you promise to exhale very carefully out the window; and so just about the only good thing about F&Fs is that they're basically one long OTS, although even here you have to go all the way outside in the cold and look at Flint, and the techs are required to get permission from their producers and let them know exactly where they'll be. Outside the Riverfront's side door off the parking lot, where it's so cold and windy you have to smoke with mittens on (a practice *Rolling Stone* in no way recommends), Jim C. and his longtime friend and partner Frank C. detail various other Trail faux pas and expand with no small sympathy on the brutality of these campaign reporters' existence: living out of suitcases and trying to keep their clothes pressed; praying that that night's hotel has room service; subsisting on the Campaign Diet, which is basically sugar and caffeine (diabetes is apparently the Black Lung of political journalism). Plus constant deadlines, and the pencils' only friends on the Trail are also their competitors, whose articles they're always reading but trying to do it secretly so they don't look insecure. Four young men in jackets over sweatshirts with the hoods all the way up are circling the press's Pimpmobile bus and boosting each other up to try the windows, and the two veteran techs just roll their eyes and wave. The Pimpmobile's driver is nowhere in sight — no one knows where drivers go during F&Fs (though there are theories). Also not recommended is trying to smoke in a high wind while jumping up and down in place. Plus, the NBC techs say, it's not just campaigns:

political media are always on the road in some type of box for
weeks at a time, very alone, connected to loved ones only by cell
phone and 1-800 answering service. *Rolling Stone* speculates that
this is maybe why everybody in the McCain2000 press corps, from
techs to 12M, sports a wedding band — it's important to feel like
there's someone to come home to. (His wife's slightly obsessive
micromanagement of his health aside, Jim C. credits her presence
on the Trail with preserving his basic sanity, at which Frank C. drolly
credits his own wife's absence from the Trail with preserving same.)
Neither tech smokes filtereds. *Rolling Stone* mentions being in hotels
every night, which before the faux pas shut him down as a source
the unnamed sound guy had said was probably the McCain campaign media's number-one stressor. The Shrub apparently stays in
five-star places with putting greens and spurting-nymph fountains
and a speed-dial number for the house masseur. Not McCain2000,
which favors Marriott, Courtyard by Marriott, Hampton Inn, Signature Inn, Radisson, Holiday Inn, Embassy Suites. *Rolling Stone,* who
is in no way cut out to be a road journalist, invokes the soul-killing
anonymity of chain hotels, the rooms' terrible transient sameness:
the ubiquitous floral design of the bedspreads, the multiple low-
watt lamps, the pallid artwork bolted to the wall, the schizoid whisper of ventilation, the sad shag carpet, the smell of alien cleansers,
the Kleenex dispensed from the wall, the automated wake-up call,
the lightproof curtains, the windows that do not open — ever. The
same TV with the same cable with the same voice saying "Welcome
to _____" on its menu channel's eight-second loop. The sense
that everything in the room's been touched by a thousand hands
before. The sounds of others' plumbing. *RS* asks whether it's any
wonder that over half of all US suicides take place in chain hotels.
Jim and Frank say they get the idea. Frank raises a ski glove in
farewell as the young men at the bus finally give up and withdraw.
RS references the chain hotel's central paradox: the form of hospitality with none of the feeling — cleanliness becomes sterility, the
politeness of the staff a vague rebuke. The terrible oxymoron of

"hotel *guest*." Hell could easily be a chain hotel. Is it any coincidence that McCain's POW prison was known as the Hanoi *Hilton*? Jim shrugs; Frank says you get used to it, that it's better not to dwell. Network camera and sound techs earn incredible overtime for staying in the field with a campaign over long periods. Frank C. has been with McCain2000 w/o break since early January and won't rotate out until Easter; the money will finance three months off during which he'll engineer indie records and sleep till eleven and not think once of hotels or scrums or the weird way your kidneys hurt after jouncing all day on a bus.

Monday afternoon, the first and only F&F in Michigan, is also *Rolling Stone*'s introduction to the Cellular Waltz, one of the most striking natural formations of the Trail. There's a huge empty lobby-like space you have to pass through to get from the Riverfront's side doors back to the area where the F&F and bathrooms are. It takes a long time to traverse this space, a hundred yards of nothing but flagstone walls and plaques with the sad pretentious names of the Riverfront's banquet/conference rooms — the Oak Room, the Windsor Room — but on return from the OTS now out here are also half a dozen different members of the F&F Room's press, each 50 feet away from any of the others, for privacy, and all walking in idle counterclockwise circles with a cell phone to their ear. These little orbits are the Cellular Waltz, which is probably the digital equivalent of doodling or picking at yourself as you talk on a regular landline. There's something oddly lovely about the Waltz's different circles here, which are of various diameters and stride-lengths and rates of rotation but are all identically counterclockwise and telephonic. We three slow down a bit to watch; you couldn't not. From above — if there were a mezzanine, say — the Waltzes would look like the cogs of some strange diffuse machine. Frank C. says he can tell by their faces something's up. Jim C., who's got his elderberry in one hand and cough syrup in the other, says what's interesting is that media south of the equator do the exact same Cellular Waltz, but that down there the circles are reversed.

And it turns out Frank C. was right as usual, that the reason press were dashing out and Waltzing urgently in the lobby is that sometime during our OTS word had apparently started to spread in the F&F Room that Mr. Mike Murphy of the McCain2000 High Command was coming down to do a surprise impromptu -Avail regarding a fresh two-page press release (still slightly warm from the Xerox) which Travis and Todd are passing out even now, and of which the first page is reproduced here:

FOR IMMEDIATE RELEASE   CONTACT: XXXXXXXXXX
February 7, 2000   XXXXXXXXXX

Bush Campaign Caught Red-Handed With Negative Ads, Unethical "Push-Polling"

Outraged South Carolinians Unite Against False Advertising, Universally Condemned Negative Polling Practice, McCain Volunteer Army Waiting With Tape Recorders to Catch Bush in the Act

COLUMBIA, SC — Deceptive TV ads and negative "push polls" conducted by phone in South Carolina last night by a polling firm employed by Texas Governor George W. Bush's campaign prompted outrage from Palmetto State voters who received the calls. One of these citizens joined Congressmen Lindsey Graham, SC House Majority Leader Rick Quinn and State Representative Dan Tripp at a press conference in Columbia today calling on Governor Bush to honor his pledge to run a positive campaign.

One of the most glaring distortions in the Bush TV ad is his contention that his plan puts $2 trillion into saving Social Security when, in fact, that money is required by law to be dedicated to the retirement plan. The other is the ads false contention that former Congressman Vin Webber, a prominent McCain supporter, praised the Bush plan.

"George Bush's claim that he somehow invented the Social Security surplus is as true as Al Gore's claim to have invented the Internet," said Quinn. "The Bush plan doesn't add a nickel to the Social Security trust fund. The bottom line is that John McCain's plan is right and George W. Bush's plan – and his TV ad – are both dead wrong."

Push polling is the practice, condemned by political professionals in both parties, of conducting a phony poll which actually attacks an opponent with false or misleading accusations.

One South Carolinian who received the calls took extensive notes of the questions asked. The poll, conducted by Voter Consumer Research (Bush pollster Jan Van Lohuizen's company which identified itself at the beginning of each call and provided a phone number to that firm) "pushed" call recipients with "facts" such as:

- Do you agree with the part of [McCain's] tax plan that increases^(taxes?) on contributions to colleges, charities and churches by $20 million?

The McCain tax plan does not tax charitable contributions. Under current law, a wealthy taxpayer can buy a painting for $10,000, have a "friendly" appraiser estimate its value at $100,000 and claim a deduction for the higher value by donating it to a charitable institution. This practice unfairly shifts the tax burden to middle income taxpayers.

--MORE--

XXXXXXXXXXXXXXXXXXXXXXX
XXXXXXXXXXXXXXXXXXXXXXXXXXXXXXXXXXXXXXX
XXXXXXXXXXXXXXXXXXXXXXXXXXXXXXXXXXXXXXXXXXXXXXXXXXX

Paid for by McCain 2000, Inc.

This document is unusual not only because McCain2000's press
releases are normally studies in bland irrelevance — "McCAIN TO
CONTINUE CAMPAIGNING IN MICHIGAN TODAY"; "McCAIN
HAS TWO HELPINGS OF POTATO SALAD AT SOUTH CAR-
OLINA VFW PICNIC" — but because no less a personage than Mike
Murphy has indeed now just come down to spin this abrupt change
of tone in the campaign's rhetoric. Murphy, who is only 37 but seems
older, is the McCain campaign's Senior Strategist, a professional
political consultant who's already had eighteen winning Senate and
gubernatorial campaigns and is as previously mentioned a constant
and acerbic presence in McCain's press salon aboard the Express.
He's a short, bottom-heavy man, pale in a sort of yeasty way, with
baby-fine red hair on a large head and sleepy turtle eyes behind the
same type of intentionally nerdy hornrims that a lot of musicians
and college kids now wear. He has short thick limbs and blunt
extremities and is always seen either slumped low in a chair or leaning on something. Oxymoron or no, what Mike Murphy looks like is
a giant dwarf. Among political pros, he has the reputation of being
(1) smart and funny as hell, and (2) a real attack-dog, working for
clients like Oliver North, New Jersey's Christine Todd Whitman, and
Michigan's own John Engler in campaigns that were absolute operas
of nastiness, and known for turning out what the *NY Times* delicately
calls "some of the most rough-edged commercials in the business."
He's leaning back against the F&F Room's wall in that way where you
have your hands behind your lower back and sort of bounce forward
and back on the hands, wearing exactly what he'll wear all week —
yellow twill trousers and brown Wallabies and an ancient and very
cool-looking brown leather jacket — and surrounded in a 180-degree
arc by the Twelve Monkeys, all of whom have steno notebooks or tiny
professional tape recorders out and keep clearing their throats and
pushing their glasses up with excitement.

Murphy says he's "just swung by" to provide the press corps with
some context on the strident press release and to give the corps
"advance notice" that the McCain campaign is also preparing a

special "response ad" that will start airing in South Carolina tomorrow. Murphy uses the words "response" or "response ad" nine times in two minutes, and when one of the Twelve Monkeys interrupts to ask whether it'd be fair to characterize this new ad as Negative, Murphy gives him a styptic look and spells *"r-e-s-p-o-n-s-e"* out very slowly. What he's leaning and bouncing against is the part of the wall between the room's door and the little round table still piled with uneaten sandwiches (to which latter the hour has not been kind), and the Twelve Monkeys and some field producers and lesser pencils form a half scrum around him, with various press joining the back or peeling away to go out and phone these new developments in to HQ.

Mike Murphy tells the hemispheric scrum that the press release and new ad reflect the McCain2000 campaign's decision, after much agonizing, to respond to what he says is Governor G. W. Bush's welching on the two candidates' public handshake-agreement in January to run a bilaterally positive campaign. For the past five days, mostly in New York and SC, the Shrub has apparently been running ads that characterize McCain's policy proposals in what Murphy terms a "willfully distorting" way. Plus there's the push-polling (see press release *supra*), a practice that is regarded as the absolute bottom-feeder of sleazy campaign tactics (Rep. Lindsey Graham, introducing McCain at tomorrow's THMs, will describe push-polling to South Carolina audiences as "the crack cocaine of modern politics"). But the worst, the most obviously unacceptable, Murphy emphasizes, was the Shrub standing up at a podium in SC a couple days ago with a wild-eyed and apparently notorious "fringe veteran" who publicly accused John McCain of "'abandoning his fellow veterans'" after returning from Vietnam, which, Murphy says, without going into Senator McCain's well-documented personal bio and heroic legislative efforts on behalf of vets for nearly 20 years (Murphy's voice rises an octave here, and blotches of color appear high on his cheeks, and it's clear he's personally hurt and aggrieved, which means that either he maybe really personally likes and believes in John S. McCain III or else has the frightening ability to raise angry blotches on his cheeks at will, the way certain great actors can make themselves cry on cue), is just so clearly over the line of even minimal personal decency and honor that it pretty much necessitates some kind of response.

The Twelve Monkeys, who are old pros at this sort of exchange, keep trying to steer Murphy away from what the Shrub's done and get him to give a quotable explanation of why McCain himself has decided to run this response ad, a transcript of which Travis and Todd are now distributing from a fresh copier box and which is, with various parties' indulgence, also now reproduced here —

VIDEO COPY

RADIO: TELEVISION: XX

DATE: February 06, 2000 TIME: :30

PRODUCERS: Stevens Reed Curcio & Company

CLIENT: McCain 2000   *Draft*

TITLE: "Desperate "

CODE:

VIDEO: AUDIO:

McCain: "I guess it was bound to happen.

Governor Bush's campaign is getting desperate with a negative ad about me.

The fact is, I will use the surplus money to fix Social Security, cut your taxes, and pay down the debt.

Governor Bush uses all the surplus for tax cuts, with not one new penny for Social Security or the debt.

His ad twists the truth like Clinton. We're all pretty tired of that.

As President, I'll be conservative, and always tell you the truth, no matter what.

© 2000 All Rights Reserved.
Stevens Reed Curcio & Company.

— of which ad-transcript the 12M point out that in particular the "twists the truth like Clinton" part seems Negative indeed, since in '00 comparing a Republican candidate to Bill Clinton is roughly equivalent to claiming that he worships Satan. But Mike Murphy — part of whose job as Senior Strategist is to act as a kind of diversionary lightning rod for any tactical criticism of McCain himself — says that he, Mike Murphy, was actually the driving force behind the ad's "strong response," that he "pushed real hard" for the ad and finally got "the campaign" to agree only after "a great deal of agonizing, because Senator McCain's been very clear with you guys about wanting a campaign we can all be proud of." One thing political reporters are really good at, though, is rephrasing a query ever so slightly so that they're able to keep asking the same basic question over and over when they don't get the answer they want, and after several minutes of this they finally get Murphy to bring his hands out and up in a kind of what-are-you-gonna-do and to say "Look, I'm not going to let them go around smearing my guy for five days without retaliating," which then leads to several more minutes of niggling semantic questions about the difference between "respond" and "retaliate," at the end of which Murphy, reaching slowly over and poking at one of the table's sandwiches with clinical interest, says "If Bush takes down his negative ads, we'll pull the response right away. Immediately. Quote me." Then turning to go. "That's all I swung by to tell you." The back of his leather jacket has a spot of what's either Wite-Out™ or bird guano on it. Murphy is hard not to like, though in a very different way from his candidate. Where McCain comes off almost brutally open and direct, Murphy's demeanor is sly and cagey in a twinkly-eyed way that makes you think he's making fun of his own slyness. He can also be direct, though. One of the scrum's oldest and most elite 12M calls out one last time that surely after all there aren't any guns to the candidates' heads in this race, that surely Mike (the Monkeys call him Mike) would have to admit that simply refusing to "quote, 'respond'" to Bush and thereby "staying on the high road" was something

McCain could have done; and Murphy's *dernier cri*, over his shoulder, is "You guys want a pacifist, go support Bradley."

For the remainder of the at least half hour more before John McCain is finally ready to get back on the Express (N.B.: McCain is later revealed to have had a sore throat today, apparently sending his staff into paroxysms of terror that he was coming down with the same Campaign Flu that's been ravaging the press corps [Jim C.'s own Campaign Flu will turn into bronchitis and then probably slight pneumonia, and for three days in South Carolina the whole rest of Bullshit 1's regulars will rearrange themselves to give Jim a couch to himself to sleep on during long DTs, because he's really sick, and it isn't until Friday that there's enough free time for Jim even to go get antibiotics, and still all week he's up and filming every speech and scrum, and in *RS*'s opinion he is incredibly brave and uncomplaining about the Campaign Flu, unlike the Twelve Monkeys, many of whom keep taking their temperatures and feeling their glands and whining into their cell phones to be rotated out, so that by midweek in SC there are really only nine Monkeys, then eight Monkeys, although the techs, out of respect for tradition, keep referring to them as the Twelve Monkeys], and it later emerges that the Flint F&F was so protracted because Mrs. McC. and Wendy and McCain2000 Political Director John Weaver had McCain up there gargling and breathing steam and pounding echinacea) to head over to Saginaw, the techs, while checking their equipment and gearing up for the scrum at the Riverfront's main doors, listen to *Rolling Stone*'s summary of the press release and Murphy's comments, confirm that the Shrub has indeed gone Negative (they'd heard about all this long before the Twelve Monkeys et al. because the techs and field producers are in constant touch with their colleagues on the Shrub's buses, whereas the Monkeys' Bush2000 counterparts are as aloof and niggardly about sharing info as the 12M themselves), and kill the last of the time in the Flint F&F by quietly analyzing $Bush_2$'s Negativity and McCain's response from a tactical point of view.

Leaving aside their aforementioned coolness and esprit de corps, you should be apprised that *Rolling Stone's* one and only journalistic coup this week is his happening to bumble into hanging around with these camera and sound guys. This is because network news techs — who all have worked countless campaigns, and who have neither the raging egos of journalists nor the political self-interest of the McCain2000 staff to muddy their perspective — turn out to be more astute and sensible political analysts than anybody you'll read or see on TV, and their assessment of today's Negativity developments is so extraordinarily nuanced and sophisticated that only a small portion of it can be ripped off and summarized here.

Going Negative is risky. Polls have shown that most voters find Negativity big-time distasteful, and if a candidate is perceived as getting nasty, it usually costs him. So the techs all agree that the first big question is why Bush2000 started playing the Negativity card. One possible explanation is that the Shrub was so personally shocked and scared by McCain's win in New Hampshire that he's now lashing out like a spoiled child and trying to hurt McCain however he can. The techs reject this, though. Spoiled child or no, Governor Bush is a creature of his campaign advisors, and these advisors are the best that $70,000,000 and the full faith and credit of the GOP Establishment can buy, and they are not spoiled children but seasoned tactical pros, and if Bush2000 has gone Negative there must be solid political logic behind the move.

This logic turns out to be indeed solid, even inspired, and the NBC, CBS, and CNN techs flesh it out while the ABC cameraman puts several emergency sandwiches in his lens bag for tonight's flight south on a campaign plane whose provisioning is notoriously inconsistent. The Shrub's attack leaves McCain with two options. If he does not retaliate, some SC voters will credit McCain for keeping to the high road. But it could also come off as wimpy, and so compromise McCain's image as a tough, take-no-shit guy with the courage to face down the Washington kleptocracy. Not responding might also look like "appeasing aggression," which for a candidate whose background is military and who spends a lot of time talking about rebuilding the armed forces and being less of a candy-ass in foreign policy would not be good, especially in a state with a higher percentage of both vets and gun nuts than any other (which SC is). So McCain pretty much has to hit back, the techs agree. But this is extremely dangerous, for by retaliating — which of course (despite all Murphy's artful dodging) means going Negative himself — McCain runs the risk of looking like just another ambitious, win-at-any-cost politician, when of course so much time and effort and money have already gone into casting him as the exact opposite of that. Plus an even bigger reason McCain can't afford to let the Shrub "pull him down to his level" (this in the phrase of the CBS cameraman, a Louisianan who's quite a bit shorter than the average tech and so besides all his other equipment has to lug a little aluminum stepladder around to stand on with his camera during scrums, which decreases his mobility but is compensated for by what the other techs agree is an almost occult talent for always finding the perfect place to set up his ladder and film at just the right angle for what his HQ wants — Jim C. says the tiny southerner is "technically about as good as they come") is that if Bush then turns around and retaliates against the retaliation and so McCain then has to re-retaliate against Bush's retaliation, and so on and so forth, then the whole GOP race could quickly degenerate into just the sort of boring, depressing, cynical, charge-and-countercharge contest that turns voters off and keeps them away from the polls . . . especially Young Voters, cynicism-wise, *Rolling Stone* and the underage pencil from the free Detroit weekly thing venture to point out, both now scribbling just as furiously with the techs as the 12M were with Murphy. The techs say well OK maybe but that the really important tactical point here is that John S. McCain *cannot* afford to have voters get turned off, since his whole strategy is based on exciting the people and inspiring them and pulling more voters *in*, especially those who'd stopped voting because they'd gotten so disgusted and bored with all the Negativity and bullshit of politics. In other words, *RS* and the Detroit-free-weekly kid propose to the techs, it's maybe actually in the Shrub's own political self-interest to let the GOP race get ugly and Negative and have voters get so bored and cynical and disgusted with the whole thing that they don't even bother to vote. Well no shit Sherlock H., the ABC techs in essence respond, good old Frank C. then explaining more patiently that, yes, if there's a low voter turnout, then the majority of the people who get off their ass and *do* vote will be the Diehard Republicans, meaning the Christian Right and the party faithful, and these are the groups that vote as they're told, the ones controlled by the GOP Establishment, an Establishment that as already mentioned has got all its cash and credibility invested in the Shrub. CNN's Mark A. takes time out from doing special stretching exercises that increase blood-flow to his arms (sound techs are very arm-conscious, since positioning a boom mike correctly in a scrum requires holding ten-foot sticks and 4.7-pound boom mikes [that's 4.7 without the weasel] horizontally out by their fully extended arms for long periods [which try this with an industrial broom or extension pruner sometime if you think it's easy], with the added proviso that the heavy mike at the end can't wobble or dip into the cameras' shot or [God forbid, and there are horror stories] clunk the candidate on the top of the head) in order to insert that this also explains why the amazingly lifelike Al Gore, over in the Democratic race, has been so relentlessly Negative and depressing in his attacks on Bill Bradley. Since Gore, like the Shrub, has his party's Establishment behind him, with all its organization and money and the Diehards who'll fall into line and vote as they're told, it's in Big Al's (and his party's bosses') interest to draw as *few* voters as possible into the Democratic primaries, because the lower the overall turnout, the more the Establishment voters' ballots actually count. Which fact then in turn, the short but highly respected CBS cameraman says, helps explain why, even though our elected representatives are always wringing their hands and making concerned

noises about low voter turnouts, nothing substantive ever gets done
to make politics less ugly or depressing or to actually induce more
people to vote: our elected representatives are incumbents, and
low turnouts favor incumbents for the same reason soft money
does.

Let's pause here one second for a quick *Rolling Stone* PSA.
Assuming you are demographically a Young Voter, it is again worth
a moment of your valuable time to consider the implications of
the techs' last couple points. If you are bored and disgusted by politics and don't bother to vote, you are in effect voting for the
entrenched Establishments of the two major parties, who please
rest assured are not dumb, and who are keenly aware that it is in
their interests to keep you disgusted and bored and cynical and to
give you every possible psychological reason to stay at home doing
one-hitters and watching MTV on primary day. By all means stay
home if you want, but don't bullshit yourself that you're not voting.
In reality, there is *no such thing as not voting:* you either vote by voting, or you vote by staying home and tacitly doubling the value of
some Diehard's vote.

So anyway, by this time all the press in the Flint F&F Room are
demodemizing and ejecting diskettes and packing up their stuff
and getting ready to go cover John McCain's 1800h speech at the
GOP Lincoln Day Dinner in Saginaw, where a Republican dressed
as Uncle Sam will show up on eight-foot stilts and totter around the
dim banquet hall through the whole thing and nearly crash into
the network crews' riser several times and irritate the hell out of
everyone, and where the Twelve Monkeys will bribe or bullshit the
headwaiter into seating them at a no-show table and feeding them
supper while all the rest of the press corps has to stand in the back
of the hall and try to help the slightly mad *Economist* guy cabbage
breadsticks when nobody's looking. Watching the techs gear up to
go scrum around McCain as he boards the Straight Talk Express is
a little like watching soldiers outfit themselves for combat: there
are numerous multipart packs and cases to strap across backs and

chests and to loop around waists and connect and lock down, and pieces of high-priced machinery to load with filters and tape and bulbs and reserve power cells and connect to each other with complex cords and co-ax cable, and weasels to wrap around high-filter boom mikes, and sticks to choose and carefully telescope out all the way till they look like the probosces of some monstrous insect and bob, slightly — the soundmen's sticks and mikes do — as the techs in the scrum keep pace with McCain and try to keep his head in the center of their shot and right underneath the long stick's mike in case he says something newsworthy. McCain has on a fresh blue pinstripe suit, and his complexion is hectic with CF fever or tactical adrenaline, and as he passes through the Riverfront lobby toward the scrum there's a faint backwash of quality aftershave, and from behind him you can see Cindy McCain using her exquisitely manicured hands to whisk invisible lint off his shoulders, and at moments like this it's difficult not to feel enthused and to really like this man and want to support him in just about any sort of feasible way you can think of.

Plus there's the single best part of every pre-scrum technical gear-up: watching the cameramen haul their heavy $40,000 rigs to their shoulders like rocket launchers and pull the safety strap tight under their opposite arm and ram the clips home with practiced ease, their postures canted under the camera's weight. It is Jim C.'s custom always to say *"Up, Simba"* in a fake-deep bwana voice as he hefts the camera to his right shoulder, and he and Frank C. like to do a little pantomime of the way football players will bang their helmets together to get pumped for a big game, although obviously the techs do it carefully and make sure their equipment doesn't touch or tangle cords.

But so the techs' assessment, then, is that Bush$_2$'s going Negative is both tactically sound and politically near-brilliant, and that it forces McCain's own strategists to walk a very tight wire indeed. What McCain has to try to do is retaliate without losing the inspiring high-road image that won him New Hampshire. This is why

Mike Murphy took valuable huddle-with-candidate time to come down to the F&F and spoon-feed the Twelve Monkeys all this stuff about Bush's attacks being so far over the line that McCain had no choice but to "respond." Because the McCain2000 campaign has got to spin today's retaliation the same way nations spin war — i.e., McCain has to make it appear that he is not actually being aggressive himself but is merely repelling aggression. It will require enormous discipline and cunning for McCain2000 to pull this off. And tomorrow's "response ad" — in the techs' opinion, as the transcript's passed around — this ad is not a promising start, discipline-and-cunning-wise, especially the "twists the truth like Clinton" line that the 12M jumped on Murphy for. This line's too mean. McCain2000 could have chosen to put together a much softer and smarter ad patiently "correcting" certain "unfortunate errors" in Bush's ads and "respectfully requesting" that the push-polling cease (with everything in quotes here being Jim C.'s suggested terms) and striking just the right high-road tone. The actual ad's "twists like Clinton" does not sound high-road; it sounds angry, aggressive. And it will allow Bush to do a React and now say that it's *McCain* who's violated the handshake-agreement and broken the 11th Commandment (= "Thou Shalt Not Speak Ill of Another Republican," which Diehard GOPs take very seriously) and gone way over the line . . . which the techs say will of course be bullshit, but it might be effective bullshit, and it's McCain's aggressive ad that's giving the Shrub the opening to do it.

If it's a mistake, then why is McCain doing it? By this time the techs are on the bus, after the hotel-exit scrum but before the Saginaw-entrance scrum, and since it's only a ten-minute ride they have their cameras down and sticks retracted but all their gear still strapped on, which forces them to sit up uncomfortably straight and wince at bumps, and in the Pimpmobile's mirrored ceiling they look even more like sci-fi combat troops on their way to some alien beachhead. The techs' basic analysis of the motivation behind "twists the truth like Clinton" is that McCain is genuinely, personally pissed off at the Shrub, and that he has taken Mike Murphy's leash off and let Murphy do what he does best, which is gutter-fight. McCain, after all, is known to have a temper (though he's been extremely controlled in the campaign so far and never shown it in public), and Jim C. thinks that maybe the truly ingenious thing the Shrub's strategists did here was find a way to genuinely, personally piss McCain off and make him want to go Negative even though John Weaver and the rest of the staff High Command had to have warned him that he'd be playing right into Bush2000's hands. This analysis suddenly reminds *Rolling Stone* of the thing in *The Godfather* where Sonny Corleone's fatal flaw is his temper, which Barzini and Tattaglia exploit by getting Carlo to beat up Connie and make Sonny so insanely angry that he drives off to kill Carlo and gets assassinated in Barzini's ambush at that tollbooth on the Richmond Parkway. Jim C., sweating freely and trying not to cough with 40 pounds of gear on, says he supposes there are some similarities, and Randy van R. (the taciturn but cinephilic CNN cameraman) speculates that the Shrub's brain-trust may actually have based their whole strategy on Barzini's ingenious ploy in *The Godfather,* whereupon Frank C. observes that Bush$_2$'s analog to slapping Connie Corleone around was standing up with the wacko Vietnam vet who claimed that McCain abandoned his comrades, which at first looked kind of stupid and unnecessarily nasty of Bush but from another perspective might have been sheer genius if it made McCain so angry that his desire to retaliate outweighed his political judgment. Because, Frank C. warns, this retaliation, and Bush's response to it, and McCain's response to Bush's response — this will be all that the Twelve Monkeys and the rest of the pro corps are interested in, and if McCain lets things get too ugly he won't be able to get anybody to pay attention to anything else.

It would, of course, have been just interesting as hell for *Rolling Stone* to have gotten to watch the top-level meetings at which John McCain and John Weaver and Mike Murphy and the rest of the campaign's High Command hashed all this out and decided on the

press release and response ad, but of course strategy sessions like
these are journalistically impenetrable, if for no other reason than
that it is the media who are the true object and audience for whatever strategy these sessions come up with, the critics who'll decide
how well it all plays (with Murphy's special little "advance notice"
spiel in the Flint F&F being the strategy's opening performance, as
everyone in the room was aware but no one said aloud).

But it turns out to be enough just getting to hear the techs kill
time by deconstructing today's big moves, because events of the
next few days bear out their analysis pretty much 100 percent. On
Tuesday morning, on the Radisson's TV in North Savannah SC,
both *Today* and *GMA* lead with "The GOP campaign takes an ugly
turn" and show the part of McCain's new ad where he says "twists
the truth like Clinton"; and sure enough by midday the good old
Shrub has put out a React where he accuses John S. McCain of violating the handshake-agreement and going Negative and says (the
Shrub does) that he (the Shrub) is "personally offended and outraged" at being compared to Bill Clinton; and at six THMs and
-Avails in a row all around South Carolina McCain carps about
the push-polling and "Governor Bush's surrogates' attacking [him]
and accusing [him] of abandoning America's veterans," each time
sounding increasingly reedy and peevish and with a vein that
nobody's noticed before appearing to bulge and throb in his left
temple when he starts in on the veteran thing; and then at a Press-
Avail in Hilton Head the Shrub avers that he knows less than nothing about any so-called push-polling and suggests that the whole
thing might have been fabricated as a sleazy political ploy on
McCain2000's part; and then on Wednesday AM on TV at the
Embassy Suites in Charleston there's now an even *more* aggressive
ad that Murphy's gotten McCain to let him run, which new ad
accuses Bush of unilaterally violating the handshake-agreement
and going Negative and then shows a nighttime shot of 1600 Pennsylvania Ave.'s famous facade with its palisade of blatantly ejacula-
tory fountains in the foreground and says *"Can America afford*

another politician in the White House that we can't trust?," about which nobody mentions the grammatical problems but Frank C. says that the shot of the White House is really going low with the knife, and that if McCain loses South Carolina it may very well be because of this ad; and sure enough by Wednesday night focus polls are showing that South Carolina voters are finding McCain's new ad Negative and depressing, polls that the Shrub then seizes on and crows about while meanwhile Bush2000's strategists, "in response" to McCain's "outrageous" equation of $Bush_2$ with W. J. Clinton, which "impugns [Bush's] character and deeply offends [him]," start running a new ad of their own that shows a clip of the handshake in New Hampshire and then some photo of McCain looking angry and vicious and says "John McCain shook hands and promised a clean campaign, then attacked Governor Bush with misleading ads," then apparently just for good measure tosses in a sound bite from 4 Feb.'s *NBC Nightly News* that says "McCain solicited money from organizations appearing before his Senate Committee . . . and pressured agencies on behalf of his contributors," about which Jim C. (who, recall, works for NBC News) says the original *NBC Nightly News* report was actually just about Bush supporters' *charges* that McCain had done these things, and thus that the ad's bite is decontextualized in a really blatantly sleazy and misleading way, but of course by this time — Thursday, 10 Feb., 0745h, proceeding in convoy formation to the day's first THMs in Spartanburg and Greenville — it doesn't matter, because there've been so many deeply offended charges and countercharges that McCain's complaining about the deceptive NBC bite would just be one more countercharge, which Jim C. says is surely why Bush2000 felt they could distort the bite and get away with it, which verily they appear to have done, because SC polls have both McCain's support and the primary's projected voter turnout falling like rocks, and the techs are having to spend all their time helping their field producers find the "fighting words" in every speech's tape because that's all the networks want, and everyone on Bullshit 1 & 2 is starting to get severely dispirited and bored, and even the 12M's strides have lost a certain pigeon-toed spring . . .

. . . And then out of nowhere comes the dramatic tactical climax mentioned way above, which hits the media like a syringe of epinephrine and makes all five networks' news that night. It occurs at the Spartanburg THM, whose venue is a small steep theater in the Fine Arts Center of a little college nobody ever did find out the name of, and is so packed by the time the McCain2000 press corps gets there that even the aisles are full, so that everybody except the techs and their producers is out in the lobby, which is itself teeming with college kids who couldn't get a seat either and are standing around taking notes for something called Speech Com 210 — McCain's visit's apparently some sort of class assignment — and rather delighting *Rolling Stone* by continually looking over the 12M's shoulders to see what they're writing. Next to the free-pastry-and-sign-up-for-McCain2000-volunteering table is a huge oak column or stanchion or something, to each of whose four sides has been attached somehow a 24-inch color monitor that's tapping CNN's video feed, which stays tight on McCain's face against the backdrop's huge flag (Where do they *get* these giant flags? What happens to them when there's no campaign? Where do they go? Where do you even store flags that size? Or is there maybe just one, which McCain2000's advance team has to take down afterward and hurtle with to the next THM to get it put up before McCain and the cameras arrive? Do Gore and the Shrub and all the other candidates each have their own giant flag?), and if you pick your path carefully you can orbit the column very quickly and see McCain delivering his 22.5 to all points of the compass at once. The lobby's front wall is glass, and in the gravel courtyard just outside is a breathtaking 20-part Cellular Waltz going on around two local news vans throbbing at idle and raising their 40-foot microwave transmitters, plus four well-dressed local male heads with hand mikes doing their stand-ups, each attached to his tech by a cord. Compared to Schieffer and Bloom and the network talent on the

ST Express, the local male heads always seem almost alienly lurid: their makeup makes their skin orange and their lips violet, and their hair's all so gelled you can see the heads' surroundings reflected in it. The local vans' transmitters' dishes, rising like great ghastly flowers on their telescoping poles, all turn to face identically south, their pistils aimed at Southeast Regional Microwave Relay #434B near Greenville.

To be honest, all the national pencils would probably be out here in the lobby even if the theater weren't full, because after a few days McCain's opening THM 22.5 becomes wrist-slittingly dull and repetitive. Journalists who've covered McCain since Christmas report that Murphy et al. have worked hard on him to become more "message-disciplined," which in politicalspeak means reducing everything as much as possible to brief, memory-friendly slogans and then punching those slogans over and over. The result is that the McCain corps' pencils have now heard every message-disciplined bit of the 22.5 — from McCain's opening joke about getting mistaken for a grampa at his children's school, to "It doesn't take much talent to get shot down," to "the Iron Triangle of money, lobbyists, and legislation," to "Clinton's feckless photo-op foreign policy," to "As president, I won't need any on-the-job training," to "I'm going to beat Al Gore like a drum," plus two or three dozen other lines that sound like crosses between a nightclub act and a motivational seminar — so many times that they just can't stand it anymore; and while they have to be at the THMs in case anything big or Negative happens, they'll go anywhere and do just about anything to avoid having to listen to the 22.5 again, plus of course to the laughter and cheers and wild applause of a THM crowd that's hearing it all for the first time, which is basically why the pencils are all now out here in the lobby ogling coeds and arguing about which silent-movie diva's the poor local heads' eyeshadow most resembles.

In fairness to McCain, he's not an orator and doesn't pretend to be. His real métier is conversation, a back-and-forth. This is because he's bright in a fast, flexible way that most other candidates aren't. He also genuinely seems to find people and questions and arguments energizing — the latter maybe because of all his years debating in Congress — which is why he favors Town Hall Q&As and constant chats with press in his rolling salon. So, while the media marvel at his accessibility because they've been trained to equate it with vulnerability, they don't seem to realize they're playing totally to McCain's strength when they converse with him instead of listening to his speeches. In conversation he's smart and alive and human and seems actually to listen and respond directly to you instead of to some demographic abstraction you might represent. It's his speeches and 22.5s that are canned and stilted, and also sometimes scary and right-wingish, and when you listen closely to these it's as if some warm pleasant fog suddenly lifts and it strikes you that you're not at all sure it's John McCain you want choosing the head of the EPA or the at least two new justices who'll probably be coming onto the Supreme Court in the next term, and you start wondering all over again what makes the guy so attractive.

But then the doubts again dissolve when McCain starts taking questions at THMs, which by now is what's under way in Spartanburg. McCain always starts this part by telling the crowd that he invites "questions, comments, and the occasional insult from any US Marines who might be here today" (which, again, gets radically less funny with repetition [apparently the Navy and Marines tend not to like each other]). The questions always run the great vox-populi gamut, from Talmudically bearded guys asking about Chechnya and tort reform to high-school kids reading questions off printed sheets their hands shake as they hold, from moms worried about their babies' future SSI to ancient vets in Legion caps who call McCain "Lieutenant" and want to trade salutes, plus the obligatory walleyed fundamentalists trying to pin him down on whether Christ really called homosexuality an abomination (w/ McCain, to his credit, pointing out that they don't even have the right Testament), and arcane questions about index-fund regulation and postal privatization, and HMO horror stories, and Internet porn, and tobacco litigation, and people who believe the Second Amendment entitles them to own grenade launchers. The questions are random and unscreened, and the candidate fields them all, and he's never better or more human than in these exchanges, especially when the questioner is angry or wacko — McCain will say "I respectfully disagree" or "We have a difference of opinion" and then detail his objections in lucid English with a gentleness that's never condescending. For a man with a temper and a reputation for suffering fools ungladly, McCain is unbelievably patient and decent with people at THMs, especially when you consider that he's 63, sleep-deprived, in chronic pain, and under enormous pressure not to gaffe or get himself in trouble. He doesn't. No matter how stale and message-disciplined the 22.5 at the beginning, in the Town Hall Q&As you get an overwhelming sense that this is a decent, honorable man trying to tell the truth to people he really sees. You will not be alone in this impression.

Among the techs and non-simian pencils, the feeling is that McCain's single finest human moment of the campaign so far was at the Warren MI Town Hall Meeting on Monday, in the Q&A, when a middle-aged man in a sportcoat and beret, a man who didn't look in any way unusual but turned out to be insane — meaning literally, as in *DSM IV*–grade schizophrenic — came to the mike and said that the government of Michigan has a mind-control machine and influences brainwaves and that not even wrapping roll after roll of aluminum foil around your head with only the tiniest pinpricks for eyes and breathing stopped them from influencing brainwaves, and he says he wants to know whether if McCain is president he will use Michigan's mind-control machine to catch the murderers and pardon the Congress and compensate him personally for 60 long years of government mind control, and can he get it in writing. The question is not funny; the room's silence is the mortified kind. Think how easy it would have been for a candidate here to blanch or stumble, or to have hard-eyed aides remove the

man, or (worst) to make fun of the guy in order to defuse everyone's horror and embarrassment and try to score humor points
with the crowd, at which most of the younger pencils would probably have fainted dead away from cynical disgust because the poor
guy is still standing there at the mike and looking earnestly up at
McCain, awaiting an answer. Which McCain, incredibly, *sees* — the
man's humanity, the seriousness of these issues to him — and says
yes, he will, he'll promise to look into it, and yes he'll put this promise in writing, although he "believe[s] [they] have a difference of
opinion about this mind-control machine," and in sum he defuses
the insane man and treats him respectfully without patronizing
him or pretending to be schizophrenic too, and does it all so
quickly and gracefully and with such basic decency that if it was
some sort of act then McCain is the very devil himself. Which the
techs, later, after the post-THM Press-Avail and scrum, degearing
aboard the ghastly Pimpmobile, say McCain is not (the devil) and
that they were, to a man, moved by the unfakable humanity of the
exchange, and yet at the same time also impressed with McCain's
professionalism in disarming the guy, and Jim C. urges *Rolling Stone*
not to be so cynical as to reject out of hand the possibility that the
two can coexist — human genuineness and political professionalism — because it's the great yin-and-yang paradox of the McCain2000
campaign, and is so much more interesting than the sort of robotic
unhuman all-pro campaign he's used to that Jim says he almost
doesn't mind the grind this time.

Maybe they really can coexist — humanity and politics, shrewdness and decency. But it gets complicated. In the Spartanburg
Q&A, after two China questions and one on taxing Internet com-
merce, as most of the lobby's pencils are still at the glass making
fun of the local heads, a totally demographically average 30-
something middle-class soccer mom in rust-colored slacks and
those round, overlarge glasses totally average 30-something soccer
moms always wear gets picked and stands and somebody brings her
the mike. It turns out her name is Donna Duren, of right here in

Spartanburg SC, and she says she has a fourteen-year-old son named Chris, in whom Mr. and Mrs. Duren have been trying to inculcate family values and respect for authority and a noncynical idealism about America and its duly elected leaders. They want him to find heroes he can believe in, she says. Donna Duren's whole story takes a while, but nobody's bored, and even out here on the stanchion's monitors you can sense a change in the THM's theater's voltage, and the national pencils come away from the front's glass and start moving in and elbowing people aside (which they're really good at) to get close to the monitors' screens. Mrs. Duren says that Chris — clearly a sensitive kid — was "made very very upset" by the Lewinsky scandal and the R-rated revelations and the appalling behavior of Clinton and Starr and Tripp and pretty much everybody on all sides during the impeachment thing, and Chris had a lot of very upsetting and uncomfortable questions that Mr. and Mrs. D. struggled to answer, and that basically it was a really hard time but they got through it. And then last year, at more or less a trough in terms of idealism and respect for elected authority, she says, Chris had discovered John McCain and McCain2000.com, and got interested in the campaign, and the parents had apparently read him some G-rated parts of McCain's *Faith of My Fathers,* and the upshot is that young Chris finally found a public hero he could believe in: John S. McCain III. It's impossible to know what McCain's face is doing during this story because the monitors are taking CNN's feed and Randy van R. of CNN is staying hard and steady on Donna Duren, who appears so iconically prototypical and so thoroughly exudes the special quiet dignity of an average American who knows she's average and just wants a decent, noncynical life for herself and her family that she can say things like "family values" and "hero" without anybody rolling their eyes. But then last night, Mrs. D. says, as they were all watching some wholesome nonviolent TV in the family room, the phone suddenly rang upstairs, and Chris went up and got it, and Mrs. D. says a little while later he came back down into the family room crying and just terribly upset and told them the phone call had been a man who started talking to him about the 2000 campaign and asked Chris if he knew that John McCain was a liar and a cheater and that anybody who'd vote for John McCain was either stupid or un-American or both. That caller had been a push-poller for Bush2000, Mrs. Duren says, knuckles on her mike-hand white and voice almost breaking, distraught in a totally average and moving parental way, and she says she just wanted Senator McCain to know about it, about what happened to Chris, and wants to know whether anything can be done to keep people like this from calling innocent young kids and plunging them into disillusionment and confusion about whether they're stupid for trying to have heroes they believe in.

At which point (0853h) two things happen out here in the Fine Arts Center lobby. The first is that the national pencils disperse in a radial pattern, each dialing his cell phone, and the network field producers all come barreling through the theater doors pulling their cell phone antennas out with their teeth, and everybody tries to find a little empty area to Waltz in while they call the gist of this riveting Negativity-related development in to networks and editors and try to raise their counterparts in the Bush2000 press corps to see if they can get a React from the Shrub on Mrs. Duren's story, at the end of which story the second thing happens, which is that CNN's Randy van R. finally pans to McCain and you can see McCain's facial expression, which is pained and pale and looks actually more distraught even than Mrs. Duren's face had looked. And what McCain does, after staring down at the floor for a few seconds, is . . . apologize. He doesn't lash out at Bush₂ or at push-polling or appear to try to capitalize politically in any way. He looks sad and compassionate and regretful and says that the only reason he got into this race in the first place was to try to help inspire young Americans to feel better about devoting themselves to something, and that a story like what Mrs. Duren took the trouble to come down here to the THM this morning and tell him is just about the worst thing he could hear, and that if it's OK with Mrs. D. he'd like to call her son — he asks his name again, and Randy van R. pans smoothly back to Donna Duren as she says "Chris" and then pans smoothly back to McCain — Chris and apologize personally on the phone and tell Chris that yes there are unfortunately some bad people out there and he's sorry Chris had to hear stuff like what he heard but that it's never a mistake to believe in something, that politics is still worthwhile as a process to get involved in, and he really does look upset, McCain does, and almost as what seems like an afterthought he says that maybe one thing Donna Duren and other concerned parents and citizens can do is call the Bush2000 campaign and tell them to stop this push-polling, that Governor Bush is a good man with a family of his own and it's difficult to believe he'd ever endorse his campaign doing things like this if he knew about it, and that he (McCain) will be calling Governor Bush again personally for the umpteenth time to ask him to stop the Negativity, and McCain's eyes now actually look wet, as in teary, which maybe is just a trick of the TV lights but is nevertheless disturbing, the whole thing is disturbing, because McCain seems upset in a way that's a little too . . . well, almost *dramatic*. He takes a couple more THM questions, then stops abruptly and says he's sorry but he's just so upset about the Chris Duren Incident that he's having a hard time concentrating, and he asks the THM crowd's forgiveness, and thanks them, and forgets his message-discipline and doesn't finish with he'll always. Tell them. The truth, but they applaud like mad anyway, and the four-faced column's monitors' feed is cut as Randy and Jim C. et al. go shoulder-held to join the scrum as McCain starts to exit.

And now none of this is simple at all, especially McCain's almost exaggerated-seeming distress about Chris Duren, which really did seem a little much; and a large set of disturbing and possibly cynical interconnected thoughts and questions start whirling around in the old journalistic head. Like the fact that Donna Duren's story was a far, far more devastating indictment of the Shrub's campaign tactics than anything McCain himself could say, and is it possible that McCain, on the theater's stage, wasn't aware of this? Is it possible that he didn't see all the TV field producers shouldering their way through the aisles' crowds with their cell phones and know instantly that Mrs. Duren's story and his reaction were going to get big network play and make Bush2000 look bad? Is it possible that some part of McCain could realize that what happened to Chris Duren is very much to his own political advantage, and yet he's still such a decent, uncalculating guy that all he feels is horror and regret that a kid was disillusioned? Was it human compassion that made him apologize first instead of criticizing the Shrub, or is McCain maybe just shrewd enough to know that Mrs. D.'s story had already nailed Bush to the wall and that by apologizing and looking distraught McCain could help underscore the difference between his own human decency and Bush's uncaring Negativity? Is it possible that he really had tears in his eyes? Is it (ulp) possible that he somehow *made* himself get tears in his eyes because he knew what a decent, caring, non-Negative guy it would make him look like? And come to think of it hey, why would a push-poller even be interested in trying to push-poll someone who's too young to vote? Does Chris Duren maybe have a really deep-sounding phone voice or something? But wouldn't you think a push-poller'd ask somebody's age before launching into his routine? And how come nobody asked this question, not even the jaded 12M out in the lobby? What could they have been thinking?

Bullshit 1 is empty except for Jay, who's grabbing an OTC way back in the ERPP, and through the port windows you can see all the techs and heads and talent in a king-size scrum around Mrs. Donna Duren in the gravel courtyard, and there's the additional cynical thought that doubtless some enterprising network crew is even now pulling up in front of poor Chris Duren's junior high (which unfortunately tonight on TV turns out to be exactly what happened). The bus idles empty for a long time — the post-event scrums and stand-ups last longer than the whole THM did — and then when the BS1 regulars finally do pile in they're all extremely busy trying to type and phone and file, and all the techs have to get their SX and DVS Digital Editors out (the CBS machine's being held steady on their cameraman's little stepladder in the aisle because all the tables and the ERPP are full) and help their producers find and time the clip of Mrs. Duren's story and McCain's response so they can feed it to HQ right away, and the Twelve Monkeys have as one body stormed the Straight Talk Express, which is just up ahead on I-85 and riding very low in the stern from all the weight in McCain's rear salon. The point is that none of the usual media pros are available for *Rolling Stone* to interface with about the Chris Duren Incident and maybe get help from in terms of trying to figure out what to be cynical about and what not to and which of the many disturbing questions the whole Incident provokes are paranoid or irrelevant versus which ones might be humanly and/or journalistically valid . . . such as was McCain really serious about calling Chris Duren? How could he have even gotten the Durens' phone number when Mrs. D. was scrummed solid the whole time he and his staff were leaving? Does he plan to just look in the phone book or something? And where were Mike Murphy and John Weaver through that whole thing, who can usually be seen Cell-Waltzing back in the shadows at every THM but today were nowhere in sight? And is Murphy maybe even now in the Express's salon in his red chair next to McCain, leaning in toward the candidate's ear and whispering very calmly and coolly about the political advantages of what just happened and about various tasteful but effective ways they can capitalize on it and use it to get out of the tight tactical box that Bush$_2$'s going Negative put them in in the first place? What's McCain's reaction if that's what Murphy's doing — like is he listening, or is he still too upset to listen, or is he somehow both? Is it possible that McCain — maybe not even consciously — played up his reaction to Mrs. Duren's story and framed his distress in order to give himself a plausible, good-looking excuse to get out of the Negative spiral that's been hurting him so badly in the polls

that Jim and Frank say he may well lose South Carolina if things
keep on this way? Is it too cynical even to consider such a thing?

At the following day's first Press-Avail, John S. McCain III issues
a plausible, good-looking, highly emotional statement to the whole
scrummed corps. This is on a warm pretty 11 Feb. morning outside
the Embassy Suites (or possibly Hampton Inn) in Charleston, right
after Baggage Call. McCain informs the press that the case of
young Chris Duren has caused him such distress that after a great
deal of late-night soul-searching he's now ordered his staff to cease
all Negativity and to pull all the McCain2000 response ads in South
Carolina regardless of whether the Shrub pulls his own Negative
ads or not.

And of course, framed as it is by the distressed context of the
Chris Duren Incident, McCain's decision now in no way makes him
look wimpy or appeasing, but rather like a truly decent, honorable,
high-road guy who doesn't want young people's political idealism
fucked with in any way if he can help it. It's a stirring and high-
impact statement, and a masterful -Avail, and everybody in the
scrum seems impressed and in some cases deeply and personally
moved, and nobody (including *Rolling Stone*) ventures to point out
aloud that, however unfortunate the phone call was for the Durens,
it turned out to be just fortunate as *hell* for John S. McCain and
McCain2000 in terms of this week's tactical battle, that actually the
whole thing couldn't have worked out better for McCain2000 if it
had been . . . well, like *scripted,* if like say Mrs. Donna Duren had
been a trained actress or even gifted partisan amateur who'd been
somehow secretly approached and rehearsed and paid and planted
in that crowd of over 300 random unscreened questioners where
her raised hand in that sea of average voters' hands was seen and
chosen and she got to tell a moving story that made all five networks last night and damaged $Bush_2$ badly and now has released
McCain from this week's tactical box. Any way you look at it (and
there's a nice long DT in which to think about it), yesterday's

Incident and THM were an almost incredible stroke of political luck for McCain . . . or else maybe a stroke of something else, something that no one — not the Twelve Monkeys, not Alison Mitchell or the marvelously cynical Australian *Globe* lady or even the totally sharp and unsentimental Jim C. — ever once broaches or mentions out loud, which might be understandable, since maybe even considering whether it was even *possible* would be so painful that it'd make it impossible to go on, which is what the press and staff and Straight Talk caravan and McCain himself have to do all day, and the next, and the next — go on.

SUCK IT UP

Another paradox: It is all but impossible to talk about the really important stuff in politics without using terms that have become such awful clichés they make your eyes glaze over and are difficult to even hear. One such term is "leader," which all the big candidates use all the time — as in "providing leadership," "a proven leader," "a new leader for a new century," etc. — and have reduced to such a platitude that it's hard to try to think about what "leader" really means and whether indeed what today's Young Voters want is a leader. The weird thing is that the word "leader" itself is cliché and boring, but when you come across somebody who actually *is* a real leader, that person isn't boring at all; in fact he's the opposite of boring.

Obviously, a real leader isn't just somebody who has ideas you agree with, nor is it just somebody you happen to believe is a good guy. A real leader is somebody who, because of his own particular power and charisma and example, is able to inspire people, with "inspire" being used here in a serious and noncliché way. A real leader can somehow get us to do certain things that deep down we think are good and want to be able to do but usually can't get ourselves to do on our own. It's a mysterious quality, hard to define, but we always know it when we see it, even as kids. You can probably remember seeing it in certain really great coaches, or teachers, or some extremely cool older kid you "looked up to" (interesting phrase) and wanted to be like. Some of us remember seeing the quality as kids in a minister or rabbi, or a scoutmaster, or a parent, or a friend's parent, or a boss in some summer job. And yes, all these are "authority figures," but it's a special kind of authority. If you've ever spent time in the military, you know how incredibly easy it is to tell which of your superiors are real leaders and which aren't, and how little rank has to do with it. A leader's true authority is a power you voluntarily give him, and you grant him this authority not in a resigned or resentful way but happily; it feels right. Deep down, you almost always like how a real leader makes you feel, how you find yourself working harder and pushing yourself and thinking in ways you wouldn't be able to if there weren't this person you respected and believed in and wanted to please.

In other words, a real leader is somebody who can help us overcome the limitations of our own individual laziness and selfishness and weakness and fear and get us to do better, harder things than we can get ourselves to do on our own. Lincoln was, by all available evidence, a real leader, and Churchill, and Gandhi, and King. Teddy and Franklin Roosevelt, and probably de Gaulle, and certainly Marshall, and maybe Eisenhower. (Although of course Hitler was a real leader too, a very potent one, so you have to watch out; all it is is a weird kind of personal power.)

Probably the last real leader we had as US president was JFK, 40 years ago. It's not that Kennedy was a better human being than the seven presidents we've had since: we know he lied about his WWII record, and had spooky Mob ties, and screwed around more in the White House than poor old Clinton could ever dream of. But JFK had that special leader-type magic, and when he said things like "Ask not what your country can do for you; ask what you can do for your country," nobody rolled their eyes or saw it as just a clever line. Instead, a lot of them felt inspired. And the decade that followed, however fucked up it was in other ways, saw millions of Young Voters devote themselves to social and political causes that had nothing to do with getting a plum job or owning expensive stuff or finding the best parties; and the 60s were, by most accounts, a generally cleaner and happier time than now.

It is worth considering why. It's worth thinking hard about why, when John McCain says he wants to be president in order to inspire a generation of young Americans to devote themselves to causes greater than their own self-interest (which means he's saying he wants to be a real leader), a great many of those young Americans will yawn or roll their eyes or make some ironic joke instead of feeling inspired the way they did with Kennedy. True, JFK's audience was in some ways more innocent than we are: Vietnam hadn't happened yet, or Watergate, or the S&L scandals, etc. But there's also something else. The science of sales and marketing was still in its drooling infancy in 1961 when Kennedy was saying "Ask not . . ." The young people he inspired had not been skillfully marketed to all their lives. They knew nothing of spin. They were not totally, terribly familiar with salesmen.

Now you have to pay close attention to something that's going to seem obvious at first. There is a difference between a great leader and a great salesman. There are also similarities, of course. A great salesman is usually charismatic and likable, and he can often get us to do things (buy things, agree to things) that we might not go for on our own, and to feel good about it. Plus a lot of salesmen are basically decent people with plenty about them to admire. But even a truly great salesman isn't a leader. This is because a salesman's ultimate, overriding motivation is self-interest — if you buy what he's selling, the salesman profits. So even though the salesman may have a very powerful, charismatic, admirable personality, and might even persuade you that buying is in *your* interests (and it really might be) — still, a little part of you always knows that what the salesman's ultimately after is something for himself. And this awareness is painful . . . although admittedly it's a tiny pain, more like a twinge, and often unconscious. But if you're subjected to great salesmen and sales pitches and marketing concepts for long enough — like from your earliest Saturday-morning cartoons, let's say — it is only a matter of time before you start believing deep down that everything is sales and marketing, and that whenever somebody seems like they care about you or about some noble idea or cause, that person is a salesman and really ultimately doesn't give a shit about you or some cause but really just wants something for himself.

Some people believe that President Ronald W. Reagan (1981–89) was our last real leader. But not many of them are Young Voters. Even in the 80s, most younger Americans, who could smell a marketer a mile away, knew that what Reagan really was was a great salesman. What he was selling was the idea of himself as a leader. And if you're under, say, 35, this is what pretty much every US president you've grown up with has been: a very talented sales-man, surrounded by smart, expensive political strategists and media consultants and spinmasters who manage his "campaign" (as in also "advertising campaign") and help him sell us on the idea that it's in our interests to vote for him. But the real interests that drove these guys were their own. They wanted, above all, To Be President, wanted the mind-bending power and prominence, the historical immortality — you could smell it on them. (Young Voters tend to have an especially good sense of smell for this sort of thing.) And this is why these guys weren't real leaders: because it was obvi-ous that their deepest, most elemental motives were selfish, there was no chance of them ever inspiring us to transcend our own selfishness. Instead, they usually helped reinforce our market-conditioned belief that everybody's ultimately out for himself and that life is about selling and profit and that words and phrases like "service" and "justice" and "community" and "patriotism" and "duty" and "Give government back to the people" and "I feel your pain" and "Compassionate Conservatism" are just the politics industry's proven sales pitches, exactly the same way "Anti-Tartar" and "Fresher Breath" are the toothpaste industry's pitches. We may vote for them, the same way we may go buy toothpaste. But we're not inspired. They're not the real thing.

It's not just a matter of lying or not lying, either. Everyone knows that the best marketing uses the truth — i.e., sometimes a brand of toothpaste really *is* better. That's not the point. The point, leader-wise, is the difference between merely believing somebody and believing *in* him.

Granted, this is a bit simplistic. All politicians sell, always have. FDR and JFK and MLK and Gandhi were great salesmen. But that's not all they were. People could smell it. That weird little extra something. It had to do with "character" (which, yes, is also a cliché — suck it up).

All of this is why watching John McCain hold press conferences and -Avails and Town Hall Meetings (we're all at the North Charleston THM right now, 0820h on Wednesday, 9 Feb., in the horrible lobby of something called the Carolina Ice Palace) and be all conspicuously honest and open and informal and idealistic and no-bullshit and say "I run for president not to Be Somebody, but to Do Something" and "We're on a national crusade to give government back to the people" in front of these cheering crowds just seems so much more goddamn *complicated* than watching old b/w clips of John Kennedy's speeches. It feels impossible, in February 2000, to tell whether John McCain is a real leader or merely a very talented political salesman, an entrepreneur who's seen a new market-niche and devised a way to fill it.

Because here's yet another paradox. Spring 2000 — midmorning in America's hangover from the whole Lewinsky-and-impeachment thing — represents a moment of almost unprecedented cynicism and disgust with national politics, a moment when blunt, I-don't-give-a-shit-if-you-elect-me honesty becomes an incredibly attractive and salable and electable quality. A moment when an anticandidate can be a real candidate. But of course if he becomes a real

candidate, is he still an anticandidate? Can you sell someone's
refusal to be for sale?

There are many elements of the McCain2000 campaign —
naming the bus "Straight Talk," the timely publication of *Faith
of My Fathers*, the much-hyped "openness" and "spontaneity" of
the Express's media salon, the message-disciplined way McCain
thumps "Always. Tell you. The truth" — that indicate that some
very shrewd, clever marketers are trying to market this candidate's
rejection of shrewd, clever marketing. Is this bad? Or just confusing? Suppose, let's say, you've got a candidate who says polls are
bullshit and totally refuses to tailor his campaign style to polls, and
suppose then that new polls start showing that people really like
this candidate's polls-are-bullshit stance and are thinking about
voting for him because of it, and suppose the candidate reads these
polls (who wouldn't?) and then starts saying even more loudly and
often that polls are bullshit and that he won't use them to decide
what to say, maybe turning "Polls are bullshit" into a campaign line
and repeating it in every speech and even painting *Polls Are Bullshit*
on the side of his bus. . . . Is he a hypocrite? Is it hypocritical that
one of McCain's ads' lines in South Carolina is "Telling the truth
even when it hurts him politically," which of course since it's an
ad means that McCain is trying to get political benefit out of his
indifference to political benefit? What's the difference between
hypocrisy and paradox?

Unsimplistic enough for you now? The fact of the matter is that
if you're a true-blue, market-savvy Young Voter, the only thing
you're certain to feel about John McCain's campaign is a very modern and American type of ambivalence, a sort of interior war
between your deep need to believe and your deep belief that the
need to believe is bullshit, that there's nothing left anywhere but
sales and salesmen. At the times your cynicism's winning, you'll
find that it's possible to see even McCain's most attractive qualities
as just marketing angles. His famous habit of bringing up his own

closet's skeletons, for example — bad grades, messy divorce, indictment as one of the Keating Five — this could be real honesty and
openness, or it could be McCain's shrewd way of preempting criticism by criticizing himself before anyone else can do it. The mod-
esty with which he talks about his heroism as a POW — "It doesn't
take much talent to get shot down"; "I wasn't a hero, but I was fortunate enough to serve my time in the company of heroes" — this
could be real humility, or it could be a clever way to make himself
seem both heroic *and* humble.

You can run the same kind of either/or analysis on almost
everything about this candidate. Even the incredible daily stamina
he shows on the Trail — this could be a function of McCain's natural energy and enjoyment of people, or it could be gross ambition,
a hunger for election so great that it drives him past sane human
limits. The operative word here is "sane": the Shrub stays at luxury
hotels like the Charleston Inn and travels with his own personal pil-
low and likes to sleep till nine, whereas McCain crashes at hellish
chain places and drinks pop out of cans and moves like only
methedrine can make a normal person move. Last night the Straight
Talk caravan didn't get back to the Embassy Suites until 2340, and
McCain was reportedly up with Murphy and Weaver planning ways
to respond to Bush$_2$'s response to the Negative ad McCain's running in response to Bush$_2$'s new Negative ad for three hours after
that, and you know getting up and showering and shaving and putting on a nice suit has to take some time if you're a guy who can't
raise his arms past his shoulders, plus he had to eat breakfast, and
the ST Express hauled out this morning at 0738h, and now here
McCain is at 0822 almost running back and forth on the raised
stage in a Carolina Ice Palace lobby so off-the-charts hideous that
the press all pass up the free crullers. (The lobby's lined with red
and blue rubber — yes, rubber — and 20 feet up a green iron
spiral staircase is an open mezzanine with fencing of mustard-
colored pipe from which hang long purple banners for the Low-
country Youth Hockey Association, and you can hear the rink's

organ someplace inside and a symphony of twitters and boings
from an enormous video arcade just down the bright-orange hall,
and on either side of the THM stage are giant monitors composed
of nine identical screens arrayed 3 × 3, and the monitor on the left
has nine identical McCain faces talking while the one on the right
has just one big McCain face cut into nine separate squares, and
every square foot of the nauseous lobby is occupied by wildly sup-
portive South Carolinians, and it's at least 95 degrees, and the
whole thing is so sensuously assaultive that all the media except Jim
C. and the techs turn around and listen facing away, most drinking
more than one cup of coffee at once.) And even on four hours'
sleep at the very outside now McCain on the stage is undergoing
the same metamorphosis that happens whenever the crowd is
responsive and laughs at his jokes and puts down coffee and kids to
applaud when he says he'll beat Al Gore like a drum. In person,
McCain is not a sleek gorgeous telegenic presence like Rep. Mark
Sanford or the Shrub. McCain is short and slight and stiff in a bit of
a twisted way. He tends to look a little sunken in his suit. His voice
is a thin tenor and not hypnotic or stirring per se. But onstage, taking questions and pacing like something caged, his body seems to
dilate and his voice takes on a resonance, and unlike the Shrub
he is bodyguardless and the stage wide open and the questions
unscreened and he answers them well, and the best Town Meetings' crowds' eyes brighten, and unlike Gore's dead bird's eyes or
the Shrub's smug glare McCain's own eyes are wide and candid and
full of a very attractive inspiring light that's either devotion to
causes beyond him or a demagogue's love of the crowd's love or an
insatiable hunger to become the most powerful white male on
earth. Or all three.

  The point, to put it as simply as possible, is that there's a tension between what John McCain's appeal is and the way that appeal
must be structured and packaged in order to get him elected. To
get you to buy. And the media — which is, after all, the box in
which John McCain is brought to you, and is for the most part your

only access to him, and is itself composed of individual people, voters, some of them Young Voters — the media see this tension, feel it, especially the buses' McCain2000 corps. Don't think they don't. And don't forget they're human, or that the way they're going to resolve this tension and decide how to see McCain (and thus how to let you see McCain) will depend way less on political ideology than on each reporter's own little interior battles between cynicism and idealism and marketing and leadership. The far-Right *National Review,* for example, calls McCain "a crook and a showboat," while the old-Left *New York Review of Books* feels that "McCain isn't the anti-Clinton . . . McCain is more like the unClinton, in the way 7Up was the unCola: different flavor, same sugar content," and the politically indifferent *Vanity Fair* quotes Washington insiders of unknown affiliation saying "People should never underestimate [McCain's] shrewdness. His positions, in many instances, are very calculated in terms of media appeal."

Well no shit. Here in SC, the single most depressing and cynical episode of the whole week involves shrewd, calculated appeal. (At least in certain moods it looks like it does [maybe].) Please recall 10 February's Chris Duren Incident in Spartanburg and McCain's enormous distress and his promise to phone and apologize personally to the disillusioned kid. So the next afternoon, at a pre-F&F Press-Avail back in North Charleston, the new, unilaterally non-Negative McCain informs the press corps that he's going up to his hotel room right now to call Chris Duren. The phone call is to be "a private one between this young man and me," McCain says. Then Todd the Press Liaison steps in looking very stern and announces that only network techs will be allowed in the room, and that while they can film the whole call, only the first ten seconds of audio will be permitted. "Ten seconds, then we kill the sound," Todd says, looking hard at Frank C. and the other audio guys. "This is a private call, not a media event." Let's think about this. If it's a "private call," why let TV cameras film McCain making it? And why only ten seconds of sound? Why not either full sound or no sound at all?

The answer is modern and American and pretty much right out of Marketing 101. The campaign wants to publicize McCain's keeping his promise and calling a traumatized kid, but *also* wants to publicize the fact that McCain is calling him "privately" and not just exploiting Chris Duren for crass political purposes. There's no other possible reason for the ten-second audio cutoff, which cutoff will require networks that run the film to explain why there's no sound after the initial Hello, which explanation will then of course make McCain look doubly good, both caring and nonpolitical. Does the shrewd calculation of media appeal here mean that McCain doesn't really care about Chris Duren, doesn't really want to buck him up and restore the kid's faith in the political process? Not necessarily. But what it does mean is that McCain2000 wants to have it both ways, rather like big corporations that give to charity and then try to reap PR benefits by hyping their altruism in their ads. Does stuff like this mean that the gifts and phone call aren't "good"? The answer depends on how gray-area-tolerant you are about sincerity vs. marketing, or sincerity plus marketing, or leadership plus the packaging and selling of same.

But if you, like poor old *Rolling Stone,* have come to a point on the Trail where you've started fearing your own cynicism almost as much as you fear your own credulity and the salesmen who feed on it, you may find your thoughts returning again and again to a certain dark and box-sized cell in a certain Hilton half a world and three careers away, to the torture and fear and offer of release and a certain Young Voter named McCain's refusal to violate a Code. There were no techs' cameras in that box, no aides or consultants, no paradoxes or gray areas; nothing to sell. There was just one guy and whatever in his character sustained him. This is a huge deal. In your mind, that Hoa Lo box becomes sort of a special dressing room with a star on the door, the private place behind the stage where one imagines "the real John McCain" still lives. And but now the paradox here is that this box that makes McCain "real" is, by definition, locked. Impenetrable. Nobody gets in or out. This is huge, too; you should keep it in mind. It is why, however many behind-the-scenes pencils get put on the case, a "profile" of John McCain is going to be just that: one side, exterior, split and diffracted by so many lenses there's way more than one man to see. Salesman or leader or neither or both, the final paradox — the really tiny central one, way down deep inside all the other campaign puzzles' spinning boxes and squares that layer McCain — is that whether he's truly "for real" now depends less on what is in his heart than on what might be in yours. Try to stay awake.

2000

CONSIDER THE LOBSTER

THE ENORMOUS, pungent, and extremely well-marketed Maine
Lobster Festival is held every late July in the state's midcoast region,
meaning the western side of Penobscot Bay, the nerve stem of
Maine's lobster industry. What's called the midcoast runs from Owl's
Head and Thomaston in the south to Belfast in the north. (Actually,
it might extend all the way up to Bucksport, but we were never able
to get farther north than Belfast on Route 1, whose summer traffic is,
as you can imagine, unimaginable.) The region's two main communities are Camden, with its very old money and yachty harbor and
five-star restaurants and phenomenal B&Bs, and Rockland, a serious
old fishing town that hosts the festival every summer in historic
Harbor Park, right along the water.[1]

  Tourism and lobster are the midcoast region's two main industries, and they're both warm-weather enterprises, and the Maine
Lobster Festival represents less an intersection of the industries
than a deliberate collision, joyful and lucrative and loud. The

---

[1] There's a comprehensive native apothegm: "Camden by the sea, Rockland by the smell."

assigned subject of this *Gourmet* article is the 56th Annual MLF, 30 July–3 August 2003, whose official theme this year was "Lighthouses, Laughter, and Lobster." Total paid attendance was over 100,000, due partly to a national CNN spot in June during which a senior editor of *Food & Wine* magazine hailed the MLF as one of the best food-themed galas in the world. 2003 festival highlights: concerts by Lee Ann Womack and Orleans, annual Maine Sea Goddess beauty pageant, Saturday's big parade, Sunday's William G. Atwood Memorial Crate Race, annual Amateur Cooking Competition, carnival rides and midway attractions and food booths, and the MLF's Main Eating Tent, where something over 25,000 pounds of fresh-caught Maine lobster is consumed after preparation in the World's Largest Lobster Cooker near the grounds' north entrance. Also available are lobster rolls, lobster turnovers, lobster sauté, Down East lobster salad, lobster bisque, lobster ravioli, and deep-fried lobster dumplings. Lobster thermidor is obtainable at a sit-down restaurant called the Black Pearl on Harbor Park's northwest wharf. A large all-pine booth sponsored by the Maine Lobster Promotion Council has free pamphlets with recipes, eating tips, and Lobster Fun Facts. The winner of Friday's Amateur Cooking Competition prepares Saffron Lobster Ramekins, the recipe for which is now available for public downloading at www.mainelobsterfestival.com. There are lobster T-shirts and lobster bobblehead dolls and inflatable lobster pool toys and clamp-on lobster hats with big scarlet claws that wobble on springs. Your assigned correspondent saw it all, accompanied by one girlfriend and both his own parents — one of which parents was actually born and raised in Maine, albeit in the extreme northern inland part, which is potato country and a world away from the touristic midcoast.[2]

For practical purposes, everyone knows what a lobster is. As usual, though, there's much more to know than most of us care about —

[2] N.B. All personally connected parties have made it clear from the start that they do not want to be talked about in this article.

it's all a matter of what your interests are. Taxonomically speaking, a lobster is a marine crustacean of the family Homaridae, characterized by five pairs of jointed legs, the first pair terminating in large pincerish claws used for subduing prey. Like many other species of benthic carnivore, lobsters are both hunters and scavengers. They have stalked eyes, gills on their legs, and antennae. There are a dozen or so different kinds worldwide, of which the relevant species here is the Maine lobster, *Homarus americanus*. The name "lobster" comes from the Old English *loppestre*, which is thought to be a corrupt form of the Latin word for locust combined with the Old English *loppe*, which meant spider.

Moreover, a crustacean is an aquatic arthropod of the class Crustacea, which comprises crabs, shrimp, barnacles, lobsters, and freshwater crayfish. All this is right there in the encyclopedia. And arthropods are members of the phylum Arthropoda, which phylum covers insects, spiders, crustaceans, and centipedes/millipedes, all of whose main commonality, besides the absence of a centralized brain-spine assembly, is a chitinous exoskeleton composed of segments, to which appendages are articulated in pairs.

The point is that lobsters are basically giant sea insects.[3] Like most arthropods, they date from the Jurassic period, biologically so much older than mammalia that they might as well be from another planet. And they are — particularly in their natural brown-green state, brandishing their claws like weapons and with thick antennae awhip — not nice to look at. And it's true that they are garbagemen of the sea, eaters of dead stuff,[4] although they'll also eat some live shellfish, certain kinds of injured fish, and sometimes one another.

But they are themselves good eating. Or so we think now. Up until sometime in the 1800s, though, lobster was literally low-class food, eaten only by the poor and institutionalized. Even in the harsh penal environment of early America, some colonies had laws

---

[3] Midcoasters' native term for a lobster is, in fact, "bug," as in "Come around on Sunday and we'll cook up some bugs."

[4] Factoid: Lobster traps are usually baited with dead herring.

against feeding lobsters to inmates more than once a week because it was thought to be cruel and unusual, like making people eat rats. One reason for their low status was how plentiful lobsters were in old New England. "Unbelievable abundance" is how one source describes the situation, including accounts of Plymouth Pilgrims wading out and capturing all they wanted by hand, and of early Boston's seashore being littered with lobsters after hard storms — these latter were treated as a smelly nuisance and ground up for fertilizer. There is also the fact that premodern lobster was cooked dead and then preserved, usually packed in salt or crude hermetic containers. Maine's earliest lobster industry was based around a dozen such seaside canneries in the 1840s, from which lobster was shipped as far away as California, in demand only because it was cheap and high in protein, basically chewable fuel.

Now, of course, lobster is posh, a delicacy, only a step or two down from caviar. The meat is richer and more substantial than most fish, its taste subtle compared to the marine-gaminess of mussels and clams. In the US pop-food imagination, lobster is now the seafood analog to steak, with which it's so often twinned as Surf 'n' Turf on the really expensive part of the chain steakhouse menu.

In fact, one obvious project of the MLF, and of its omnipresently sponsorial Maine Lobster Promotion Council, is to counter the idea that lobster is unusually luxe or unhealthy or expensive, suitable only for effete palates or the occasional blow-the-diet treat. It is emphasized over and over in presentations and pamphlets at the festival that lobster meat has fewer calories, less cholesterol, and less saturated fat than chicken.[5] And in the Main Eating Tent, you can get a "quarter" (industry shorthand for a 1¼-pound lobster), a four-ounce cup of melted butter, a bag of chips, and a soft roll w/ butter-pat for around $12.00, which is only slightly more expensive than supper at McDonald's.

---

[5] Of course, the common practice of dipping the lobster meat in melted butter torpedoes all these happy fat-specs, which none of the council's promotional stuff ever mentions, any more than potato industry PR talks about sour cream and bacon bits.

Be apprised, though, that the Maine Lobster Festival's democratization of lobster comes with all the massed inconvenience and aesthetic compromise of real democracy. See, for example, the aforementioned Main Eating Tent, for which there is a constant Disneyland-grade queue, and which turns out to be a square quarter mile of awning-shaded cafeteria lines and rows of long institutional tables at which friend and stranger alike sit cheek by jowl, cracking and chewing and dribbling. It's hot, and the sagged roof traps the steam and the smells, which latter are strong and only partly food-related. It is also loud, and a good percentage of the total noise is masticatory. The suppers come in styrofoam trays, and the soft drinks are iceless and flat, and the coffee is convenience-store coffee in more styrofoam, and the utensils are plastic (there are none of the special long skinny forks for pushing out the tail meat, though a few savvy diners bring their own). Nor do they give you near enough napkins considering how messy lobster is to eat, especially when you're squeezed onto benches alongside children of various ages and vastly different levels of fine-motor development — not to mention the people who've somehow smuggled in their own beer in enormous aisle-blocking coolers, or who all of a sudden produce their own plastic tablecloths and spread them over large portions of tables to try to reserve them (the tables) for their own little groups. And so on. Any one example is no more than a petty inconvenience, of course, but the MLF turns out to be full of irksome little downers like this — see for instance the Main Stage's headliner shows, where it turns out that you have to pay $20 extra for a folding chair if you want to sit down; or the North Tent's mad scramble for the Nyquil-cup-sized samples of finalists' entries handed out after the Cooking Competition; or the much-touted Maine Sea Goddess pageant finals, which turn out to be excruciatingly long and to consist mainly of endless thanks and tributes to local sponsors. Let's not even talk about the grossly inadequate Port-A-San facilities or the fact that there's nowhere to wash your hands before or after eating. What the Maine Lobster Festival really

is is a midlevel county fair with a culinary hook, and in this respect
it's not unlike Tidewater crab festivals, Midwest corn festivals, Texas
chili festivals, etc., and shares with these venues the core paradox
of all teeming commercial demotic events: It's not for everyone.[6]
Nothing against the euphoric senior editor of *Food & Wine*, but I'd
be surprised if she'd ever actually been here in Harbor Park, amid
crowds of people slapping canal-zone mosquitoes as they eat deep-
fried Twinkies and watch Professor Paddywhack, on six-foot stilts in
a raincoat with plastic lobsters protruding from all directions on
springs, terrify their children.

Lobster is essentially a summer food. This is because we now prefer
our lobsters fresh, which means they have to be recently caught,
which for both tactical and economic reasons takes place at depths
less than 25 fathoms. Lobsters tend to be hungriest and most active

---

[6] In truth, there's a great deal to be said about the differences between working-class
Rockland and the heavily populist flavor of its festival versus comfortable and elitist Camden with its expensive view and shops given entirely over to $200 sweaters and great rows
of Victorian homes converted to upscale B&Bs. And about these differences as two sides
of the great coin that is US tourism. Very little of which will be said here, except to
amplify the above-mentioned paradox and to reveal your assigned correspondent's own
preferences. I confess that I have never understood why so many people's idea of a fun
vacation is to don flip-flops and sunglasses and crawl through maddening traffic to loud,
hot, crowded tourist venues in order to sample a "local flavor" that is by definition ruined
by the presence of tourists. This may (as my festival companions keep pointing out) all
be a matter of personality and hardwired taste: the fact that I do not like tourist venues
means that I'll never understand their appeal and so am probably not the one to talk
about it (the supposed appeal). But, since this FN will almost surely not survive magazine-
editing anyway, here goes:
    As I see it, it probably really is good for the soul to be a tourist, even if it's only once
in a while. Not good for the soul in a refreshing or enlivening way, though, but rather in
a grim, steely-eyed, let's-look-honestly-at-the-facts-and-find-some-way-to-deal-with-them
way. My personal experience has not been that traveling around the country is broaden-
ing or relaxing, or that radical changes in place and context have a salutary effect, but
rather that intranational tourism is radically constricting, and humbling in the hardest
way — hostile to my fantasy of being a true individual, of living somehow outside and
above it all. (Coming up is the part that my companions find especially unhappy and
repellent, a sure way to spoil the fun of vacation travel:) To be a mass tourist, for me, is
to become a pure late-date American: alien, ignorant, greedy for something you cannot
ever have, disappointed in a way you can never admit. It is to spoil, by way of sheer on-
tology, the very unspoiledness you are there to experience. It is to impose yourself on
places that in all non-economic ways would be better, realer, without you. It is, in lines
and gridlock and transaction after transaction, to confront a dimension of yourself that
is as inescapable as it is painful: As a tourist, you become economically significant but
existentially loathsome, an insect on a dead thing.

(i.e., most trappable) at summer water temperatures of 45–50 degrees. In the autumn, most Maine lobsters migrate out into deeper water, either for warmth or to avoid the heavy waves that pound New England's coast all winter. Some burrow into the bottom. They might hibernate; nobody's sure. Summer is also lobsters' molting season — specifically early- to mid-July. Chitinous arthropods grow by molting, rather the way people have to buy bigger clothes as they age and gain weight. Since lobsters can live to be over 100, they can also get to be quite large, as in 30 pounds or more — though truly senior lobsters are rare now because New England's waters are so heavily trapped.[7] Anyway, hence the culinary distinction between hard- and soft-shell lobsters, the latter sometimes a.k.a. shedders. A soft-shell lobster is one that has recently molted. In midcoast restaurants, the summer menu often offers both kinds, with shedders being slightly cheaper even though they're easier to dismantle and the meat is allegedly sweeter. The reason for the discount is that a molting lobster uses a layer of seawater for insulation while its new shell is hardening, so there's slightly less actual meat when you crack open a shedder, plus a redolent gout of water that gets all over everything and can sometimes jet out lemonlike and catch a tablemate right in the eye. If it's winter or you're buying lobster someplace far from New England, on the other hand, you can almost bet that the lobster is a hard-shell, which for obvious reasons travel better.

As an à la carte entrée, lobster can be baked, broiled, steamed, grilled, sautéed, stir-fried, or microwaved. The most common method, though, is boiling. If you're someone who enjoys having lobster at home, this is probably the way you do it, since boiling is so easy. You need a large kettle w/ cover, which you fill about half full with water (the standard advice is that you want 2.5 quarts of water per lobster). Seawater is optimal, or you can add two tbsp salt per quart from the tap. It also helps to know how much your

---

[7] Datum: In a good year, the US industry produces around 80,000,000 pounds of lobster, and Maine accounts for more than half that total.

lobsters weigh. You get the water boiling, put in the lobsters one at a time, cover the kettle, and bring it back up to a boil. Then you bank the heat and let the kettle simmer — ten minutes for the first pound of lobster, then three minutes for each pound after that. (This is assuming you've got hard-shell lobsters, which, again, if you don't live between Boston and Halifax is probably what you've got. For shedders, you're supposed to subtract three minutes from the total.) The reason the kettle's lobsters turn scarlet is that boiling somehow suppresses every pigment in their chitin but one. If you want an easy test of whether the lobsters are done, you try pulling on one of their antennae — if it comes out of the head with minimal effort, you're ready to eat.

A detail so obvious that most recipes don't even bother to mention it is that each lobster is supposed to be alive when you put it in the kettle. This is part of lobster's modern appeal — it's the freshest food there is. There's no decomposition between harvesting and eating. And not only do lobsters require no cleaning or dressing or plucking, they're relatively easy for vendors to keep alive. They come up alive in the traps, are placed in containers of seawater, and can — so long as the water's aerated and the animals' claws are pegged or banded to keep them from tearing one another up under the stresses of captivity[8] — survive right up until they're boiled. Most of us have been in supermarkets or restaurants that feature tanks of live lobsters, from which you can pick out your supper while it watches you point. And part of the overall spectacle of the Maine Lobster Festival is that you can see actual lobstermen's vessels docking at the

---

[8] N.B. Similar reasoning underlies the practice of what's termed "debeaking" broiler chickens and brood hens in modern factory farms. Maximum commercial efficiency requires that enormous poultry populations be confined in unnaturally close quarters, under which conditions many birds go crazy and peck one another to death. As a purely observational side-note, be apprised that debeaking is usually an automated process and that the chickens receive no anesthetic. It's not clear to me whether most *Gourmet* readers know about debeaking, or about related practices like dehorning cattle in commercial feed lots, cropping swine's tails in factory hog farms to keep psychotically bored neighbors from chewing them off, and so forth. It so happens that your assigned correspondent knew almost nothing about standard meat-industry operations before starting work on this article.

wharves along the northeast grounds and unloading fresh-caught product, which is transferred by hand or cart 150 yards to the great clear tanks stacked up around the festival's cooker — which is, as mentioned, billed as the World's Largest Lobster Cooker and can process over 100 lobsters at a time for the Main Eating Tent.

So then here is a question that's all but unavoidable at the World's Largest Lobster Cooker, and may arise in kitchens across the US: Is it all right to boil a sentient creature alive just for our gustatory pleasure? A related set of concerns: Is the previous question irksomely PC or sentimental? What does "all right" even mean in this context? Is the whole thing just a matter of personal choice?

As you may or may not know, a certain well-known group called People for the Ethical Treatment of Animals thinks that the morality of lobster-boiling is not just a matter of individual conscience. In fact, one of the very first things we hear about the MLF . . . well, to set the scene: We're coming in by cab from the almost indescribably odd and rustic Knox County Airport[9] very late on the night before the festival opens, sharing the cab with a wealthy political consultant who lives on Vinalhaven Island in the bay half the year (he's headed for the island ferry in Rockland). The consultant and cabdriver are responding to informal journalistic probes about how people who live in the midcoast region actually view the MLF, as in is the festival just a big-dollar tourist thing or is it something local residents look forward to attending, take genuine civic pride in, etc. The cabdriver (who's in his seventies, one of apparently a whole platoon of retirees the cab company puts on to help with the summer rush, and wears a US-flag lapel pin, and drives in what can only be called a very *deliberate* way) assures us that locals do endorse and enjoy the MLF, although he himself hasn't gone in years, and now come to think of it no one he and his wife know has, either. However, the demilocal consultant's been to recent festivals a couple times (one gets the impression it was at his wife's behest), of which his most vivid impression was that

---

[9] The terminal used to be somebody's house, for example, and the lost-luggage-reporting room was clearly once a pantry.

"you have to line up for an ungodly long time to get your lobsters, and meanwhile there are all these ex–flower children coming up and down along the line handing out pamphlets that say the lobsters die in terrible pain and you shouldn't eat them."

And it turns out that the post-hippies of the consultant's recollection were activists from PETA. There were no PETA people in obvious view at the 2003 MLF,[10] but they've been conspicuous at many of the recent festivals. Since at least the mid-1990s, articles in everything from the *Camden Herald* to the *New York Times* have described PETA urging boycotts of the Maine Lobster Festival, often deploying celebrity spokesmen like Mary Tyler Moore for open letters and ads saying stuff like "Lobsters are extraordinarily sensitive" and "To me, eating a lobster is out of the question." More concrete is the oral testimony of Dick, our florid and extremely gregarious rental-car liaison,[11] to the effect that PETA's been around so much during recent years that a kind of brittlely tolerant homeostasis now obtains between the activists and the festival's locals, e.g.: "We had some incidents a couple years ago. One lady took most of her clothes off and painted herself like a lobster, almost got herself arrested. But for the most part they're let alone. [Rapid series of small ambiguous laughs, which with Dick happens a lot.] They do their thing and we do our thing."

---

[10] It turned out that one Mr. William R. Rivas-Rivas, a high-ranking PETA official out of the group's Virginia headquarters, was indeed there this year, albeit solo, working the festival's main and side entrances on Saturday, 2 August, handing out pamphlets and adhesive stickers emblazoned with "Being Boiled Hurts," which is the tagline in most of PETA's published material about lobsters. I learned that he'd been there only later, when speaking with Mr. Rivas-Rivas on the phone. I'm not sure how we missed seeing him *in situ* at the festival, and I can't see much to do except apologize for the oversight — although it's also true that Saturday was the day of the big MLF parade through Rockland, which basic journalistic responsibility seemed to require going to (and which, with all due respect, meant that Saturday was maybe not the best day for PETA to work the Harbor Park grounds, especially if it was going to be just one person for one day, since a lot of diehard MLF partisans were off-site watching the parade (which, again with no offense intended, was in truth kind of cheesy and boring, consisting mostly of slow homemade floats and various midcoast people waving at one another, and with an extremely annoying man dressed as Blackbeard ranging up and down the length of the crowd saying "Arrr" over and over and brandishing a plastic sword at people, etc.; plus it rained)).

[11] By profession, Dick is actually a car salesman; the midcoast region's National Car Rental franchise operates out of a Chevy dealership in Thomaston.

This whole interchange takes place on Route 1, 30 July, during a four-mile, 50-minute ride from the airport[12] to the dealership to sign car-rental papers. Several irreproducible segues down the road from the PETA anecdotes, Dick — whose son-in-law happens to be a professional lobsterman and one of the Main Eating Tent's regular suppliers — explains what he and his family feel is the crucial mitigating factor in the whole morality-of-boiling-lobsters-alive issue: "There's a part of the brain in people and animals that lets us feel pain, and lobsters' brains don't have this part."

Besides the fact that it's incorrect in about nine different ways, the main reason Dick's statement is interesting is that its thesis is more or less echoed by the festival's own pronouncement on lobsters and pain, which is part of a Test Your Lobster IQ quiz that appears in the 2003 MLF program courtesy of the Maine Lobster Promotion Council:

> The nervous system of a lobster is very simple, and is in fact most similar to the nervous system of the grasshopper. It is decentralized with no brain. There is no cerebral cortex, which in humans is the area of the brain that gives the experience of pain.

Though it sounds more sophisticated, a lot of the neurology in this latter claim is still either false or fuzzy. The human cerebral cortex is the brain-part that deals with higher faculties like reason, metaphysical self-awareness, language, etc. Pain reception is known to be part of a much older and more primitive system of nociceptors and prostaglandins that are managed by the brain stem and thalamus.[13]

---

[12] The short version regarding why we were back at the airport after already arriving the previous night involves lost luggage and a miscommunication about where and what the midcoast's National franchise was — Dick came out personally to the airport and got us, out of no evident motive but kindness. (He also talked nonstop the entire way, with a very distinctive speaking style that can be described only as manically laconic; the truth is that I now know more about this man than I do about some members of my own family.)

[13] To elaborate by way of example: The common experience of accidentally touching a hot stove and yanking your hand back before you're even aware that anything's going on is explained by the fact that many of the processes by which we detect and avoid painful stimuli do not involve the cortex. In the case of the hand and stove, the brain is bypassed altogether; all the important neurochemical action takes place in the spine.

On the other hand, it is true that the cerebral cortex is involved in what's variously called suffering, distress, or the emotional experience of pain — i.e., experiencing painful stimuli as unpleasant, very unpleasant, unbearable, and so on.

Before we go any further, let's acknowledge that the questions of whether and how different kinds of animals feel pain, and of whether and why it might be justifiable to inflict pain on them in order to eat them, turn out to be extremely complex and difficult. And comparative neuroanatomy is only part of the problem. Since pain is a totally subjective mental experience, we do not have direct access to anyone or anything's pain but our own; and even just the principles by which we can infer that other human beings experience pain and have a legitimate interest in not feeling pain involve hard-core philosophy — metaphysics, epistemology, value theory, ethics. The fact that even the most highly evolved nonhuman mammals can't use language to communicate with us about their subjective mental experience is only the first layer of additional complication in trying to extend our reasoning about pain and morality to animals. And everything gets progressively more abstract and convoluted as we move farther and farther out from the higher-type mammals into cattle and swine and dogs and cats and rodents, and then birds and fish, and finally invertebrates like lobsters.

The more important point here, though, is that the whole animal-cruelty-and-eating issue is not just complex, it's also uncomfortable. It is, at any rate, uncomfortable for me, and for just about everyone I know who enjoys a variety of foods and yet does not want to see herself as cruel or unfeeling. As far as I can tell, my own main way of dealing with this conflict has been to avoid thinking about the whole unpleasant thing. I should add that it appears to me unlikely that many readers of *Gourmet* wish to think about it, either, or to be queried about the morality of their eating habits in the pages of a culinary monthly. Since, however, the assigned subject of this article is what it was like to attend the 2003 MLF, and thus to spend several days in the midst of a great mass of Americans all eating lobster, and thus to be more or less impelled to think hard about lobster and the experience of buying and eating lobster, it turns out that there is no honest way to avoid certain moral questions.

There are several reasons for this. For one thing, it's not just that lobsters get boiled alive, it's that you do it yourself — or at least it's done specifically for you, on-site.[14] As mentioned, the World's Largest Lobster Cooker, which is highlighted as an attraction in the festival's program, is right out there on the MLF's north grounds for everyone to see. Try to imagine a Nebraska Beef Festival[15] at which part of the festivities is watching trucks pull up and the live cattle get driven down the ramp and slaughtered right there on the World's Largest Killing Floor or something — there's no way.

The intimacy of the whole thing is maximized at home, which of course is where most lobster gets prepared and eaten (although note already the semiconscious euphemism "prepared," which in the case of lobsters really means killing them right there in our kitchens). The basic scenario is that we come in from the store and make our little preparations like getting the kettle filled and boiling, and then we lift the lobsters out of the bag or whatever retail container they came home in . . . whereupon some uncomfortable things start to happen. However stuporous a lobster is from the trip home, for instance, it tends to come alarmingly to life when placed

---

[14] Morality-wise, let's concede that this cuts both ways. Lobster-eating is at least not abetted by the system of corporate factory farms that produces most beef, pork, and chicken. Because, if nothing else, of the way they're marketed and packaged for sale, we eat these latter meats without having to consider that they were once conscious, sentient creatures to whom horrible things were done. (N.B. "Horrible" here meaning really, really horrible. Write off to PETA or peta.org for their free "Meet Your Meat" video, narrated by Mr. Alec Baldwin, if you want to see just about everything meat-related you don't want to see or think about. (N.B.$_2$ Not that PETA's any sort of font of unspun truth. Like many partisans in complex moral disputes, the PETA people are fanatics, and a lot of their rhetoric seems simplistic and self-righteous. But this particular video, replete with actual factory-farm and corporate-slaughterhouse footage, is both credible and traumatizing.))

[15] Is it significant that "lobster," "fish," and "chicken" are our culture's words for both the animal and the meat, whereas most mammals seem to require euphemisms like "beef" and "pork" that help us separate the meat we eat from the living creature the meat once was? Is this evidence that some kind of deep unease about eating higher animals is endemic enough to show up in English usage, but that the unease diminishes as we move out of the mammalian order? (And is "lamb"/"lamb" the counterexample that sinks the whole theory, or are there special, biblico-historical reasons for that equivalence?)

in boiling water. If you're tilting it from a container into the steaming kettle, the lobster will sometimes try to cling to the container's sides or even to hook its claws over the kettle's rim like a person trying to keep from going over the edge of a roof. And worse is when the lobster's fully immersed. Even if you cover the kettle and turn away, you can usually hear the cover rattling and clanking as the lobster tries to push it off. Or the creature's claws scraping the sides of the kettle as it thrashes around. The lobster, in other words, behaves very much as you or I would behave if we were plunged into boiling water (with the obvious exception of screaming[16]). A blunter way to say this is that the lobster acts as if it's in terrible pain, causing some cooks to leave the kitchen altogether and to take one of those little lightweight plastic oven-timers with them into another room and wait until the whole process is over.

There happen to be two main criteria that most ethicists agree on for determining whether a living creature has the capacity to suffer and so has genuine interests that it may or may not be our moral duty to consider.[17] One is how much of the neurological hardware required for pain-experience the animal comes equipped with — nociceptors, prostaglandins, neuronal opioid receptors, etc. The other criterion is whether the animal demonstrates behavior associated with pain. And it takes a lot of intellectual gymnastics and

---

[16] There's a relevant populist myth about the high-pitched whistling sound that sometimes issues from a pot of boiling lobster. The sound is really vented steam from the layer of seawater between the lobster's flesh and its carapace (this is why shedders whistle more than hard-shells), but the pop version has it that the sound is the lobster's rabbit-like death-scream. Lobsters communicate via pheromones in their urine and don't have anything close to the vocal equipment for screaming, but the myth's very persistent — which might, once again, point to a low-level cultural unease about the boiling thing.

[17] "Interests" basically means strong and legitimate preferences, which obviously require some degree of consciousness, responsiveness to stimuli, etc. See, for instance, the utilitarian philosopher Peter Singer, whose 1974 *Animal Liberation* is more or less the bible of the modern animal-rights movement:

It would be nonsense to say that it was not in the interests of a stone to be kicked along the road by a schoolboy. A stone does not have interests because it cannot suffer. Nothing that we can do to it could possibly make any difference to its welfare. A mouse, on the other hand, does have an interest in not being kicked along the road, because it will suffer if it is.

behaviorist hairsplitting not to see struggling, thrashing, and lid-clattering as just such pain-behavior. According to marine zoologists, it usually takes lobsters between 35 and 45 seconds to die in boiling water. (No source I could find talks about how long it takes them to die in superheated steam; one rather hopes it's faster.)

There are, of course, other ways to kill your lobster on-site and so achieve maximum freshness. Some cooks' practice is to drive a sharp heavy knife point-first into a spot just above the midpoint between the lobster's eyestalks (more or less where the Third Eye is in human foreheads). This is alleged either to kill the lobster instantly or to render it insensate, and is said at least to eliminate some of the cowardice involved in throwing a creature into boiling water and then fleeing the room. As far as I can tell from talking to proponents of the knife-in-head method, the idea is that it's more violent but ultimately more merciful, plus that a willingness to exert personal agency and accept responsibility for stabbing the lobster's head honors the lobster somehow and entitles one to eat it (there's often a vague sort of Native American spirituality-of-the-hunt flavor to pro-knife arguments). But the problem with the knife method is basic biology: Lobsters' nervous systems operate off not one but several ganglia, a.k.a. nerve bundles, which are sort of wired in series and distributed all along the lobster's underside, from stem to stern. And disabling only the frontal ganglion does not normally result in quick death or unconsciousness.

Another alternative is to put the lobster in cold saltwater and then very slowly bring it up to a full boil. Cooks who advocate this method are going on the analogy to a frog, which can supposedly be kept from jumping out of a boiling pot by heating the water incrementally. In order to save a lot of research-summarizing, I'll simply assure you that the analogy between frogs and lobsters turns out not to hold — plus, if the kettle's water isn't aerated seawater, the immersed lobster suffers from slow suffocation, although usually not decisive enough suffocation to keep it from still thrashing and clattering when the water gets hot enough to kill it. In fact, lobsters boiled incrementally often display a whole bonus set of gruesome, convulsionlike reactions that you don't see in regular boiling.

Ultimately, the only certain virtues of the home-lobotomy and slow-heating methods are comparative, because there are even worse/crueler ways people prepare lobster. Time-thrifty cooks sometimes microwave them alive (usually after poking several vent-holes in the carapace, which is a precaution most shellfish-microwavers learn about the hard way). Live dismemberment, on the other hand, is big in Europe — some chefs cut the lobster in half before cooking; others like to tear off the claws and tail and toss only these parts into the pot.

And there's more unhappy news respecting suffering-criterion number one. Lobsters don't have much in the way of eyesight or hearing, but they do have an exquisite tactile sense, one facilitated by hundreds of thousands of tiny hairs that protrude through their carapace. "Thus it is," in the words of T. M. Prudden's industry classic *About Lobster,* "that although encased in what seems a solid, impenetrable armor, the lobster can receive stimuli and impressions from without as readily as if it possessed a soft and delicate skin." And lobsters do have nociceptors,[18] as well as invertebrate versions of the prostaglandins and major neurotransmitters via which our own brains register pain.

Lobsters do not, on the other hand, appear to have the equipment for making or absorbing natural opioids like endorphins and enkephalins, which are what more advanced nervous systems use to try to handle intense pain. From this fact, though, one could conclude either that lobsters are maybe even *more* vulnerable to pain, since they lack mammalian nervous systems' built-in analgesia, or, instead, that the absence of natural opioids implies an absence of the really intense pain-sensations that natural opioids are designed to mitigate. I for one can detect a marked upswing in mood as I con-

---

[18] This is the neurological term for special pain-receptors that are "sensitive to potentially damaging extremes of temperature, to mechanical forces, and to chemical substances which are released when body tissues are damaged."

template this latter possibility. It could be that their lack of endorphin/enkephalin hardware means that lobsters' raw subjective experience of pain is so radically different from mammals' that it may not even deserve the term "pain." Perhaps lobsters are more like those frontal-lobotomy patients one reads about who report experiencing pain in a totally different way than you and I. These patients evidently do feel physical pain, neurologically speaking, but don't dislike it — though neither do they like it; it's more that they feel it but don't feel anything *about* it — the point being that the pain is not distressing to them or something they want to get away from. Maybe lobsters, who are also without frontal lobes, are detached from the neurological-registration-of-injury-or-hazard we call pain in just the same way. There is, after all, a difference between (1) pain as a purely neurological event, and (2) actual suffering, which seems crucially to involve an emotional component, an awareness of pain as unpleasant, as something to fear/dislike/want to avoid.

Still, after all the abstract intellection, there remain the facts of the frantically clanking lid, the pathetic clinging to the edge of the pot. Standing at the stove, it is hard to deny in any meaningful way that this is a living creature experiencing pain and wishing to avoid/escape the painful experience. To my lay mind, the lobster's behavior in the kettle appears to be the expression of a *preference;* and it may well be that an ability to form preferences is the decisive criterion for real suffering.[19] The logic of this (preference —→ suffering) relation may be easiest to see in the negative case. If you cut certain kinds of worms in half, the halves will often keep crawling around and going about their vermiform business as if nothing had happened. When we assert, based on their post-op behavior, that these worms appear not to be suffering, what we're really saying is that there's no sign the worms know anything bad has happened or would *prefer* not to have gotten cut in half.

---

[19] "Preference" is maybe roughly synonymous with "interests," but it is a better term for our purposes because it's less abstractly philosophical — "preference" seems more personal, and it's the whole idea of a living creature's personal experience that's at issue.

Lobsters, though, are known to exhibit preferences. Experiments have shown that they can detect changes of only a degree or two in water temperature; one reason for their complex migratory cycles (which can often cover 100-plus miles a year) is to pursue the temperatures they like best.[20] And, as mentioned, they're bottom-dwellers and do not like bright light — if a tank of food-lobsters is out in the sunlight or a store's fluorescence, the lobsters will always congregate in whatever part is darkest. Fairly solitary in the ocean, they also clearly dislike the crowding that's part of their captivity in tanks, since (as also mentioned) one reason why lobsters' claws are banded on capture is to keep them from attacking one another under the stress of close-quarter storage.

In any event, at the MLF, standing by the bubbling tanks outside the World's Largest Lobster Cooker, watching the fresh-caught lobsters pile over one another, wave their hobbled claws impotently, huddle in the rear corners, or scrabble frantically back from the glass as you approach, it is difficult not to sense that they're unhappy, or frightened, even if it's some rudimentary version of these feelings . . . and, again, why does rudimentariness even enter into it? Why is a

---

[20] Of course, the most common sort of counterargument here would begin by objecting that "like best" is really just a metaphor, and a misleadingly anthropomorphic one at that. The counterarguer would posit that the lobster seeks to maintain a certain optimal ambient temperature out of nothing but unconscious instinct (with a similar explanation for the low-light affinities upcoming in the main text). The thrust of such a counterargument will be that the lobster's thrashings and clankings in the kettle express not unpreferred pain but involuntary reflexes, like your leg shooting out when the doctor hits your knee. Be advised that there are professional scientists, including many researchers who use animals in experiments, who hold to the view that nonhuman creatures have no real feelings at all, merely "behaviors." Be further advised that this view has a long history that goes all the way back to Descartes, although its modern support comes mostly from behaviorist psychology.

To these what-looks-like-pain-is-really-just-reflexes counterarguments, however, there happen to be all sorts of scientific and pro–animal rights counter-counterarguments. And then further attempted rebuttals and redirects, and so on. Suffice it to say that both the scientific and the philosophical arguments on either side of the animal-suffering issue are involved, abstruse, technical, often informed by self-interest or ideology, and in the end so totally inconclusive that as a practical matter, in the kitchen or restaurant, it all still seems to come down to individual conscience, going with (no pun) your gut.

primitive, inarticulate form of suffering less urgent or uncomfortable for the person who's helping to inflict it by paying for the food it results in? I'm not trying to give you a PETA-like screed here — at least I don't think so. I'm trying, rather, to work out and articulate some of the troubling questions that arise amid all the laughter and saltation and community pride of the Maine Lobster Festival. The truth is that if you, the festival attendee, permit yourself to think that lobsters can suffer and would rather not, the MLF begins to take on the aspect of something like a Roman circus or medieval torture-fest.

Does that comparison seem a bit much? If so, exactly why? Or what about this one: Is it possible that future generations will regard our present agribusiness and eating practices in much the same way we now view Nero's entertainments or Mengele's experiments? My own initial reaction is that such a comparison is hysterical, extreme — and yet the reason it seems extreme to me appears to be that I believe animals are less morally important than human beings;[21] and when it comes to defending such a belief, even to myself, I have to acknowledge that (a) I have an obvious selfish interest in this belief, since I like to eat certain kinds of animals and want to be able to keep doing it, and (b) I haven't succeeded in working out any sort of personal ethical system in which the belief is truly defensible instead of just selfishly convenient.

Given this article's venue and my own lack of culinary sophistication, I'm curious about whether the reader can identify with any of these reactions and acknowledgments and discomforts. I'm also concerned not to come off as shrill or preachy when what I really am is more like confused. For those *Gourmet* readers who enjoy well-prepared and -presented meals involving beef, veal, lamb, pork, chicken, lobster, etc.: Do you think much about the (possible) moral status and (probable) suffering of the animals involved? If

---

[21] Meaning *a lot* less important, apparently, since the moral comparison here is not the value of one human's life vs. the value of one animal's life, but rather the value of one animal's life vs. the value of one human's taste for a particular kind of protein. Even the most diehard carniphile will acknowledge that it's possible to live and eat well without consuming animals.

you do, what ethical convictions have you worked out that permit you not just to eat but to savor and enjoy flesh-based viands (since of course refined *enjoyment,* rather than mere ingestion, is the whole point of gastronomy)? If, on the other hand, you'll have no truck with confusions or convictions and regard stuff like the previous paragraph as just so much fatuous navel-gazing, what makes it feel truly okay, inside, to just dismiss the whole thing out of hand? That is, is your refusal to think about any of this the product of actual thought, or is it just that you don't want to think about it? And if the latter, then why not? Do you ever think, even idly, about the possible reasons for your reluctance to think about it? I am not trying to bait anyone here — I'm genuinely curious. After all, isn't being extra aware and attentive and thoughtful about one's food and its overall context part of what distinguishes a real gourmet? Or is all the gourmet's extra attention and sensibility just supposed to be sensuous? Is it really all just a matter of taste and presentation?

These last few queries, though, while sincere, obviously involve much larger and more abstract questions about the connections (if any) between aesthetics and morality — about what the adjective in a phrase like "The Magazine of Good Living" is really supposed to mean — and these questions lead straightaway into such deep and treacherous waters that it's probably best to stop the public discussion right here. There are limits to what even interested persons can ask of each other.

2004

JOSEPH FRANK'S DOSTOEVSKY

HAVE A PROLEGOMENOUS LOOK at two quotations. The first is from Edward Dahlberg, a Dostoevsky-grade curmudgeon if ever in English there was one:

> The citizen secures himself against genius by icon worship. By the touch of Circe's wand, the divine troublemakers are translated into porcine embroidery.[1]

The second is from Turgenev's *Fathers and Sons:*

> "At the present time, negation is the most useful of all — and we deny —"
> "Everything?"
> "Everything!"
> "What, not only art and poetry . . . but even . . . horrible to say . . ."
> "Everything," repeated Bazarov, with indescribable composure.

---

[1] From "Can These Bones Live?" in *The Edward Dahlberg Reader,* New Directions, 1957.

As the backstory goes, in 1957 one Joseph Frank, then thirty-eight, a Comparative Lit professor at Princeton, is preparing a lecture on existentialism, and he starts working his way through Fyodor Mikhailovich Dostoevsky's *Notes from Underground.* As anyone who's read it can confirm, *Notes* (1864) is a powerful but extremely weird little novel, and both these qualities have to do with the fact that the book is at once universal and particular. Its protagonist's self-diagnosed "disease" — a blend of grandiosity and self-contempt, of rage and cowardice, of ideological fervor and a self-conscious inability to act on his convictions: his whole paradoxical and self-negating character — makes him a universal figure in whom we can all see parts of ourselves, the same kind of ageless literary archetype as Ajax or Hamlet. But at the same time, *Notes from Underground* and its Underground Man are impossible really to understand without some knowledge of the intellectual climate of Russia in the 1860s, particularly the frisson of utopian socialism and aesthetic utilitarianism then in vogue among the radical intelligentsia, an ideology that Dostoevsky loathed with the sort of passion that only Dostoevsky could loathe with.

Anyway, Professor Frank, as he's wading through some of this particular-context background so that he can give his students a comprehensive reading of *Notes,* begins to get interested in using Dostoevsky's fiction as a kind of bridge between two distinct ways of interpreting literature, a purely formal aesthetic approach vs. a social-dash-ideological criticism that cares only about thematics and the philosophical assumptions behind them.[2] That interest, plus forty years of scholarly labor, has yielded the first four volumes of a projected five-book study of Dostoevsky's life and times and writing. All the volumes are published by Princeton U. Press. All

[2] Of course, contemporary literary theory is all about showing that there's no real distinction between these two ways to read — or rather it's about showing that aesthetics can pretty much always be reduced to ideology. For me, one reason Frank's overall project is so worthwhile is that it shows a whole different way to marry formal and ideological readings, an approach that isn't nearly as abstruse and (sometimes) reductive and (all too often) joy-killing as literary theory.

four are titled *Dostoevsky* and then have subtitles: *The Seeds of Revolt, 1821–1849* (1976); *The Years of Ordeal, 1850–1859* (1984); *The Stir of Liberation, 1860–1865* (1986); and this year, in incredibly expensive hardcover, *The Miraculous Years, 1865–1871.* Professor Frank must now be about seventy-five, and judging by his photo on *The Miraculous Years*'s back jacket he's not exactly hale,[3] and probably all serious scholars of Dostoevsky are waiting bated to see whether Frank can hang on long enough to bring his encyclopedic study all the way up to the early 1880s, when Dostoevsky finished the fourth of his Great Novels,[4] gave his famous Pushkin Speech, and died. Even if the fifth volume of *Dostoevsky* doesn't get written, though, the appearance now of the fourth ensures Frank's status as the definitive literary biographer of one of the best fiction writers ever.

** Am I a good person? Deep down, do I even really want to be a good person, or do I only want to *seem* like a good person so that people (including myself) will approve of me? Is there a difference? How do I ever actually know whether I'm bullshitting myself, morally speaking? **

In a way, Frank's books aren't really literary biographies at all, at least not in the way that Ellmann's book on Joyce and Bate's on Keats are. For one thing, Frank is as much a cultural historian as he is a biographer — his aim is to create an accurate and exhaustive context for FMD's works, to place the author's life and writing within a coherent account of nineteenth-century Russia's intellectual life. Ellmann's *James Joyce*, pretty much the standard by which most literary bios are measured, doesn't go into anything like Frank's detail on ideology or

---

[3] The amount of library time he must have put in would take the stuffing out of anybody, I'd imagine.

[4] Among the striking parallels with Shakespeare is the fact that FMD had four works of his "mature period" that are considered total masterpieces — *Crime and Punishment, The Idiot, Demons* (a.k.a. *The Demons,* a.k.a. *The Devils,* a.k.a. *The Possessed*), and *The Brothers Karamazov* — all four of which involve murders and are (arguably) tragedies.

politics or social theory. What Frank is about is showing that a comprehensive reading of Dostoevsky's fiction is impossible without a detailed understanding of the cultural circumstances in which the books were conceived and to which they were meant to contribute. This, Frank argues, is because Dostoevsky's mature works are fundamentally ideological and cannot truly be appreciated unless one understands the polemical agendas that inform them. In other words, the admixture of universal and particular that characterizes *Notes from Underground*[5] really marks all the best work of FMD, a writer whose "evident desire," Frank says, is "to dramatize his moral-spiritual themes against the background of Russian history."

Another nonstandard feature of Frank's bio is the amount of critical attention he devotes to the actual books Dostoevsky wrote. "It is the production of such masterpieces that makes Dostoevsky's life worth recounting at all," his preface to *The Miraculous Years* goes, "and my purpose, as in the previous volumes, is to keep them constantly in the foreground rather than treating them as accessory to the life per se." At least a third of this latest volume is given over to close readings of the stuff Dostoevsky produced in this amazing half decade — *Crime and Punishment, The Gambler, The Idiot, The Eternal Husband,* and *Demons.*[6] These readings aim to be explicative rather than argumentative or theory-driven; their aim is to show as clearly as possible what Dostoevsky himself wanted the books to mean. Even though this approach assumes that there's no

---

[5] Volume III, *The Stir of Liberation,* includes a very fine explicative reading of *Notes,* tracing the book's genesis as a reply to the "rational egoism" made fashionable by N. G. Chernyshevsky's *What Is to Be Done?* and identifying the Underground Man as basically a parodic caricature. Frank's explanation for the widespread misreading of *Notes* (a lot of people don't read the book as a *conte philosophique,* and they assume that Dostoevsky designed the Underground Man as a serious Hamlet-grade archetype) also helps explain why FMD's more famous novels are often read and admired without any real appreciation of their ideological premises: "The parodistic function of [the Underground Man's] character has always been obscured by the immense vitality of his artistic embodiment." That is, in some ways Dostoevsky was too good for his own good.

[6] This last one Frank refers to as *The Devils.* One sign of the formidable problems in translating literary Russian is the fact that lots of FMD's books have alternative English titles — the first version of *Notes from Underground* I ever read called itself *Memoirs from a Dark Cellar.*

such thing as the Intentional Fallacy,[7] it still seems prima facie justified by Frank's overall project, which is always to trace and explain
the novels' genesis out of Dostoevsky's own ideological engagement with Russian history and culture.[8]

** What exactly does "faith" mean? As in "religious faith," "faith in
God," etc. Isn't it basically crazy to believe in something that there's
no proof of? Is there really any difference between what we call

---

[7] Never once in four volumes does Professor Frank mention the Intentional Fallacy[7(a)] or
try to head off the objection that his biography commits it all over the place. In a way this
silence is understandable, since the tone Frank maintains through all of his readings is
one of maximum restraint and objectivity: he's not about imposing any particular theory
or method of decoding Dostoevsky, and he steers clear of fighting with critics who've
chosen to apply their various axes' edges to FMD's work. When Frank does want to question or criticize a certain reading (as in occasional attacks on Bakhtin's *Problems of Dostoevsky's Poetics*, or in a really brilliant response to Freud's "Dostoevsky and Parricide" in
the appendix to Volume I), he always does so simply by pointing out that the historical
record and/or Dostoevsky's own notes and letters contradict certain assumptions the
critic has made. His argument is never that somebody else is wrong, just that they don't
have all the facts.

What's also interesting here is that Joseph Frank came of age as a scholar at just the
time when the New Criticism was becoming entrenched in the US academy, and the
good old Intentional Fallacy is pretty much a cornerstone of New Criticism; and so, in
Frank's not merely rejecting or arguing against the IF but proceeding as if it didn't even
exist, it's tempting to imagine all kinds of marvelous patricidal currents swirling around
his project — Frank giving an enormous silent raspberry to his old teachers. But if we
remember that New Criticism's removal of the author from the interpretive equation did
as much as anything to clear the way for poststructural literary theory (as in e.g. Decon-
struction, Lacanian psychoanalysis, Marxist/Feminist Cultural Studies, Foucaultian/
Greenblattian New Historicism, & c.), and that literary theory tends to do to the text
itself what New Criticism had done to the author of the text, then it starts to look as if
Joseph Frank is taking a sharp early turn away from theory[7(b)] and trying to compose a
system of reading and interpretation so utterly different that it (i.e., Frank's approach)
seems a more telling assault on lit theory's premises than any frontal attack could be.

[7(a)] In case it's been a long time since freshman lit, the Intentional Fallacy = "The
judging of the meaning or success of a work of art by the author's expressed or ostensible
intention in producing it." The IF and the Affective Fallacy (= "The judging of a work of
art in terms of its results, especially its emotional effect") are the big two prohibitions of
objective-type textual criticism, especially the New Criticism.

[7(b)] (said theory being our own age's big radical-intellectual fad, rather as nihilism
and rational egoism were for FMD's Russia)

[8] It seems only fair to warn you, though, that Frank's readings of the novels are extremely
close and detailed, at times almost microscopically so, and that this can make for slow
going. And also that Frank's explications seem to require that his reader have Dostoevsky's novels fresh in mind — you end up getting immeasurably more out of his discussions if you go back and actually reread whatever novel he's talking about. It's not clear
that this is a defect, though, since part of the appeal of a literary bio is that it serves as a
motive/occasion for just such rereading.

faith and some primitive tribe's sacrificing virgins to volcanoes because they believe it'll produce good weather? How can somebody have faith before he's presented with sufficient reason to have faith? Or is somehow *needing* to have faith a sufficient reason for having faith? But then what kind of need are we talking about? **

To really appreciate Professor Frank's achievement — and not just the achievement of having absorbed and decocted the millions of extant pages of Dostoevsky drafts and notes and letters and journals and bios by contemporaries and critical studies in a hundred different languages — it is important to understand how many different approaches to biography and criticism he's trying to marry. Standard literary biographies spotlight an author and his personal life (especially the seamy or neurotic stuff) and pretty much ignore the specific historical context in which he wrote. Other studies — especially those with a theoretical agenda — focus almost exclusively on context, treating the author and his books as simple functions of the prejudices, power dynamics, and metaphysical delusions of his era. Some biographies proceed as if their subjects' own works have all been figured out, and so they spend all their time tracing out a personal life's relation to literary meanings that the biographer assumes are already fixed and inarguable. On the other hand, many of our era's "critical studies" treat an author's books hermetically, ignoring facts about that author's circumstances and beliefs that can help explain not only what his work is about but why it has the particular individual magic of a particular individual writer's personality, style, voice, vision, etc.[9]

*   *   *

---

[9] That distinctive singular stamp of himself is one of the main reasons readers come to love an author. The way you can just tell, often within a couple paragraphs, that something is by Dickens, or Chekhov, or Woolf, or Salinger, or Coetzee, or Ozick. The quality's almost impossible to describe or account for straight out — it mostly presents as a vibe, a kind of perfume of sensibility — and critics' attempts to reduce it to questions of "style" are almost universally lame.

** Is the real point of my life simply to undergo as little pain and as much pleasure as possible? My behavior sure seems to indicate that this is what I believe, at least a lot of the time. But isn't this kind of a selfish way to live? Forget selfish — isn't it awful lonely? **

So, biographically speaking, what Frank's trying to do is ambitious and worthwhile. At the same time, his four volumes constitute a very detailed and demanding work on a very complex and difficult author, a fiction writer whose time and culture are alien to us. It seems hard to expect much credibility in recommending Frank's study here unless I can give some sort of argument for why Dostoevsky's novels ought to be important to us as readers in 1996 America. This I can do only crudely, because I'm not a literary critic or a Dostoevsky expert. I am, though, a living American who both tries to write fiction and likes to read it, and thanks to Joseph Frank I've spent pretty much the whole last two months immersed in Dostoevskynalia.

Dostoevsky is a literary titan, and in some ways this can be the kiss of death, because it becomes easy to regard him as yet another sepia-tinted Canonical Author, belovedly dead. His works, and the tall hill of criticism they've inspired, are all required acquisitions for college libraries . . . and there the books usually sit, yellowly, smelling the way really old library books smell, waiting for somebody to have to do a term paper. Dahlberg is mostly right, I think. To make someone an icon is to make him an abstraction, and abstractions are incapable of vital communication with living people.[10]

*　　*　　*

---

[10] One has only to spend a term trying to teach college literature to realize that the quickest way to kill an author's vitality for potential readers is to present that author ahead of time as "great" or "classic." Because then the author becomes for the students like medicine or vegetables, something the authorities have declared "good for them" that they "ought to like," at which point the students' nictitating membranes come down, and everyone just goes through the requisite motions of criticism and paper-writing without feeling one real or relevant thing. It's like removing all oxygen from the room before trying to start a fire.

** But if I decide to decide there's a different, less selfish, less lonely point to my life, won't the reason for this decision be my desire to be less lonely, meaning to suffer less overall pain? Can the decision to be less selfish ever be anything other than a selfish decision? **

And it's true that there are features of Dostoevsky's books that are alien and off-putting. Russian is notoriously hard to translate into English, and when you add to this difficulty the archaisms of nineteenth-century literary language, Dostoevsky's prose/dialogue can often come off mannered and pleonastic and silly.[11] Plus there's the stiltedness of the culture Dostoevsky's characters inhabit. When people are ticked off, for instance, they do things like "shake their

---

[11] . . . especially in the Victorianish translations of Ms. Constance Garnett, who in the 1930s and '40s cornered the Dostoevsky & Tolstoy–translation market, and whose 1935 rendering of *The Idiot* has stuff like (scanning almost at random):

> "Nastasya Filippovna!" General Epanchin articulated reproachfully.
>
> . . .
>
> "I am very glad I've met you here, Kolya," said Myshkin to him. "Can't you help me? I must be at Nastasya Filippovna's. I asked Ardelion Alexandrovitch to take me there, but you see he is asleep. Will you take me there, for I don't know the streets, nor the way?"
>
> . . .
>
> The phrase flattered and touched and greatly pleased General Ivolgin: he suddenly melted, instantly changed his tone, and went off into a long, enthusiastic explanation.
>
> . . .

And even in the acclaimed new Knopf translations by Richard Pevear and Larissa Volokhonsky, the prose (in, e.g., *Crime and Punishment*) is still often odd and starchy:

> "Enough!" he said resolutely and solemnly. "Away with mirages, away with false fears, away with spectres! . . . There is life! Was I not alive just now? My life hasn't died with the old crone! May the Lord remember her in His kingdom and — enough, my dear, it's time to go! Now is the kingdom of reason and light and . . . and will and strength . . . and now we shall see! Now we shall cross swords!" he added presumptuously, as if addressing some dark force and challenging it.

Umm, why not just "as if challenging some dark force"? Can you challenge a dark force without addressing it? Or is there in the original Russian something that keeps the above phrase from being redundant, stilted, just plain bad in the same way a sentence like "'Come on!' she said, addressing her companion and inviting her to accompany her" is bad? If so, why not acknowledge that in English it's still bad and just go ahead and fix it? Are literary translators not supposed to mess with the original syntax at all? But Russian is an inflected language — it uses cases and declensions instead of word order — so translators are already messing with the syntax when they put Dostoevsky's sentences into uninflected English. It's hard to understand why these translations have to be so clunky.

fists" or call each other "scoundrels" or "fly at" each other.[12] Speakers use exclamation points in quantities now seen only in comic strips. Social etiquette seems stiff to the point of absurdity — people are always "calling on" each other and either "being received" or "not being received" and obeying rococo conventions of politeness even when they're enraged.[13] Everybody's got a long and hard-to-pronounce last name and Christian name — plus a patronymic, plus sometimes a diminutive, so you almost have to keep a chart of characters' names. Obscure military ranks and bureaucratic hierarchies abound; plus there are rigid and totally weird class distinctions that are hard to keep straight and understand the implications of, especially because the economic realities of old Russian society are so strange (as in, e.g., the way even a destitute "former student" like Raskolnikov or an unemployed bureaucrat like the Underground Man can somehow afford to have servants).

The point is that it's not just the death-by-canonization thing: there is real and alienating stuff that stands in the way of our appreciating Dostoevsky and has to be dealt with — either by learning enough about all the unfamiliar stuff that it stops being so confusing, or else by accepting it (the same way we accept racist/sexist elements in some other nineteenth-century books) and just grimacing and reading on anyway.

But the larger point (which, yes, may be kind of obvious) is that some art is worth the extra work of getting past all the impediments to its appreciation; and Dostoevsky's books are definitely worth the work. And this is so not just because of his bestriding the Western canon — if anything, it's despite that. For one thing that canonization and course assignments obscure is that Dostoevsky isn't just

---

[12] What on earth does it mean to "fly at" somebody? It happens dozens of times in every FMD novel. What, "fly at" them in order to beat them up? To yell at them? Why not *say* that, if you're translating?

[13] Q.v. a random example from Pevear and Volkhonsky's acclaimed new Knopf rendering of *Notes from Underground:*

> "Mr. Ferfichkin, tomorrow you will give me satisfaction for your present words!" I said loudly, pompously addressing Ferfichkin.
> "You mean a duel, sir? At your pleasure," the man answered.

great — he's also fun. His novels almost always have ripping good plots, lurid and intricate and thoroughly dramatic. There are murders and attempted murders and police and dysfunctional-family feuding and spies, tough guys and beautiful fallen women and unctuous con men and wasting illnesses and sudden inheritances and silky villains and scheming and whores.

Of course, the fact that Dostoevsky can tell a juicy story isn't enough to make him great. If it were, Judith Krantz and John Grisham would be great fiction writers, and by any but the most commercial standards they're not even very good. The main thing that keeps Krantz and Grisham and lot of other gifted storytellers from being artistically good is that they don't have any talent for (or interest in) characterization — their compelling plots are inhabited by crude and unconvincing stick figures. (In fairness, there are also writers who are good at making complex and fully realized human characters but don't seem able to insert those characters into a believable and interesting plot. Plus others — often among the academic avant-garde — who seem expert/interested in neither plot nor character, whose books' movement and appeal depend entirely on rarefied meta-aesthetic agendas.)

The thing about Dostoevsky's characters is that they are *alive*. By which I don't just mean that they're successfully realized or developed or "rounded." The best of them live inside us, forever, once we've met them. Recall the proud and pathetic Raskolnikov, the naive Devushkin, the beautiful and damned Nastasya of *The Idiot*,[14] the fawning Lebyedev and spiderish Ippolit of the same novel; *C&P*'s ingenious maverick detective Porfiry Petrovich (with-

---

[14] (. . . who was, like Faulkner's Caddie, "doomed and knew it," and whose heroism consists in her haughty defiance of a doom she also courts. FMD seems like the first fiction writer to understand how deeply some people love their own suffering, how they use it and depend on it. Nietzsche would take Dostoevsky's insight and make it a cornerstone of his own devastating attack on Christianity, and this is ironic: in our own culture of "enlightened atheism" we are very much Nietzsche's children, his ideological heirs, and without Dostoevsky there would have been no Nietzsche, and yet Dostoevsky is among the most profoundly religious of all writers.)

out whom there would probably be no commercial crime fiction w/ eccentrically brilliant cops); Marmeladov, the hideous and pitiful sot; or the vain and noble roulette addict Aleksey Ivanovich of *The Gambler;* the gold-hearted prostitutes Sonya and Liza; the cynically innocent Aglaia; or the unbelievably repellent Smerdyakov, that living engine of slimy resentment in whom I personally see parts of myself I can barely stand to look at; or the idealized and all-too-human Myshkin and Alyosha, the doomed human Christ and triumphant child-pilgrim, respectively. These and so many other FMD creatures are alive — retain what Frank calls their "immense vitality" — not because they're just skillfully drawn types or facets of human beings but because, acting within plausible and morally compelling plots, they dramatize the profoundest parts of all humans, the parts most conflicted, most serious — the ones with the most at stake. Plus, without ever ceasing to be 3-D individuals, Dostoevsky's characters manage to embody whole ideologies and philosophies of life: Raskolnikov the rational egoism of the 1860s' intelligentsia, Myshkin mystical Christian love, the Underground Man the influence of European positivism on the Russian character, Ippolit the individual will raging against death's inevitability, Aleksey the perversion of Slavophilic pride in the face of European decadence, and so on and so forth. . . .

The thrust here is that Dostoevsky wrote fiction about the stuff that's really important. He wrote fiction about identity, moral value, death, will, sexual vs. spiritual love, greed, freedom, obsession, reason, faith, suicide. And he did it without ever reducing his characters to mouthpieces or his books to tracts. His concern was always what it is to be a human being — that is, how to be an actual *person,* someone whose life is informed by values and principles, instead of just an especially shrewd kind of self-preserving animal.

** Is it possible really to love other people? If I'm lonely and in pain, everyone outside me is potential relief — I need them. But can you really love what you need so badly? Isn't a big part of love

caring more about what the other person needs? How am I supposed to subordinate my own overwhelming need to somebody
else's needs that I can't even feel directly? And yet if I can't do this,
I'm damned to loneliness, which I definitely don't want . . . so I'm
back at trying to overcome my selfishness for self-interested reasons. Is there any way out of this bind? **

It's a well-known irony that Dostoevsky, whose work is famous for its
compassion and moral rigor, was in many ways a prick in real life —
vain, arrogant, spiteful, selfish. A compulsive gambler, he was usually broke, and whined constantly about his poverty, and was always
badgering his friends and colleagues for emergency loans that he
seldom repaid, and held petty and long-standing grudges over
money, and did things like pawn his delicate wife's winter coat so
he could gamble, etc.[15]

But it's just as well known that Dostoevsky's own life was full of
incredible suffering and drama and tragedy and heroism. His Moscow childhood was evidently so miserable that in his books Dostoevsky never once sets or even mentions any action in Moscow.[16] His
remote and neurasthenic father was murdered by his own serfs
when FMD was seventeen. Seven years later, the publication of his
first novel,[17] and its endorsement by critics like Belinsky and Herzen,
made Dostoevsky a literary star at the same time he was starting to

---

[15] Frank doesn't sugar-coat any of this stuff, but from his bio we learn that Dostoevsky's
character was really more contradictory than prickish. Insufferably vain about his literary
reputation, he was also tormented his whole life by what he saw as his artistic inadequa-
cies; a leech and a spendthrift, he also voluntarily assumed financial responsibility for his
stepson, for the nasty and ungrateful family of his deceased brother, and for the debts of
Epoch, the famous literary journal that he and his brother had co-edited. Frank's new Volume IV makes it clear that it was these honorable debts, rather than general deadbeat-
ism, that sent Mr. and Mrs. FMD into exile in Europe to avoid debtors' prison, and that it
was only at the spas of Europe that Dostoevsky's gambling mania went out of control.
[16] Sometimes this allergy is awkwardly striking, as in e.g. the start of part 2 of *The Idiot*, when
Prince Myshkin (the protagonist) has left St. Petersburg for six full months in Moscow:
"of Myshkin's adventures during his absence from Petersburg we can give little information," even though the narrator has access to all sorts of other events outside St. P. Frank
doesn't say much about FMD's Muscophobia; it's hard to figure what exactly it's about.
[17] = *Poor Folk*, a standard-issue "social novel" that frames a (rather goopy) love story with
depictions of urban poverty sufficiently ghastly to elicit the approval of the socialist Left.

get involved with the Petrashevsky Circle, a group of revolutionary intellectuals who plotted to incite a peasant uprising against the tsar. In 1849, Dostoevsky was arrested as a conspirator, convicted, sentenced to death, and subjected to the famous "mock execution of the Petrashevtsy," in which the conspirators were blindfolded and tied to stakes and taken all the way to the *"Aim!"* stage of the firing-squad process before an imperial messenger galloped in with a supposed "last-minute" reprieve from the merciful tsar. His sentence commuted to imprisonment, the epileptic Dostoevsky ended up spending a decade in balmy Siberia, returning to St. Petersburg in 1859 to find that the Russian literary world had all but forgotten him. Then his wife died, slowly and horribly; then his devoted brother died; then their journal *Epoch* went under; then his epilepsy started getting so bad that he was constantly terrified that he'd die or go insane from the seizures.[18] Hiring a twenty-two-year-old stenographer to help him complete *The Gambler* in time to satisfy a publisher with whom he'd signed an insane deliver-by-a-certain-date-or-forfeit-all-royalties-for-everything-you-ever-wrote contract, Dostoevsky married this lady six months later, just in time to flee *Epoch*'s creditors with her, wander unhappily through a Europe whose influence on Russia he despised,[19] have a beloved daughter

---

[18] It is true that FMD's epilepsy — including the mystical illuminations that attended some of his preseizure auras — gets comparatively little discussion in Frank's bio; and reviewers like the *London Times*'s James L. Rice (himself the author of a book on Dostoevsky and epilepsy) have complained that Frank "gives no idea of the malady's chronic impact" on Dostoevsky's religious ideals and their representation in his novels. The question of proportion cuts both ways, though: q.v. the *New York Times Book Review*'s Jan Parker, who spends at least a third of his review of Frank's Volume III making claims like "It seems to me that Dostoevsky's behavior does conform fully to the diagnostic criteria for pathological gambling as set forth in the American Psychiatric Association's diagnostic manual." As much as anything, reviews like these help us appreciate Joseph Frank's own evenhanded breadth and lack of specific axes to grind.

[19] Let's not neglect to observe that Frank's Volume IV provides some good personal dirt. W/r/t Dostoevsky's hatred of Europe, for example, we learn that his famous 1867 spat with Turgenev, which was ostensibly about Turgenev's having offended Dostoevsky's passionate nationalism by attacking Russia in print and then moving to Germany, was also fueled by the fact that FMD had previously borrowed fifty thalers from Turgenev and promised to pay him back right away and then never did. Frank is too restrained to make the obvious point: it's much easier to live with stiffing somebody if you can work up a grievance against him.

who died of pneumonia almost right away, writing constantly, pen-
niless, often clinically depressed in the aftermath of tooth-rattling
grand mal seizures, going through cycles of manic roulette binges
and then crushing self-hatred. Frank's Volume IV relates a lot of
Dostoevsky's European tribulations via the journals of his new young
wife, Anna Snitkin,[20] whose patience and charity as a spouse might
well qualify her as a patron saint of today's codependency groups.[21]

** What is "an American"? Do we have something important in
common, as Americans, or is it just that we all happen to live inside
the same boundaries and so have to obey the same laws? How
exactly is America different from other countries? Is there really
something unique about it? What does that uniqueness entail? We
talk a lot about our special rights and freedoms, but are there also
special responsibilities that come with being an American? If so,
responsibilities to whom? **

Frank's bio does cover all this personal stuff, in detail, and he doesn't
try to downplay or whitewash the icky parts.[22] But his project requires that Frank strive at all times to relate Dostoevsky's personal
and psychological life to his books and to the ideologies behind

---

[20] Another bonus: Frank's volumes are replete with marvelous and/or funny tongue-rolling
names — Snitkin, Dubolyobov, Strakhov, Golubov, von Voght, Katkov, Nekrasov, Pisarev.
One can see why Russian writers like Gogol and FMD made a fine art of epithetic names.
[21] Random example from her journal: "'Poor Feodor, he does suffer so much, and is
always so irritable, and liable to fly out about trifles. . . . It's of no consequence, because the
other days are good, when he is so sweet and gentle. Besides, I can see that when he
screams at me it is from illness, not from bad temper.'" Frank quotes and comments on
long passages of this kind of stuff, but he shows little awareness that the Dostoevskys'
marriage was in certain ways quite sick, at least by 1990s standards — see e.g. "Anna's forbearance, whatever prodigies of self-command it may have cost her, was amply compensated for (at least in her eyes) by Dostoevsky's immense gratitude and growing sense of
attachment."
[22] Q.v. also, for instance, Dostoevsky's disastrous passion for the bitch-goddess Appolinari
Suslova, or the mental torsions he performed to justify his casino binges . . . or the fact,
amply documented by Frank, that FMD really was an active part of the Petrashevsky Circle
and as a matter of fact probably did deserve to be arrested under the laws of the time,
this *pace* a lot of other biographers who've tried to claim that Dostoevsky just happened
to be dragged by friends to the wrong radical meeting at the wrong time.

JOSEPH FRANK'S DOSTOEVSKY   269

them. The fact that Dostoevsky is first and last an ideological writer[23] makes him an especially congenial subject for Joseph Frank's contextual approach to biography. And the four extant volumes of *Dostoevsky* make it clear that the crucial, catalyzing event in FMD's life, ideologically speaking, was the mock execution of 22 December 1849 — a five- or ten-minute interval during which this weak, neurotic, self-involved young writer believed that he was about to die. What resulted inside Dostoevsky was a type of conversion experience, though it gets complicated, because the Christian convictions that inform his writing thereafter are not those of any one church or tradition, and they're also bound up with a kind of mystical Russian nationalism and a political conservatism[24] that led the next century's Soviets to suppress or distort much of Dostoevsky's work.[25]

** Does this guy Jesus Christ's life have something to teach me even if I don't, or can't, believe he was divine? What am I supposed to

---

[23] In case it's not obvious, "ideology" is being used here in its strict, unloaded sense to mean any organized, deeply held system of beliefs and values. Granted, by this sort of definition, Tolstoy and Hugo and Zola and most of the other nineteenth-century titans were also ideological writers. But the big thing about Dostoevsky's gift for character and for rendering the deep conflicts within (not just between) people is that it enables him to dramatize extremely heavy, serious themes without ever being preachy or reductive, i.e., without ever blinking the difficulty of moral/spiritual conflicts or making "goodness" or "redemption" seem simpler than they really are. You need only compare the protagonists' final conversions in Tolstoy's *The Death of Ivan Ilych* and FMD's *Crime and Punishment* in order to appreciate Dostoevsky's ability to be moral without being moralistic.
[24] Here is another subject that Frank treats brilliantly, especially in Vol. III's chapter on *House of the Dead*. Part of the reason FMD abandoned the fashionable socialism of his twenties was his years of imprisonment with the absolute dregs of Russian society. In Siberia, he came to understand that the peasants and urban poor of Russia actually loathed the comfortable upper-class intellectuals who wanted to "liberate" them, and that this loathing was in fact quite justified. (If you want to get some idea of how this Dostoevskyan political irony might translate into modern US culture, try reading *House of the Dead* and Tom Wolfe's "Mau-Mauing the Flak Catchers" at the same time.)
[25] The political situation is one reason why Bakhtin's famous *Problems of Dostoevsky's Poetics*, published under Stalin, had to seriously downplay FMD's ideological involvement with his own characters. A lot of Bakhtin's praise for Dostoevsky's "polyphonic" characterizations, and for the "dialogic imagination" that supposedly allowed him to refrain from injecting his own values into his novels, is the natural result of a Soviet critic's trying to discuss an author whose "reactionary" views the State wanted forgotten. Frank, who takes out after Bakhtin at a number of points, doesn't really make clear the constraints that Bakhtin was operating under.

make of the claim that someone who was God's relative, and so
could have turned the cross into a planter or something with just a
word, still voluntarily let them nail him up there, and died? Even if
we suppose he was divine — did he *know?* Did he know he could
have broken the cross with just a word? Did he know in advance
that death would just be temporary (because I bet I could climb up
there, too, if I knew that an eternity of right-hand bliss lay on the
other side of six hours of pain)? But does any of that even really
matter? Can I still believe in JC or Mohammed or Whoever even if I
don't believe they were actual relatives of God? Except what would
that mean: "believe in"? **

What seems most important is that Dostoevsky's near-death experience changed a typically vain and trendy young writer — a very talented writer, true, but still one whose basic concerns were for his
own literary glory — into a person who believed deeply in moral/
spiritual values[26] . . . more, into someone who believed that a life

---

[26] Not surprisingly, FMD's exact beliefs are idiosyncratic and complicated, and Joseph
Frank is thorough and clear and detailed in explaining their evolution through the novels'
thematics (as in, e.g., the toxic effects of egoistic atheism on the Russian character in
Notes and *C&P;* the deformation of Russian passion by worldly Europe in *The Gambler;*
and, in *The Idiot's* Myshkin and *The Brothers Karamazov's* Zossima, the implications of a
human Christ subjected literally to nature's physical forces, an idea central to all the
fiction Dostoevsky wrote after seeing Holbein the Younger's "Dead Christ" at the Basel
Museum in 1867).
   But what Frank has done really phenomenally well here is to distill the enormous
amounts of archival material generated by and about FMD, making it comprehensive
instead of just using selected bits of it to bolster a particular critical thesis. At one point,
somewhere near the end of Vol. III, Frank even manages to find and gloss some obscure
author-notes for "Socialism and Christianity," an essay Dostoevsky never finished, that
help clarify why he is treated by some critics as a forerunner of existentialism:

   "Christ's incarnation . . . provided a new ideal for mankind, one that has retained
   its validity ever since. N.B. Not one atheist who has disputed the divine origin of
   Christ has denied the fact that He is the ideal of humanity. The latest on this —
   Renan. This is very remarkable." And the law of this new ideal, according to Dostoevsky, consists of "the return to spontaneity, to the masses, but freely. . . . Not forcibly,
   but on the contrary, in the highest degree willfully and consciously. It is clear that
   this higher willfulness is at the same time a higher renunciation of the will."

lived without moral/spiritual values was not just incomplete but depraved.[27]

The big thing that makes Dostoevsky invaluable for American readers and writers is that he appears to possess degrees of passion, conviction, and engagement with deep moral issues that we — here, today[28] — cannot or do not permit ourselves. Joseph Frank does an admirable job of tracing out the interplay of factors that made this engagement possible — FMD's own beliefs and talents, the ideological and aesthetic climates of his day, etc. Upon his finishing Frank's books, though, I think that any serious American reader/writer will find himself driven to think hard about what exactly it is that makes many of the novelists of our own place and time look so thematically shallow and lightweight, so morally impoverished, in comparison to Gogol or Dostoevsky (or even to lesser lights like Lermontov and Turgenev). Frank's bio prompts us to ask ourselves why we seem to require of our art an ironic distance from deep convictions or desperate questions, so that contemporary writers have to either make jokes of them or else try to work them in under cover of some formal trick like intertextual quotation or incongruous juxtaposition, sticking the really urgent stuff inside asterisks as part of some multivalent defamiliarization-flourish or some such shit.

Part of the explanation for our own lit's thematic poverty obviously includes our century and situation. The good old modernists, among their other accomplishments, elevated aesthetics to the

---

[27] The mature, postconversion Dostoevsky's particular foes were the Nihilists, the radical progeny of the 1840s' yuppie socialists, whose name (i.e., the Nihilists' name) comes from the same all-negating speech in Turgenev's *Fathers and Sons* that got quoted at the outset. But the real battle was wider, and much deeper. It is no accident that Joseph Frank's big epigraph for Vol. IV is from Kolakowski's classic *Modernity on Endless Trial*, for Dostoevsky's abandonment of utilitarian socialism for an idiosyncratic moral conservatism can be seen in the same basic light as Kant's awakening from "dogmatic slumber" into a radical Pietist deontology nearly a century earlier: "By turning against the popular utilitarianism of the Enlightenment, [Kant] also knew exactly that what was at stake was not any particular moral code, but rather a question of the existence or nonexistence of the distinction between good and evil and, consequently, a question of the fate of mankind."

[28] (maybe under our own type of Nihilist spell)

level of ethics — maybe even metaphysics — and Serious Novels after Joyce tend to be valued and studied mainly for their formal ingenuity. Such is the modernist legacy that we now presume as a matter of course that "serious" literature will be aesthetically distanced from real lived life. Add to this the requirement of textual self-consciousness imposed by postmodernism[29] and literary theory, and it's probably fair to say that Dostoevsky et al. were free of certain cultural expectations that severely constrain our own novelists' ability to be "serious."

But it's just as fair to observe, with Frank, that Dostoevsky operated under cultural constraints of his own: a repressive government, state censorship, and especially the popularity of post-Enlightenment European thought, much of which went directly against beliefs he held dear and wanted to write about. For me, the really striking, inspiring thing about Dostoevsky isn't just that he was a genius; he was also brave. He never stopped worrying about his literary reputation, but he also never stopped promulgating unfashionable stuff in which he believed. And he did this not by ignoring (now a.k.a. "transcending" or "subverting") the unfriendly cultural circumstances in which he was writing, but by confronting them, engaging them, specifically and by name.

It's actually not true that our literary culture is nihilistic, at least not in the radical sense of Turgenev's Bazarov. For there are certain tendencies we believe are bad, qualities we hate and fear. Among these are sentimentality, naïveté, archaism, fanaticism. It would probably be better to call our own art's culture now one of congenital skepticism. Our intelligentsia[30] distrust strong belief, open conviction. Material passion is one thing, but ideological passion disgusts us on some deep level. We believe that ideology is now the province of the rival SIGs and PACs all trying to get their slice of the big green pie . . . and, looking around us, we see that indeed

---

[29] (whatever exactly that is)
[30] (which, given this review's venue, means basically us)

it is so. But Frank's Dostoevsky would point out (or more like hop up and down and shake his fist and fly at us and shout) that if this is so, it's at least partly because we have abandoned the field. That we've abandoned it to fundamentalists whose pitiless rigidity and eagerness to judge show that they're clueless about the "Christian values" they would impose on others. To rightist militias and conspiracy theorists whose paranoia about the government supposes the government to be just way more organized and efficient than it really is. And, in academia and the arts, to the increasingly absurd and dogmatic Political Correctness movement, whose obsession with the mere forms of utterance and discourse show too well how effete and aestheticized our best liberal instincts have become, how removed from what's really important — motive, feeling, belief.

Have a culminative look at just one snippet from Ippolit's famous "Necessary Explanation" in *The Idiot:*

> "Anyone who attacks individual charity," I began, "attacks human nature and casts contempt on personal dignity. But the organization of 'public charity' and the problem of individual freedom are two distinct questions, and not mutually exclusive. Individual kindness will always remain, because it is an individual impulse, the living impulse of one personality to exert a direct influence upon another. . . . How can you tell, Bahmutov, what significance such an association of one personality with another may have on the destiny of those associated?"

Can you imagine any of our own major novelists allowing a character to say stuff like this (not, mind you, just as hypocritical bombast so that some ironic hero can stick a pin in it, but as part of a ten-page monologue by somebody trying to decide whether to commit suicide)? The reason you can't is the reason he wouldn't: such a novelist would be, by our lights, pretentious and overwrought and silly. The straight presentation of such a speech in a Serious Novel today would provoke not outrage or invective, but worse — one raised eyebrow and a very cool smile. Maybe, if the novelist was really major, a dry bit of mockery in *The New Yorker.* The novelist would be (and this is our own age's truest vision of hell) laughed out of town.

So he — we, fiction writers — won't (can't) dare try to use serious art to advance ideologies.[31] The project would be like Menard's *Quixote*. People would either laugh or be embarrassed for us. Given this (and it is a given), who is to blame for the unseriousness of our serious fiction? The culture, the laughers? But they wouldn't (could not) laugh if a piece of morally passionate, passionately moral fiction was also ingenious and radiantly human fiction. But how to make it that? How — for a writer today, even a talented writer today — to get up the guts to even try? There are no formulas or guarantees. There are, however, models. Frank's books make one of them concrete and alive and terribly instructive.

1996

---

[31] We will, of course, without hesitation use art to parody, ridicule, debunk, or criticize ideologies — but this is very different.

HOST

(1)

Mr. John Ziegler, thirty-seven, late of Louisville's WHAS, is now on the air, "Live and Local," from 10:00 PM to 1:00 AM every weeknight on Southern California's KFI, a 50,000-watt megastation whose hourly ID and sweeper, designed by the station's Imaging

FCC regulations require a station ID to be broadcast every hour. This ID comprises a station's call letters, band and frequency, and the radio market it's licensed to serve. Just about every serious commercial station (which KFI very much is) appends to its ID a sweeper, which is the little tagline by which the station wishes to be known. KABC, the other giant AM talk station in Los Angeles, deploys the entendre-rich "Where America Comes First." KFI's own main sweeper is "More *Stimulating* Talk Radio," but it's also got secondary sweepers that it uses to intro the half-hour news, traffic updates at seventeen and forty-six past the hour, and station promos. "Southern California's Newsroom," "The Radio Home of Fox News," and "When You See News Break, Don't Try to Fix It Yourself — Leave That to Professionals" are the big three that KFI's running this spring. The content and sound of all IDs, sweepers, and promos are the responsibility of the station's Imaging department, apparently so named because they involve KFI's image in the LA market. Imaging is sort of the radio version of branding — the sweepers let KFI communicate its special personality and 'tude in a compressed way.

There are also separate, subsidiary taglines that KFI develops specially for its local programs. The main two they're using for the *John Ziegler Show* so far are "Live and Local" and "Hot, Fresh Talk Served Nightly."

department and featuring a gravelly basso whisper against licks from Ratt's '84 metal classic "Round and Round," is: "KFI AM-640, Los Angeles — More *Stimulating* Talk Radio." This is either the eighth or ninth host job that Mr. Ziegler's had in his talk radio career, and far and away the biggest. He moved out here to LA over Christmas — alone, towing a U-Haul — and found an apartment not far

> The whisperer turns out to be one Chris Corley, a voiceover actor best known for movie trailers. Corley's C^2 Productions is based in Ft. Myers FL.

from KFI's studios, which are in an old part of the Koreatown district, near Wilshire Center.

The *John Ziegler Show* is the first local, nonsyndicated late-night program that KFI has aired in a long time. It's something of a gamble for everyone involved. 10:00–1:00 qualifies as late at night in Southern California, where hardly anything reputable's open after nine.

It is currently right near the end of the program's second segment on the evening of May 11, 2004, shortly after Nicholas Berg's taped beheading by an al-Qaeda splinter in Iraq. Dressed, as is his custom, for golf, and wearing a white billed cap w/ corporate logo, Mr. Ziegler is seated by himself in the on-air studio, surrounded by monitors and sheaves of Internet printouts. He is trim, clean-shaven, and handsome in the bland way that top golfers and local

> (By the standards of the US radio industry, this makes him almost movie-star gorgeous.)

TV newsmen tend to be. His eyes, which off-air are usually flat and unhappy, are alight now with passionate conviction. Only some of the studio's monitors concern Mr. Z.'s own program; the ones up near the ceiling take muted, closed-caption feeds from Fox News, MSNBC, and what might be C-SPAN. To his big desk's upper left is a wall-mounted digital clock that counts down seconds. His computer monitors' displays also show the exact time.

Across the soundproof glass of the opposite wall, another monitor in the Airmix room is running an episode of *The Simpsons*, also muted, which both the board op and call screener are watching with half an eye.

Pendent in front of John Ziegler's face, attached to the same type of hinged, flexible stand as certain student desk lamps, is a Shure-brand broadcast microphone that is sheathed in a gray foam filtration sock to soften popped p's and hissed sibilants. It is into this microphone that the host speaks:

"And I'll tell you why — it's because we're *better* than they are."

A Georgetown BA in Government and Philosophy, scratch golfer, former TV sportscaster, possible world-class authority on the O.J. Simpson trial, and sometime contributor to MSNBC's *Scarborough Country*, Mr. Ziegler is referring here to America versus what he terms "the Arab world." It's near the end of his "churn," which is the industry term for a host's opening monologue, whose purpose is both to introduce a show's nightly topics and to get listeners emotionally stimulated enough that they're drawn into the program and don't switch away. More than any other mass medium, radio enjoys a captive audience — if only because so many of the listeners are driving — but in a major market there are dozens of AM stations to listen to, plus of course FM and satellite radio, and even a very seductive and successful station rarely gets more than a 5 or 6 percent audience share.

"We're not perfect, we suck a lot of the time, but we are *better* as a people, as a culture, and as a society than they are, and we need to recognize that, so that we can possibly even *begin* to deal with the evil that we are facing."

When he's impassioned, Mr. Z.'s voice rises and his arms wave around (which obviously only those in the Airmix room can see). He also fidgets, bobs slightly up and down in his executive desk chair, and weaves. Although he must stay seated and can't pace around the room, the host does not have to keep his mouth any set distance from the microphone, since the board op, 'Mondo Hernandez, can adjust his levels on the mixing board's channel 7 so that Mr. Z.'s volume always stays in range and never peaks or fades. 'Mondo, whose price for letting outside parties hang around Airmix is one large bag of cool-ranch Doritos per evening, is an

Prophet is the special OS for KFI's computer system — "like Windows for a radio station," according to Mr. Ziegler's producer.

immense twenty-one-year-old man with a ponytail, stony Meso-american features, and the placid, grandmotherly eyes common to giant mammals everywhere. Keeping the studio signal from peaking is one of 'Mondo's prime directives, along with making sure that each of the program's scheduled commercial spots is loaded into Prophet and run at just the right time, where-

'Mondo's lay explanation of what peaking is consists of pointing at the red area to the right of the two volumeters' bobbing needles on the mixing board: "It's when the needles go into the red." The overall mission, apparently, is to keep the volume and resonance of a host's voice high enough to be stimulating but not so high that they exceed the capacities of an AM analog signal or basic radio receiver. One reason why callers' voices sound so much less rich and authoritative than hosts' voices on talk radio is that it is harder to keep telephone voices from peaking.

"Analog" is slightly misleading, because in fact KFI's signal is digitized for transmission from the studio down to the transmitter facility in La Mirada, where it's then converted back to analog for broadcast. But it is true that AM signals are more limited, quality-wise, than FM. The FCC prohibits AM signal frequencies of more than 10,000 kilohertz, whereas FM signals get 15,000 kHz — mainly because the AM part of the electromagnetic spectrum is more crowded than the FM part.

upon he must confirm that the ad has run as scheduled in the special Airmix log he signs each page of, so that the station can bill advertisers for their spots. 'Mondo, who started out two years ago as an unpaid intern and now earns ten dollars an hour, works 7:00–1:00 on weeknights and also board-ops KFI's special cooking show on Sunday mornings.

Another reason is mike processing, which evens and fills out the host's voice, removing raspy or metallic tones, and occurs automatically in Airmix. There's no such processing for callers' voices.

In the unlikely event of further interest, here is a simplified version of the technical path taken by Mr. Z.'s voice during broadcast: Through channel 7 of 'Mondo's board and the wall of processors, levelers, and compressors in Airmix, through the Eventide BD-980 delayer and Aphex compellor in KFI's master control room, through a duo of Moseley 6000-series digital encoders and to the microwave transmitter on the roof, whence it is beamed at 951.5 MHz to the repeater-site antenna on Briarcrest Peak in the Hollywood Hills, then beamed from the repeater at 943.5 MHz to KFI's forties-era transmitter in Orange County, where its signal is decoded by more Moseley 6000s, further processed and modulated and brought up to maximum legal frequency, and pumped up KFI's 757-foot main antenna, whose 50,000 watts cost $6,000 a month in electricity and cause phones in a five-mile radius to play ghostly KFI voices whenever the weather's just right.

As long as he's kept under forty hours a week, which he somehow always just barely is, the station is not obliged to provide 'Mondo with employee benefits.

The Nick Berg beheading and its Internet video compose what is known around KFI as a "Monster," meaning a story that has both high news value and tremendous emotional voltage. As is SOP in political talk radio, the emotions most readily accessed are anger, outrage, indignation, fear, despair, disgust, contempt, and a certain kind of apocalyptic glee, all of which the Nick Berg thing's got in spades. Mr. Ziegler, whose program is in only its fourth month at KFI, has been fortunate in that 2004 has already been chock-full of Monsters — Saddam's capture, the Abu Ghraib scandal, the Scott Peterson murder trial, the Greg Haidl gang-rape trial, and preliminary hearings in the rape trial of Kobe Bryant. But tonight is the most angry, indignant, disgusted, and impassioned that Mr. Z.'s

---

Here is a sample bit of "What the *John Ziegler Show* Is All About," a long editorial intro to the program that Mr. Ziegler delivered snippets of over his first several nights in January:

> The underlying premise of the *John Ziegler Show* is that, thanks to its socialistic leanings, incompetent media, eroding moral foundation, aging demographics, and undereducated masses, the United States, as we know it, is doomed. In my view, we don't know how much longer we still have to enjoy it, so we shouldn't waste precious moments constantly worrying or complaining about it. However, because not everyone in this country is yet convinced of this seemingly obvious reality, the show does see merit in pointing out or documenting the demise of our nation and will take great pains to do so. And because most everyone can agree that there is value in attempting to delay the sinking of the *Titanic* as long as possible, whenever feasible the *John Ziegler Show* will attempt to do its part to plug whatever holes in the ship it can. With that said, the show realizes that, no matter how successful it (or anyone else) may be in slowing the downfall of our society, the final outcome is still pretty much inevitable, so we might as well have a good time watching the place fall to pieces.

Be advised that the intro's stilted, term-paperish language, which looks kind of awful in print, is a great deal more effective when the spiel is delivered out loud — the stiffness gives it a slight air of self-mockery that keeps you from being totally sure just how seriously John Ziegler takes what he's saying. Meaning he gets to have it both ways. This half-pretend pretension, which is ingenious in all sorts of ways, was pioneered in talk radio by Rush Limbaugh, although with Limbaugh the semi-self-mockery is more tonal than syntactic.

gotten on-air so far, and the consensus in Airmix is that it's resulting in some absolutely first-rate talk radio.

John Ziegler, who is a talk radio host of unflagging industry,
broad general knowledge, mordant wit, and extreme conviction,
makes rather a specialty of media criticism. One object of his disgust and contempt in the churn so far has been the US networks'
spineless, patronizing decision not to air the Berg videotape and
thus to deny Americans "a true and accurate view of the barbarity,
the utter *depravity*, of these people." Even more outrageous, to Mr.
Z., is the mainstream media's lack of outrage about Berg's taped
murder versus all that same media's hand-wringing and invective
over the recent photos of alleged prisoner abuse at Abu Ghraib
prison, which he views as a clear indication of the deluded, blame-
America-first mentality of the US press. It is an associated contrast
between Americans' mortified response to the Abu Ghraib photos
and reports of the Arab world's phlegmatic reaction to the Berg
video that leads to his churn's climax, which is that we are plainly,
unambiguously better than the Arab world — whereupon John
Ziegler invites listeners to respond if they are so moved, repeats the
special mnemonic KFI call-in number, and breaks for the :30 news
and ads, on time to the second, as 'Mondo takes ISDN feed from
Airwatch and the program's associate producer and call screener,
Vince Nicholas — twenty-six and hiply bald — pushes back from
his console and raises both arms in congratulation, through the
glass.

It goes without saying that there are all different kinds of stimulation. Depending on one's politics, sensitivities, and tastes in

ISDN, in which the *D* stands for "Digital," is basically a phone line of very
high quality and expense. ISDN is the main way that stations take feed for
syndicated programs from companies like Infinity Broadcasting, Premiere
Radio Networks, etc. KFI has its own News department, but on nights and
weekends it uses a service called Airwatch that provides off-hour news and
traffic for stations in the LA area. When, at :17 and :46 every hour, Mr. Z.
intros a report from "Alan LaGreen in the KFI Traffic Center," it's really
Alan LaGreen of Airwatch, who's doing traffic reports for different stations
at different times all hour and has to be very careful to give the right call
letters for the Traffic Center he's supposedly reporting from.

argumentation, it is not hard to think of objections to John Ziegler's climactic claim, or at least of some urgent requests for clarification. Like: Exactly what and whom does "the Arab world" refer to? And why are a few editorials and televised man-on-the-street interviews sufficient to represent the attitude and character of a whole diverse region? And why is al-Jazeera's showing of the Berg video so awful if Mr. Z. has just castigated the US networks for *not* showing it? Plus, of course, what is "better" supposed to mean here? More moral? More diffident about our immorality? Is it not, in our own history, pretty easy to find some Berg-level atrocities committed by US nationals, or agencies, or even governments, and approved by much of our populace? Or perhaps this: Leaving aside whether John Ziegler's assertions are true or coherent, is it even remotely helpful or productive to make huge, sweeping claims about some other region's/culture's inferiority to us? What possible effect can such remarks have except to incite hatred? Aren't they sort of irresponsible?

It is true that no one on either side of the studio's thick window expresses or even alludes to any of these objections. But this is not because Mr. Z.'s support staff is stupid, or hateful, or even necessarily on board with sweeping jingoistic claims. It is because they understand the particular codes and imperatives of large-market talk radio. The fact of the matter is that it is not John Ziegler's job to be responsible, or nuanced, or to think about whether his on-air comments are produc-

tive or dangerous, or co-gent, or even defen-sible. That is not to say that the host would not defend his "We're bet-ter" — strenuously — or that he does not believe it's true. It is to say that he has exactly

It is maybe more significant that not one of the listeners who call in tonight and wait on hold for ten, twenty, or in one case forty-plus minutes to respond to John Ziegler has any problem with his assertions of Arab inferiority. And this is not (unlike Rush's call-screening protocols) just a matter of whom Vince and Mr. Z. allow on the air. Vince's screening conversations with callers are clearly audible in the Airmix room — even the ones who don't get through agree; or, if they disagree, it's that they don't think the comparison goes far enough.

one on-air job, and that is to be stimulating. An obvious point, but it's one that's often overlooked by people who complain about propaganda, misinformation, and irresponsibility in commercial talk radio. Whatever else they are, the above-type objections to "We're better than the Arab world" are calls to accountability. They are the sorts of criticisms one might make of, say, a journalist, someone whose job description includes being responsible about what he says in public. And KFI's John Ziegler is not a journalist — he is an entertainer. Or maybe it's better to say that he is part of

See, e.g., Mr. John Kobylt, of KFI's top-rated afternoon *John & Ken Show*, in a recent *LA Times* profile: "The truth is, we do everything for ratings. Yes, that's our job. I can show you the contract. . . . This is not *Meet the Press*. It's not the *Jim Lehrer NewsHour*."

a peculiar, modern, and very popular type of news industry, one that manages to enjoy the authority and influence of journalism without the stodgy constraints of fairness, objectivity,

Or you could call it atavistic, a throwback to the days before Joseph Pulitzer started warning everyone that "A cynical, mercenary, demagogic press will produce in time a people as base as itself." The truth is that what we think of as objectivity in journalism has been a standard since only the 1900s, and mainly in the US. Have a look at some European dailies sometime.

KFI management's explanation of "stimulating" is apposite, if a bit slippery. Following is an excerpted transcript of a mid-May Q&A with Ms. Robin Bertolucci, the station's intelligent, highly successful, and sort of hypnotically intimidating Program Director. (The haphazard start is because the interviewing skills behind the Q parts are marginal; the excerpt gets more interesting as it goes along.)

Q: Is there some compact way to describe KFI's programming philosophy?
A: "What we call ourselves is 'More *Stimulating* Talk Radio.'"
Q: Pretty much got that part already.
A: "That is the slogan that we try to express every minute on the air. Of being stimulating. Being informative, being entertaining, being energetic, being dynamic . . . The way we do it is a marriage of information and stimulating entertainment."
Q: What exactly is it that makes information entertaining?
A: "It's attitudinal, it's emotional."
Q: Can you explain this attitudinal component?
A: "I think *'stimulating'* really sums it up. It's what we really try to do."
Q: [Strangled frustration-noises.]
A: "Look, our station logo is in orange and black, and white — it's a stark, aggressive look. I think that typifies it. The attitude. A little in-your-face. We're not . . . stodgy."

and responsibility that make trying to tell the truth such a drag for everyone involved. It is a frightening industry, though not for any of the simple reasons most critics give.

Distributed over two walls of KFI's broadcast studio, behind the monitors and clocks, are a dozen promotional KFI posters, all in the station's eye-catching Halloween colors against the sweeper's bright white. On each poster, the word "Stimulating" is both italicized and underscored. Except for the door and soundproof window, the entire studio is lined in acoustic tile with strange Pollockian patterns of tiny holes. Much of the tile is grayed and decaying, and the carpet's no color at all; KFI has been in this facility for nearly thirty years and will soon be moving out. Both the studio and Airmix are kept chilly because of all the electronics. The overhead

> KFI has large billboards at traffic nodes all over metro Los Angeles with the same general look and feel, although the billboards often carry both the sweeper and extra tag phrases: "Raving Infomaniacs," "The Death of Ignorance," "The Straight Poop," and (against a military-camouflage background) "Intelligence Briefings."

lights are old inset fluorescents, the kind with the slight flutter to them; nothing casts any sort of shadow. On one of the studio walls is also pinned the special set of playing cards distributed for last year's invasion of Iraq, these now with hand-drawn Xs over the faces of those Baathists captured or killed so far. The great L-shaped table that Mr. Z. sits at nearly fills the little room; it's got so many coats

> The Airmix room's analogue to the cards is a bumper sticker next to the producer's station:
> WHO WOULD THE FRENCH VOTE FOR?
> — *AMERICANS FOR BUSH*

of brown paint on it that the tabletop looks slightly humped. At the L's base is another Shure microphone, used by Ken Chiampou of 3:00–7:00's *John & Ken,* its hinged stand now partly folded up so that the mike hangs like a wilted flower. The oddest thing about the studio is a strong scent of decaying bananas, as if many cast-off peels or even whole bananas were rotting in the room's wastebaskets, none of which look to have been emptied anytime recently.

(He never leaves his chair during breaks, for example, not even to use the restroom.)

Mr. Ziegler, who has his ascetic side, drinks only bottled water in the studio, and absolutely never snacks, so there is no way he is the source of the banana smell.

It is worth considering the strange media landscape in which political talk radio is a salient. Never before have there been so many different national news sources — different now in terms of both medium and ideology. Major newspapers from anywhere are available online; there are the broadcast networks plus public TV, cable's CNN, Fox News, CNBC, et al., print and Web magazines, Internet bulletin boards, *The Daily Show,* e-mail newsletters, blogs. All this is well-known; it's part of the Media Environment we live in. But there are some very odd prices and ironies here. One is that the increasing control of US mass media by a mere handful of corporations has created a situation of extreme fragmentation, a kaleidoscope of information options. Another is that the ever-increasing number of ideologically based news outlets creates precisely the kind of relativism that cultural conservatives decry, a kind of epistemic free-for-all in which "the truth" is wholly a matter of perspective and agenda. In some respects all this variety is probably good, productive of difference and dialogue and so on. But it can also be confusing and stressful for the average citizen. Short of signing on to a particular mass ideology and patronizing only those partisan news sources that ratify what you want to believe,

Both on- and off-air, Mr. Ziegler avows that "the fragmentation [of US news media] is a big factor in the destruction of America. There's now so many places they [= politicians and public figures] can go, why go anyplace that's going to ask the real questions?"

(Again, though, it's not as if viciously partisan news is new, historically speaking — see, e.g., the battles between Hearst- and Pulitzer-controlled newspapers in the late 1800s.)

EDITORIAL ASIDE It's hard to understand Fox News tags like "Fair and Balanced," "No-Spin Zone," and "We Report, You Decide" as anything but dark jokes, ones that delight the channel's conservative audience precisely because their claims to objectivity so totally enrage liberals, whose own literal interpretation of the taglines then makes the left seem dim, humorless, and stodgy.

it is increasingly hard to determine which sources to pay attention to and how exactly to distinguish real information from spin.

EDITORIAL CONTENT Of course, this is assuming you believe that information and spin are different things — and one of the dangers of partisan news's metastasis is the way it enables the conviction that the two aren't really distinct at all. Such a conviction, if it becomes endemic, alters democratic discourse from a "battle of ideas" to a battle of sales pitches for ideas (assuming, again, that one chooses to distinguish ideas from pitches, or actual guilt/innocence from lawyers' arguments, or binding commitments from the mere words "I promise," and so on and so forth).

This fragmentation and confusion have helped give rise to what's variously called the "meta-media" or "explaining industry." Under most taxonomies, this category includes media critics for news dailies, certain high-end magazines, panel shows like CNN's *Reliable Sources*, media-watch blogs like instapundit.com and talkingpointsmemo.com, and a large percentage of political talk radio. It is no accident that one of the signature lines Mr. Ziegler likes to deliver over his opening bumper music at :06 is ". . . the show where we take a look at the news of the day, we provide you the facts, and then we give you the truth." For this is how much of 2004's political talk radio understands its function: to explore the day's news in a depth and detail that other media do not, and to interpret, analyze, and explain that news.

N.B.: In a recent and very astute political-culture study called *Sore Winners*, the *LA Weekly*'s John Powers comes at the problem from a slightly different angle: "Just as the proliferation of blurbs in movie ads has made all critics appear to be idiots or flacks, so the rabbitlike proliferation of news sources — many of them slipshod, understaffed, or insanely partisan — has inevitably devalued the authority of any individual source."

Granted, most political talk radio shows include non-news stuff, often personal elements designed to help develop a host's on-air persona and heighten the listener's sense of a relationship with a real person. On the *John Ziegler Show*, Mr. Z. often talks about his past jobs and personal travails, and has a periodic "Ask John Anything" feature whose title is self-explanatory. The modifier "political" is mostly meant to exclude certain kinds of specialty talk radio, such as Dave Ramsey's syndicated program on personal finance, Kim Komando's computer advice show, Dr. Dean Edell, Howard Stern, etc.

Which all sounds great, except of course "explaining" the news really means editorializing, infusing the actual events of the day with the host's own opinions. And here is

Quick sample intros: Mike Gallagher, a regular Fox News contributor whose program is syndicated by Salem Radio Network, has an upcoming book called *Surrounded by Idiots: Fighting Liberal Lunacy in America*. Neal Boortz, who's carried by Cox Radio Syndication and JRN, bills himself as "High Priest of the Church of the Painful Truth," and his recent ads in trade publications feature the quotation "How can we take airport security seriously until ethnic profiling is not only permitted, but *encouraged*?"

where the real controversy starts, because these opinions are, as just one person's opinions, exempt from strict journalistic standards of truthfulness, probity, etc., and yet they are often delivered by the talk radio host not as opinions but as revealed truths, truths intentionally ignored or suppressed by a "mainstream media" that's "biased" in favor of liberal interests. This is, at any rate, the rhetorical template for Rush Limbaugh's program, on which most syndicated and large-market political talk radio is modeled, from ABC's Sean Hannity and Talk Radio Network's Laura Ingraham to G. G. Liddy, Rusty Humphries, Michael Medved, Mike Gallagher, Neal Boortz, Dennis Prager, and, in many respects, Mr. John Ziegler.

PURELY INFORMATIVE It's true that there are, in some large markets and even syndication, a few political talk radio hosts who identify as moderate or liberal. The best known of these are probably Ed Schultz, Thom Hartmann, and Doug Stephan. But only a few, and only Stephan has anything close to a national audience. And the tribulations of Franken et al.'s Air America venture are well-known. The point is that it is neither inaccurate nor unfair to say that today's political talk radio is, in general, overwhelmingly conservative.

(whose show is really only semi-political)

It is not that all these hosts are what Limbaugh's become and Hannity's been from the beginning: wholly owned subsidiaries of the Republican Party, far more interested in partisan politics than in any battle of ideas. But it's fair to say that all these other programs present the listener with the same basic problem as EIB and Hannitization, which is that they profess to be explaining and aiding interpretation by stripping away ideology but are in fact promulgating ideology, offering nothing more than

(Just on general principles, Michael Savage is not going to be included or referred to in any way, ever.)

Mr. Z. identifies himself as a Libertarian, though he's not a registered member of the Libertarian Party because he feels they "can't get their act together," which he does not seem to intend as a witticism.

(and to the DNC, and to progressive PACs, and political scientists, and psephologists) a particular political slant on the news, and claiming — as gifted spinners always claim — that it's not they but the Other Side who are spinning and slanting and promoting an agenda. The result is to make whatever we decide to call "the news" even more diffuse and confusing — unless, again, the listener happens to share the hosts' politics, in which case what political talk radio offers is just a detailed, stimulating confirmation of stuff that the listener already believes.

The numbers here are based on 2003 Arbitron weekly Cume figures for listeners 12+. (Explanations of the jargon are coming up.)

With some 1,400 US stations now broadcasting talk radio, with 14.5 million regular listeners to Limbaugh and 11 million to Hannity, 2.5 million each to Boortz and Gallagher, and well over a million each day to Liddy, Humphries, Medved, and Ingraham, part of what is so unsettling to liberals and moderates is that it's unclear whether (a) political talk radio is merely serving up right-wingers their daily ration of red meat, or (b) it's functioning as propaganda that causes undecided listeners to become more conservative because the hosts are such seductive polemicists, or (c) both. It's known that talk radio played a big part in keeping the Whitewater and Lewinsky scandals alive

NON-EDITORIAL ASIDE One clear way that talk radio and conservative cable do affect politics: repetition. Which they're really, really good at. If a story, allegation, or factoid gets sufficiently hammered on in the conservative media, over and over and day after day, it is almost inevitable that the mainstream press will pick it up, if only because it eventually becomes real news that the conservative media is making such heavy weather of the item. In many cases, the "Conservative commentators are charging that . . ." part then drops off the item (if only because it's unsexy jot-and-tittle clutter compared to the charge itself), and the story takes on a life of its own.

long enough to hamstring the Clinton presidency, and that hosts' steady iteration of exaggerated stories about Al Gore's supposed Internet-invention and *Love Story* claims did damage to his candidacy. It's known that the vastly increased popularity of talk radio over the past decade coincides with the growth and mobilization of the GOP's right wing, with the proliferation of partisan media, with the alliance of neoconservatism and evangelical Christianity, and with what seems like the overnight disappearance

That certain systemic vices of our mainstream press (e.g., laziness, cupidity) are partly responsible for the success of this tactic seems too obvious to belabor.

Forget the sixties: One would have to go back to Hamiltonian Federalists vs. Jeffersonian Democratic-Republicans c. 1800 to find this kind of bilateral venom.

of restraint, tolerance, and civility — even a pretense of mutual respect — in US political discourse. It's known that 58 percent of talk radio listeners earn more than $50,000 a year, that 34 percent of those listeners over twenty-five are college graduates, and that political talk radio's audience is more likely to vote than people who listen to other kinds of radio formats. What's not known is what any of this really means.

(. . . though opinions abound, e.g.:)

One of the more plausible comprehensive theories is that political talk radio is one of several important "galvanizing venues" for the US right. This theory's upshot is that talk radio functions as a kind of electronic town hall meeting where passions can be inflamed and arguments honed under the loquacious tutelage of the hosts. What's compelling about this sort of explanation is not just its eschewal of simplistic paranoia about disinformation/agitprop (comparisons of Limbaugh and Hannity to Hitler and Goebbels are dumb, unhelpful, and easy for conservatives to make fun of), but the fact that it helps explain what is a deeper, much more vexing mystery for nonconservatives. This mystery is why the right is now where the real energy is in US political life, why the conservative message seems so much more straightforward and stimulating, why they're all having so much more goddamn *fun* than the left of the *Times* and *The Nation* and NPR and the DNC. It seems reasonable to say that political talk radio is part of either a fortuitous set of circumstances or a wildly successful strategy for bringing a large group of like-minded citizens together, uniting them in a coherent set of simple ideas, energizing them, and inciting them to political action. That the US left enjoyed this sort of energized coalescence in the 1960s and '70s but has (why not admit the truth?) nothing like it now is what lends many of the left's complaints about talk radio a bitter, whiny edge . . . which edge the right has even more fun laughing at, and which the theory can also account for.

VERY EDITORIAL Is this the really maddening question for anyone else sitting out here watching it all? Why is conservatism so hot right now? What accounts for its populist draw? It can't just be 9/11; it predates 9/11. But since just when has the right been so energized? Has there really been some reactionary Silent Majority out there for decades, frustrated but atomized, waiting for an inciting spark? If so, was Ronald Reagan that spark? But there wasn't this kind of right-wing populist verve to the Reagan eighties. Did it start with Gingrich's rise to Speaker, or with the intoxicating hatred of all things Clinton? Or has the country as a whole just somehow moved so far right that hard-core conservatism now feeds, stormlike, on the hot vortical energy of the mainstream?

Or is it the opposite — that the US has moved so far and so fast toward cultural permissiveness that we've reached a kind of apsidal point? It might be instructive to try seeing things from the perspective of, say, a God-fearing

Continued on next page

Continued from previous page
hard-working rural-Midwestern military vet. It's not that hard. Imagine gazing through his eyes at the world of MTV and the content of video games, at the gross sexualization of children's fashions, at Janet Jackson flashing her aureole on what's supposed to be a holy day. Imagine you're him having to explain to your youngest what oral sex is and what it's got to do with a US president. Ads for penis enlargers and Hot Wet Sluts are popping up out of nowhere on your family's computer. Your kids' school is teaching them WWII and Vietnam in terms of Japanese internment and the horrors of My Lai. Homosexuals are demanding holy matrimony; your doctor's moving away because he can't afford the lawsuit insurance; illegal aliens want driver's licenses; Hollywood elites are bashing America and making millions from it; the president's ridiculed for reading his Bible; priests are diddling kids left and right. Shit, the country's been *directly attacked*, and people aren't supporting our commander in chief.

Assume for a moment that it's not silly to see things this man's way. What cogent, compelling, relevant message can the center and left offer him? Can we bear to admit that we've actually helped set him up to hear "We're *better* than they are" not as twisted and scary but as refreshing and redemptive and true? If so, then now what?

(In the real Midwest, this word is pronounced with a long *i*.)

"Spot load" is the industry term for the number of minutes per hour given over to commercials. The point of the main-text sentence is that a certain percentage of the spots that run on KFI from nine to noon are Rush's/PRN's commercials, and they are the ones who get paid by the advertisers. The exact percentages and distributions of local vs. syndicator's commercials are determined by what's called "the Clock," which is represented by a pie-shaped distribution chart that Ms. Bertolucci has on file but will show only a very quick glimpse of, since the spot-load apportionments for syndicated shows in major markets involve complex negotiations between the station and the syndicator, and KFI regards its syndicated Clocks as proprietary info — management doesn't want other stations to know what deals they've cut with PRN.

KFI AM-640 carries Rush Limbaugh's program every weekday, 9:00 AM to noon, via live ISDN feed from Premiere Radio Networks, which is one of the dozen syndication networks that own talk radio shows so popular that it's worth it for local stations to air them even though it costs the stations a portion of their spot load. The same goes for Dr. Laura Schlessinger, who's based in Southern California and used to broadcast her syndicated show from KFI until the mid-nineties, when Premiere built its own LA facility and

In White Star Productions' *History of Talk Radio* video, available at better libraries everywhere, there is footage of Dr. Laura doing her show right here at KFI, although she's at a mike in what's now the Airmix room — which according to 'Mondo used to be the studio, with what's now the studio serving as Airmix. (Why they switched rooms is unclear, but transferring all the gear must

Continued on next page

Continued from previous page
have been a serious hassle.) In the video, the little gray digital clock propped up counting seconds on Dr. Laura's desk is the same one that now counts seconds on the wall to Mr. Ziegler's upper left in the studio — i.e., it's the very same clock — which not only is strangely thrilling but also further testifies to KFI's thriftiness about capital expenses.

was able to offer Schlessinger more sumptuous digs. Dr. Laura airs M–F from noon to 3:00 on KFI. Besides 7:00–10:00 PM's Phil Hendrie (another KFI host whose show went into national syndication, and who now has his own private dressing room and studio over at Premiere), the only other weekday syndication the station uses is *Coast to Coast with George Noory,* which covers and analyzes news of the paranormal throughout the wee hours.

Whatever the social effects of talk radio or the partisan agendas of certain hosts, it is a fallacy that political talk radio is motivated by ideology. It is not. Political talk radio is a business, and it is motivated by revenue. The conservatism that dominates today's AM airwaves does so because it generates high Arbitron ratings, high ad rates, and maximum profits.

The persistence of this fallacy among left-wing opponents of talk radio is extraordinary — it's actually one of the main premises behind the Air America launch. As summarized by *The Public Interest*'s William G. Mayer, the usual claim here is that right-wing radio is "owned by large, profit-hungry corporations or wealthy, profit-driven individuals, who use their companies to push a conservative, pro-capitalist agenda." Mayer's analysis also identifies the gross economic illogic of this claim. Suppose that I am the conservative and rabidly capitalist owner of a radio company. I believe that free-market conservatism is Truth and that the US would be better off in every way if everybody were conservative. This, for me, makes conservatism a "public good" in the Intro Econ sense of the term — i.e., a conservative electorate is a public good in the same way that a clean environment or a healthy populace is a public good. And the same basic economics that explains corporate contributions to air pollution and obesity explains why my radio company has zero incentive to promote the public good of conservatism. Because the time and money my one company would spend trying to spread the Truth would yield (at best) only a tiny increase in the conservatism of the whole country — and yet the advantages of that increased conservatism would be shared by everyone, including my radio competitors, even though they wouldn't have put themselves out one bit to help shift public opinion. In other words, I alone would have paid for a benefit that my competition could also enjoy, free. All of which plainly would not be good business . . . which is why it is actually in my company's best interests to "underinvest" in promulgating ideology.

Coast to Coast used to start at 10:00 PM and run all through the night, which involved rebroadcasting certain hours of the show from 2:00 to 5:00 AM. KFI's big experiment this year began with moving Noory's program back to a 1:00 AM start and cutting the rebroadcast, leaving the 10:00–1:00 slot open for a Live and Local show.

Radio has become a more lucrative business than most people know. Throughout most of the past decade, the industry's revenues have increased by more than 10 percent a year. The average cash-flow margin for major radio companies is now 40 percent, compared to more like 15 percent for large TV networks; and the mean price paid for a radio station has gone from eight to more than thirteen times cash flow. Some of this extreme profitability, and thus the structure of the industry, is due to the 1996 Federal Telecommunications Act, which allowed radio companies to acquire up to eight stations in a given market and to control as much as 35 percent of a market's total ad revenues. The emergence of huge, dominant radio conglomerates like Clear Channel and Infinity is a direct consequence of the '96 Act (which the FCC, aided by the very conservative DC Court of Appeals, has lately tried to make even more permissive). And these radio conglomerates enjoy not just substantial economies of scale but almost unprecedented degrees of business integration.

(Plus it eliminated limits on the number of different markets a company could enter.)

Clear Channel bought KFI — or rather the radio company that owned KFI — sometime around 2000. It's all a little fuzzy, because it appears that Clear Channel actually bought, or absorbed, the radio company that had just bought KFI from another radio company, or something like that.

KFI's local talk rival, KABC, is owned by Disney.

Example: Clear Channel Communications Inc. now owns KFI AM-640, plus two other AM stations and five FMs in the Los

Angeles market. It also owns Premiere Radio Networks. It also turns out to own the Airwatch news/traffic service. And it designs and manufactures Prophet, the KFI operating system, which is state-of-the-art and much too expensive for most independent stations. All told, Clear Channel currently owns some 1,200 radio sta-

It turns out that one of the reasons its old Korea-town studios are such a latrine is that KFI's getting ready to move very soon to a gleaming new complex in Burbank that will house five of Clear Channel's stations and allow them to share a lot of cutting-edge technical equipment and software. Some of the reasons for the consolidation involve AM radio's complex, incremental move from analog to digital broadcast, a move that's a lot more economical if stations can be made to share equipment. The Burbank hub facility will also feature a new and improved mega-Prophet OS that all five stations can use and share files on, which for KFI means convenient real-time access to all sorts of new preloaded bumper music and sound effects and bites.

As the board op, 'Mondo Hernandez is also responsible for downloading and cueing up the sections of popular songs that intro the *John Ziegler Show* and background Mr. Z.'s voice when a new segment starts. Bumper music is, of course, a talk radio convention: Rush Limbaugh has a franchise on the Pretenders, and Sean Hannity always uses that horrific Martina McBride "Let freedom ring/ Let the guilty pay" song. Mr. Z. favors a whole rotating set of classic rock hooks, but his current favorites are Van Halen's "Right Now" and a certain extra-jaunty part of the theme to *Pirates of the Caribbean,* because, according to 'Mondo, "They get John pumped." In case anyone else is curious, the answer to how talk radio gets to use copyrighted songs in its programs is BMI and ASCAP, which 'Mondo explains are the two big licensing entities that stations pay for the use of clients' music. He isn't sure what the acronyms stand for, but he does know that KFI uses BMI — or rather Clear Channel pays BMI a yearly fee that entitles it to unlimited use of the agency's inventory for all its stations, both talk and music. Hence another serious economy of scale for Clear Channel — it's unclear how small, independent stations manage the fees.

N.B.: Mr. Z. usually refers to himself as either "Zig" or "the Zig-meister," and has made a determined effort to get everybody at KFI to call him Zig, with only limited success so far.

(This, it turns out, is Broadcast Music Inc., which "collects fees on behalf of more than two hundred thousand artists worldwide.")

(Despite suspicions, amateur investigation produced no evidence that Clear Channel or any of its subsidiaries owns BMI.)

(This means that the negotiations between KFI and Premiere over the terms of syndication for Rush, Dr. Laura, et al. are actually negotiations between two parts of the same company, which either helps explain or renders even more mysterious KFI's reticence about detailing the Clocks for their PRN shows.)

tions nationwide, one of which happens to be Louisville Kentucky's WHAS, the AM talk station from which John Ziegler was fired, amid spectacular gossip and controversy, in August of '03. Which means that Mr. Ziegler now works in Los Angeles for the same company that just fired him in Louisville, such that his firing now appears — in retrospect, and considering the relative sizes of the Louisville and LA markets — to have been a promotion. All of which turns out to be a strange and revealing story about what a talk radio host's life is like.

(2)

For obvious reasons, critics of political talk radio concern themselves mainly with the programs' content. Talk station management, on the other hand, tends to think of content as a subset of personality, of how stimulating a given host is. As for the hosts — ask Mr. Ziegler off-air what makes him good at his job, and he'll shrug glumly and say "I'm not really all that talented. I've got passion, and I work really hard." Taken so for granted that nobody in the business seems aware of it is something that an outsider, sitting in Airmix and watching John Ziegler at the microphone, will notice right away.

"Passion" is a big word in the industry, and John Ziegler uses the word in connection with himself a lot. It appears to mean roughly the same as what Ms. Bertolucci calls "edginess" or "attitude."

Hosting talk radio is an exotic, high-pressure gig that not many people are fit for, and being truly good at it requires skills so specialized that many of them don't have names.

To appreciate these skills and some of the difficulties involved, you might wish to do an experiment. Try sitting alone in a room with a clock, turning on a tape recorder, and starting to speak into it. Speak about anything you want — with the proviso that your topic, and your opinions on it, must be of interest to some group of strangers who you imagine will be listening to the tape. Naturally, in order to be even minimally interesting, your remarks should be intelligible and their reasoning sequential — a listener will have to be able to follow the logic of what you're saying — which means that you will have to know enough about your topic to organize your statements in a coherent way. (But you cannot do much of this organizing beforehand; it has to occur at

> Part of the answer to why conservative talk radio works so well might be that extreme conservatism provides a fairly neat, clear, univocal template with which to organize one's opinions and responses to the world. The current term of approbation for this kind of template is "moral clarity."

the same time you're speaking.) Plus ideally what you're saying should be not just comprehensible and interesting but compelling, stimulating, which means that your remarks have to provoke and sustain some kind of emotional reaction in the listeners, which in turn will require you to construct some kind of identifiable persona for yourself — your comments will need to strike the listener as coming from an actual human being, someone with a real per-

> It is, of course, much less difficult to arouse genuine anger, indignation, and outrage in people than it is to induce joy, satisfaction, fellow feeling, etc. The latter are fragile and complex, and what excites them varies a great deal from person to person, whereas anger et al. are more primal, universal, and easy to stimulate (as implied by expressions like "He really pushed my buttons").

sonality and real feelings about whatever it is you're discussing. And

> This, too: Consider the special intimacy of talk radio. It's usually listened to solo — radio is the most solitary of broadcast media. And half-an-ear background listening is much more common with music formats than with talk. This is a human being speaking to you, with a pro-caliber voice, eloquently and with passion, in what feels like a one-to-one; it doesn't take long before you start to feel you know him. Which is why it's often such a shock when you see a real host, his face — you discover you've had a picture of this person in your head without knowing it, and it's always wrong. This dissonant shock is one reason why Rush and Dr. Laura, even with their huge built-in audiences, did not fare well on TV.

> (as the industry is at pains to remind advertisers)

it gets trickier: You're trying to communicate in real time with some-one you cannot see or hear responses from; and though you're communicating in speech, your remarks cannot have any of the frag-mentary, repetitive, garbled qualities of real interhuman speech, or speech's ticcy unconscious "umm"s or "you know"s, or false starts or stutters or long pauses while you try to think of how to phrase what you want to say. You're also, of course, denied the physical inflec-tions that are so much a part of spoken English — the facial expres-sions, changes in posture, and symphony of little gestures that accompany and buttress real talking. Everything unspoken about you, your topic, and how you feel about it has to be conveyed through pitch, volume, tone, and pacing. The pacing is especially important: It can't be too slow, since that's low-energy and dull, but it can't be too rushed or it'll sound like babbling. And so you have somehow to keep all these different imperatives and strictures in mind at the same time, while also filling exactly, say, eleven minutes, with no dead air and no going over, such that at 10:46 you have

---

The exact-timing thing is actually a little less urgent for a host who's got the resources of Clear Channel behind him. This is because in KFI's Airmix room, nestled third from the bottom in one of the two eight-foot stacks of processing gear to the left of 'Mondo's mixing board, is an Akai DD1000 Mag-neto optical disk recorder, known less formally as a "Cashbox." What this is is a sound compressor, which exploits the fact that even a live studio program is — because of the FCC-mandated seven-second delay — taped. Here is how 'Mondo, in exchange for certain vending-machine comestibles, explains the Cashbox: "All the shows are supposed to start at six past. But if they put more spots in the log, or say like if traffic goes long, now we're all of a sudden start-ing at seven past or something. The Cashbox can take a . . . twenty-minute segment and turn it into a nineteen." It does this by using computerized sound processing to eliminate pauses and periodically accelerate Mr. Z.'s delivery just a bit. The trick is that the Cashbox can compress sound so art-fully that you don't hear the speed-up, at least not in a nineteen-for-twenty exchange ("You get down to eighteen it's risky, or down around seventeen you can definitely hear it"). So if things are running a little over, 'Mondo has to use the Cashbox — very deftly, via controls that look really complicated — in order to make sure that the Clock's adhered to and Airwatch breaks, pro-mos, and ad spots all run as specified. A gathering suspicion as to why the Akai DD1000 is called the Cashbox occasions a Q: Does the station ever press 'Mondo or other board ops to use the Cashbox and compress shows in order to make room for additional ads? A: "Not really. What they'll do is just put an extra spot or two in the log, and then I've just got to do the best I can."

wound things up neatly and are in a position to say "KFI is the station with the most frequent traffic reports — Alan LaGreen is in the

> The only elocutionary problem Mr. Z. ever exhibits is a habit of confusing the words "censure" and "censor."

↑

KFI Traffic Center" (which, to be honest, Mr. Z. sometimes leaves himself only three or even two seconds for and has to say extremely fast, which he can always do without a flub). So then, ready: Go.

It's no joke. See for example the *John Ziegler Show*'s producer, Emiliano Limon, who broke in at KFI as a weekend overnight host before moving across the glass:

"What's amazing is that when you get new people who think that they can do a talk radio program, you watch them for the first time. By three minutes into it, they have that look on their face like, 'Oh my God, I've got ten minutes left, what am I going to say?' And that's what happened to me a lot. So you end up talking about yourself [which, for complex philosophical reasons, the producer disapproves of], or you end up yammering." Emiliano is a large, very calm and competent man in his mid-thirties who either wears the same black *LA Times* T-shirt every day or owns a whole closetful of them. He was pulled off other duties to help launch KFI's experimental Live and Local evening show, an assignment that obviously involves working closely with Mr. Z., which Emiliano seems to accept as his karmic punishment for being so unflappable and easy to get along with. He laughs more than everyone else at KFI put together.

"I remember one time, I just broke after five minutes, I was just done, and they were going 'Hey, what are you doing, you have another ten minutes!' And I was like, 'I don't know what else to say!' And that's what happens. For those people who think 'Oh, I could do talk radio,' well, there's more to it. A lot of people can't take it once they get that taste of, you know, 'Geez, I gotta fill all this time *and* sound interesting?'

"Then, as you keep on doing it over the days, there's something that becomes absolutely clear to you. You're not really acting on the radio. It's *you*. If no one really responds and the ratings aren't good, it means they don't like *you*." Which is worth keeping very much in mind.

* * *

Another much-bruited theory about ideology and talk radio is exemplified by stuff like the following, which is © 2002 by the *New Statesman:* "Why is talk radio so overwhelmingly right-wing? [It's] because those on the left are prone to be inclusive, tolerant and reflective, qualities that make for a boring radio show." Assuming that one accepts this very generous characterization of the left, the big question becomes just why tolerance and reflection make for "boring radio." An unstated premise behind the theory, though, is that the main reason its audience listens to political talk radio is for entertainment,

> There are elements at KFI, of whom Emiliano Limon is one, who believe that people listen to their station primarily to be informed (details forthcoming).

excitement — and yet it's far from clear why this is so. The same *New Statesman* article includes a supporting bite from an industry source: "Lefties cannot cut it because talk radio is the World Wrestling Foundation with ideas." Notice that the analogy here reveals, or depends on, some further assumptions about talk radio's audience, assumptions that are (given the sorts of people who tend to like pro wrestling) pretty unflattering.

Certain random statistical facts about talk radio listeners were tossed around above; they were contextless because they *are* contextless. Arbitron Inc. and some of its satellites can help measure how many are listening for how long and when, and they provide some rough age data and demographic specs. A lot of the rest is guesswork, and Program Directors don't like to talk about it.

From outside, though, one of the best clues to how a radio station understands its audience is spots. Which commercials it runs, and when, indicate how the station is pitching its listeners' tastes and receptivities to sponsors. In how often particular spots are repeated lie clues

> For instance, one has only to listen to *Coast to Coast w/ Noory*'s ads for gold as a hedge against hyperinflation, special emergency radios you can hand-crank in case of extended power failure, miracle weight-loss formulas, online dating services, etc., to understand that KFI and the syndicator regard this show's audience as basically frightened, credulous, and desperate.

to the length of time the station thinks people are listening, to how

> (ad-wise, a lucrative triad indeed)

attentive it thinks they are, etc. Specific example: Just from its spot load, we can deduce that KFI trusts its audience to sit still for an extraordinary amount of advertising. An average hour of the *John Ziegler Show* consists of four program segments: :06–:17, :23–:30, :37–:46, and :53–:00, or thirty-four minutes of Mr. Z. actually talking. Since KFI's newscasts are never more than ninety seconds, and since quarterly traffic reports are always bracketed by live-read spots for Traffic Center sponsors, that makes each hour at least 40

UNALLOYED INFORMATION A live read is when a host or newsperson reads the ad copy himself on-air. They're sort of a radio tradition, but the degree to which KFI weaves live reads into its programming represents a whole new dimension in broadcast marketing. Live-read spots are more expensive for advertisers, especially the longer, more detailed ones read by the programs' hosts, since these ads (a) can sound at first like an actual talk segment and (b) draw on the personal appeal and credibility of the host. And the spots themselves are often clearly set up to exploit these features — see for instance John Kobylt's live read for LA's Cunning Dental Group during afternoons' *John & Ken:* "Have you noticed how bad the teeth are of all the contestants in these reality shows? I saw some of this the other day. Discolored, chipped, misshaped, misaligned, rotted-out teeth, missing teeth, not to mention the bleeding, oozing, pus-y gums. You go to Cunning Dental Group, they'll take all your gross teeth and in one or two visits fix them and give you a bright shiny smile. . . ."

Even more expensive than live reads are what's called "endorsements," which are when a host describes, in ecstatically favorable terms, his own personal experience with a product or service. Examples here include Phil Hendrie's weight loss on Cortislim, John Kobylt's "better than 20-20" laser-surgery outcome with Saddleback Eye Center, and Mr. Bill Handel's frustrations with various dial-up ISPs before discovering DSL Extreme. These ads, which are KFI's most powerful device for exploiting the intimacy and trust of the listener-host relationship, also result in special "endorsement fees" paid directly to the host. Kobylt, Hendrie, and Handel each do regular endorsements for half a dozen different advertisers. John Ziegler, on the other hand, has yet to do any live reads or endorsements at KFI. His explanations for this tend to vary. Sometimes Mr. Z. calls endorsements "disgusting" and says "The majority of talk show hosts in this country are complete and total whores." At other times he'll intimate that he's had feelers, but that none of the products/services he's been offered are ones that would "do my image much good." KFI management has declined to comment on the new host's endorsement situation, but it seems pretty clear that, in this market, John Ziegler hasn't yet built the kind of long-term affection and credibility that can be sold.

(It's unclear how one spells the adjectival form of "pus," though it sounds okay on-air.)

KFI's Handel, whose 5:00–9:00 AM show is an LA institution in morning drive, describes his program as "in-your-face, informational, with a lot of racial humor."

percent ads; the percentage is even higher if you count sweepers for the station and promos for other KFI shows. And this is the load just on a local program, one for which the Clock doesn't have to be split with a syndicator.

It's not that KFI's unaware of the dangers here. Station management reads its mail, and, as Emiliano Limon puts it, "If there's one complaint listeners always have, it's the spot load." But the only important issue is whether all the complaints translate into actual listener behavior. KFI's spot load is an instance of the kind of multivariable maximization problem that MBA programs thrive on. It is obviously in the station's financial interests to carry just as high a volume of ads as it can without hurting ratings — the moment listeners begin turning away from KFI because of too many commercials, the Arbitron numbers go down, the rates charged for ads have to be reduced, and profitability suffers.

But anything more specific is, again, guesswork. When asked about management's thinking here, or whether there's any particular formula KFI uses to figure out how high a spot load the market will bear, Ms. Bertolucci will only smile and shrug as if pleasantly stumped: "We have more commercials than

> A talk radio marketing consultant at Cleveland's McVay Media explains crushing spot loads and a proliferation of live reads and endorsements in terms of three phenomena: (1) "Consolidation — and the ambitious revenue goals necessary to service debt that owners incurred when they paid for [all] their [many] stations"; (2) "Technology brought new competition — radio is under the gun from MP3 downloads, XM and Sirius, [etc.]"; (3) "Attention spans got *lots* shorter." The solution: "We're developing ways to embed advertiser brand and content into radio programming."

> It's a little more complicated than that, really, because excessive spots can also affect ratings in less direct ways — mainly by lowering the quality of the programming. Industry analyst Michael Harrison, of *Talkers* magazine, complains that "the commercial breaks are so long today that it is hard for hosts to build upon where they left off. The whole audience could have changed. There is the tendency to go back to the beginning and re–set up the premise. . . . It makes it very difficult to do what long-form programming is supposed to do."

we've ever had, and our ratings are the best they've ever been."

How often a particular spot can run over and over before listeners just can't stand it anymore is something

SEMI-EDITORIAL Even in formal, on-record, and very PR-savvy interviews, the language of KFI management is filled with little unconscious bits of jargon — "inventory" for the total number of ad minutes available, "product" for a given program, or (a favorite) "to monetize," which means to extract ad revenue from a given show — that let one know exactly where KFI's priorities lie. Granted, the station is a business, and broadcasting is not charity work. But given how intimate and relationship-driven talk radio is, it's disheartening when management's only term for KFI's listeners, again and again, is "market."

else no one will talk about, but the evidence suggests that KFI sees its audience as either very patient and tolerant or almost catatonically inattentive. Canned ads for local sponsors like Robbins Bros. Jewelers, Sit 'n Sleep Mattress, and the Power Auto Group play every couple hours, 24/7, until one knows every hitch and nuance. National saturation campaigns for products like Cortislim vary things somewhat by using both endorsements and canned spots.

CONSUMER ADVISORY As it happens, the latter two here are products of Berkeley Premium Nutraceuticals, an Ohio company with annual sales of more than $100 million, as well as over 3,000 complaints to the BBB and the Attorney General's Office in its home state alone. Here's why. The radio ads say you can get a thirty-day free trial of Enzyte by calling a certain toll-free number. If you call, it turns out there's a $4.90 S&H charge for the free month's supply, which the lady on the phone wants you to put on your credit card. If you acquiesce, the company then starts shipping you more Enzyte every month and auto-billing your card for at least $35 each time, because it turns out that by taking the thirty-day trial you've signed up for Berkeley's "Automatic Purchase" program — which the operator neglected to mention. And calling Berkeley Nutraceuticals to get the automatic shipments and billings stopped usually doesn't work; they'll stop only if some kind of consumer agency sends a letter. It's the same with Altovis and its own "free trial." In short, the whole thing is one of those irksome, hassle-laden marketing scams, and KFI runs dozens of spots per day for Berkeley products. The degree to which the station is legally responsible for helping a company rip off members of its audience is, by FTC and FCC rules, nil. But it's hard not to see it as another indication of the station's true regard for its listeners.

Pitches for caveat emptor–type nostrums like Avacor (for hair loss), Enzyte ("For natural male enhancement!"), and Altovis ("Helps fight daily fatigue!") often repeat once an hour through the night. As of spring '04, though, the most frequent and concussive spots on KFI are for mortgage and home-refi companies. In just a few slumped, glazed hours of listening, a member of this station's audi-

> FYI: Enzyte, which bills itself as a natural libido and virility enhancer (it also has all those "Smiling Bob & Grateful Wife" commercials on cable TV), contains tribulis terristris, panax ginseng, ginko biloba, and a half dozen other innocuous herbal ingredients. The product costs Berkeley, in one pharmacologist's words, "nothing to make." But it's de facto legal to charge hundreds of dollars a year for it, and to advertise it as an OTC Viagra — the FDA doesn't regulate herbal meds unless people are actually falling over from taking them, and the Federal Trade Commission doesn't have anything like the staff to keep up with the advertising claims, so it's all basically an unregulated market.

ence can hear both canned and live-read ads for Green Light Financial, HMS Capital, Home Field Financial, Benchmark Lending. Over and over. Pacific Home Financial, Lenox National Lending, U.S. Mortgage Capital, Crestline Funding, Home Savings Mortgage, Advantix Lending. Reverse mortgages, negative amortization, adjustable rates, APR, FICO . . . where did all these firms come from? What were these guys doing five years ago?

> (Calls to KFI's Sales department re consumers' amply documented problems with Enzyte and Altovis were, as the journalists say, not returned.)

Why is KFI's audience seen as so especially ripe and ready for refi? Betterloans.com, lendingtree.com, Union Bank of California, bethebroker.net, on and on and on.

Emiliano Limon's "It's *you*" seems true to an extent. But there is also the issue (somewhat paradoxically) of persona, meaning the on-air personality that a host adopts in order to heighten the sense of a real person behind the mike. It is, after all, unlikely that Rush Limbaugh always feels as jaunty and confident as he seems on the air, or that Howard Stern really is deeply fascinated by porn starlets every waking minute of the day. But it's not the same as outright acting. A host's persona, for the most part, is probably more like the way we are all slightly different with some people than we are with others.

In some cases, though, the personas are more contrived and extreme. In the slot preceding Mr. Z.'s on KFI is the *Phil Hendrie Show*, which is actually a cruel and complicated kind of meta-talk radio. What happens every night on this program is that Phil Hendrie brings on some wildly offensive guest — a man who's leaving his wife because she's had a mastectomy, a Little League coach who advocates corporal punishment of players, a retired colonel who claims that females' only proper place in the military is as domestics and concubines for the officers — and first-time or casual listeners will call in and argue with the guests and (not surprisingly) get very angry and upset. Except the whole thing's a put-on. The

(who really is a gifted mimic)

guests are fake, their different voices done by Hendrie with the aid of mike processing and a first-rate board op, and the show's real entertainment is the callers, who don't know it's all a

Apparently, one reason why Hendrie's show was perfect for national syndication was that the wider dissemination gave Hendrie a much larger pool of uninitiated listeners to call in and entertain the initiated listeners.

gag — Hendrie's real audience, which is in on the joke, enjoys hearing these callers get more and more outraged and sputtery as the "guests" yank their chain. It's all a bit like the old *Candid Camera* if the joke perpetrated over and over on that show were con-

The overwhelming question, obviously, is why anyone would enjoy listening to people get fooled into becoming more and more offended and upset. To which there seems no good answer. At some point we have simply to bow our heads in acceptance of the fact that some Americans enjoy stuff that seems like it ought to make any right-thinking person want to open a vein. There are, after all, functional US adults who like evangelical television, the Home Shopping Network, and radio Muzak. It is the Democratic Adventure.

vincing somebody that a loved one had just died. So obviously Hendrie — whose show now draws an estimated one million listeners a week — lies on the outer frontier of radio persona.

A big part of John Ziegler's on-air persona, on the other hand, is that he doesn't have one. This could be just a function of all the time he's spent in the abattoir of small-market radio, but in Los Angeles it plays as a canny and sophisticated meta-radio move. Part of his January introduction to himself and his program is: "The key to the *John Ziegler Show* is that I am almost completely real. Nearly every show begins with the credo 'This is the show where the host says what he believes and believes what he says.' I do not make up my opinions or exaggerate my stories simply to stir the best debate on that particular broadcast."

Though Mr. Z. won't ever quite say so directly, his explicit I-have-no-persona persona helps to establish a contrast with weekday afternoons' John Kobylt, whose on-air voice is similar to Ziegler's in

National talk radio hosts like Limbaugh, Prager, Hendrie, Gallagher, et al. tend to have rich baritone radio voices that rarely peak, whereas today's KFI has opted for a local-host sound that's more like a slightly adenoidal second tenor. The voices of Kobylt, Bill Handel, Ken Chiampou, weekend host Wayne Resnick, and John Ziegler all share not only this tenor pitch but also a certain quality that is hard to describe except as sounding stressed, aggrieved, Type A: the Little Guy Who's Had It Up To Here. Kobylt's voice in particular has a snarling, dyspeptic, fed-up quality — a perfect aural analogue to the way drivers' faces look in jammed traffic — whereas Mr. Ziegler's tends to rise and fall more, often hitting extreme upper registers of outraged disbelief[.] Off-air, Mr. Z.'s speaking voice is nearly an octave lower than it sounds on his program, which is mysterious, since 'Mondo denies doing anything special to the on-air voice except maybe setting the default volume on the board's channel 7 a bit low because "John sort of likes to yell a lot." And Mr. Ziegler bristles at the suggestion that he, Kobylt, or Handel has anything like a high voice on the air: "It's just that we're passionate. Rush doesn't get all that passionate. You try being passionate and having a low voice."

pitch and timbre. Kobylt and his side-kick Ken Chiampou have a hugely (as in if you listen to an upset person say "I can't be*lieve* it!")

popular show based around finding stories and causes that will make white, middle-class Californians feel angry and disgusted, then hammering away at these stories/causes day after day. Their personas are what the *LA Times* calls "brash" and Chiampou him-

CONTAINS EDITORIAL ELEMENTS It should be conceded that there is at least one real and refreshing journalistic advantage that bloggers, fringe-cable newsmen, and most talk radio hosts have over the mainstream media: They are neither the friends nor the peers of the public officials they cover. Why this is an advantage involves an issue that tends to get obscured by the endless fight over whether there's actually a "liberal bias" in the "elite" mainstream press. Whether one buys the bias thing or not, it is clear that leading media figures are part of a very different social and economic class than most of their audience. See, e.g., a snippet of Eric Alterman's recent *What Liberal Media?*:

> No longer the working-class heroes of *The Front Page/His Gal Friday* lore, elite journalists in Washington and New York [and LA] are rock-solid members of the political and financial Establishment about whom they write. They dine at the same restaurants and take their vacations on the same Caribbean islands. . . . What's more, like the politicians, their jobs are not subject to export to China or Bangladesh [*sic*].

This is why the really potent partisan label for the *NYT/Time/*network–level press is not "liberal media" but "elite media" — because the label's true. And talk radio is very deliberately *not* part of this elite media. With the exception of Limbaugh and maybe Hannity, these hosts are not stars, or millionaires, or sophisticates. And a large part of their on-air persona is that they are of and for their audience — the Little Guy — and against corrupt incompetent pols and their "spokesholes," against smooth-talking lawyers and PC whiners and idiot bureaucrats, against illegal aliens clogging our highways and emergency rooms, paroled sex offenders living among us, punitive vehicle taxes, and stupid, self-righteous, agenda-laden laws against public smoking, SUV emissions, gun ownership, the right to watch the Nick Berg decapitation video over and over in slow motion, etc.

In other words, the talk host's persona and appeal are deeply, totally populist, and if it's all somewhat fake — if John Kobylt can shift a little too easily from the apoplectic Little Guy of his segments to the smooth corporate shill of his live reads — then that's just life in the big city.

(discussed at some length below)

self calls "rabid dogs," which latter KFI has developed into the promo line "The Junkyard Dogs of Talk Radio." What John & Ken really are is professional oiks. Their program is

(Except of course some of your more slippery right-wing commentators alter this to "elit*ist* media," which sounds similar but is really a far more loaded and hateful term.)

credited with helping jump-start the '03 campaign to recall Governor Gray Davis, although they were equally disgusted by most of the candidates who wanted to replace him (q.v. Kobylt: "If there's anything I don't like more than politicians, it's those wormy little nerds who act as campaign handlers and staff. . . . We just happened to on our own decide that Davis was a rotting stool that ought to be flushed"). In '02 they organized a parade of SUVs in Sacramento to protest stricter vehicle emissions laws; this year they spend at least an hour a day attacking various government officials and their "spokesholes" for failing to enforce immigration laws and trying to bullshit the citizens about it; and so on. But the *John & Ken Show*'s real specialty is gruesome, high-profile California trials, which they often cover on-site, Kobylt eschewing all PC pussyfooting and legal niceties to speak his mind about defendants like 2002's David Westerfield and the current Scott Peterson, both "scumbags that are guilty as sin." The point being that Mr. John Kobylt broadcasts in an almost perpetual state of affronted rage; and, as more than one KFI staffer has ventured to observe off the record, it's improbable

> Besides legendary stunts like tossing broccoli at "vegetable-head" jurors for taking too long to find Westerfield guilty, Kobylt is maybe best known for shouting "Come out, Scott! No one believes you! You can't hide!" at a window's silhouette as the *J&K Show* broadcast live from in front of Peterson's house, which scene got re-created in at least one recent TV movie about the Scott & Laci case.

that any middle-aged man could really go around this upset all the time and not drop dead. It's a persona, in other words, not exactly fabricated but certainly exaggerated . . . and of course it's also demagoguery of the most classic and unabashed sort.

> The *John & Ken Show* pulls higher ratings in Southern California than the syndicated Rush and Dr. Laura, which is pretty much unheard of.

But it makes for stimulating and profitable talk radio. As of Arbitron's Winter '04 Book, KFI AM-640 has become the No. 1 talk station in the

> (terms defined just below)

country, beating out New York's WABC in both Cume and AQH for the coveted 25–54 audience. KFI also now has the second-highest market share of any radio station in Los Angeles, trailing only FM hip-hop giant KPWR. In just one year, KFI has gone from being the eighteenth to the seventh top-billing station in the country, which is part of why it received the 2003 News/Talk Station of the Year Award from *Radio and Records* magazine. Much of this success is attributed to Ms. Robin Bertolucci, the Program Director brought in from Denver shortly after Clear Channel acquired KFI, whom Mr. Z. describes as "a real superstar in the business right now." From all reports, Ms. Bertolucci has done everything from re-designing the station's ID and sweeper and sound and overall in-your-face vibe to helping established hosts fine-tune their personas and create a distinc-tively KFI-ish style and 'tude for their shows.

Every Wednesday afternoon, Ms. Berto-lucci meets with John Ziegler to review the previous week and chat about how the show's going. The Pro-gram Director's large

> In truth, just about everyone at KFI except Ms. B. refers to Arbitron as "Arbitraryon." This is because it's 100 percent diary-based, and diary surveys are notoriously iffy, since a lot of subjects neglect to fill out their diaries in real time (especially when they're listening as they drive), tending instead to wait till the night before they're due and then trying to do them from memory. Plus it's widely held that certain ethnic minorities are chronically mis- or overrepresented in LA's Books, evidently because Arbitron has a hard time recruiting these minorities as subjects, and when it lands a few it tends to stick with them week after week.

private office is located just off the KFI prep room (in which prep room Mr. Z's own office is a small computer table with a crude homemade THIS AREA RESERVED FOR JOHN ZIEGLER sign taped to it). Ms. B. is soft-spoken, polite, unpretentious, and almost com-pletely devoid of moving parts. Here is her on-record explanation of the Program Director's role w/r/t the *John Ziegler Show:*

"It's John's show. He's flying the airplane, a big 747. What I am, I'm the little person in the control tower. I have a different per-spective —"

"I *have* no perspective!" Mr. Z. interrupts, with a loud laugh, from his seat before her desk.

"— which might be of value. Like, 'You may want to pull up because you're heading for a mountain.'" They both laugh. It's an outrageous bit of understatement: Nine months ago John Ziegler's career was rubble, and Ms. B. is the only reason he's here, and she's every inch his boss, and he's nervous around her — which you can tell by the way he puts his long legs out and leans back in his chair with his hands in his slacks' pockets and yawns a lot and tries to look exaggeratedly relaxed.

> (Plus he omits to wear his golf cap in her office, and his hair shows evidence of recent combing.)

The use of some esoteric technical slang occasions a brief Q&A on how exactly Arbitron works while Mr. Z. joggles his sneaker impatiently. Then they go over the past week. Ms. B. gently chides the new host for not hitting

> In the Winter '04 Arbitron report, KFI's overall Share was 4.7, up from 4.2 for Fall '03. In a radio market as crowded as LA's, this kind of half-point jump in Share is a phenomenal achievement.

the Greg Haidl trial harder, and for usually discussing the case in his show's second hour instead of the first. Her thrust: "It's a big story

> Arbitron Inc., a diary-based statistical sampling service, is more or less the Nielsen of US radio. The company puts out quarterly ratings reports for every significant market in the country. These reports, of which the one for LA is the size of a small telephone directory, are known in the business as "Books." Arbitron is a paid service: Radio stations must subscribe in order to be included, which they have to be, since the Arbitron Book is basically what determines the rates that can be charged to advertisers. There are all kinds of demographic breakdowns, but the major category for talk radio is Listeners Age 25–54. The measurements for determining how a given radio station is doing are Rating and Share, each of which is subcategorized in terms of Cume, AQH, and TSL. As Ms. B. explains it, a station's overall Rating answers the question "Out of the entire metro-LA population of c. 10,407,400, how many are listening to us?" whereas Share answers "Out of every hundred radios that are on, how many are tuned to our station?" The subcategorical "Cume" stands for Cumulative, "AQH" for Average Quarter Hour, and "TSL" for Time Spent Listening — all of which Ms. B. can explain by analogy to a party. Say KFI is a cocktail party: Cume is how many people came to your party, total. But guests come and go. So AQH is as if every fifteen minutes you had everyone at the party freeze and you counted them all, then averaged all these different counts at the evening's end. With TSL being how long the average guest stayed at your party.
>
> Since Arbitron also generates average numbers for each three-hour period of the day, individual shows' performance can be measured and tracked over time. The *John Ziegler Show*'s comparative Book so far looks like this:
>
> *JZS* Winter '04 AQH Share = 2.9 vs. *Coast to Coast* Winter '03 AQH Share = 4.6
> *JZS* Winter '04 AQH Rating = 0.1 vs. *Coast to Coast* Winter '03 AQH Rating = 0.2.

Continued on next page

Continued from previous page
Which doesn't look all that good. But no one at KFI expects the new program to be a ratings hit right away; *Coast to Coast* is an established nighttime show with a loyal audience. "I'm committed to [Mr. Z.'s] show," Ms. Bertolucci says. (This is on a different day from the Wednesday confab.) "What I'm looking for is not insane ratings right off the get-go. The thing I am looking for is steady and incremental growth." Ms. B. also insists that dissatisfaction with *Coast to Coast's* quarterly Book was not one of the reasons for moving the show back to deep overnights and going Live and Local from ten to one. That decision was driven by "other pressures," which Ms. B. declines to specify but very likely involve the Clock for *Coast to Coast* and the percentage of ad revenue that KFI had to cede to its syndicator. With a local show, all the spots are KFI's own.

Clearly, though, the *John Ziegler Show* is Ms. B.'s baby; it was she who sold top management on the *Coast to Coast* move, the Live and Local experiment, and the program's host. So

Q: What will be the consequences for you if the gamble doesn't pay off?

A: "You mean if the show doesn't work do I get fired?"

Q: [Nervous laughter.]

A: "I have a lot invested in the success of the show. It was a risk to take. But [quick cool smile] my fate is not solely linked to the success of any individual show."

Q: How long do you get to prove that Mr. Z.'s show can succeed? A year? Three years?

A: "Three years in this business is a long time. [Smiles now w/ a hint of sadness, or perhaps pity at Q's naïveté.] The business now is more impatient. When KFI started [meaning in its current talk format], it took eight or nine years before it got any traction. The business pressures as they are right now, there's a great impatience and need for success, and we don't have long periods of time to see if shows hit or miss. Radio's not as bad as TV yet — we don't have overnight ratings yet — but there's a lot of the same pressure."

Q: Why is there so much extra pressure now?

A: "The radio companies are bigger, the monetary pressures are greater, the companies are publicly traded. There are big, large corporations."

Q: So the odd thing here is that radio consolidation seems to up the pressure instead of reduce it — the competition is between fewer companies, but it's way fiercer competition.

A: "Well, the media live in the same business world that probably a lot of your magazine's readers live in, which is, you know, quarter by quarter, how are we doing, are we making our numbers. [Tiny ambiguous smile.] Maybe we've just become a more impatient society."

for us. It's got sex, it's got police, class issues, kids running amok, video, the courts, and who gets away with what. And it's in Orange County." When Mr. Ziegler (whose off-air method of showing annoyance or frustration is to sort of hang his head way over to one side) protests that both Bill Handel and John & Ken have already covered the story six ways from Sunday every day and there is no way for him to do anything fresh or stimulating with it, Ms. B. nods slowly and responds: "If we were KIIS-FM, and we had a new Christina Aguilera song, and they played it heavy on the morning show and the after-

(As you may have noticed, Ms. B. has a thing for analogies.)

noon show, wouldn't you still play it on the evening show?" At which Mr. Z. sort of lolls his head from side to side several times — "All right. I see your point. All right" — and on tonight's (May 19) program he does lead with and spend much of the first hour on the latest Haidl developments.

FOR THOSE OUTSIDE SOUTHERN CA Haidl, the teenage son of an Orange County Asst. Sheriff, is accused, together with some chums, of gang-raping an unconscious girl at a party two or three years ago. Rocket scientists all, the perps had videotaped the whole thing and then managed to lose the tape, which eventually found its way to police.

In a week without a real Monster story like Abu Ghraib or Nick Berg, the what-to-hit-hard-first issue is sub-tended by a larger question, which is whether the host should think of his program more as one

There is a People Meter–brand overnight rating service now available for commercial radio, but evidently most stations and media buyers hate the idea — the whole current system is based around Arbitron.

three-hour show or as three one-hour shows. Mr. Z.'s prep and orchestration tend to imply the former, but Ms. B. — citing certain Arbitron–sup-plement services' microdata on the whereabouts and TSL of the average 10:00–1:00 listener — quietly invites him to maybe think more in terms of three discrete broadcast hours, in which a certain amount of repetition might be all right. It's just something for him to consider, of course, offered from a different,

(meaning whether or not in the car)

noncockpit perspective, and Mr. Z. nods thoughtfully throughout. That evening, though, over a large restaurant steak, he is
a great deal more
voluble and sardonic on

> Ascetic or no, Mr. Z.'s tastes in Q&A food are
> rather more expensive than 'Mondo's.

the (1×3)–vs.–(3×1)
question: "She changes her fucking mind on that in every meeting.
Rush does his show as one three-hour thing, and he does okay, I
think you'd agree." And the host's response to the pilot-and-con-
trol-tower analogy as a way to explain Ms. Bertolucci's relationship
to his show, as well as to an outsider's observation that Ms. B. seems
both really smart and totally in Mr. Z.'s corner, is a worldly
shrug over his ribeye: "She's the PD. She'll fuck me over if it's in
her interests to."

By way of post-meeting analysis, it is worth noting that a certain
assumption behind Ms. B.'s Christina Aguilera analogy — namely,
that a criminal trial is every bit as much an entertainment product
as a Top 40 song —
was not questioned
or even blinked at

> Mr. Z.'s explanatory overview of his professional
> broadcasting life so far: "My ass is sore from being
> fucked by so many stations." (See also below.)

by either participant. This is, doubtless, one reason for KFI's recent
success — the near total conflation of news and entertainment. It
also explains why KFI's twice-hourly newscasts (which are always extremely short, and densely interwoven with station promos and
live-read ads) concentrate so heavily on lurid, tabloidish stories.
Post–Nick Berg, the station's newscasts in May and early June tend
to lead with child-molestation charges against local clerics and
teachers, revelations in
the Peterson and Haidl
trials, and developments
in the Kobe Bryant and

> (= part of the same mid-May Q&A in which Ms.
> B. batted her interlocuter around like a pet's
> toy mouse w/r/t the meaning of "stimulating")

Michael Jackson cases. Respecting Ms. Bertolucci's on-record
description of KFI's typical listener — "An information-seeking
person that wants to know what's going on in the world and wants

> Again, this claim seems a little tough to reconcile with the actual news that KFI concentrates on, but — as Mr. Z. himself once pointedly observed during a Q&A — interviewing somebody is not the same as arguing with him over every last little thing.

to be communicated to in an interesting, entertaining, stimulating sort of way" — it seems fair to observe that KFI provides a peculiar and very selective view of what's going on in the world.

Ms. B.'s description turns out to be loaded in a number of ways. The role of news and information versus personal and persona-driven stuff on the *John Ziegler Show,* for example, is a matter that Mr. Z. and his producer see very differently. Emiliano Limon, who's worked at the station for over a decade and believes he knows its audience, sees "two distinct eras at KFI. The first was the opinion-driven, personal, here's-my-take-on-things era. The second is the era we're in

> [meaning, again, at the station in its current talk format, which started sometime in the eighties. KFI itself has been on the air since 1922 — the "FI" actually stands for "Farm Information."]

right now, putting the information first." Emiliano refers to polls he's seen indicating that most people in Southern California get their news from local TV newscasts and Jay Leno's monologue on the *Tonight* show. "We go

> (with whom Emiliano, from all indications, does not enjoy a very chummy or simpatico relationship, although he's always a master of tact and circumspection on the subject of Mr. Z.)

on the presumption that the average driver, average listener, isn't reading the news the way we are. We read *everything.*" In fact, this voracious news-reading is a big part of Emiliano's job. He is, like most talk radio producers, a virtuoso on the Internet, and he combs through a daily list of sixty national papers, 'zines, and blogs, and he believes that his and KFI's main function is to provide "a kind of executive news summary" for busy listeners. In a different, nonprandial Q&A, though, Mr. Ziegler's take on the idea of his show's providing news is wholly different: "We're trying to get away from that, actually. The original thought was that this would be mostly an informational show, but now we're trying to get a little

The upshot here is that there's a sort of triangular dissonance about the *John Ziegler Show* and how best to stimulate LA listeners. From all available evidence, Robin Bertolucci wants the program to be mainly info-driven (according to KFI's particular definition of info), but she wants the information heavily editorialized and infused with 'tude and in-your-face energy. Mr. Ziegler interprets this as the PD's endorsing his talking a lot about himself, which Emiliano Limon views as an antiquated, small-market approach that is not going to interest people in Los Angeles, who tend to get more than their share of colorful personality and idiosyncratic opinion just in the course of their normal day. If Emiliano is right, then Mr. Z. may simply be too old-school and self-involved for KFI, or at least not yet aware of how different the appetites of a New York or LA market are from those of a Louisville or Raleigh.

more toward personality" . . . which, since Mr. Z. makes a point of not having a special on-air persona, means more stuff about himself, John Ziegler — his experiences, his résumé, his political and cultural outlook and overall philosophy of life.

(who does tend to be the clearest and most persuasive person at KFI)

(3)

If we're willing to disregard the complicating precedents of Joe Pyne and Alan Burke, then the origins of contemporary political talk radio can be traced more or less directly to three phenomena of the 1980s.

(famous "confrontational" talk hosts of the sixties)

(We're also pretermitting the fifties' Long John Nebel, inventor of the seven-second delay; plus of course the protofascist broadcasts of Fr. Charles Coughlin during the Depression.)

The first of these involved AM music stations' getting absolutely murdered by FM, which could broadcast music in stereo and allowed for much better fidelity on high and low notes. The human voice, on the other hand, is mid-range and doesn't require high fidelity. The eighties' proliferation of talk formats on the AM band also provided new careers for some music deejays — e.g., Don

As of 1981, there were around seventy-five news/talk radio stations in the US. There are now almost twenty times that.

You'll doubtless recall the offset factoid about AM's 10,000 kHz vs. FM's 15,000 from page 278.

Imus, Morton Downey Jr. — whose chatty personas didn't fit well
with FM's all-about-the-music ethos.

The second big factor was the repeal, late in Ronald Reagan's
second term, of what was known as the Fairness Doctrine. This was
a 1949 FCC rule designed to minimize any possible restrictions on
free speech caused by limited access to broadcasting outlets. The
idea was that, as one of the conditions for receiving an FCC broadcast license, a station had to "devote reasonable attention to the
coverage of controversial issues of public importance," and consequently had to provide "reasonable, although not necessarily
equal" opportunities for opposing sides to express their views.
Because of the Fairness Doctrine, talk stations had to hire and program "symmetrically": If you had a three-hour program whose
host's politics were on one side of the ideological spectrum, you
had to have another program whose host more or less spoke for the
other side. Weirdly enough, up through the mid-eighties it was usually the US right that ben-
efited most from the
Doctrine. Pioneer talk syndicator Ed McLaughlin,
who managed San Francisco's KGO in the 1960s, recalls now that "I
had more liberals on the air than I had conservatives or even moderates for that matter, and I had a hell of a time finding the other
voice."

KGO happens to be the station where Ms.
Robin Bertolucci, fresh out of Cal-Berkeley,
first broke into talk radio.

This main-text ¶ contains
editorial elements.

└The Fairness Doctrine's repeal was
part of the sweeping deregulations of the Reagan era, which aimed
to liberate all sorts of industries from government interference
and allow them to compete freely in the marketplace. The old,
Rooseveltian logic of the Doctrine had been that since the airwaves
belonged to everyone, a license to profit from those airwaves con-
ferred on the broadcast industry some special obligation to serve
the public interest. Commercial radio broadcasting was not, in
other words, originally conceived as just another for-profit industry;
it was supposed to meet a higher standard of social responsibility.

After 1987, though, just another | (except, obviously, for some
industry is pretty much what radio | restrictions on naughty language)
became, and its only real responsibility now is to attract and retain
listeners in order to generate revenue. In other words, the sort of
distinction explicitly drawn by FCC chairman Newton Minow in
the 1960s, namely that between "the public interest" and "merely
what interests the public," no longer exists.

CONTAINS WHAT MIGHT BE PERCEIVED AS EDITORIAL ELEMENTS It seems only fair
and balanced to observe, from the imagined perspective of a Neal Boortz or
John Ziegler, that Minow's old distinction reflected exactly the sort of controlling, condescending, nanny-state liberal attitude that makes government regulation such a bad idea. For how and why does a federal
bureaucrat like Newton Minow get to decide what "the public interest" is?
Why not respect the American people enough to let the public itself decide
what interests it? Of course, this sort of objection depends on precisely the
collapse of "the public interest" into "what happens to interest the public"
that liberals object to. For the distinction between these two is *itself* liberal,
as is the idea of a free press's and broadcast media's special responsibilities
— "liberal" in the sense of being rooted in a professed concern for the common good over and above the preferences of individual citizens. The point
is that the debate over things like the Fairness Doctrine and the proper
responsibility of broadcasters quickly hits ideological bedrock on both sides.

DITTO (which does indeed entail government's arrogating the power to
decide what that common good is, it's true. On the other hand, the idea is
that at least government officials are elected, or appointed by elected representatives, and thus are somewhat accountable to the public they're deciding
for. What appears to drive liberals most crazy about the right's conflation of
"common good"/"public interest" with "what wins in the market" is the conviction that it's all a scam, that what the deregulation of industries like broadcasting, health care, and energy really amounts to is the subordination of the
public's interests to the financial interests of large corporations. Which is, of
course, all part of a very deep, serious national argument about the role and
duties of government that America's having with itself right now. It is an
argument that's not being plumbed at much depth on political talk radio,
though — at least not the more legitimate, non-wacko claims of some on the
left [a neglect that then strengthens liberal suspicions that all these conservative talk hosts are just spokesholes for their corporate masters . . . and
around and around it all goes].)

(which there have been periodic attempts in Congress to resurrect)

The crucial connection with the FD's repeal was not Rush's show but that show's syndicatability. A station could now purchase and air three daily hours of Limbaugh without being committed to programming another three hours of Sierra Club or Urban League or something.

More or less on the heels of the Fairness Doctrine's repeal came the West Coast and then national syndication of *The Rush Limbaugh Show* through Mr. McLaughlin's EFM Media. Limbaugh is the third great progenitor of today's political talk radio partly because he's a host of extraordinary, once-in-a-generation talent and charisma —

EFM Media, named for Edward F. McLaughlin, was a sort of Old Testament patriarch of modern syndication, although Mr. McL. tended to charge subscribing stations cash instead of splitting the Clock, because he wanted a low spot load that would give Rush maximum airtime to build his audience.

bright, loquacious, witty, complexly authoritative — whose show's blend of news, entertainment, and partisan analysis became the model for legions of imitators. But Rush was also the first great promulgator of the Mainstream Media's Liberal Bias idea. This

In truth, Limbaugh's disdain for the "liberal press" somewhat recalls good old Spiro Agnew's attacks on the Washington press corps (as in "nattering nabobs," "hopeless, hysterical hypochondriacs," etc.), with the crucial difference being that Agnew's charges always came off as thuggish and pathetic *in the "liberal press,"* which at that time was the only vector for their transmission. Because of his own talent and the popularity of his show, Rush has been able to move partisan distrust for the "mainstream liberal media" into the mainstream itself.

turned out to be a brilliantly effective gambit, since the MMLB concept functioned simultaneously as a standard around which Rush's audience could rally, as an articulation of the need for a right-wing (i.e., unbiased) media, and as a mechanism by which any criticism

STRENUOUSLY NON-EDITORIAL So maybe Fox News's "Fair and Balanced" isn't meant just as a cynical joke. A partisan news source can plausibly deny being biased if it understands itself as basically a corrective — a balancing force — against the manifest bias of other news sources. Meaning that the whole back-and-forth argument over Fox News, too, devolves into a debate about whether the MMLB is real.

or refutation of conservative ideas could be dismissed (either as biased or as the product of indoctrination by biased media). Boiled way down, the MMLB thesis is

(although Fox et al.'s dependence, raison d'être–wise, on the same MMLB they spend so much time howling about does look a bit suspicious)

JUST CLEAR-EYED, DISPASSIONATE REASON Notwithstanding all sorts of interesting other explanations, the single biggest reason why left-wing talk radio experiments like Air America or the Ed Schultz program are not likely to succeed, at least not on a national level, is that their potential audience is just not dissatisfied enough with today's mainstream news sources to feel that they have to patronize a special type of media to get the unbiased truth.

able both to exploit and to perpetuate many conservatives' dissatisfaction with extant media sources — and it's this dissatisfaction that cements political talk radio's large and loyal audience.

In the best Rush Limbaugh tradition, Mr. Ziegler takes pride in his on-air sense of humor. His media criticism is often laced with wisecracks, and he likes to leaven his show's political and cultural analyses with timely ad-lib gags, such as "It's maybe a good thing that Catholics and Muslims don't tend to marry — if they had a kid, he'd grow up and then, what, abuse some child and then blow him up?" And he has a penchant for comic maxims ("Fifty percent of all marriages are confirmed failures, while the other fifty percent end in divorce"; "The female figure is the greatest known evidence that there might be a God, but the female psyche is an indication that this God has a very sick sense of humor") that he uses on the air and then catalogues as "Zieglerisms" on his KFI Website.

Mr. Z. can also, when time and the demands of prep permit, go long-form. In his program's final hour for May 22, he delivers a mock commencement address to the Class of 2004, a piece of prepared sit-down comedy that is worth excerpting, verbatim, as a sort of keyhole into the professional psyche of Mr. John Ziegler:

> Class of 2004, congratulations on graduation. . . . I wish to let you in on a few secrets that those of you who are not completely brain-dead will eventually figure out your own, but, if you listen to me, will save a lot of time and frustration. First of all, most of what you have been taught in your academic career is not true. I am not just talking

Again, this is all better, and arguably funnier, when delivered aloud in Mr. Z.'s distinctive way.

about the details of history that have been distorted to promote the liberal agenda of academia. I am also referring to the big-picture lessons of life as well. The sad truth is that, contrary to what most of you have been told, you *cannot* do or be anything you want. The vast majority of you . . . will be absolutely miserable in whatever career

EDITORIAL QUIBBLE It's unclear just when in college Mr. Z. thinks students are taught that they can do or be anything. A good part of what he considers academia's leftist agenda, after all, consists in teaching kids about social and economic stratification, inequalities, uneven playing fields — all the US realities that actually limit possibilities for some people.

you choose or are forced to endure. You will most likely hate your boss because they will most likely be dumber than you think you are, and they will inevitably screw you at every chance they get. . . . The boss will not be the

only stupid person you encounter in life. The vast majority of people are *much, much* dumber than you have

(if conservatively disposed, please substitute "allegedly")

ever been led to believe. Never forget this. And just like people are far dumber than you have been led to believe, they are also *far* more dishonest than anyone is seemingly willing to admit to you. If you have any doubt as to whether someone is telling you the truth, it is a safe bet to assume that they are lying to you. . . . Do not trust anyone unless you have some sort of significant leverage over him or her and they *know* that you have that leverage over them. Unless this condition exists, anyone — and I mean *anyone* — can and probably will stab you in the back.

That is about one sixth of the address, and for the most part it speaks for itself.

One of many intriguing things about Mr. Ziegler, though, is the contrast

The best guess re Mr. Z.'s brutal on-record frankness is that either (a) the host's on- and off-air personas really are identical, or (b) he regards speaking to a magazine correspondent as just one more part of his job, which is to express himself in a maximally stimulating way (there was a tape recorder out, after all).

between his cynicism about backstabbing and the naked, seemingly self-destructive candor with which he'll discuss his life and career. This candor becomes almost paradoxical in Q&As with an outside correspondent, a stranger

(for a magazine, moreover, that pretty much everyone around KFI regards as a chattering-class organ of the most elitist liberal kind)

whom Mr. Z. has no particular reason to trust at those times when he winces after saying something and asks that it be struck from the record. As it happens, however, nearly all of what follows is on-record stuff from an autobiographical timeline constructed by John Ziegler in late May '04, over yet another medium-rare steak. Especially interesting is the timeline's mixture of raw his-

(Meaning he spoke while also eating, and watching a Lakers play-off game on a large-screen high-def TV, which latter was the only real condition he placed on the interview.)

torical fact and passionate editorial opinion, which Mr. Z. blends so seamlessly that one really can believe he discerns no difference between them.

1967–89: Mr. John Ziegler grows up in suburban Philadelphia, the elder son of a financial manager and a homemaker. All kinds of unsummarizable evidence indicates that Mr. Z. and his mother are very close. In 1984, he is named High School Golfer of the Year by the *Bucks County Courier Times*. He's also a three-year golf letterman at Georgetown, where his liberal arts studies turn out to be "a great way to prepare for a life of being unemployed, which I've done quite a bit of."

(especially the one at Raleigh's WLFL Fox 22 — "My boss there was the worst boss in the history of bosses")

1989–95: Mr. Z.'s original career is in local TV sports. He works for stations in and around Washington DC, in Steubenville OH, and finally in Raleigh NC. Though sports news is what he's wanted to do ever since he was a little boy, he hates the jobs: "The whole world of sports and local news is so disgusting . . . local TV news is half a step above prostitution."

1994–5: Both personally and professionally, this period constitutes a dark night of the soul for John Ziegler. Summer '94: O.J. Simpson's ex-wife is brutally murdered. Fall '94: Mr. Ziegler's mother is killed in a car crash. Winter '95: During his sportscast, Mr. Z. makes "an incredibly tame joke about O.J. Simpson's lack of innocence" w/r/t his wife's murder, which draws protest from Raleigh's black community. John Ziegler is eventually fired from WLFL because the station "caved in to Political Correctness." The whole nasty incident marks the start of (a) Mr. Z.'s deep, complex hatred for all things PC, and (b) "my history with O.J." He falls into a deep funk, decides to give up sports broadcasting, "pretty much gave up on life, actually." Mr. Z. spends his days watching the Simpson trial on cable television, often sitting through repeat broadcasts of the coverage late at night; and when O.J. is finally acquitted, "I was nearly suicidal." Two psychiatrist golf buddies talk him into going on antidepressants, but much of the time O.J. is still all Mr. Ziegler can think and talk about. "It got so bad — you'll find this funny — at [?!] one point I was so depressed that it was my goal, assuming that he'd be acquitted and that [O.J.'s] Riviera Country Club wouldn't have the guts to kick him out, that I was going to become a caddy at Riviera, knock him off, and see whether or not [a certain lawyer Mr. Z. also played golf with, whose name is here omitted] could get me off on jury nullification. That's how obsessed I was." The lawyer/golfer/friend's reaction to this plan is not described.

Late '95: Mr. Z. decides to give life and broadcasting another shot. Figuring that "maybe my controversial nature would work better on talk radio," he takes a job as a weekend fill-in host for a station in Fuquay-Varina NC — "the worst talk radio station on the planet . . . to call the station owner a redneck was insulting to rednecks" — only to be abruptly fired when the station switches to an automated Christian-music format.

Early '96: "I bought, actually *bought*, time on a Raleigh talk radio station" in order to start "putting together a Tape," although Mr. Z. is good

A Tape is sort of the radio/TV equivalent of an artist's portfolio.

enough on the air that they soon put him on as a paid

host. What happens, though, is that this station uses a certain programming consultant, whose name is being omitted — "a pretty big name in the industry, who [however] is a *snake,* and, I believe, extremely overrated — and he at first really took a shine to me, and then told me, *told me,* to do a show on how I got fired from the TV job, and I did the show," which evidently involves retelling the original tame O.J. joke, after which the herpetic consultant stands idly by as the station informs Mr. Z. that "'We're done with you, no thank you,' which was another blow."

1996–7: Another radio consultant recommends Mr. Z. for a job at WWTN, a Nashville talk station, where he hosts an evening show that makes good Book and is largely hassle-free for several months. Of his brief career at WWTN, the host now believes that

(the whole story of which is very involved and takes up almost half a microcassette)

"I kind of self-destructed there, actually, in retrospect. I got frustrated with management. I was right, but I was stupid as well." The trouble starts when Tiger Woods wins the 1997 Masters. As part of his com-

(whom the host reveres — a standing gag on his KFI program is that Mr. Z. is a deacon in the First Church of Tiger Woods)

mentary on the tournament, Mr. Z. posits on-air that Tiger constitutes living proof of the fact that "not all white people are racists." His supporting argument is that "no white person would ever think of Tiger as a nigger," because whites draw a mental distinction "between people who just happen to be black and people who act like niggers." His reason for broadcasting the actual word "nigger"? "This all goes back to O.J. I hated the fact that the media treated viewers and listeners like children by saying 'Mark Fuhrman used the N-word.' I despised that, and I think it gives the word too much power. Plus there's the whole hypocrisy of how black people can use it and white people can't. I was young and naive and thought I could stand on principle." As part of that principled stand, Mr. Z. soon redeploys the argument and the word

As Mr. Z. explains it, consultants work as freelance advisers to different stations' Program Directors — "They sort of give the PD a cover if he hires somebody and it doesn't work out."

in a discussion of boxer Mike Tyson, whereupon he is fired, "even though there was very little listener reaction." As Mr. Z. understands it, the reason for his dismissal is that "a single black employee complained," and WWTN's owner, "a lily-white company," feared that it was vulnerable to a discrimination lawsuit.

1998–9: Mr. Z. works briefly as a morning fill-in at Nashville's WLAC, whose studios are right across the street from the station that just fired him. From there, he is hired to do overnights at WWDB, an FM talk station in Philadelphia, his hometown. There are again auspicious beginnings . . . "except my boss, [the PD who hired him], is completely unstable and ends up punching out a consultant, and gets fired. At that point I'm totally screwed — I have nobody who's got my back, and everybody's out to get me." Mr. Z. is suddenly fired to make room for syndicated raunchmeister Tom Leykis, then is quickly rehired when listener complaints get Leykis's program taken off the air . . . then is refired a week later when the station juggles its schedule again. Mr. Z. on his time at WWDB: "I should have sued those bastards."

> **FOR THOSE UNFAMILIAR WITH TOM LEYKIS**
> Imagine Howard Stern without the cleverness.

Q: So what exactly is the point of a host's having a contract if the station can evidently just up and fire you whenever they feel like it? A: "The only thing a contract's worth in radio is how much they're going to pay you when they fire you. And if they fire you 'For Cause,' then they don't have to pay you anything."

2000: John Ziegler moves over to WIP, a famous Philadelphia sports-talk station. "I hated it, but I did pretty well. I can do sports, obviously, and it was also a big political year." But there is both a general problem and a specific problem. The general problem is that "The boss there, [name omitted], is an evil, evil, evil, *evil* man. If God said 'John, you get one person to kill for free,' this would be the man I would kill. And I would make it brutally

painful." The specific problem arises when "... Mike
Tyson holds a press conference, and calls himself a nigger. And I can't resist — I mean, here I've gotten fired in
the past for using the word in relation to a person who
calls *himself* that

> In the Q&A itself, Mr. Z. goes back and forth between actually using the N-word and merely referring to it as "the N-word," without apparent pattern or design.

now. I mean, my
God. So I tell the
story [of having
used the word
and gotten fired for it] on the air, but I do not use the
N-word — I *spell* the N-word, every single time, to cover
my ass, and to also make a point of the absurdity of
the whole thing. And we get one, *one* postcard, from a
total lunatic black person — misspellings, just clearly
a lunatic. And [Mr. Z.'s boss at WIP] calls me in and
says 'John, I think you're a racist.' Now, first of all, *this guy*

EDITORIAL OPINION This is obviously a high-voltage area to get into, but for
what it's worth, John Ziegler does not appear to be a racist as "racist" is generally understood. What he is is more like very, very insensitive — although
Mr. Z. himself would despise that description, if only because "insensitive" is
now such a PC shibboleth. Actually, though, it is in the very passion of his
objection to terms like "insensitive," "racist," and "the N-word" that his real
problem lies. Like many other post-Limbaugh hosts, John Ziegler seems
unable to differentiate between (1) cowardly, hypocritical acquiescence to
the tyranny of Political Correctness and (2) judicious, compassionate cau-
tion about using words that cause pain to large groups of human beings,
especially when there are all sorts of less upsetting words that can be used.
Even though there is plenty of stuff for reasonable people to dislike about
Political Correctness as a dogma, there is also something creepy about the
brutal, self-righteous glee with which Mr. Z. and other conservative hosts
defy all PC conventions. If it causes you real pain to hear or see something,
and I make it a point to inflict that thing on you merely because I object to
your reasons for finding it painful, then there's something wrong with my
sense of proportion, or my recognition of your basic humanity, or both.

THIS, TOO (And let's be real: Spelling out a hurtful word is no improvement. In some ways it's worse than using the word outright, since spelling it
could easily be seen as implying that the people who are upset by the word
are also too dumb to spell it. What's puzzling here is that Mr. Ziegler seems
much too bright and self-aware not to understand this.)

(just one person's opinion . . .)

is a racist, I mean he is a *real* racist. I am anything but a racist, but to be called that by *him* just made my blood boil. I mean, life's too short to be working overnights for this fucking bastard." A day or two later Mr. Z. is fired, For Cause, for spelling the N-word on-air.

> Mr. Z. explains that he's referring here to the constant moving around and apartment-hunting and public controversy caused by the firings. His sense of grievance and loss seems genuine. But one should also keep in mind how vital, for political talk hosts in general, is this sense of embattled persecution — by the leftist mainstream press, by slick Democratic opera-tives, by liberal lunatics and identity politics and PC and rampant cynical pandering. All of which provides the constant conflict required for good narrative and stimulating radio. Not, in John Ziegler's case, that any of his anger and self-pity is contrived — but they can be totally real and still function as parts of the skill set he brings to his job.

Q: It sounds like you've got serious personal reasons for disliking Political Correctness. A: "Oh my God, yes. My whole life has been ruined by it. I've lost relationships, I can't get married, I can't have kids, all because of Po-litical Correctness. I can't put anybody else through the crap I've been through. I can't do it."

2001: While writing freelance columns for the *Philadelphia Enquirer* and *Philadelphia Daily News,* Mr. Ziegler also gets work at a small twenty-four-hour Comcast cable TV network in Philly, where he's a writer and commentator on a prime-time issues-related talk show. Although Comcast is "an evil, evil, evil company, [which] created that network for the sole pur-pose of giving blowjobs to politicians who vote on Comcast legislation," Mr. Z. discovers that "I'm actually really good

> A corollary possibility: The reason why the world as interpreted by many hosts is one of such thoroughgoing selfishness and cynicism and fear is that these are qualities of the talk radio industry they are part of, and they (like professionals everywhere) tend to see their industry as a reflection of the real world.

at talk TV. I was the best thing that ever happened to this show. I actually ended up winning an Emmy, which is ironic." His problem this time is that his show's executive producer, who is also the wife of a senior Comcast executive, "ends up falling in love with me. She's a complete nut job and totally unprofessional . . . a very pretty lady on the air, but it takes her about three hours to look that way. I think she was a

> Mr. Z. is consistently cruel, both on and off the air, in his remarks about women. He seems unaware of it. There's no clear way to explain why, but one senses that his mother's death hurt him very deeply.

very lonely person — her husband was probably fucking around." The whole thing ends up with Mr. Z. threatening to sue for sexual harassment and negotiating an out-of-court settlement with Comcast Inc.

!?

2002: John Ziegler is hired as the mid-morning host at Clear Channel's WHAS in Louisville, which Arbitron lists as the fifty-fifth-largest radio market in the US. According to a local paper, the host's "stormy thirteen-month tenure in Louisville was punctuated by intrigue, outrage, controversy and litigation." According to John Ziegler, "the whole story would make a great movie — in fact my whole life would make a great movie, but this in particular would make a great movie." Densely compressed synopsis: For several quarters, Mr. Z.'s program is a great success in Louisville: "I'm doing huge numbers — in one Book I got a fifteen Share, which is ridiculous." He is also involved in a very public romance with one Darcie Divita, a former LA Lakers cheerleader who is part of a morning news show on the local Fox TV affiliate. The relationship is apparently Louisville's version of Ben & J.Lo, and its end is not amicable. In August

> Here, some of John Ziegler's specific remarks about Darcie Divita are being excised at his request. It turns out that Ms. Divita is suing both the host and WHAS — Mr. Z.'s deposition is in a few weeks.

'03, prompted by callers' questions on his regular "Ask John Anything" feature, Mr. Z. makes certain on-air comments about Darcie Divita's breasts, underwear, genital grooming, and libido. Part of the enduring controversy over John Ziegler's firing, which occurs a few days later, is exactly how much those comments and/or subsequent complaints from listeners and the Louisville media had to do with it. Mr. Z.

has a long list of reasons for believing that his PD was really just looking for an excuse to can him. As for all the complaints, the host remains bitter and perplexed: (1) "The comments I made about Darcie's physical attributes were extremely positive in nature"; (2) "Darcie had, in the past, *volunteered* information about her cleavage on my program"; (3) "I've gone much further with other public figures without incident . . . I mocked [Kentucky Governor] Paul Patton for his inability to bring Tina Conner to orgasm, [and] no one from management ever even mentioned it to me."

John Ziegler on why he thinks he was hired for the Live and Local job by KFI: "They needed somebody 'available.'" And on the corporate logic behind his hiring: "It's among the most bizarre things I've ever been involved in. To simultaneously

(after what Ms. Bertolucci characterizes as "a really big search around the country")

be fired by Clear Channel and negotiate termination in a market where I had immense value and be courted by the same company in a market where I had no current value is beyond explicable."

Mr. Z. explains the scare quotes around "available" as meaning that the experimental gig didn't offer the sort of compensation that could lure a large-market host away from another station. He will describe his current KFI salary only as "in the low six figures."

Mr. Z. on talk radio as a career: "This is a terrible business. I'd love to quit this business." On why, then, he accepted KFI's offer: "My current contract would be by far the toughest for them to fire me of anyplace I've been."

Mr. Z. on the single most challenging thing about hosting a talk radio program: "The hardest thing is choosing what to talk about, especially in this day and age. How in the world are you supposed to know what thirty or forty thousand nameless, faceless people want to hear you talk about? Plus you're constantly editing yourself because of PC." Q: With all respect, your show does not exactly seem, umm, hamstrung by PC delicacy. Can you think of any recent PC-type self-editing you've had to do regard-

INFORMATIVE + EDITORIAL Mr. Z.'s said this on the air, too, several times. So have John & Ken. It grates. On the surface, there's something ballsy and refreshing about someone who'll flatly state "I know the bastard's guilty," but this is only if you don't really think about it. The truth is that the hosts do *not* know whether Scott Peterson is guilty. Nor do they have any special inside dope on the crime or the prosecution's case — they know nothing that everybody else who watches the news doesn't know. They just happen to watch a whole, whole lot of news.

Ideology aside, this may be the most striking thing about talk radio personalities: They are the most media-saturated Americans of all. The prep these hosts do for every show consists largely of sitting there absorbing huge quantities of mass-media news and analysis and opinion . . . then of using the Internet to access still more media. Some of the results of this are less ironic than surreal. John Ziegler, for instance, is so

(See below.)

steeped in news coverage of the Peterson trial that he appears to forget that the news is inevitably partial and skewed, that there might be crucial elements of the case that are not available for public consumption. He forgets that you simply can't believe everything you see and hear and read in the press. Given the axioms of conservative talk radio and Mr. Z.'s own acuity as a media critic, this seems like a very strange thing to forget.

ing, say, this year's lurid trials? Haidl, Bryant, Jackson? Scott Peterson? A: "I'm not that interested in the Peterson story because I know he's guilty. . . . Frankly, though, I think one of the areas of the Kobe [Bryant] case that hasn't been fully talked about is the fact that, as a six-foot-eight black guy, I think most people probably presume Kobe is hung like a horse, and that that, apparently, could have been vital to the injuries that the woman allegedly incurred. And I've alluded to that on the air, but you have to be careful — as soon as you enter an area like that, red and yellow lights start going off in your brain. You start thinking, 'How can I phrase this in a way that won't get me in trouble but still allows me to tell the truth?'"

* * *

Compared with many talk radio hosts, John Ziegler is unusually polite to on-air callers. Which is to say that he doesn't yell at them, call them names, or hang up while they're speaking, although he does get frustrated with some calls. But there are good and bad kinds of frustration, stimulation-wise. Hence the delicate art of call screening. The screener's little switchboard and computer console are here in the Airmix room, right up next to the studio window.

JZS producer Emiliano Limon: "There are two types of callers. You've got your hard-core talk radio callers, who just like hearing themselves on-air" — these listeners will sometimes vary the first names and home cities they give the screener, trying to disguise the fact that they've been calling in night after night — "and then there are the ones who just, for whatever reason, respond to the topic." Of these latter, a certain percentage are wackos, but some wackos actually make good on-air callers. Assoc. prod. and screener Vince Nicholas: "The trick is knowing what kooks to get rid of and what to let through. People that are kooky on a particular issue — some of these Zig likes; he can bust on them and have fun with them. He likes it."

'Mondo Hernandez confirms on-record that Vince's screener-voice sounds like someone talking around a huge bong hit.

Vince (who is either a deep professional admirer or a titanic suck-up) states several times that John Ziegler is excellent with callers, dutifully referring to him each time as "Zig."

Vince isn't rude or brusque with the callers he screens out; he simply becomes more and more laconic and stoned-sounding over the headset as the person rants on, and finally just says "Whoa, gotta go." Especially obnoxious

RATHER LESS EDITORIAL THAN IT MIGHT BE Thus we need to add colored lights and warnings about potential trouble to the list of stuff the professional hosts's brain must hold and sift while the on-air talk proceeds apace. But of course there is also the professed imperative of "telling the truth." Again, let's try to put aside issues of ideology, of people's various sensitivities, and of the medical realities of rape. It may be the sheer amount of tactical on-air calculation required of a host that keeps Mr. Z. from considering an obvious question: Is "the truth" the same as a coarse racial stereotype that may be on some of his listeners' minds? Would it not be closer to the real truth simply to ignore such a stereotype? Or would ignoring this stereotype smack too much of stodgy hypocrisy or PC hand-wringing? Maybe the real journalism-vs.-talk-radio conflict isn't about "responsibility" so much as it is about the specific sorts of truths one feels responsible to.

and persistent callers can be placed on Hold at the screener's switchboard, locking up their phone until Vince decides to let them go. Those whom the screener lets through enter a different, computerized Hold system in which eight callers at a time can be kept queued up and waiting, each designated on Mr. Z.'s monitor by a different colored box displaying a first name, city, one-sentence summary of the caller's thesis, and the elapsed time waiting. The host chooses, cafeteria-style, from this array.

In his selections, Mr. Z. has an observable preference for female callers. Emiliano's explanation: "Since political talk radio is so white male–driven, it's good to get female voices in there." It turns out that this is an industry convention — the roughly 50-50 gender mix of callers one hears on most talk radio is because screeners admit a much higher percentage of female callers to the system.

One of the last things that Emiliano Limon always does before airtime is to use the station's NexGen Audio Editing System to load various recorded sound bites from the day's broadcast news onto a Prophet file that goes with the "Cut Sheet." This is a numbered list of bites available for tonight's *John Ziegler Show*, of which both Mr. Z. and 'Mondo get a copy. Each bite must be precisely timed. It is an intricate, exacting process of editing and compilation, during which Mr. Z. often drums his fingers

(a Clear Channel product)

NexGen displays a Richterish-looking sound wave, of which all different sizes of individual bits can be highlighted and erased in order to tighten the pacing and compress the sound bite. It's different from 'Mondo's Cashbox, which tightens things automatically according to preset specs; using NexGen requires true artistry. Emiliano knows the distinctive vocal wave patterns of George W. Bush, Bill O'Reilly, Sean Hannity, and certain others well enough that he can recognize them on the screen without any sound or ID. He is so good at using NexGen that he manages to make the whole high-stress Cut Sheet thing look dull.

gers and looks pointedly at his watch as the producer ignores him and always very slowly and placidly edits and compresses and loads and has the Cut Sheet ready at the very last second. Emiliano is the sort of extremely chilled-out person who can seem to be leaning back at his station with his feet up on the Airmix table even when he isn't leaning back at all. He's wearing the *LA Times* shirt again. His own view on listener calls is that they are "overrated in talk radio," that they're rarely cogent or stimulating, but that hosts tend to be "overconcerned with taking calls and whether people are calling. Consider: This is the only type of live performance with absolutely no feedback from the audience. It's natural for the host

> Please note that the producer manages to be interesting and authoritative while presenting all this as merely opinion. He does not, for example, ever use the word "know," even though it's an established fact that only around 0.1 percent of talk radio listeners ever call in to a program.

to key in on the only real-time response he can get, which is the calls. It takes a long time with a host to get him to forget about the calls, to realize the calls have very little to do with the wider audience."

Vince, meanwhile, is busy at the screener's station. A lady with a heavy accent keeps calling in to say that she has vital information: A Czech newspaper has revealed that John Kerry is actually a Jew, that his grandfather changed his distinctively Jewish surname, and that this fact is being suppressed in the US media and must be exposed. Vince finally tries putting her on

> 'Mondo and Vince clearly enjoy each other, exchanging "*puto*" and "*chilango*" with brotherly ease. When Vince takes a couple days off, it becomes difficult to get 'Mondo to say anything about anything, Doritos or no.

punitive Hold, but her line's light goes out, which signifies that the lady has a cell phone and has disengaged by simply turning it off. Meaning that she can call back again as much as she likes, and that Vince is going to have get actively rude. 'Mondo's great mild eyes rise from the log: "*Puto*, man, what's that about?" Vince, very flat and bored: "Kerry's a Jew." Emiliano: "Another big advent is the

cell phone. Before cells, you got mostly homebound invalids calling in. [Laughs.] Now you get the driving invalid."

(4)

Historically, the two greatest ratings periods ever for KFI AM-640
have been the Gray Davis gubernatorial recall and the O.J. Simp-

Q [based on seeing some awfully high minute-counts in some people's
colored boxes on Vince's display]: How long will callers wait to get on
the air?

Emiliano Limon: "We get some who'll wait for the whole show. [Laughs.] If
they're driving, what else do they have to do?"

Q: If a drunk driver calls in, do you have to notify the police or something?

A: "Well, this is why screening is tricky. You'll get, say, somebody calling in
saying they're going to commit suicide — sometimes you have to refer
the call. But sometimes you're getting pranked. Keep in mind, we're in
an area with a lot of actors and actresses anxious to practice their craft.
[Now his feet really are up on the table.] I remember we had Ross Perot
call in one time, it sounded just like him, and actually he really was due
to be on the show but not for an hour, and now he's calling saying he
needs to be on right now because of a schedule change. Very convinc-
ing, sounded just like him, and I had to go 'Uh, Mr. Perot, what's the
name of your assistant press liaison?' Because I'd just talked to her a
couple days prior. And he's [doing vocal impression]: 'Listen here, you
all going to put me on the air or not?' And I'm: 'Umm, Mr. Perot, if you
understand the question, please answer the question.' And he hangs
up. [Laughs.] But you would have *sworn* this was Ross Perot."

son trial. Now, in early June '04, the tenth anniversary of the
Ron Goldman–Nicole
Brown Simpson mur-
ders is approaching,
and O.J. starts to pop
up once again on the
cultural radar. And Mr.
John Ziegler happens

Some of his personal reasons for this have
been made clear. But the Simpson case also
rings a lot of professional cherries for Mr.
Ziegler as a host: sports, celebrity, race, racism,
PC and the "race card," the legal profession,
the US justice system, sex, misogyny, misce-
genation, and a lack of shame and personal
accountability that Mr. Z. sees as just plain evil.

to be more passionate about the O.J. Simpson thing than maybe
any other single issue, and feels that he "know[s] more about the

case than anyone not directly involved," and is able to be almost unbearably stimulating about O.J. Simpson and the utter indubitability of his guilt. And the confluence of the murders' anniversary, the case's tabloid importance to the nation and business importance to KFI, and its deep personal resonance for Mr. Z. helps produce what at first looks like the absolute Monster talk radio story of the month.

On June 3, in the third segment of the *John Ziegler Show*'s second hour, after lengthy discussions of the O.J. anniversary and the Michael Jackson case, Mr. Z. takes a phone call from one "Daryl in Temecula," an African-American gentleman who is "absolutely astounded they let a Klansman on the radio this time of night." The call, which lasts seven minutes and eighteen seconds and runs well over the :46 break, ends with John Ziegler telling the audience "That's as angry as I've ever gotten in the history of my career"; and Vince Nicholas, looking awed and spent at his screener's station, pronounces the whole thing "some of the best talk radio I ever heard."

> This annoys Alan LaGreen of Airwatch enough to cause him to snap at 'Mondo on an off-air channel (mainly because Alan LaGreen now ends up having to be the KFI Traffic Center during an interval in which he's supposed to be the Traffic Center for some country station); plus it pushes 'Mondo's skills with the Cashbox right to their limit in the hour's segment four.

Certain portions of the call are untranscribable because they consist mainly of Daryl and Mr. Z. trying to talk over each other. Daryl's core points appear to be (1) that Mr. Z. seems to spend all his time talking about black men like Kobe and O.J. and Michael Jackson — "Don't white people commit crimes?" — and (2) that O.J. was, after all, found innocent in a court of law, and yet Mr. Z. keeps "going on about 'He's guilty, he's guilty —'"

"He *is*," the host inserts.

Daryl: "He was acquitted, wasn't he?"

"That makes no difference as to whether or not he did it."

"O.J., Kobe: You just thrive on these black guys."

It turns out to be impossible, off the air, to Q&A Mr. Ziegler about his certainty re O.J.'s guilt. Bring up anything that might sound like reservations, and Mr. Z. won't say a word — he'll just angle his head way over to the side and look at you as if he can't tell whether you're trying to jerk him around or you're simply out of your mind.

It is here that Mr. Z. begins to pick up steam. "Oh yeah, Daryl, right, I'm a racist. As a matter of fact, I often say 'You know what? I just wish another black guy would commit a crime

It's different if you ask about O.J. Simpson *l'homme*, or about specific details of his personality and marriage and lifestyle and golf game and horrible crimes. For instance, John Ziegler has a detailed and fairly plausible-sounding theory about O.J.'s motive for the murders, which boils down to Simpson's jealous rage over his ex-wife's having slept with Mr. Marcus Allen, a former Heisman Trophy winner and current NFL star. Mr. Z. can defend this theory with an unreproducibly long index of facts, names, and media citations, all of which you can ask him about if you keep your face and tone neutral and simply write down what he says without appearing to quibble or object or in any way question the host's authority on the subject.

(as of '94)

because I hate black people so much.'"

Daryl: "I think you do have more to talk about on black guys; I think that's more

(For instance, you cannot ask something like whether Nicole's liaison with Marcus Allen is a documented fact or just part of Mr. Z.'s personal theory — this will immediately terminate the Q&A.)

'*news*'" . . . which actually would be kind of an interesting point to explore, or at least address; but Mr. Z. is now stimulated:

"As a matter of fact, Daryl, oftentimes when we go through who's committed the crimes, there are times when the white people who control the media, we get together and go 'Oh, we can't talk about that one, because that was a white guy.' This is all a big conspiracy, Daryl. Except, to be serious for a second, Daryl, what really upsets me, assuming you're a black guy, is that you ought to be *ten* times more pissed off at O.J. Simpson than I am, because you know why?"

Daryl: "You can't tell me how I should feel. As a forty-year-old black man, I've seen racism for forty years."

Mr. Z. is starting to move his upper body back and forth excitedly in his chair. "I bet you have. I bet you have. And here's why you ought to be pissed off: Because, out of all the black guys who *deserved* to get a benefit of the doubt because of the history of racism, which is real in this country, and which is insidious, the one guy — *the one guy* — who gets the benefit of all of that pain and suffering over a hundred years of history in this country is the one guy who deserves it less than anybody else, who sold his race out, who tried to talk white, who only had white friends, who had his ass kissed all over the place because he decided he wasn't really a black guy, who was the first person in the history of this country ever accepted by white America, who was actually able to do commercial endorsements because he pretended to be white, and *that's the guy? That's the guy? That's the guy* who gets the benefit of that history, and that doesn't piss you off, *that doesn't piss you off?*" And then an abrupt

> In case memories of the trial have dimmed, Mr. Z. is referring here to the defense team's famous playing of the race card, the suggestion that the LAPD wanted to frame O.J. because he was a miscegenating black, etc.

> TINY EDITORIAL CORRECTION Umm, four hundred?

> John Ziegler is now screeching — except that's not quite the right word. Pitch and volume have both risen ('Mondo's at the channel 7 controls trying to forestall peaking), but his tone is meant to connote a mix of incredulity and outrage, with the same ragged edge to his stressed syllables as — no kidding — Jackson's and Sharpton's. Daryl of Temecula, meantime, has been silenced by the sheer passion of the host's soliloquy . . . and we should note that Daryl really has stopped speaking; it's not that Mr. Z. has turned off the volume on the caller's line (which is within his power, and which some talk radio hosts do a lot, but Mr. Z. does not treat callers this way).

> (voice breaking a bit here)

> Mr. Z. means first *black* person — he's now so impassioned he's skipping words. It never once sounds like babbling, though.

decrescendo: "Daryl, I can assure you that the last thing I am is racist on this. This is the last guy who should benefit."

EDITORIAL OPINION Again, it's nothing so simple as that he doth protest too much; but it would be less discomfiting if Mr. Z. didn't feel he could so totally *assure* Daryl of this — i.e., if Mr. Z. weren't so certain that his views are untainted by racism. Not to mention that the assurance resonates strangely against all the host's vented spleen about a black man's "selling out his race" by "pretending to be white."

Not, again, that Mr. Z. wears a pointy hood — but he seems weirdly unconscious of the fact that Simpson's ostensible bet-

(Is it wimpy or white-guiltish to believe that we're all at least a little bit racist in some of our attitudes or beliefs, or at any rate that it's not totally impossible that we are?)

rayal of his race is something that only a member of that race really has the right to get angry about. No? If a white person gets angry about a black person's "pretending to be white," doesn't the anger come off far less as sympathy with the person's betrayed race than as antipathy for somebody who's trying to crash a party he doesn't

(Better than "the right" here might be "the rhetorical authority.")

belong at? (Or is Mr. Z. actually to be admired here for not giving a damn about how his anger comes off, for not buying into any of that it's-okay-for-a-black-person-to-say-it-but-not-okay-for-a-white-person stuff? And if so, why is it that his "selling out"–complaints seem creepy and obtuse instead of admirable [although, of course, how his complaints "seem" might simply depend on the politics and sensitivities of the individual listener (such that the whole thing becomes not so much stimulating as exhausting)]?)

*   *   *

And then June 4, the night following the Daryl interchange, turns out to be a climactic whirlwind of production challenges, logistical brinksmanship, meta-media outrage, Simpsonian minutia, and Monster-grade stimulation. As is SOP, it starts around 7:00 PM in KFI's large central prep room, which is where all the local hosts and their producers come in early to prepare for their shows.

The standard of professionalism in talk radio is one hour of prep for each hour on the air. But Mr. Ziegler, whose specialty in media criticism entails extra-massive daily consumption of Internet and cable news, professes to be "pretty much always prepping," at least during the times he's not asleep (3:00–10:00 AM) or playing golf (which since he's moved to LA he does just about every day, quite possibly by himself — all he'll say about it is "I have no life here").

The prep room, which station management sometimes refers to as the production office, is more or less the nerve center of KFI, a large, complexly shaped space perimetered with battered little canted desks and hutches and two-drawer file cabinets supporting tabletops of composite planking. There are beat-up computers and pieces of sound equipment and funny Scotch-taped bits of office humor (such as, e.g., pictures with staffers' heads Photoshopped onto tabloid celebrities' bodies). Like the studio and Airmix, the prep room is also a DPH-grade mess: Half the overhead fluorescents are either out or flickering nauseously, and the gray carpet crunches underfoot,

> There is also another large TV in the prep room, this one wired to a TiVo digital recording system so that anything from the day's cable news can be tagged, copied, and loaded into NexGen and Prophet. The TV gets only one channel at a time, but apparently certain cable stuff can also be accessed on one of the prep room computers by a producer who knows what he's doing.

and the wastebaskets are all towering fire hazards, and many of the tabletops are piled with old books and newspapers. Plus there are a great many USPS mail containers (the cloudy-plastic ones that say FEDERAL PROPERTY and list penalties for unauthorized use) stacked up at various points all over the room, filled with various old

> Examples of volumes pulled at random from the tabletops' clutter: Dwight Nichols's *God's Plans for Your Finances,* the Hoover Institution's *Education and Capitalism: How Overcoming Our Fear of Markets and Economics Can Improve America's Schools,* and Louis Barajas's *The Latino Journey to Financial Greatness.*

tapes, VHS cassettes, cast-off clothing, hats, nonsequential sheets of paper — it's unclear whether all this is stuff that's being thrown out, or moved to the new facility, or what. One window, which is hot to the touch, over-

> One example of the ways in which the prep room's condition is actually kind of entertaining: On the wall over the TiVo television is a standard newsroom row of clocks for different parts of the world — Jerusalem, London, Karachi, Kabul, Tokyo. Except most of the clocks' batteries are low, and the times are way off. Instead of replacing the batteries, someone has put a very precise homemade sign under each clock: "LONDON, ENGLAND: + 8 HOURS," "TOKYO, JAPAN: + 17 HOURS" . . . which of course renders the clocks themselves pointless.

looks KFI's gated parking lot and security booth and the office of a Korean podiatrist across the street.

Overall, the layout and myriad tactical functions of the prep room are too complicated to try to describe this late in the game. At one end, it gives onto the KFI newsroom, which is a whole galaxy unto itself. At the other, comparatively uncluttered end is a set of thick, distinguished-looking doors leading off into the offices of the Station Manager, Director of Marketing & Promotions, Program Director, and so on, with also a semiattached former closet for the PD's assistant, a very (who's usually long gone by the time the *JZS* staff starts prepping) kindly and eccentric lady who's been at KFI for over twenty years and wears a high-tech headset that one begins, only over time, to suspect isn't really connected to anything.

There are three main challenges facing tonight's *John Ziegler Show.* One is that Emiliano Limon is off on certain personal business that he doesn't want described, and therefore Mr. Vince Nicholas is soloing as producer for the very first time. Another is that last night's on-air exchange with Daryl of Temecula is the type of intensely stimulating talk radio event that cries out for repetition and commentary; Mr. Z. wants to rerun certain snippets of the call in a very precise order so that he can use them as jumping-off points for detailing his own "history with O.J." and explaining why he's so incandescently passionate about the case.

The third difficulty is that Simpson's big anniversary Q&A with Ms. Katie Couric is airing tonight on NBC's *Dateline,* and the cuts and discussions of the Daryl call are going to have to be interwoven with excerpts from what Mr. Z. refers to several times as "Katie's blowjob interview." An additional complication is

There's a strong oral subtheme to John Ziegler's distaste for these tenth-anniversary tête-à-têtes. When a Fox promo comes on for Greta Van Susteren's own O.J. interview, Mr. Z. repeatedly shouts in a deep announcer voice: "Monday at ten: Greta sucks O.J.'s cock!," making everyone in the prep room nervous because they're not sure whether or how hard they should laugh.

that *Dateline* airs in Los Angeles from 8:00 to 10:00 PM, and it has also now run teases for stories on the health hazards of the Atkins Diet and the dangerously lax security in US hotels. Assuming that *Dateline* waits and does the O.J. interview last (which it is clearly in the program's business interests to do), then the interview's bits will have to be recorded off TiVo, edited on NexGen, loaded onto Prophet, and queued up for the Cut Sheet all very quickly, since Mr. Z.'s opening segment starts at 10:06 and it's hard to fiddle with logistics once his show's under way.

Thus Vince spends 7:00–8:00 working two side-by-side computers, trying simultane-

> "You're going to need to kick some ass tonight, bud," Mr. Z. tells Vince as he highlights bites in a transcript of Daryl's call, eliciting something close to a salute.

ously to assemble the cuts from last night's call, load an MSNBC interview with Nicole Brown Simpson's sister directly into NexGen, and track down a Web transcript of tonight's *Dateline* (which on the East Coast has already aired) so that he and Mr. Z. can choose and record bites from the Couric thing in real time. 'Mondo, who is back board-opping the ISDN feed of 7:00–10:00's *Phil Hendrie Show,* nevertheless comes in from Airmix several times to stand behind Vince at the terminals, ostensibly to see what's going on but really to lend moral support. 'Mondo's shadow takes up almost half the prep room's east wall.

John Ziegler, who is understandably quite keyed up, spends a lot of the pre-*Dateline* time standing around with an extremely pretty News department intern named Kyra, watching the MSNBC exchange with half an eye while doing his trademark stress-relieving thing of holding two golf balls and trying to align the dimples so that one ball stays balanced atop the other. He is

> Nobody ever ribs Mr. Z. about the manual golf ball thing vis-à-vis, say, Captain Queeg's famous ball bearings. It is not that he wouldn't get the allusion; Mr. Z. is just not the sort of person one kids around with this way. After one mid-May appearance on *Scarborough Country* re some San Diego schoolteachers getting suspended for showing the Nick Berg decapitation video in class, a certain unnamed person tried joshing around with him, in an offhand and light-hearted way, about a supposed very small facial tic that had kept appearing unbeknownst to John Ziegler whenever he'd used the phrase "wussification of America" on-camera; and Mr. Z. was, let's just say, unamused, and gave the person a look that chilled him to the marrow.

wearing a horizontally striped green-and-white golf shirt, neatly pressed black shorts, and gleaming New Balance sneakers. He keeps saying he cannot be*lieve* they're even giving Simpson airtime. No one points out that his shock seems a bit naive given the business realities of network TV news, realities about which John Ziegler is normally very savvy and cynical. Kyra does venture to observe, quietly, that the Simpson thing draws even bigger ratings than today's Scott Peterson, who —

"Don't even compare the two," Mr. Z. cuts her off. "O.J.'s just in his own world in terms of arrogance."

The designated *JZS* intern, meanwhile, is at the prep room's *John & Ken Show* computer, working (in Vince's stead)

> (a UC-Irvine undergrad, name omitted)

on a comic review feature called "What Have We Learned This Week?," which is normally a Friday standard but which there may or may not be time for tonight. At 7:45 PM it is still 90 degrees out, and smoggy. The windows' light makes people look greenish in the areas where the room's fluorescents are low. A large spread of take-out chicken sits uneaten and expensively congealing. Mr. Z.'s intern spends nearly an hour composing

> (negotiated ahead of time with Vince as the price for letting a mute, unobtrusive outside party observe tonight's prep)

> 'Mondo eventually starts taking plates of food back into Airmix with him.

a mock poem to Ms. Amber Frey, the mistress to whom Scott Peterson allegedly read romantic verse over the phone. The poem's final version, which is "Roses are red,/Violets are blue./If I find out you're pregnant,/I'll drown your ass, too," takes such a long time because of confusions about just how to conjugate "drown" as a future contingent.

"And to top it off," Mr. Z. is telling Kyra as her smile becomes

> (meaning the Bundy Drive crime scene, which Mr. Z. has evidently walked every inch of)

brittle and she starts trying to edge away, "to top it off, he leaves Nicole's body in a place where the most likely people to find it are his *children*. It's just a fluke that couple found her. I don't know if you've ever walked by there, but it's really dark at night, and they

were in a, like [gesturing, one golf ball in each hand], cave formation out at the front."

Sure enough, *Dateline* runs the anti-Atkins story first. For reasons
involving laser printers and a special editing room off the on-air news
cubicle, there's suddenly a lot of running back and forth.

> 'Mondo can neither confirm nor deny whether these supposedly outraged
> uninitiated callers are maybe *themselves* fakes, just more disembodied voices
> that Hendrie and his staff are creating, and thus whether maybe the real dupes
> are us, the initiated audience, for believing that the callers are genuine dupes.
> 'Mondo has not, he confesses, ever considered this possibility, but he agrees
> that it would constitute "a serious mind-fuck" for KFI listeners.

In Airmix, 'Mondo is eating Koo Koo Roo's chicken while
watching *Punk'd,* an MTV show where friends of young celebrities
collude with the producers to make the celebrities think they're in
terrible legal trouble. 'Mondo is very careful about eating anywhere near the mixing board. It's always around 60 degrees in this
room. On the board's channel 6 and the overhead speakers, Phil
Hendrie is pretending to mediate between apoplectic callers and a
man who's filing sexual-harassment charges against female coworkers who've gotten breast implants. For unknown reasons, a waist-
high pile of disconnected computer keyboards has appeared in the
Airmix room's north corner, just across the wall from KFI's Imaging studio, whose door is always double-locked.

It is only right and proper that John Ziegler gets the spot
directly in front of the prep room's TV, with everyone else's office
chairs sort of fanned out to either side behind him. Seated back
on his tailbone with his legs out and ankles crossed, Mr. Z. is
able simultaneously to watch
Dateline's are-you-in-danger-at-
luxury-hotels segment, to hear
and help rearrange Vince's
cuts from the MSNBC ex-
change, and to highlight
those parts of the O.J.–Katie
Couric transcript that he
wants to make absolutely

> (which Vince was able to find online,
> but which had to be specially reconfig-
> ured and printed in order to restore the
> original line breaks and transcript for-
> mat of, this being one cause of all the
> running around between 8:00 and 8:30,
> as well as another reason why it took the
> *JZS* intern so long to finish his quatrain,
> which he is even now fidgeting in his
> chair and trying to decide on just the
> right moment to show to Mr. Z.)

sure to have Vince load from TiVo into Prophet when the greedy bastards at *Dateline* finally deign to air the interview. It must be said, too,
that Vince is an impressive surprise as a producer — he's a veritable
blur of all-business competence and technical savvy. There are none
of Emiliano's stoic shrugs, *sotto* wisecracks, or passive-aggressive lan-
guor. Nor, tonight, is Vince's own slackerish stoner persona anywhere
in view. It's the same type of change as when you place a fish back in
the water and it seems to turn electric in your hand. Watching Vince
and the host work so well as a team induces the night's first strange
premonitory jolt: Emiliano's days are numbered.

The broadcast studio is strange
when no one's in here. Through the
soundproof window, 'Mondo's head
looks small and far-away as he works

> Sure enough, within just weeks
> Emiliano Limon will have left
> KFI for a job at New York's
> WCBS.

his levels. It seems like a lonely, cloistered place in which to try to
be passionate about the world. Mr. Z.'s padded host chair is old and
lists slightly to port; it's the same chair that John Kobylt sits in, and
mornings' Bill Handel, and maybe
even Dr. Laura back in the day. The
studio wastebaskets have been
emptied, but the banana scent still lingers. It might simply be that

> (It is a medical commonplace that
> bananas are good for ulcers.)

John and/or Ken eats a lot of bananas during afternoon drive. All
the studio's television monitors are on, though none is tuned to
NBC. On the Fox News monitor up over the digital clock, Sean
Hannity and Susan Estrich are rerunning the Iowa Caucuses clip
of Howard Dean screaming at the start of his concession speech.
They play the scream over and over. Ms. Estrich is evidently filling
in on *Hannity and Colmes*. "They have hatred for George W. Bush,
but they don't have ideas," Sean Hannity says. "Where are the
ideas on the left? Where is the thinking liberal?" Susan Estrich
says, "I don't know. I don't have a full-time job on TV, so I can't
tell you."

All multi-tasking ends when *Dateline,* after two teases and an
extra-long spot break, finally commences the interview segment. It

is Katie Couric and O.J. Simpson
and Simpson's attorney in a living
room that may or may not be real.
One tends to forget how unusually,
screen-fillingly large O.J.'s head is.

> Vince's broad back is to the TV
> and everyone around it as he
> uploads real-time TiVo feed into
> NexGen and edits per his host's
> written specs.

Mr. Ziegler is now angled forward with his elbows on his knees
and his fingers steepled just under his nose. Although he does,
every so often, let loose with a "Katie Couric *sucks!*" or "Katie
Couric should be fucking *shot!*," for the most part a person seated
on the host's far flank has to watch his upper face — his right
eye's and nostril's dilations — to discern when Mr. Z.'s reacting
strongly or thinking about how he'll respond to some specific bit
of Simpson's "sociopathic BS" when it's his turn to talk.

It's odd: If you've spent some time watching him perform in
the studio, you can predict just what John Ziegler will look like,
how his head and arms will move and eyes fill with life as he says
certain things it's all but sure he'll say on-air tonight, such as "I
have some very, very strong opinions about how this interview was
conducted," and "Katie Couric is a disgrace to journalism everywhere," and that O.J.'s self-presentation was "delusional and arrogant beyond all belief," and that the original trial jury was "a
collection of absolute nimrods," and that to believe in Simpson's
innocence, as Ms. Couric says a poll shows some 70 percent of
African-Americans still do, "you have to be either crazy, deluded, or
stupid — there are no other explanations."

> All of this John Ziegler will and does say on his program . . . although
> what no one in the prep room now can know is that tonight's second-
> hour Airwatch flash on the imminent death of Ronald W. Reagan will
> cut short Mr. Z.'s analysis and require a total, on-the-fly change of
> both subject and mood.

> (who is in so many ways the efficient cause, ideologically
> and statutorily, of today's partisan media, and whose
> passing will turn out to be June's true Monster . . .)

To be fair, though, there truly are some dubious, unsettling things about the *Dateline* interview, such as for instance that NBC

> The only bit of genuine fun is during the interview's first commercial break, when the opening ad is for Hertz — *Hertz*, of O.J.-running-through-airports-spots fame — and Mr. Z. throws his head back and asks if he's really seeing what he's seeing. Even Vince turns around in his chair to look. Hertz's placement of an ad here is a brilliant, disgusting, unforgettable piece of meta-metamedia marketing. It's impossible not to laugh . . . and yet Mr. Z. doesn't. (Neither do the room's two interns, though that's only because they're too young to get the meta-reference.)

has acceded to O.J. Simpson's "No Editing" condition for appearing, which used to be a total taboo for serious news organizations. Or that O.J. gets to sit there looking cheery and unguarded even

> COULD BE PERCEIVED AS PARTLY EDITORIAL On the other hand, lamentable or no, this looks to be just another consequence of fragmentation/competition in the news industry, where mere access to newsmakers becomes the prize to bid for. Consider it from NBC's point of view: Had *Dateline* refused to cede editorial control, some other news show would have granted it and snagged O.J. for prime time. After all, since journalistic integrity is pretty clearly another "public good," simple business logic dictates that NBC underinvest in that integrity and do whatever's necessary to get O.J. onto *Dateline* for its advertisers. It's the good old Free Market in action.

(given, of course, that broadcast news is now understood as just a for-profit business like any other)

though he has his lawyer almost in his lap; or that most of Katie Couric's questions turn out to be Larry King–size fluffballs; or that O.J. Simpson responds to one of her few substantive questions — about 1994's eerie, slow-motion Bronco chase and its bearing on how O.J.'s case is still perceived — by harping on the fact that the chase "never ever, in three trials that I had, it never came up," as if that had anything to do with whatever his behavior in the Bronco really signified (and at which non-answer, and Ms. Couric's failure to press or follow up, Mr. Z. moans and smears his hand up and down over his face). Or that O.J.'s cheerful expression never changes when Katie Couric, leaning forward and speaking with a delicacy that's either decent or obscene, inquires whether his children ever ask him about the

Plus of course there's the creepy question of why O.J. Simpson is doing a murder-anniversary TV interview at all. What does he possibly stand to gain from sitting there on-camera and letting tens of millions of people search his big face for guilt or remorse? Why subject himself to America's ghoulish fascination? And make no mistake — it is fascinating. The interview and face are riveting television entertainment. It's almost impossible to look away, or not to feel that special kind of guilty excitement in the worst, most greedy and indecent parts of yourself. You can really feel it: This is why drivers slow down to gape at accidents, why reporters put mikes in the faces of bereaved relatives, why the Haidl gang-rape trial is a hit single that merits heavy play, why the cruelest forms of reality TV and tabloid news and talk radio generate such numbers. But that doesn't mean the fascination is good, or even feels good. Aren't there parts of ourselves that are just better left unfed? If it's true that there are, and that we sometimes choose what we wish we wouldn't, then there is a very serious unanswered question at the heart of KFI's sweeper: "More *Stimulating*" of what?

JUST THE SORT OF PARALYTIC DITHERING THAT MAKES THE MORAL CLARITY OF "WE'RE *BETTER* THAN THEY ARE" SO APPEALING

Is this not a crucial part of Minow's old distinction between what interests us and what's truly in our interests — that there are parts of people that we should choose, as a community, not to cater to and gratify and strengthen?

But what if it's good sound business to cater to those parts? Then what? Government regulation? Of which industries, by exactly whom, and based on what criteria? And what about the First Amendment?

For instance, it's troubling that her delivery is that of someone who's choosing her words with great care, when clearly the words have already been chosen and the question scripted. Which would seem to mean she's acting.

crime. And when someone in the arc of chairs around John Ziegler says, almost to himself, that the one pure thing to hope for here is that Simpson's kids believe he's innocent, Mr. Z. gives a snort of reply and states, very flatly, "They know, and he knows they know, that he did it." To which, in KFI's prep room, the best response would probably be compassion, empathy. Because one can almost feel it: what a bleak and merciless world this host lives in — believes, nay, knows for an absolute *fact* he lives in. I'll take doubt.

(It goes without saying that this is just one person's opinion.)

Personal Acknowledgments

The following people deserve special thanks for their help with the foregoing: Marian Berelowitz, Karen Carlson, Mimi Bailey Davis, Susanna Einstein, Jonathan Franzen, Steven Geller, Karen L. Green, Colin Harrison, Ben Healy, Glenn Kenny, Ron Lindblom, Joel Lovell, Martin Maehr, David Malley, Bessmarie Moll, Marie Mundaca, Cullen Murphy, Michael Pietsch, Ellen Rosenbush, Lee Smith, Martha Spaulding, Harry Thomas, Monona S. Thompson, Bill Tonelli, Betsy Uhrig, James D. Wallace, Sally F. Wallace, Evan Wright, Zainab Zakari, and Jocelyn Zuckerman.